EXAM CRAM™

# Solaris 8 System Administrator

Darrell L. Ambro

CORIOLIS™

**Limits of Liability and Disclaimer of Warranty**

The author and publisher of this book have used their best efforts in preparing the book and the programs contained in it. These efforts include the development, research, and testing of the theories and programs to determine their effectiveness. The author and publisher make no warranty of any kind, expressed or implied, with regard to these programs or the documentation contained in this book.

The author and publisher shall not be liable in the event of incidental or consequential damages in connection with, or arising out of, the furnishing, performance, or use of the programs, associated instructions, and/or claims of productivity gains.

**Trademarks**

Trademarked names appear throughout this book. Rather than list the names and entities that own the trademarks or insert a trademark symbol with each mention of the trademarked name, the publisher states that it is using the names for editorial purposes only and to the benefit of the trademark owner, with no intention of infringing upon that trademark.

The Coriolis Group, LLC
14455 N. Hayden Road
Suite 220
Scottsdale, Arizona 85260

(480)483-0192
FAX (480)483-0193
www.coriolis.com

Library of Congress Cataloging-in-Publication Data
Ambro, Darrell L.
Solaris 8 system administrator/ by Darrell L. Ambro
p. cm. -- (Exam cram)
Includes index.
ISBN 1-57610-921-6
1. Electronic data processing personnel--Certification. 2. Operating systems (Computers) Certification--Study guides. 3. Solaris (Computer file) I. Title. II. Series.
QA76.3.A526 2001
005.4'4769--dc21 2001042168

Printed in the United States of America
10 9 8 7 6 5 4 3 2

**President and CEO**
Roland Elgey

**Publisher**
Al Valvano

**Associate Publisher**
Katherine R. Hartlove

**Acquisitions Editor**
Sharon Linsenbach

**Product Marketing Manager**
Jeff Johnson

**Project Editor**
Dan Young

**Technical Reviewer**
Sheldon Barry

**Production Coordinator**
Thomas Riker

**Cover Designer**
Laura Wellander

CORIOLIS™

The Coriolis Group, LLC • 14455 North Hayden Road, Suite 220 • Scottsdale, Arizona 85260

# A Note from Coriolis

Our goal has always been to provide you with the best study tools on the planet to help you achieve your certification in record time. Time is so valuable these days that none of us can afford to waste a second of it, especially when it comes to exam preparation.

Over the past few years, we've created an extensive line of *Exam Cram* and *Exam Prep* study guides, practice exams, and interactive training. To help you study even better, we have now created an e-learning and certification destination called **ExamCram.com**. (You can access the site at **www.examcram.com**.) Now, with every study product you purchase from us, you'll be connected to a large community of people like yourself who are actively studying for their certifications, developing their careers, seeking advice, and sharing their insights and stories.

We believe that the future is all about collaborative learning. Our **ExamCram.com** destination is our approach to creating a highly interactive, easily accessible collaborative environment, where you can take practice exams and discuss your experiences with others, sign up for features like "Questions of the Day," plan your certifications using our interactive planners, create your own personal study pages, and keep up with all of the latest study tips and techniques.

We hope that whatever study products you purchase from us—*Exam Cram* or *Exam Prep* study guides, *Personal Trainers*, *Personal Test Centers*, or one of our interactive Web courses—will make your studying fun and productive. Our commitment is to build the kind of learning tools that will allow you to study the way you want to, whenever you want to.

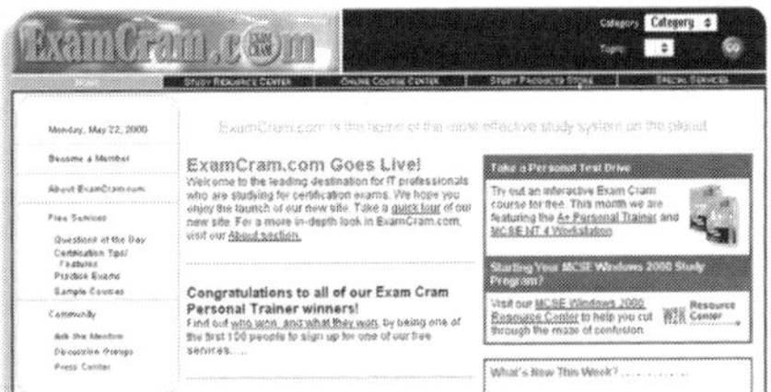


***Visit ExamCram.com now to enhance your study program.***

Help us continue to provide the very best certification study materials possible. Write us or email us at **learn@examcram.com** and let us know how our study products have helped you study. Tell us about new features that you'd like us to add. Send us a story about how we've helped you. We're listening!

Good luck with your certification exam and your career. Thank you for allowing us to help you achieve your goals.

***ExamCram.com Connects You to the Ultimate Study Center!***

*For my parents, my brother and his family, my wife and kids.*

*And in memory of Alfred Chabarek (1920–2000).*

# About the Author

**Darrell L. Ambro** is a Distinguished Member of Technical Staff with Lucent Technologies. He has been with Lucent and its predecessors for 24 years and has been using various forms of Unix since 1977.

During his career, Darrell has been involved in a variety of projects supporting both military and civilian organizations of the U.S. Government. These projects involved Local Area Network (LAN) design, operation, implementation and troubleshooting, application development and systems integration, system security and intrusion detection, database design, system administration, system test, proposal development, acceptance test/sales support, software maintenance and tier 2 support. Recently Darrell has become involved in supporting Lucent's corporate computer infrastructure.

In addition to being a Sun Certified System Administrator for Solaris 2.6, Solaris 7 and Solaris 8, Darrell is also a Sun Certified Network Administrator for Solaris 8, a Novell Certified NetWare Engineer (CNE) and a Microsoft Certified System Engineer (MCSE).

Darrell is a third degree black belt in Tae Kwon Do under the training of Grand Master Seung Gyoo Dong of Richmond, VA.

# Acknowledgments

Thanks to Sharon Linsenbach, Dan Young, Tiffany Taylor, Sheldon Barry, Thomas Riker, April Nielsen, and Jesse Dunn at The Coriolis Group who provided guidance and assistance in the development and production of my second book.

My wife, Lilli and my kids, Shane and Eva, for giving me the time to get it done. I love you.

My food chain at Lucent Technologies, Dennis Stinehelfer, Mark Decker and Chris Thomas for not objecting to me taking vacation on short notice. This allowed me to keep up with the writing schedule for this book.

My co-workers and friends for providing encouragement.

# Contents at a Glance

# Table of Contents

# Introduction

Welcome to *Solaris 8 System Administrator Exam Cram*. This book will help you get ready to take—and pass—the two exams required to obtain the Sun Certified System Administrator for Solaris 8 certification. In this Introduction, I talk about Sun's certification program in general and how the *Exam Cram* series can help you prepare for the Solaris 8 certification exams.

*Exam Cram* books help you understand and appreciate the subjects and materials you need to pass Solaris certification exams. The books are aimed strictly at test preparation and review. They do not teach you everything you need to know about a topic. Instead, I present and dissect the questions and problems that you're likely to encounter on a test.

Nevertheless, to completely prepare yourself for any Solaris test, I recommend that you begin by taking the Self-Assessment included in this book immediately following this Introduction. This tool will help you evaluate your knowledge base against the requirements for a Solaris 8 System Administrator under both ideal and real circumstances.

Based on what you learn from that exercise, you might decide to begin your studies with some classroom training or by reading one of the many system administration guides available from Sun and third-party vendors. I also strongly recommend that you install, configure, and fool around with Solaris 8 and other software that you'll be tested on, because nothing beats hands-on experience and familiarity when it comes to understanding the questions you're likely to encounter on a certification test. Book learning is essential, but hands-on experience is the best teacher of all!

## The Sun Certified System Administrator for Solaris 8

The certification program currently includes two separate tests. A brief description of each test follows:

- *Sun Certified System Administrator for the Solaris 8 Operating Environment, Part 1 (Exam 310-0011)*—The first exam (Part 1) covers basic system administration.

Knowledge tested includes installing the operating system, software package administration, patches, the boot process, system security and file permissions, account administration, disk and file system management, backup, and recovery.

- *Sun Certified System Administrator for the Solaris 8 Operating Environment, Part 2 (Exam 310-012)*—The second exam (Part 2) covers advanced topics and several add-on software packages that are used to enhance system administration capabilities. Knowledge tested includes the Solaris 8 network environment and network clients; device administration; virtual disk management systems; Network File System (NFS), along with automounting and caching; naming services such as DNS, NIS, and NIS+; along with automated installation using JumpStart.

To become a certified system administrator, an individual must pass both exams. You must pass Part 1 exam before you can take the Part 2 exam. This order is preferred anyway, since the knowledge tested builds from the first exam to the second.

It's not uncommon for the entire process to take a year or so, and many individuals find that they must take a test more than once to pass. The primary goal of the *Exam Cram* series is to make it possible, given proper study and preparation, to pass both of the exams on the first try.

Because certification is associated with a particular version of the Solaris operating system, there is no requirement to ever recertify. However, once a Solaris version becomes obsolete, being certified on that version will have very little value. It would be in your best interest to work on the certification for the next version of Solaris.

In the past, Sun has used the certification requirements and test objectives from the previous version as a starting point for the next version. Therefore, once certified on a version of Solaris, you should be very familiar with most of the test objectives for certification in the next version of Solaris. I estimate that about 25 percent of the test objectives changed between Solaris 7 and Solaris 8.

The best place to keep tabs on Sun's certification program is on the Sun Web site. The current URL for Sun's System Administrator program is at **http://suned.sun.com/US/certification/sysadmin.html**. Sun's certification Web site changes frequently, so if this URL doesn't work, try using the Search tool on Sun's site (**www.sun.com**) with either "certification" or the quoted phrase "certified system administrator" as the search string. This will help you find the latest and most accurate information about the company's certification programs.

## Taking a Certification Exam

Alas, testing is not free. You'll be charged $150 for each test you take, whether you pass or fail. In the United States and Canada, tests are administered by Sylvan Prometric.

First, you must purchase an examination voucher from Sun Educational Services. In the U.S., they can be contacted at 1-800-422-8020. This requires the use of a credit card. The voucher can be used for up to one year from the date of purchase.

Next, contact Sylvan Prometric to register for the exam. In the U.S., their number is 1-800-795-3926. You can also use the Sylvan Web site (**www.2test.com**).

To schedule an exam, call at least one day in advance. To cancel or reschedule an exam, you must call at least one day before the scheduled test time (or you may be charged the $150 fee). When calling Sylvan Prometric, please have the following information ready for the telesales staffer who handles your call:

- Your name, organization, mailing address, and social security number.
- The name of the exam you want to take.
- The number of the Sun voucher. (This information may not be needed, because the Sylvan Prometric staffer may already have it.)

An appointment confirmation will be sent to you by mail if you register more than five days before an exam, or will be sent by fax if less than five days before the exam. A Candidate Agreement letter, which you must sign to take the examination, will also be provided.

On the day of the test, try to arrive at least 15 minutes before the scheduled time slot. You must supply two forms of identification, one of which must be a photo ID.

All exams are completely closed book. In fact, you will not be permitted to take anything with you into the testing area. I suggest that you review the most critical information about the test you're taking just before the test. (*Exam Cram* books provide a brief reference—The Cram Sheet, located inside the front of this book—that lists the essential information from the book in distilled form.) You will have some time to compose yourself, to mentally review this critical information, and even to take a sample orientation exam before you begin the real thing. I suggest you take the orientation test before taking your first exam; they're all more or less identical in layout, behavior, and controls, so you probably won't need to do this more than once.

When you complete a Solaris 8 certification exam, the testing software will tell you whether you've passed or failed. Results are broken into several topical areas. Whether you pass or fail, I suggest you ask for—and keep—the detailed report that the test administrator prints for you. You can use the report to help you prepare for another go-round, if necessary, and even if you pass, the report shows areas you may need to review to keep your edge. If you need to retake an exam, you'll have to call Sylvan Prometric, schedule a new test date, and pay another $150.

# Tracking Certification Status

Sun maintains a database that indicates the exams you have passed and your corresponding test scores. This database is accessible at **www.galton.com/~sun**. After you pass both exams, you'll be certified as a System Administrator for Solaris 8. Official certification normally takes anywhere from four to six weeks (generally within 30 days), so don't expect to get your certificate overnight. Once certified, you will receive a package with a Welcome Kit that contains a number of elements:

- A System Administrator for Solaris 8 certificate, suitable for framing
- A logo sheet, which includes camera-ready artwork, for use on letterhead, business cards, etc.
- A Sun Certified System Administrator lapel pin

Many people believe that the benefits of certification go well beyond the perks that Sun provides to newly anointed members of this elite group. I am starting to see more job listings that request or require applicants to have a Solaris certification, and many individuals who complete the program can qualify for increases in pay and/or responsibility. As an official recognition of hard work and broad knowledge, Solaris certification is a badge of honor in many IT organizations.

# How to Prepare for an Exam

At a minimum, preparing for Solaris 8 exams requires that you obtain and study the following materials:

- The Solaris 8 documentation in printed form, on CD-ROM as delivered with Solaris 8 (AnswerBook2), or on the Web at **docs.sun.com**.
- The exam test objectives and sample questions on the Sun certification page (**http://suned.sun.com/US/certification/solaris/sysadmin.html**). Also see the Test Objectives section of Chapter 1. A table is included that provides a chapter to test objective cross-reference.

- This *Exam Cram* book. It's the first and last thing you should read before taking the exam.

In addition, you'll probably find any or all of the following materials useful in your quest for Solaris 8 system administration expertise:

- *Hands-on Experience*—Obtain a copy of Solaris 8 from the **www.sun.com** Web site. As you work through the book, try the commands and explore the details. Experience is the best way to learn and remember the details that you'll need to know to pass the exams. The Solaris 8 operating system can be downloaded for free or obtained on CD-ROM for the cost of media and shipping.
- *Classroom Training*—Sun offers classroom and computer-based training that you will find useful to help you prepare for the exam. But a word of warning: These classes are fairly expensive (in the range of $440 per day of training). However, they do offer a condensed form of learning to help you "brush up" on your Solaris knowledge. The tests are closely tied to the classroom training provided by Sun, so I would suggest taking the classes to get the Solaris-specific (and classroom-specific) terminology under your belt.
- *Other Publications*—You'll find direct references to other publications and resources in this book, and there's no shortage of materials available about Solaris; however, many are not written specifically for Solaris 8. For that reason, I have not referenced a large number of these publications. To help you sift through some of the publications out there, I end each chapter with a "Need To Know More?" section that provides pointers to more complete and exhaustive resources covering the chapter's subject matter. This section tells you where to look for further details.

These required and recommended materials represent a nonpareil collection of sources and resources for Solaris 8 System Administrator topics and software. In the section that follows, I explain how this book works and give you some good reasons why this book should also be on your required and recommended materials list.

# About This Book

Each topical *Exam Cram* chapter follows a regular structure, along with graphical cues about especially important or useful material. Here's the structure of a typical chapter:

- *Opening Hotlists* Each chapter begins with lists of the terms, tools, and techniques that you must learn and understand before you can be fully conversant with the chapter's subject matter. I follow the hotlists with one or two introductory paragraphs to set the stage for the rest of the chapter.

- *Topical Coverage*—After the opening hotlists, each chapter covers a series of topics related to the chapter's subject. Throughout this section, I highlight material most likely to appear on a test using a special Exam Alert layout, like this:

> This is what an Exam Alert looks like. Normally, an Exam Alert stresses concepts, terms, software, or activities that will most likely appear in one or more certification test questions. For that reason, any information found offset in Exam Alert format is worthy of unusual attentiveness on your part. Indeed, most of the facts appearing in The Cram Sheet appear as Exam Alerts within the text.

  Even if material isn't flagged as an Exam Alert, *all* the contents of this book are associated, at least tangentially, to something test-related. This book is tightly focused for quick test preparation, so you'll find that what appears in the meat of each chapter is critical knowledge.

  I have also provided tips that will help build a better foundation of system administration knowledge. Although the information may not be on the exam, it is highly relevant and will help you become a better test-taker.

> This is how tips are formatted. Keep your eyes open for these, and you'll become a test guru in no time!

- *Practice Questions*—This section presents a series of mock test questions and explanations of both correct and incorrect answers.
- *Details And Resources*—Every chapter ends with a section titled "Need to Know More?". This section provides direct pointers to Sun and third-party resources that offer further details on the chapter's subject matter. In addition, this section tries to rate the quality and thoroughness of each topic's coverage. If you find a resource you like in this collection, use it; but don't feel compelled to use all these resources. On the other hand, I recommend only resources I use on a regular basis, so none of my recommendations will be a waste of your time or money.

The bulk of the book follows this chapter structure slavishly, but there are a few other elements that I would like to point out. Chapters 11 and 22 include sample tests that provide a good review of the material presented throughout the book to ensure you're ready for the exam. Chapters 12 and 23 provide answer keys to the sample tests. Finally, look for The Cram Sheet, which appears inside the front of this *Exam Cram* book. It is a valuable tool that represents a condensed and compiled collection of facts, figures, and tips that I think you should memorize before taking the test. Because you can dump this information out of your head onto a piece of paper before answering any exam questions, you can master this information by brute force—you need to remember it only long enough to write it down when you walk into the test room. You might even want to look at it in the car or in the lobby of the testing center just before you walk in to take the test.

# How to Use This Book

If you're prepping for a first-time test, I've structured the topics in this book to build on one another. Therefore, some topics in later chapters make more sense after you've read earlier chapters. That's why I suggest you read this book from front to back for your initial test preparation.

If you need to brush up on a topic or you have to bone up for a second try, use the index or table of contents to go straight to the topics and questions that you need to study. Beyond the tests, I think you'll find this book useful as a tightly focused reference to some of the most important aspects of topics associated with being a system administrator, as implemented under Solaris 8.

Given all the book's elements and its specialized focus, I've tried to create a tool that you can use to prepare for—and pass—both of the Solaris 8 System Administrator examinations. Please share your feedback on the book with me, especially if you have ideas about how I can improve it for future test-takers. I'll consider everything you say carefully, and I try to respond to all suggestions. You can reach me via email at **solaris@unixcert.net**. Or you can send your questions or comments to **cipq@coriolis.com**. Please remember to include the title of the book in your message.

For up-to-date information on certification, online discussion forums, sample tests, content updates, and more, visit the Certification Insider Press Web site at **www.certificationinsider.com**.

Thanks, and enjoy the book!

# Self-Assessment

I've included a Self-Assessment in this *Exam Cram* to help you evaluate your readiness to tackle Sun Certified System Administrator for Solaris 8 certification. It should also help you understand what you need to master the topic of this book—namely, Exam 310-011, "Sun Certified System Administrator for Solaris 8 Operating Environment, Part 1" and Exam 310-012, "Sun Certified System Administrator for Solaris 8 Operating Environment, Part 2". But before you tackle this Self-Assessment, let's talk about the concerns you may face when pursuing a Solaris 8 System Administrator certification, and what an ideal candidate might look like.

## Solaris 8 System Administrators in the Real World

In the next section, I describe an ideal Solaris 8 System Administrator candidate, knowing full well that only a few actual candidates meet this ideal. In fact, my description of that ideal candidate might seem downright scary. But take heart, because, although the requirements to obtain a Solaris 8 System Administrator certification may seem pretty formidable, they are by no means impossible to meet. However, you should be keenly aware that it does take time, requires some expense, and consumes a substantial effort.

You can get all the real-world motivation you need from knowing that many others have gone before you. You can follow in their footsteps. If you're willing to tackle the process seriously and do what it takes to obtain the necessary experience and knowledge, you can take—and pass—the certification tests. In fact, the *Exam Crams* and the companion *Exam Preps* are designed to make it as easy as possible for you to prepare for these exams. But prepare you must!

The same, of course, is true for other Solaris certifications, including:

- Solaris 8 Network Administrator, which concentrates on the networking aspects but requires only one exam. The Solaris 8 System Administrator certification is a prerequisite.
- Solaris 7 System Administrator, which is similar to the Solaris 8, but addresses the previous version of Solaris and requires two exams.

- Solaris 7 Network Administrator, which concentrates on the networking aspects of the Solaris 7 environment and requires only one exam.

# The Ideal Solaris 8 System Administrator Candidate

Just to give you some idea of what an ideal Solaris 8 System Administrator candidate is like, here are some relevant statistics about the background and experience such an individual might have. Don't worry if you don't meet these qualifications (or, indeed, if you don't even come close), because this world is far from ideal, and where you fall short is simply where you'll have more work to do. The ideal candidate will have:

- Academic or professional training in Unix operating systems and more specifically the AT&T System V Release 4 (SVR4) Unix operating system on which Solaris is based.
- Three-plus years of professional system administration experience, including experience installing and upgrading operating systems, performance tuning, troubleshooting problems, creating users, and managing backup and recovery scenarios.

I believe that well under half of all certification candidates meet these requirements. In fact, most probably meet less than half of these requirements (that is, at least when they begin the certification process). But, because all those who have their certifications already survived this ordeal, you can survive it, too—especially if you heed what this Self-Assessment can tell you about what you already know and what you need to learn.

# Put Yourself to the Test

The following series of questions and observations is designed to help you figure out how much work you'll face in pursuing Solaris certification and what kinds of resources you may consult on your quest. Be absolutely honest in your answers, or you'll end up wasting money on exams you're not ready to take. There are no right or wrong answers, only steps along the path to certification. Only you can decide where you really belong in the broad spectrum of aspiring candidates.

Two things should be clear from the outset, however:

- Even a modest background in computer science will be helpful.
- Hands-on experience with Solaris operating system and technologies is an essential ingredient to certification success.

## Educational Background

1. Have you ever taken any computer-related classes? [Yes or No]

   If yes, proceed to Question 2; if no, proceed to Question 4.

2. Have you taken any classes on the Unix operating system? [Yes or No]

   If yes, you will probably be able to handle the discussions that relate to the Solaris operating system and system administration. If you're rusty, brush up on the basic Unix concepts and networking. If the answer is no, consider some basic reading in this area. I strongly recommend a good Solaris system administration book such as *A Practical Guide to Solaris* by Mark Sobell (1999). Or, if this title doesn't appeal to you, check out reviews for other, similar titles at your favorite online bookstore. However, don't expect a long list. Solaris 8 is still new in terms of available titles.

3. Have you taken any networking concepts or technologies classes? [Yes or No]

   If yes, you will probably be able to handle the networking terminology, concepts, and technologies (but brace yourself for frequent departures from normal usage). If you're rusty, brush up on basic networking concepts and terminology. If your answer is no, you might want to check out some titles on the Transport Communication Protocol/Internet Protocol (TCP/IP).

4. Have you done any reading on Unix or networks? [Yes or No]

   If yes, review the requirements from Questions 2 and 3. If you meet those, move to the next section, "Hands-On Experience." If you answered no, consult the recommended reading for both topics. This kind of strong background will be of great help in preparing you for the Solaris exams.

## Hands-On Experience

Another important key to success on all of the Solaris tests is hands-on experience. If I leave you with only one realization after taking this Self-Assessment, it should be that there's no substitute for time spent installing, configuring, and using the various Solaris command and tools upon which you'll be tested repeatedly and in depth.

5. Have you installed, configured, and worked with Solaris 8? [Yes or No]

   - If yes, make sure you understand basic concepts as covered in Exam 310-011.

   If you haven't worked with Solaris 8, you must obtain a copy of it for either SPARC or Intel x86 compatible platforms. Then, learn about the installation and administration.

TIP: You can obtain the exam objectives, practice questions, and other information about Solaris exams from the Sun's Training and Certification page on the Web at **http://suned.sun.com**.

Before you even think about taking any Solaris exam, make sure you've spent enough time with Solaris 8 to understand how it may be installed and configured, how to maintain such an installation, and how to troubleshoot that software when things go wrong. This will help you in the exam—as well as in real life.

TIP: If you have the funds or your employer will pay your way, consider taking a class at a Sun training and education center.

## Testing Your Exam-Readiness

Whether you attend a formal class on a specific topic to get ready for an exam or use written materials to study on your own, some preparation for the Solaris certification exams is essential. At $150 a try, pass or fail, you want to do everything you can to pass on your first try. That's where studying comes in.

I have included in this book several practice exam questions for each chapter and a sample test, so if you don't score well on the chapter questions, you can study more and then tackle the sample tests at the end of each part. If you don't earn a score of at least 66 percent on the Part I test and 70 percent on the Part II test, you'll want to investigate the other practice test resources available via the Web (locate them using your favorite search engine).

For any given subject, consider taking a class if you've tackled self-study materials, taken the test, and failed anyway. If you can afford the privilege, the opportunity to interact with an instructor and fellow students can make all the difference in the world. For information about Sun classes, visit the Certification Program page at **http://suned.sun.com**.

If you can't afford to take a class, visit the Certification Program page anyway, because it also includes free sample questions. Even if you can't afford to spend much at all, you should still invest in some low-cost practice exams from commercial vendors, because they can help you assess your readiness to pass a test better than any other tool. Check with the **www.unixcert.net** Web site for other available resources.

6. Have you taken a practice exam on your chosen test subject? [Yes or No]

   If yes—and you scored 66 percent or better on Part I and 70 percent or better on Part II—you're probably ready to tackle the real thing. If your score isn't above that crucial threshold, keep at it until you break that barrier. If you answered no, obtain all the free and low-budget practice tests you can find (or afford) and get to work. Keep at it until you can comfortably break the passing threshold.

TIP

There is no better way to assess your test readiness than to take a good-quality practice exam and pass with a score of 66 percent or better on Part I and 70 percent or better on Part II. When I'm preparing, I shoot for 80 plus percent, just to leave room for the "weirdness factor" that sometimes shows up on Solaris exams.

## Assessing Your Readiness for Exams 310-011 and 310-012

In addition to the general exam-readiness information in the previous section, other resources are available to help you prepare for the exams. Two Web sites come to mind. These are **www.solarisguide.com** and **www.solariscentral.org**. Also the comp newsgroups **comp.unix.solaris** and **comp.sys.sun.admin** available via news services or via **google.com**. Groups at **groups.google.com** are good. These are great places to ask questions about topics you are having trouble understanding and get good answers, or simply to observe the questions that others ask (along with the answers, of course). The Sun Blueprints Programs at **www.sun.com/blueprints** provide in-depth articles on various Solaris topics.

I'd also like to recommend that you check out one or more of these books as you prepare to take the exam:

- Mulligan, John P. *Solaris 8 Essential Reference*. New Riders, 2001.
- Sun Microsystems. The three volume *System Administration Guide* for Solaris 8 (Sun Micro Systems, 2000).

One last note: Hopefully, it makes sense to stress the importance of hands-on experience in the context of the exams. As you review the material for the exams, you'll realize that hands-on experience with Solaris 8 commands, tools, and utilities is invaluable.

## Onward, through the Fog!

Once you've assessed your readiness, undertaken the right background studies, obtained the hands-on experience that will help you understand the products and technologies at work, and reviewed the many sources of information to help you prepare for a test, you'll be ready to take a round of practice tests. When your scores come back positive enough to get you through the exam, you're ready to go after the real thing. If you follow my assessment regime, you'll not only know what you need to study, but when you're ready to make a test date at Sylvan. Good luck!

# Part I

## Exam 310-011

1

# Solaris 8 Certification Exams

**Terms you'll need to understand:**

✓ Multiple-choice question formats

✓ Radio button

✓ Checkbox

✓ Exhibit

✓ Drag and drop

✓ Fill in the blank (free choice)

✓ Careful reading

✓ Process of elimination

**Techniques you'll need to master:**

✓ Assessing your exam-readiness

✓ Preparing to take a certification exam

✓ Practicing (to make perfect)

✓ Making the best use of the testing software

✓ Budgeting your time

✓ Saving the hardest questions until last

✓ Guessing (as a last resort)

As experiences go, test-taking is not something that most people anticipate eagerly, no matter how well they're prepared. In most cases, familiarity helps ameliorate test anxiety. In plain English, this means that you probably won't be as nervous when you take your fourth or fifth certification exam as you will be when you take your first one.

Whether it's your first test or your tenth, understanding the exam-taking particulars (how much time to spend on questions, the setting you'll be in, and so on) and the testing software will help you concentrate on the material rather than on the environment. Likewise, mastering a few basic test-taking skills should help you recognize—and perhaps even outfox—some of the tricks and gotchas you're bound to find in some of the test questions.

In this chapter, I'll explain the testing environment and software, as well as describe some proven test-taking strategies that you should be able to use to your advantage.

# Assessing Exam-Readiness

Before you take any Solaris exam, I strongly recommend that you read through and take the Self-Assessment included with this book (it appears just before this chapter). This will help you compare your knowledge base to the requirements for obtaining the Solaris 8 System Administrator certification and will help you identify parts of your background or experience that might be in need of improvement, enhancement, or further learning. If you get the right set of basics under your belt, obtaining Solaris certification will be that much easier.

Once you've gone through the Self-Assessment, you can remedy those topical areas where your background or experience might not measure up to that of an ideal certification candidate. But you can also tackle subject matter for individual tests at the same time, so you can continue making progress while you're catching up in some areas.

Once you've worked through this *Exam Cram*, have read the supplementary materials, and have taken the practice tests in Chapters 11 and 22, you'll have a pretty clear idea of when you should be ready to take the real exam. Although I strongly recommend that you keep practicing until your scores top the 66 percent mark on Part I and the 70 percent mark on Part II, 71 and 75 percent, respectively, would be a good goal to give yourself some margin for error in a real exam situation (where stress will play more of a role than when you practice). Once you hit that point, you should be ready to go. But if you get through the practice exam in this book without attaining that score, you should keep taking practice tests and studying the materials until you get there. You'll find more information about other practice test vendors in the Self-Assessment along with even more pointers on how to study and prepare. But now, on to the exam itself!

## The Test Objectives

The test objectives for both exams are posted on Sun's Web site at **http://suned.sun.com/US/certification/solaris/sysadmin.html**. Tables 1.1 and 1.2 provide a quick chapter to test objective cross-reference.

## The Testing Situation

When you arrive at the Sylvan Prometric Testing Center where you scheduled your test, you'll need to sign in with a test coordinator. He or she will ask you to produce two forms of identification, one of which must be a photo ID. Once you've signed in and your time slot arrives, you'll be asked leave any books, bags, or other items you brought with you, and you'll be escorted into a closed room. Typically, that room will be furnished with anywhere from one to half a dozen computers, and each workstation will be separated from the others by dividers designed to keep you from seeing what's happening on someone else's computer.

**Table 1.1 Chapter to Exam 310-011 (Part I) Test Objectives.**

| Chapter | Test Objective |
|---|---|
| 2 | System Concepts |
| 3 | Installation |
| 4 | The Boot Prom, Initialization, and Shutdown |
| 5 | Security |
| 6 | User Administration |
| 7 | Process Control |
| 8 | Disk Configuration and Format |
| 9 | File Systems. Files and Directories, Backup, and Recovery |
| 10 | Basic Command Syntax, Editor, Remote Connection |

**Table 1.2 Chapter to Exam 310-012 (Part II) Test Objectives.**

| Chapter | Test Objective |
|---|---|
| 13 | Client Server Relationship and Solaris Network Environment |
| 14 | Solaris Syslog |
| 15 | Disk Management |
| 16 | Solaris Pseudo File Systems and Swap Space |
| 17 | Role-Based Access Control (RBAC) |
| 18 | NFS, AutoFS, and CacheFS |
| 19 | Naming Services and NIS |
| 20 | Solaris Management Console and Solstice AdminSuite |
| 21 | JumpStart — Automatic Installation |

You'll be furnished with a pen or pencil and a blank sheet of paper or, in some cases, an erasable plastic sheet and an erasable felt-tip pen. You're allowed to write down any information you want on this sheet, and you can write stuff on both sides of the page. I suggest that you memorize as much as possible of the material that appears on the Cram Sheet (inside the front of this book) and then write that information down on the blank sheet as soon as you sit down in front of the test machine. You can refer to the sheet any time you like during the test, but you'll have to surrender it when you leave the room.

Most test rooms feature a wall with a large window. This allows the test coordinator to monitor the room, to prevent test-takers from talking to one another, and to observe anything out of the ordinary that might be going on. The test coordinator will have preloaded the Solaris certification exam that you've signed up for, and you'll be permitted to start as soon as you're seated in front of the machine.

Each Solaris certification exam permits you to take up to 90 minutes to complete the test (the test itself will tell you, and it maintains an on-screen counter/clock so that you can check the time remaining whenever you like). Part I consists of 57 questions and Part II consists of 61 questions, randomly selected from a pool of questions.

TIP: The passing score varies per exam. For Exam 310-011, the passing score is 66 percent, and for Exam 310-012, the passing score is 70 percent.

All Solaris certification exams are computer - generated and use a multiple-choice, drag-and-drop or fill-in-the-blank format. Although this might sound easy, the questions are constructed not just to check your mastery of basic Solaris system administration, but also require you to evaluate one or more sets of circumstances or requirements. Often, you'll be asked to give more than one answer to a question; likewise, you might be asked to select the best or most effective solution to a problem from a range of choices, all of which technically are correct. The tests are quite an adventure, and they involve real thinking. This book will show you what to expect and how to deal with the problems, puzzles, and predicaments that you're likely to find on the exams.

## Test Layout and Design

A typical test question is depicted in Question 1. It's a multiple-choice question that requires you to select a single correct answer. Following the question is a brief summary of each potential answer and why it was either right or wrong.

## Question 1

Which of the following is the last phase in the Solaris boot process?

❍ a. init

❍ b. Boot PROM

❍ c. BIOS

❍ d. Kernel initialization

❍ e. Boot programs

Answer a is correct. All of these are phases of either the SPARC or the Intel x86 boot process. The boot PROM and BIOS phases test hardware. Therefore, answers b and c are incorrect. The boot programs phase locates and loads boot programs, and then the kernel initialization phase loads the kernel. Therefore, answers d and e are incorrect. Only then can the init phase occur to initialize the operating system services.

This sample question corresponds closely to those you'll see on Solaris certification exams. To select the correct answer during the test, you would position the cursor over the radio button next to answer a and click the mouse to select that particular choice. The only difference between the questions on the certification exams and questions such as this one is that the real questions are not immediately followed by the answers.

The following is a question for which one or more answers are possible. This type of question provides checkboxes rather than radio buttons for marking all the appropriate selections.

## Question 2

Which of the following commands can be used to list all installed patches? [Select all that apply]

❑ a. **showrev -p**

❑ b. **patchinfo**

❑ c. **patchlist all**

❑ d. **patchadd -p**

Answers a and d are correct. Answers b and c do not exist.

For this type of question, one or more answers must be selected to answer the question correctly. For Question 2, you would have to position the cursor over the checkboxes next to items a and d and click on both to obtain credit for a correct answer.

These two types of questions can appear in many forms and constitute the foundation on which most of the Solaris certification exam questions rest. More complex questions might include so-called exhibits, which are usually tables or data-content layouts of one form or another. You'll be expected to use the information displayed in the exhibit to guide your answer to the question.

Other questions involving exhibits might use charts or diagrams to help document a workplace scenario that you'll be asked to troubleshoot or configure. Paying careful attention to such exhibits is the key to success—be prepared to toggle between the picture and the question as you work. Often, both are complex enough that you might not be able to remember all of either one.

The drag-and-drop questions are new to the Solaris exams. They provide a table consisting of two columns of data, such as technical terms and their definitions. All of the terms have to be positioned (using the mouse) in front of their respective definition to be correct. To drag a term, position the mouse over the term and depress the left mouse button. Then move the mouse to drag the term to the appropriate location. Release the mouse button to drop the term in front of its definition.

The remaining questions are fill in the blank. This involves entering the name of a command, file name, command-line argument, or Solaris-related terminology. A typical fill-in-the-blank question is shown in Question 3. This question provides a box in which to enter the answer.

## Question 3

Enter the full pathname to the file used to modify the configuration of the kernel.

______________________________

The correct answer is /etc/system.

Be sure to read this type of question very carefully. Without having any answers in front of you, there is nothing to jog your memory and it makes guessing almost impossible. Because this question specifically asked for the full pathname, an answer such as *system*, which might be considered technically correct, will be marked as wrong. Try to be as specific as possible.

## Using the Test Software Effectively

A well-known test-taking principle is to read over the entire test from start to finish first, but to answer only those questions that you feel absolutely sure of on the first pass. On subsequent passes, you can dive into more complex questions, knowing how many such questions you have to deal with.

Fortunately, the test software makes this approach easy to implement. At the bottom of each question, you'll find a checkbox that permits you to mark that question for a later visit. (Note that marking questions makes review easier, but you can return to any question by clicking the Forward and Back buttons repeatedly until you get to the question.) As you read each question, if you answer only those you're sure of and mark for review those that you're not, you can keep going through a decreasing list of open questions as you knock the trickier ones off in order.

TIP

There's at least one potential benefit to reading the test over completely before answering the trickier questions: Sometimes, you find information in later questions that sheds more light on earlier ones. Other times, information you read in later questions might jog your memory about facts, figures, or behavior that also will help with earlier questions. Either way, you'll come out ahead if you defer those questions about which you're not absolutely sure of the answer(s).

Keep working on the questions until you're absolutely sure of all your answers or until you know you'll run out of time. If unanswered questions remain, you'll want to zip through them and guess. No answer guarantees that no credit will be given for a question, and a guess has at least a chance of being correct. (Blank answers and incorrect answers are scored as equally wrong.)

TIP

At the very end of your test period, you're better off guessing than leaving questions blank or unanswered.

## Taking Testing Seriously

The most important advice I can give you about taking any test is this: Read each question carefully. Some questions are deliberately ambiguous, some use double negatives, and others use terminology in incredibly precise ways. I've taken numerous practice tests and real tests myself, and in nearly every test I've missed at least one question because I didn't read it closely or carefully enough.

Here are some suggestions on how to deal with the tendency to jump to an answer too quickly:

- Make sure you read every word in the question. If you find yourself jumping ahead impatiently, go back and start over.
- As you read, try to restate the question in your own terms. If you can do this, you should be able to pick the correct answer(s) much more easily.
- When returning to a question after your initial read-through, reread every word again—otherwise, your mind can fall quickly into a rut. Sometimes, seeing a question afresh after turning your attention elsewhere lets you see something that you missed, but the strong tendency is to see what you've seen before. Try to avoid that tendency at all costs.
- If you return to a question more than twice, try to articulate to yourself what you don't understand about the question, why the answers don't appear to make sense, or what appears to be missing. If you chew on the subject for a while, your subconscious might provide the details that are lacking or you might notice a "trick" that will point to the right answer.

Above all, try to deal with each question by thinking through what you know about being a Solaris system administrator—commands, characteristics, behaviors, facts, and figures involved. By reviewing what you know (and what you've written down on your information sheet), you'll often recall or understand things sufficiently to determine the answer to the question.

## Question-Handling Strategies

Based on the tests I've taken, a couple of interesting trends in the answers have become apparent. For those questions that take only a single answer, usually two or three of the answers will be obviously incorrect, and two of the answers will be plausible. But, of course, only one can be correct. Unless the answer leaps out at you (and if it does, reread the question to look for a trick; sometimes those are the ones you're most likely to get wrong), begin the process of answering by eliminating those answers that are obviously wrong.

Things to look for in the "obviously wrong" category include spurious command choices or file names, nonexistent software or command options, and terminology that you've never seen before. If you've done your homework for a test, no valid information should be completely new to you. In that case, unfamiliar or bizarre terminology probably indicates a totally bogus answer. As long as you're sure what's right, it's easy to eliminate what's wrong.

Numerous questions assume that the default behavior of a particular Solaris command is in effect. It's essential to know and understand the default settings for the various commands. If you know the defaults and understand what they mean, this knowledge will help you cut through many Gordian knots.

Likewise, when dealing with questions that require multiple answers, you must know and select all the correct options to get credit. This, too, qualifies as an example of why careful reading is so important.

As you work your way through the test, another counter that the exam provides will come in handy: the number of questions completed and questions outstanding. Budget your time by making sure that you've completed one-fourth of the questions one-quarter of the way through the test period. Check again three-quarters of the way through. For Exam 310-011 with 57 questions and Exam 310-012 with 61 questions, that's about 20 questions after 30 minutes and 40 questions after 60 minutes (30 minutes remaining).

If you're not through after 80 minutes, use the last 10 minutes to guess your way through the remaining questions. Remember, guesses are potentially more valuable than blank answers because blanks are always wrong, but a guess might turn out to be right. If you haven't a clue about any of the remaining questions, pick answers at random or choose all *a*s, *b*s, and so on. The important thing is to submit a test for scoring that has an answer for every question.

# Mastering the Inner Game

In the final analysis, knowledge breeds confidence, and confidence breeds success. If you study the materials in this book carefully and review all the questions at the end of each chapter, you should be aware of those areas where additional studying is required.

Next, follow up by reading some or all of the materials recommended in the "Need to Know More?" section at the end of each chapter. The idea is to become familiar enough with the concepts and situations that you find in the sample questions to be able to reason your way through similar situations on a real test. If you know the material, you have every right to be confident that you can pass the test.

Once you've worked your way through Part I, take the practice test in Chapter 11. Likewise, after studying Part II, take the practice test in Chapter 22. The tests will provide a reality check and help you identify areas that you need to study further. Make sure that you follow up and review materials related to the questions you miss before scheduling the real tests. Only when you've covered all the ground and feel comfortable with the whole scope of the practice tests should you take the real tests.

> **TIP** If you take the practice test in Chapter 11 and don't score at least 66 percent correct or don't score at least 70 percent on the practice test in Chapter 22, you'll want to practice further.

Armed with the information in this book and with the determination to augment your knowledge, you should be able to pass the certification exam. But if you don't work at it, you'll spend the test fee more than once before you finally do pass. If you prepare seriously, the exam should go flawlessly. Good luck!

# Additional Resources

By far, the best source of information about Solaris certification exams comes from Sun itself. Because its products and technologies—and the tests that go with them—change frequently, the best place to go for exam-related information is online.

If you haven't already visited the Solaris certification pages, do so right now. As I'm writing this chapter, the certification home page resides at **http://suned.sun.com/US/certification/solaris/sysadmin.html**.

*Note: It might not be there by the time you read this, or it might have been replaced by something new and different, because things change regularly on the Sun site. Should this happen, please read the section titled "Coping with Change on the Web" later in this chapter.*

This Web page will point to additional information in the certification pages. Here's what to check out:

- *Overview*—An overview of the certification process and exams.
- *Supporting Courseware*—Classroom courses and self-paced computer-based training offered by Sun that cover the information listed in the exam objectives.
- *Exam Objectives*—A detailed list of the topics that will be covered on the exams.
- *Sample Questions*—A limited number of sample questions and answers.
- *Registration*—Information on purchasing a Sun voucher and registering with Sylvan Prometric to schedule the exams.
- *FAQs*—Frequently Asked Questions; yours might get answered here.

As you browse through them—and I strongly recommend that you do—you'll probably find other things that I didn't mention here that are every bit as interesting and compelling.

## Coping with Change on the Web

Sooner or later, all the specifics I've shared with you about the Solaris certification pages, and all the other Web-based resources I mention throughout the rest of this book, will go stale or be replaced by newer information. In some cases, the URLs that you find here might lead you to their replacements; in other cases, the URLs will go nowhere, leaving you with the dreaded "404 File not found" error message.

When that happens, please don't give up. There's always a way to find what you want on the Web—if you're willing to invest some time and energy. To begin with, most large or complex Web sites—and Sun's qualifies on both counts—offer a search engine. As long as you can get to Sun's home page (and I'm sure that it will stay at **www.sun.com** for a long while yet), you can use this tool to help you find what you need.

The more focused you can make a search request, the more likely it is that the results will include information you can use. For example, you can search for the string "training and certification" to produce a lot of data about the subject in general, but if you're looking for the details on the Sun Certified System Administrator tests, you'll be more likely to get there quickly if you use a search string such as this:

```
"Administrator" AND "certification"
```

Likewise, if you want to find the training and certification downloads, try a search string such as this:

```
"training and certification" AND "download page"
```

Finally, don't be afraid to use general search tools such as **www.search.com**, **www.altavista.com**, or **www.excite.com** to search for related information. Even though Sun offers information about its certification exams online, there are plenty of third-party sources of information, training, and assistance in this area that do not have to follow a party line like Sun does. The bottom line is this: If you can't find something where the book says it lives, start looking around. If worse comes to worse, you can always email me! I just might have a clue. My email address is **solaris@unixcert.net**.

# 2

# System Concepts

### Terms you'll need to understand:

- ✓ Kernel
- ✓ Shell
- ✓ File system
- ✓ Daemon
- ✓ The *Solaris 8 Reference Manual*

### Techniques you'll need to master:

- ✓ Distinguishing between the parts of the operating system
- ✓ Distinguishing between the three shells
- ✓ Using the **man** command to view online manual pages

This chapter covers some basic concepts of the Solaris 8 operating system. The first section briefly summarizes the new features of Solaris 8. The second section addresses the structure and components of the operating system. The next section summarizes the three shells, and the last section provides an overview of the online reference manual. This chapter covers the *System Concepts* test objectives.

# New Features of Solaris 8

The following enhancements have been added to the latest release of Solaris:

- *Internet Protocol version 6 (IPv6)*—The next generation of IP, which overcomes many of the limitations associated with the current version of IP (version 4). The main advantages are a larger address space and the autoconfiguration of addresses. In Solaris 8, the network interfaces can be configured simultaneously for both IPv4 and IPv6.
- *Java 2 Software Development Kit (SDK)*—The latest version of the Java SDK makes Solaris a powerful platform for machine-independent software development.
- *Universal Disk Format (UDF) file system*—Allows easy interchange of data stored on CD-ROMs, DVDs, hard disks, and diskettes.
- *Graphical wizards*—A couple new graphical wizards have been added to improve system usability. Most notable are the Installation Wizard and the DCHP Manager. In addition, the X Server that supports X applications has been upgraded to the X11R6.4 industry standard.

# The Three Parts of the Operating System

Solaris 8, like all variations of the Unix operating system, consists of three parts: the kernel, the shell, and the file system. Each of these will be discussed in the next few sections.

## The Kernel

The *kernel* is a collection of software that manages the physical and logical resources of the computer. These management services include controlling the allocation of memory and other storage devices, controlling access to peripheral devices (input/output), and controlling the scheduling and execution of processes or tasks. For the most part, these services are transparent to the user. The user issues a request to perform a task, and the kernel deals with the complexity of the underlying hardware and allocating logical resources to accomplish the task.

The physical resources are controlled by means of software modules, referred to as *device drivers*, which understand how to communicate with hardware devices and control their operation. Typically, each device has a unique driver that is provided with the hardware and is identified by hardware manufacturer, model, and sometimes hardware version.

The logical resources include processes and memory. A *process* is a task or program. The kernel maintains internal data structures that define and control the processes; it also controls the scheduling, execution, and termination of processes. Other important kernel services are memory management and interprocess communication. Memory management involves keeping track of available memory, allocating it to processes as needed, and reclaiming it as processes release it or terminate. Interprocess communication involves handling the cooperative communication between processes.

The Solaris 8 kernel supports multiple users, each of which can be executing one or more processes or tasks. Thus, Solaris 8 is both a *multiuser* and a *multitasking* system. The Solaris 8 kernel accomplishes this level of support by allowing a task to have access to system resources for a small slice of time. A task is allowed to execute for one or more time slices and then is suspended to allow another task to execute. This approach provides time-sharing among all active tasks and gives the appearance that all tasks are running simultaneously. A task that appears to be executing all the time (and typically provides a service on demand) is referred to as a *daemon*.

## The Shell

The *shell* is a software module that provides the interface between users and the kernel. It accepts user requests and submits them to the kernel. It also accepts status information and data from the kernel and presents them to the user. Typically, the shell accepts user input from a terminal or network connection; however, input can be taken from a file, a device, or even another process. In addition, output from the kernel is typically sent to the user's terminal or network connection. Likewise, this output can be redirected to a file, a device, or another process.

The shell also provides a built-in programming language that can be used to automate repetitive tasks. This automation includes flow control along with the ability to manipulate numeric and string data.

Solaris 8 provides several different shells, each with unique strengths. Some shells provide a history/recall mechanism that allows the user to reexecute a previous command by entering a few control sequences instead of reentering the command. Other shells provide built-in math manipulation.

## The File System

A *file* is a group of bytes treated as a unit for storage, retrieval, and manipulation. The *file system* is a collection of files stored on a disk drive in a hierarchical structure. A special type of file, called a *directory*, serves as a folder and is used to organize files. A file system can be thought of as an inverted tree, with the directories being the branches and the files being the leaves. The name for the top-level directory of a Unix system, *root*, comes from this analogy.

The Unix operating system supports the file system concept by providing utilities to create, mount (make accessible), check, repair, duplicate, and back up file systems. The storage space that is accessible on a Unix system usually is divided into multiple file systems. This division allows easier maintenance and improves performance.

# The Three Most Common Shells

The Solaris 8 environment provides several shells. The three most common shells are the Bourne shell (sh), the C shell (csh), and the Korn shell (ksh).

The Bourne shell was developed by Steven Bourne at AT&T Bell Laboratories and was the shell provided with the original Unix operating system. The Unix operating system was designed and developed by Ken Thompson and Dennis Ritchie at Bell Labs during the 1970s. The most popular version was Unix System V.

EXAM ALERT: The Bourne shell is the default shell for the Solaris 8 operating system.

The C shell was developed by Bill Joy of the University of California, Berkeley and was provided with a version of the Unix operating system that was developed at the university and referred to as Berkeley Software Distribution (BSD) Unix.

The Korn shell was designed and developed by David G. Korn at AT&T Bell Laboratories. The Korn shell was derived from the Bourne shell by adding many features from the C shell along with new features of its own. Table 2.1 compares the features of the three shells.

EXAM ALERT: Use of the initialization files for each shell is an important concept that is useful when you're setting up user accounts on a Solaris 8 system. Be sure that you understand their usage and associate the file names correctly with the appropriate shells.

**Table 2.1 Features of Solaris 8 shells.**

| Feature | sh | csh | ksh | Function |
|---|---|---|---|---|
| Aliasing | No | Yes | Yes | Lets you assign a short, simple name to a complex string and then to use the name in place of the string in commands. Doing so gives the appearance of being able to add custom commands to the shell. |
| Bourne shell–compatible syntax | Yes | No | Yes | Because the Korn shell is an enhanced version of the Bourne shell, they use the same syntax. The C shell was developed separately, and its syntax is based on the C programming language. |
| Default prompt | $ | % | $ | The default prompt for both the Bourne and the Korn shells is the dollar sign ($) character, whereas the default prompt for the C shell is the system hostname followed by the percent (%) character. |
| History capability | No | Yes | Yes | The history capability of the C and the Korn shells keeps track of a user-defined number of previous commands. Instead of reentering a command, you can copy it from the history and then execute it. |
| History editing | No | Yes | No | Lets you modify and then reuse previous commands. |
| History execution | No | !*n* | fc | Repeats the previous command with few keystrokes. For csh, *n* is the number of the command in the history list. |
| Initialization file: login | .profile | .login | .profile | Stores commands that should be executed once, when a user logs in to the system. |
| Initialization file: shell startup | No | .cshrc | User defined | Stores commands that are executed every time the user starts a shell to execute a command. With the Korn shell, the user can specify the name of the shell startup initialization file using the **ENV** parameter. |
| Inline editing | No | No | Yes | Allows you to edit a command that has been entered but not yet executed. Thus, you can correct typographical errors rather than retyping the entire command. Either emacs or vi editing commands can be used when you're correcting errors. |

*(continued)*

**Table 2.1 Features of Solaris 8 shells *(continued)*.**

| Feature | sh | csh | ksh | Function |
|---|---|---|---|---|
| Logout file | No | .logout | No | Stores commands that should be executed when a user logs out. |
| Overwrite protect | No | Yes | Yes | Prevents files from being accidentally overwritten; can be set by using the **noclobber** parameter. |
| Repeat last command | No | !! | No | Handy shortcut for reexecuting the last command with only a few keystrokes. |
| Restricted version | rsh | No | rksh | Intended for users who need only limited access to the Unix system. Provides enhanced security by confining the user to a single directory and preventing the redirection of shell output. Be sure not to confuse the restricted Bourne shell (/usr/lib/rsh) with the remote shell (/usr/bin/rsh), which is used to execute commands on a remote system. The restricted version of the Korn shell is /usr/bin/rksh. |
| Source | AT&T | Berkeley | AT&T | Both the Bourne and Korn shells originated at AT&T Bell Labs, whereas the C shell came from the University of California at Berkeley. |

# The Online Reference Manual

The *Solaris 8 Reference Manual* (in printed form) is a multivolume set of manuals that document the commands, system calls, library functions, special files, and so on, that are available with the Solaris 8 operating system. This format originated with the initial version of the Unix operating system developed by AT&T Bell Labs and has been adopted as *the* definitive documentation for almost every version of the Unix operating system available.

For convenience, an online version of the *Reference Manual* is provided with the Solaris 8 system and most other versions of the Unix operating system. The *pages* or topics of the online *Reference Manual* can be viewed on the terminal/monitor screen using the **man**(1) command. The *Reference Manual* is also included in the Solaris 8 AnswerBook2 online documentation, which lets you search, display, and print *Reference Manual* pages using an HTML Web browser such as Netscape Navigator. The pages of the *Reference Manual* are referred to as *man pages*.

The *Reference Manual* is divided into *sections*. Each section addresses a related set of commands or different aspects of the operating system. Table 2.2 describes the *Reference Manual* sections.

**Table 2.2 Sections of the *Solaris 8 Reference Manual.***

| Section | Description |
|---|---|
| 1 | Commands available to all users. Included are commands that are part of the BSD Compatibility Package (1B), commands used to communicate between systems (1C), commands associated with the *Form and Menu Language Interpreter* (1F), and commands specific the SunOS system (1S). |
| 1M | Commands used for system maintenance and administration. Some are restricted to system administration login accounts (such as root). |
| 2 | Low-level operating system calls that can be used by C language programs to access and control system resources. |
| 3 | Functions available in system libraries that can be used by C language programs to access and control system resources. This section is subdivided based on library function (basic, networking, threads, curses, and so on). |
| 4 | Format of various system configuration files. Also included are descriptions of the C language data structure declarations that can be used to access some system files via a C language program. |
| 5 | Miscellaneous topics such as standards, environments, and macros. |
| 6 | Any available games or demos. |
| 7 | Special files associated with specific hardware, device drivers, and components of the STREAMS I/O subsystem. |
| 9 | Two kernel-level device drive specifications: the Device Driver Interface (DDI) and the Driver/Kernel Interface (DKI). This section is subdivided based on topic (entry points, functions, data structures, and so on). |

Note that Section 8 is not used. In the original AT&T Unix System V operating system, Section 8 was used to describe special system maintenance procedures. For Solaris, these procedures are described in the *System Administration Guide* and other guides and manuals.

Typically, each section of the *Reference Manual* is printed as a separate volume. When a man page is referenced in text, the section number may be specified in parentheses after the name of the command. This number may not be important in the online manuals, but if you are trying to locate a manual page within a stack of printed manuals more than a foot high, knowing the section number (that is, which volume) saves a lot of time and effort. Thus, **man**(1) indicates that the **man** command is located in Section 1: "User Commands."

## Using the man Command

Even though both the printed *Reference Manual* and AnswerBook2 are available, the test objectives for Part I include using the online man pages as a requirement. The **man**(1) command is used to display one or more man pages specified as

| Table 2.3 Command-line arguments for the man command. | |
|---|---|
| **Argument** | **Description** |
| ***name*** | The name of a Solaris command, file, and so on, that is described by a man page of the same name. At least one ***name*** is required by all arguments except the **-f**, **-k**, and **-M** arguments. More than one ***name*** (separated by spaces) can be specified. |
| **-** | Don't automatically send output through the **more**(1) command (which provides pagination, underlining, and so on). |
| **-a** | Display all man pages that match the specified ***name*** (regardless of section). |
| **-d** | Display debug information (search methods used, sections searched, and so on) used to locate the ***name*** man page. |
| **-f *file* ...** | List man pages that reference the specified ***file*** (requires preformatted man pages). More than one ***file*** can be specified (separated by spaces). Note that this argument is used to locate a file referenced in the man page, not a man page (therefore, it does not require a man page ***name*** argument). |
| **-F** | Force a search of all man sections for ***name*** instead of using the windex database to locate man pages (windex is associated with preformatted man pages). |
| **-k *keyword* ...** | Print a summary of all windex database entries that contain the specified ***keyword*** (preformatted man pages only). More than one ***keyword*** can be specified (separated by spaces). Note that this argument is used to locate keywords in a database, not a man page (therefore, it does not require a man page ***name*** argument). |
| **-l** | List all man pages that match the specified ***name*** (regardless of section). |
| **-M *path*** | Specify an alternate directory ***path*** for man page files. This argument can be used with any of the other arguments. |
| **-r** | Reformats the specified ***name*** man page. Instead of being displayed, the output is captured in a file for use by subsequent **man** commands. |
| **-s *section* ...** | Search only the specified ***section*** or sections (separated by spaces). |
| **-t** | Typeset the specified ***name*** man page using **troff**(1). If **-t** is used with the **-** argument, the output is not displayed, but instead is captured in a file for subsequent use by the **man** command. |
| **-T *macro*** | Use the specified **nroff**(1) *macro* package instead of the standard man page (**-man**) macro package. |

command-line arguments. Table 2.3 lists the command-line arguments available with the **man** command.

The following example shows how you can use the **man** command to display the **man**(1) man page. Note that man pages longer than one screen in length use the **more**(1) command to display one screen of the man page at a time:

```
# man man
Reformatting Page. Please wait... Done

User Commands                                          man(1)

NAME
     man - find and display reference manual pages

SYNOPSIS
     man [ - ]  [ -adFlrt ]  [ -M path ]  [ -T macro-package ]
     [-s section ]  name ...

     man [ -M path ]  -k keyword ...

     man [ -M path ]  -f file ...

DESCRIPTION
     The man command  displays  information  from  the  reference
     manuals.  It  displays complete manual pages that you select
     by name, or one-line summaries selected  either  by  keyword
     (-k),  or  by  the  name  of  an associated file (-f). If no
     manual page is located, man prints an error message.

  Source Format
     Reference Manual pages are marked up with  either   nroff(1)
     or   sgml(5)  (Standard  Generalized  Markup Language) tags.
     The man command recognizes the type of markup and  processes
     the  file accordingly.  The various source files are kept in
     separate directories depending on the type of markup.

  Location of Manual Pages
     The online Reference Manual page directories are convention-
     ally  located  in  /usr/share/man.  The  nroff  sources  are
     located in the /usr/share/man/man* directories.   The   SGML
     sources are located in the /usr/share/man/sman* directories.
     Each directory corresponds to a section of the manual. Since
.
.
.
```

The *passwd* topic shows the different **man** command-line arguments, because **passwd**(1) is a command and **passwd**(4) is a system file. The following example lists all man pages named *passwd.*

```
# man -l passwd
passwd (1)      -M /usr/share/man
passwd (4)      -M /usr/share/man
#
```

Note that both man pages are listed. In addition, an appropriate **-M** command-line argument is displayed to show the location of the man pages. The default path name for man pages is /usr/share/man.

The following example displays the **passwd**(1) man page:

```
# man passwd
Reformatting Page. Please wait... Done

User Commands                                          passwd(1)

NAME
     passwd - change login password and password attributes

SYNOPSIS
     passwd [ -r files | -r ldap  | -r nis  |  -r  nisplus  ]
     [ name ]

     passwd [  -r files  ]  [ -egh ]  [ name ]

     passwd [  -r files  ]  -s  [ -a ]

     passwd [  -r files  ]  -s  [ name ]

     passwd [  -r files  ]  [ -d | -l ]  [ -f ]  [  -n min  ]
     [ -w warn ]  [ -x max ]  name

     passwd  -r  ldap  [ -egh ]  [ name ]

     passwd  -r  nis  [ -egh ]  [ name ]

     passwd  -r  nisplus  [ -egh ]  [ -D domainname ]  [ name ]

     passwd  -r  nisplus  -s  [ -a ]

     passwd  -r  nisplus  [ -D domainname ]  -s  [ name ]

     passwd  -r  nisplus  [ -l ]  [ -f ]  [ -n min ]  [ -w warn ]
     [ -x max ]  [ -D domainname ]  name

DESCRIPTION
     The passwd command changes the password  or  lists  password
.
.
.
```

Note that **man -s 1 passwd** would have provided the same result. In the absence of a specified section, the man pages are searched by section and the first one found is printed. To display the **passwd**(4) man page, you must specify the section as in the following example:

```
# man -s 4 passwd
Reformatting Page. Please wait... Done

File Formats                                         passwd(4)

NAME
     passwd - password file

SYNOPSIS
     /etc/passwd

DESCRIPTION
     /etc/passwd is a local source of  information  about  users'
     accounts.  The password file can be used in conjunction with
     other password sources, including the NIS maps
     passwd.byname and  passwd.bygid and the NIS+ table  passwd.
     Programs use the getpwnam(3C) routines to access this infor-
     mation.

     Each  passwd entry is a single line of the form:

          username:password:uid:
          gid:gcos-field:home-dir:
          login-shell

     where

     username
          is the user's login name. It is recommended that  this
          field conform to the checks performed by  pwck(1M).

     password
          is an empty field. The encrypted password for the user
          is in the corresponding entry in the /etc/shadow file.
          pwconv(1M) relies on a special value  of  'x'  in  the
          password  field  of  /etc/passwd. If this value of 'x'
.
.
.
```

Because it is difficult to remember all the Solaris 8 commands (especially all the command-line arguments), the **man** command provides a way to get detailed information quickly. Keep in mind that multiple man pages may have the same name, so it is important to know which section could contain the information and to understand the use of the **-s** command-line argument to specify the appropriate section. If you can't remember the **man** command-line arguments, you can use **man** to display them using **man man**.

The following example uses the **-a** command-line argument to display all *passwd* man pages:

```
# man -a passwd
Reformatting Page. Please wait... Done

::::::::::::::
/usr/share/man/cat1/passwd.1
::::::::::::::

User Commands                                        passwd(1)

NAME
     passwd - change login password and password attributes

SYNOPSIS
     passwd [ -r files | -r ldap  | -r nis  |  -r  nisplus  ]
     [ name ]

     passwd [  -r files  ] [ -egh ]  [ name ]

     passwd [  -r files  ]  -s  [ -a ]

     passwd [  -r files  ]  -s  [ name ]

     passwd [  -r files  ] [ -d | -l ]  [ -f ]  [  -n min  ]
     [ -w warn ]  [ -x max ]  name

     passwd  -r  ldap  [ -egh ]  [ name ]

     passwd  -r  nis  [ -egh ]  [ name ]

     passwd  -r  nisplus  [ -egh ]  [ -D domainname ]  [ name ]

     passwd  -r  nisplus  -s  [ -a ]

     passwd  -r  nisplus  [ -D domainname ]  -s  [ name ]
```

```
     passwd  -r  nisplus  [ -l ]  [ -f ]  [ -n min ]  [ -w warn ]
     [ -x max ]  [ -D domainname ]  name
.
.
.
::::::::::::::
/usr/share/man/cat4/passwd.4
::::::::::::::
File Formats                                          passwd(4)

NAME
     passwd - password file

SYNOPSIS
     /etc/passwd

DESCRIPTION
     /etc/passwd is a local source of  information  about  users'
     accounts.  The password file can be used in conjunction with
     other password sources, including the NIS maps
     passwd.byname and  passwd.bygid and the NIS+ table  passwd.
     Programs use the getpwnam(3C) routines to access this infor-
     mation.

     Each  passwd entry is a single line of the form:

          username:password:uid:
          gid:gcos-field:home-dir:
          login-shell

     where

     username
           is the user's login name. It is recommended that  this
           field conform to the checks performed by  pwck(1M).

     password
           is an empty field. The encrypted password for the user
           is in the corresponding entry in the /etc/shadow file.
           pwconv(1M) relies on a special value  of  'x'  in  the
.
.
.
```

Note that the previous examples (which display man pages) begin with the phrase *Reformatting Page. Please wait... Done.* The man pages are stored as either **nroff**(1) source files or **sgml**(5) source files. To display the man pages, they are formatted "on the fly" by the **nroff** command. The man pages that are **sgml** are passed through an SGML preprocessor before being formatted by the **nroff** command.

Any searches for a man page are basically brute force—that is, each directory containing man pages is searched until the specified man page is located. To speed up displaying and searching, you can generate and store a preformatted version of the man pages. The preformatted version is used whenever possible. As part of the preformatting process, an index of man page keywords also is generated. This index is referred to as the *windex* database. The **catman**(1M) command formats the man pages and generates the windex database. Note that depending on the speed of the system CPU and current load, the **catman** command may take a significant amount of time to format all the man pages.

In addition, having the windex lets you search the man pages for keywords and files. The following example shows using the **-f** command-line argument to search the man pages for references to the /etc/passwd file and the -k command-line argument to search for the keyword *passwd*:

```
# man -f /etc/passwd
passwd          passwd (1)          - change login password and
                                      password attributes
passwd          passwd (4)          - password file

# man -k passwd
d_passwd        d_passwd (4)        - dial-up password file
getpw           getpw (3c)          - get passwd entry from UID
kpasswd         kpasswd (1)         - change a user's Kerberos
                                      password
nispasswd       nispasswd (1)       - change NIS+ password
                                      information
nispasswdd      rpc.nispasswdd (1m) - NIS+ password update daemon
passwd          passwd (1)          - change login password and
                                      password attributes
passwd          passwd (4)          - password file
pwconv          pwconv (1m)         - installs and updates
                                      /etc/shadow with information
                                      from /etc/passwd
rpc.nispasswdd  rpc.nispasswdd (1m) - NIS+ password update daemon
rpc.yppasswdd   rpc.yppasswdd (1m)  - server for modifying NIS
                                      password file
yppasswd        yppasswd (1)        - change your network password
                                      in the NIS database
yppasswdd       rpc.yppasswdd (1m)  - server for modifying
                                      NIS password file
#
```

You can use the **-d** command-line argument to view the search process as the **man** command attempts to locate the specified man page. The following example searches the windex database. All available sections are identified in the /usr/share/man/man.cf file as a list of section identifiers defined as the contents of the **MANSECTS** variable. Each section identifier is appended to the specified man page and used to search the windex database. Note that some of the debug output has been deleted to make the example shorter:

```
# man -d -l passwd
/usr/share/man: from man.cf,
MANSECTS=1,1m,1s,2,3,3c,3malloc,3dl,3nsl,3socket,3ldap,3krb,
3nisdb,3rac,3resolv,3rpc,3slp,3xfn,3proc,3rt,3thr,3elf,3kvm,
3kstat,3m,3mp,3pam,3sched,3aio,3bsm,3cpc,3sec,3secdb,3cfgadm,
3crypt,3devid,3devinfo,3door,3lib,3libucb,3head,7,7d,7fs,7i,
7m,7p,9,9e,9f,9s,4,5,4b,3gen,3exacct,3dmi,3snmp,3tnf,3volmgt,
3mail,3layout,3ext,1b,1c,1f,3ucb,3xnet,3curses,3plot,3xcurses,
3gss,6,l,n

mandir path = /usr/share/man
  search in = /usr/share/man/windex file
  search an entry to match passwd.1
passwd (1) -M /usr/share/man
  search an entry to match passwd.1m
  search an entry to match passwd.1s
  search an entry to match passwd.2
  search an entry to match passwd.3
  search an entry to match passwd.3c
  .
  .
  .
  search an entry to match passwd.9f
  search an entry to match passwd.9s
  search an entry to match passwd.4
passwd (4) -M /usr/share/man
  search an entry to match passwd.5
  search an entry to match passwd.4b
  search an entry to match passwd.3gen
  .
  .
  .
```

If the **nroff** or **sgml** source file for one or more manual pages is updated, the preformatted man page can also be updated using the **-r** command-line argument. The following example creates the formatted manual page for the **man** command:

```
# man -r man
Reformatting page.  Please Wait... done
#
```

# Practice Questions

## Question 1

What are the three parts of the Solaris 8 operating system? [Select all that apply]

- ❑ a. Disk drive
- ❑ b. Kernel
- ❑ c. File system
- ❑ d. System console
- ❑ e. Memory management
- ❑ f. Shell
- ❑ g. Process control

Answers b, c, and f are correct. The three parts of the Solaris 8 operating system are the kernel, the file system, and the shell. The disk drive and system console are hardware devices. Therefore, answers a and d are incorrect. Memory management and process control are functions of the kernel. Therefore, answers e and g are incorrect.

## Question 2

What is the commonly used shell provided by the Solaris 8 system?

- ❍ a. Corn shell
- ❍ b. Sea shell
- ❍ c. Bourne shell
- ❍ d. Berkeley shell

Answer c is correct. Solaris 8 provides the Bourne shell. Answers a and b are incorrect because they sound similar to the Korn and C shells, but are spelled differently. Answer d, the Berkeley shell, does not exist.

## Question 3

Which of the following files is used to store commands that should be executed when a user logs in to the system?

- ❍ a. The .cshrc file
- ❍ b. The .Profile file
- ❍ c. The .startup file
- ❍ d. The profile file
- ❍ e. The .login file

Answer e is correct. The .login file is the login initialization file for the C shell. The .cshrc file is the shell startup initialization file for the C shell. Therefore, answer a is incorrect. Answer b is similar to the name of the Bourne and Korn login initialization file, but the correct file name uses a lowercase *p*. In Unix, file names are case sensitive, so answer b is incorrect. The file .startup is not a standard initialization file. Therefore, answer c is incorrect. Answer d would be correct if it began with a period.

## Question 4

System maintenance commands are documented in which section of the *Reference Manual*?

- ❍ a. 1
- ❍ b. 1M
- ❍ c. 2
- ❍ d. 4

Answer b is correct. System maintenance commands are documented in Section 1M. User commands are documented in Section 1, system calls in Section 2, and file formats in Section 4. Therefore, answers a, c, and d are incorrect.

## Question 5

An account is set up to use the Bourne shell. Which file is used to store commands to be executed when the user logs in to the system?

❍ a. The .cshrc file

❍ b. The .profile file

❍ c. The .startup file

❍ d. The .logon file

❍ e. The .login file

Answer b is correct. The .profile file is used to store commands that are executed when the user logs in to the system. The shell startup initialization file for the C shell is .cshrc. Therefore, answer a is incorrect. Answers c and d are incorrect because they are not standard names for login initialization files. Answer e is the login initialization file for the C shell.

## Question 6

Which of the following are functions of the kernel? [Select all that apply]

❑ a. Process control

❑ b. Hardware interface and control

❑ c. Memory management

❑ d. Interprocess communication

Answers a, b, c, and d are correct. They are all functions of the kernel.

## Question 7

Which of the following shells are available in a restricted version? [Select all that apply]

❑ a. C shell

❑ b. Korn shell

❑ c. Bourne shell

Answers b and c are correct. The Korn and Bourne shells are available in a restricted version. The C shell does not provide a restricted version; therefore, answer a is incorrect.

## Question 8

Which commands can be used to display the **passwd**(4) manual page? [Select all that apply]

- ❑ a. **man -s 4 passwd**
- ❑ b. **man -a passwd**
- ❑ c. **man passwd**
- ❑ d. **man passwd -s 4**

Answers a and b are correct. Answer a displays only **passwd**(4), whereas answer b displays both **passwd**(1) and **passwd**(4). **man passwd** displays only **passwd**(1); therefore, answer c is incorrect. **man passwd -s 4** displays **passwd**(1) and generates an error message, because **-s 4** is misinterpreted as the name of manual pages (command-line arguments must be specified before the name of the manual pages). Therefore, answer d is incorrect.

# Need to Know More?

Bach, Maurice J., *The Design of the Unix Operating System* (Prentice-Hall, Englewood Cliffs, NJ, 1987), ISBN 0-13-201799-7.

Kernighan, Brian W., and Rob Pike, *The Unix Programming Environment* (Prentice-Hall, Englewood Cliffs, NJ, 1984), ISBN 0-13-937681-X.

Rosenblatt, Bill and Mike Loukides (Editor), *Learning the Korn Shell* (O'Reilly & Associates, Englewood Cliffs, NJ, 1993), ISBN 1-56-592054-6.

Sorbell, Mark G., *A Practical Guide to Solaris* (Addison-Wesley, Reading, MA, 1999), ISBN 0-201-89548-X.

Sun Microsystems, *System Reference Manual, Section 1 - User Commands*. Available in printed form (part number 806-0624-10), on the Web at **docs.sun.com**, and from the online documentation, AnswerBook2, provided with the Solaris 8 operating system.

# 3

# Installing and Maintaining Solaris 8

**Terms you'll need to understand:**

✓ Software clusters

✓ Software groups

✓ Packages

✓ Patches

**Techniques you'll need to master:**

✓ Installing Solaris 8

✓ Adding and removing packages

✓ Listing installed packages

✓ Adding and removing patches

✓ Listing installed patches

The first section of this chapter covers the Solaris 8 distribution. Next, we cover installing the operating system in detail. The last two sections summarize the commands used to perform software package administration and patch administration. The *Installation* test objectives are covered in this chapter.

# The Solaris 8 Distribution

Solaris 8 system and application software is delivered as collections of files and directories, referred to as *packages*. You can copy these packages onto the system from CD-ROM or magnetic tape as a single compressed file and uncompress them for installation.

Included with the package is information regarding the package, such as its title, storage requirements, and version. Also included are any custom scripts needed to properly install the software.

Sometimes system software is distributed in more than one package, but you need to distribute and install the packages as a unit. A collection of two or more related packages is referred to as a *software cluster*. A software cluster is a logical grouping of packages.

The Solaris 8 operating system is preconfigured into *software groups* that consist of different collections of software clusters and packages. The five software groups are shown in Table 3.1.

*Note: Some Solaris 8 documents refer to the operating system's preconfigured software groups as* software configuration clusters *or simply* clusters. *The term* software cluster *also is used to refer to a collection of packages, so this reference can create confusion. In this book, we'll use the term* software groups, *because this is the term used in the* Solaris 8 Advanced Installation Guide.

The Entire Distribution Plus OEM group is available only for SPARC platforms.

# Installing Solaris 8

Solaris 8 can be installed in four ways. Two of the methods are interactive: the Solaris Interactive Installation program (SunInstall) and Solaris Web Start are

**Table 3.1 Solaris 8 software groups.**

| Software Group | Contents |
|---|---|
| Core | Required operating system files |
| End-User System Support | Core plus windowing environments |
| Developer System Support | End-User plus development environment |
| Entire Distribution | Developer System plus enhanced features |
| Entire Distribution Plus OEM | Entire Distribution plus third-party hardware drivers |

covered in this chapter. The other two methods are automatic: JumpStart and Custom JumpStart. These are objectives for Exam 310-012 and are covered in Chapter 21.

SunInstall is an interactive Open Windows installation program can be used to install the Solaris 8 software but that does not support installation of copackaged software. You can install any copackaged software using the installation programs provided with the copackaged software after you finish installing the Solaris 8 software.

Web Start lets you install Solaris 8 using a Web browser–like interface instead of the Open Windows interface used by SunInstall. By default, all Solaris and copackaged software is installed; however, this default can be changed to let you select specific software.

By default, Web Start sets up the system disks, including the root and swap partitions. It also lets you change the size of the system partitions and provides access to the Layout File Systems utility to set up other disks. The /opt partition is created automatically for copackaged software. Web Start also lets you create additional partitions and file systems.

## Hardware Requirements

Solaris 8 can be installed on both Sun SPARC platforms and Intel x86 or compatible platforms. The hardware requirements for both are similar.

### Solaris 8 on SPARC Hardware

Solaris 8 can be installed on most sun4c, sun4u, and sun4m platform groups. Consult the *Solaris 8 Sun Hardware Platform Guide* to determine whether a particular platform is supported along with other devices and peripherals, such as disk drives, CD-ROM drives, tape drives, diskette drives, SCSI/PCI host adapters, graphic accelerators, network interfaces, and keyboard/mouse components.

EXAM ALERT

You can use the Solaris 8 installation programs to install either the 32-bit or 64-bit version of the Solaris operating system. The 64-bit version is selected by default when you install on Sun UltraSPARC systems, but you can choose the 32-bit version instead. However, you may need to upgrade the Flash PROM on some UltraSPARC sun4u platforms to provide 64-bit support. The *Solaris 8 Sun Hardware Platform Guide* provides information on determining whether the Flash PROM for a particular system must be upgraded and also provides a procedure for updating the Flash PROM.

Solaris 8 requires a minimum of 64MB of memory. The recommended space for the smallest Solaris 8 software group (End-User System) is 1.6GB of hard disk space. For the largest software group (Entire Distribution Plus OEM with 64-bit support), 2.4GB of hard disk space is required. Either a CD-ROM drive or the appropriate environment for a network installation is required.

### Solaris 8 on Intel Hardware

Solaris 8 can be installed on most Pentium or better Intel-compatible CPUs, including AMD and Cyrix processors. Consult the *Solaris 8 (Intel Platform Edition) Hardware Compatibility List* to determine whether a particular CPU is supported along with other devices and peripherals, such as system buses, disk drives, CD-ROM drives, tape drives, diskette drives, SCSI/PCI host adapters, graphic accelerators, network interfaces, and keyboard/mouse components. If the system does not have a CD-ROM drive or cannot be booted from the CD-ROM drive, a floppy disk drive is required.

Solaris 8 requires a minimum of 64MB of memory. The recommended space for the smallest Solaris 8 software group (End-User System with 32-bit support) is 1.6GB of hard disk space. For the largest software group (Entire Distribution), 2.4GB of hard disk space is recommended. Either a CD-ROM drive or the appropriate environment for a network installation is required.

## Installing Solaris 8 on a New System Using Web Start

If you're installing Solaris 8 on a single new system, the preferred installation method is to install from a local CD-ROM drive using Web Start. (Over-the-network installation is described briefly later in this chapter and in more detail in Chapter 21.) Solaris Web Start can be accessed using either a command-line interface or a graphical interface.

The installation is divided logically into three phases:

- Preparation
- Configuration
- Software installation

### Preparation

The following list summarizes the steps necessary to prepare to install Solaris 8 on a SPARC or Intel-compatible platform from a local CD-ROM drive:

1. Verify that the system hardware is supported. For SPARC system, see the *Solaris 8 Sun Platform Guide*. For Intel-compatible system, see the *Solaris 8 (Intel Platform Edition) Hardware Compatibility List*.
2. If the system is networked (will be attached to a network), decide if Dynamic Host Configuration Protocol (DHCP) will be used. If not, determine the host name, IP address, and subnet mask information.

3. Determine the domain name. If a name service is used, determine the server host name and IP address. The choice of name services are Domain Name System (DNS), Network Information Service (NIS), or NIS+.
4. Determine the disk space required by selecting a software group (End-User, Developer, Entire Distribution, or Entire Distribution Plus OEM) and identifying additional software and space for home directories.
5. Determine the language used to install Solaris.
6. Insert the appropriate Solaris 8 Installation CD-ROM (English or Multilingual) into the CD-ROM drive. For Intel-compatibles that cannot boot from the CD-ROM drive, insert the Solaris 8 Device Configuration Assistant diskette in the floppy disk drive.
7. Boot the system by turning the power on.
8. For Intel-compatible systems, the Device Configuration Assistant runs to identify the hardware configuration.
9. If you're using the Multilingual CD-ROM, the Web Start Installer prompts you for the language to use during the install. Select the appropriate language.
10. For SPARC platforms, the Installer prompts you to select Initial Install or Upgrade. Select Initial Install.
11. For Intel-compatible platforms, if an appropriate partition for Solaris is not located, a utility similar to the MS-DOS FDISK program executes to define a partition.
12. The Installer prompts you to confirm reformatting of the default disk, requests a size for the swap space, and confirms that the swap space can be located at the beginning of the disk (or prompts for a starting location if the swap space can't be located). The Installer copies the mini-root and platform-specific files to the disk and then reboots the system.
13. For SPARC platforms, the graphical Web Start interface starts automatically after the system boots.
14. For Intel-compatible platforms, the Installer prompts you for a window configuration (video card and monitor) and tests it to be certain the configuration is correct. Without a proper configuration, the graphical interface and Solaris Desktop cannot be displayed. After a few seconds, the graphical Web Start interface starts.

The install process continues with the configuration phase.

## Configuration

The following steps are used to collect the necessary configuration information using the Web Start graphical interface. In this sequence of screens, the next screen typically is displayed after you provide the required information on the current screen and click the Next button:

1. The Welcome screen is displayed.
2. On the Network Connectivity screen, select Networked (if you do not know the network configuration, contact your network administrator).
3. On the DHCP screen, select Yes to enable DHCP; otherwise, select No. If DHCP is not being used:
    - On the Host Name screen, enter the name of the host in the dialog box.
    - On the IP Address screen, enter the IP address of the system name in the dialog box.
    - On the Netmask screen, enter the subnet mask in the dialog box.
4. On the IPv6 screen, select Yes to enable IPv6; otherwise, select No.
5. On the Name Service screen, select NIS+, NIS, DNS, or None. If you select a name service:
    - On the Domain Name screen, enter the domain name in the dialog box.
    - If you selected NIS or NIS+, on the Name Server screen, select Find One or Specify One. If you select Specify One, the Name Server Information screen opens, in which you specify the server host name and IP address.
    - If you selected DNS, on the DNS Server Address screen, enter up to three IP addresses for DNS servers in the dialog boxes. On the DNS Search List screen, enter up to six domains to be searched to resolve a DNS query in the dialog boxes. If none is identified, only the domain specified for the system will be searched.
6. On the Time Zone screen, select how to specify the time zone: Geographic Region, Offset From GMT, or Time Zone File:
    - If you select Geographic Region, the Geographic Region screen opens. Select a region or country and an associated time zone.
    - If you select Offset From GMT, the Offset From GMT screen opens. Drag the slide bar until the screen displays the appropriate number of hours (plus or minus) different from GMT.
    - If you select Time Zone File, the Time Zone File screen opens. Enter the name of the time zone file (typically /usr/share/lib/zoneinfo).

7. On the Date And Time screen, enter the year, month, day, hour, and minute in the appropriate dialog boxes.
8. On the Root Password screen, enter the password for the root account.
9. On the Power Management screen, select whether power management should be turned on or off and if the selection should be prompted at each reboot.
10. On the Proxy Server Configuration screen, select Direct Connection To The Internet or Use Proxy Configuration and enter a host name and port number of the proxy server.
11. The Confirm Information screen summarizes your selections. Either click Confirm to continue with the software installation phase or click Back to change one or more selections.

The install process continues with the software installation phase.

## Software Installation

The following steps use the graphical interface of Web Start to install the Solaris 8 software on a networked SPARC or Intel-compatible system with a local CD-ROM drive. In this sequence of screens, the next screen typically is displayed after you provide the required information on the current screen and click the Next button:

1. On the Welcome screen, click Next. The Installation CD is ejected.
2. On the Insert CD screen, click OK after inserting the CD-ROM labeled *Solaris 8 Software 1 of 2* in the CD-ROM drive.
3. On the Select Type Of Install screen, select Default Install or Custom Install. *If you select Default Install, then skip Steps 4 through 10; the installation continues with Step 11.*
4. On the Select Software Localizations screen, select software localization based on geographic region.
5. On the Select System Locale screen, select the initial locale.
6. On the Select Products screen, select any additional products (such as the AnswerBook2) that should be installed.
7. On the Additional Products screen, select None if no other products are to be installed at this time, or select one of the following:
   - If you select Product CD, the Solaris 8 Software CD-ROM is ejected and the Insert CD dialog box is displayed. Click OK after inserting a product CD-ROM to be scanned. The Scanning CD screen is displayed. After the CD-ROM has been scanned, the Select Products screen is

displayed; it lists the software products found on the CD-ROM. Select the products to install. Eject the Product CD-ROM, insert the Solaris 8 software CD-ROM, and click OK.

- If you select Kiosk Download, the Scanning Download screen is displayed. After Web Start scans the Kiosk download directory (/webstart/kiosk/download), the Select Products screen is displayed; it lists the software products found in the download directory. Select the products to install and click OK.
- If you select Local Or Network File System, the Specify Network File System Path screen is displayed. Enter the appropriate path to additional products that should be installed. After Web Start scans the specified path, the Select Products screen is displayed; it lists the software products found. Select the products to install and click OK.

8. On the Select Solaris Cluster Configuration screen, select the desired software group.
9. On the Disk Selection screen, select one more disks to be used for the Solaris 8 software.
10. The Lay Out File Systems screen shows a default file system layout. To modify the file system layout, highlight a listed disk/file system entry and click Modify. A Disk dialog box opens in which you can assign the file systems on the disk to different slices and/or modify the size of each file system. Click Apply to save the configuration and return to the Lay Out File Systems screen. Click Next when you're finished modifying the layout of the disk(s).
11. The Ready To Install screen summarizes your selections. Click Install Now to start the installation or Back to change one or more selections.
12. The Installing... screen displays messages and progress bars to show the status of the software installation. When the installation of the Solaris 8 Software 1 of 2 CD-ROM is completed, the CD-ROM is ejected.
13. The Installation Summary screen displays the status of the installation. To view additional information, click Details.
14. If you select additional products, the Specify Media screen opens, in which you can select either CD or Network File System as a source:
    - If you select CD, the Insert CD dialog box is displayed. Click OK after inserting a product CD-ROM. The Reading CD, Launching Installer, Extracting, and Installing screens are displayed.

- If you select Network File System, the Specify Network File System Path screen is displayed. Enter the appropriate path to additional products that should be installed. The Launching Installer, Extracting, and Installing screens are displayed.

15. On the Reboot screen, click Reboot Now to reboot the system.

After the system reboots, log in as the root account and select either OpenWindows or CDE as a desktop for the account. You've now completed the Solaris 8 installation for a networked standalone system using Web Start.

## Upgrading an Existing Solaris System

Upgrading a system allows you to merge the existing system configuration with the new Solaris 8 operating system. However, planning and occasional manual intervention are required to accomplish the upgrade successfully.

EXAM ALERT

SunInstall and custom JumpStart (see Chapter 21) can be used to upgrade a system. Web Start and the standard JumpStart cannot be used to upgrade an existing system with an earlier version of Solaris (Solaris 7 or earlier).

### Before the Upgrade

You should complete a number of tasks before you upgrade your system:

1. Check the latest Solaris 8 Release Notes to determine whether any Solaris 8 changes or enhancements affect the current operation. This information includes software that is no longer provided with Solaris or patches that you need to install.

2. Verify that the hardware is supported as described in the preparation phase of the Web Start installation.

3. Install Solaris either using a CD-ROM or via the network. Depending on the method, verify either the proper operation of the CD-ROM drive or network connectivity.

4. Some Sun applications, such as DiskSuite, cannot be upgraded automatically. Manual configuration changes are required before the software can be used. Check the documentation provided with the applications.

5. If any third-party software is installed on the system, check with the software manufacturer to verify that the software will run on Solaris 8. You may need to purchase new versions of third-party software.

6. Back up the existing system. If the upgrade fails, you may need to restore to the existing system until the reasons for failure can be determined and resolved.

7. Collect any configuration information that you might be prompted for during the upgrade, such as hostname, network interface, IP address, subnet mask, and domain name. You can avoid having to respond to prompts during installation by preconfiguring system configuration information (as explained later in this chapter).
8. Set up a backup medium for possible use during the upgrade. In the event that disk space needs to be reallocated, you will need to copy file systems to a backup medium and then reload them after the space on the system disk(s) has been adjusted. Local devices, such as unused system disks, tape, or diskettes, along with remote files systems, can be used for the backup medium.
9. If you're using the Solaris 8 distribution CD, insert it in the system CD-ROM drive. For x86 platforms that cannot be booted from the CD-ROM drive, insert the Device Configuration Assistant diskette into the A: drive. If you're installing over the network, set up an install server and possibly a boot server.
10. Reboot the system.

### During the Upgrade

If the current layout of the system disks does not provide enough space for the upgrade, SunInstall will use the auto-layout feature to reallocate disk space as required. If the auto-layout fails or you want to use a different layout, you must manually specify the disk layout.

If the system configuration information was not preconfigured, you will need to provide the appropriate information when prompted.

### After the Upgrade

Merging of the existing system configuration with the Solaris 8 operating system may not be completely successful, and you may need to perform some manual cleanup. Check the /a/var/sadm/system/data/upgrade_clean file to determine any configuration problems that need to be reviewed and possibly modified before the system can be rebooted.

After resolving any cleanup issues, reboot the system.

## Preconfiguring System Configuration Information

You can preconfigure the system configuration information required for installation in two ways: the name service method or the sysidcfg file method:

- *Name service method*—This method adds the system information to an available name service (NIS or NIS+). During installation, the information is retrieved from the name service and used to configure the system. This is the recommended method for SPARC installations.

- *Sysidcfg method*—This method creates a file named sysidcfg that contains the configuration information. The file must conform to a defined format (keywords and syntax). The file must be available on a local drive, and the local diskette drive on the remote drive must be accessible via the network.

## Over-the-Network Installation

Typically, a system is installed with the Solaris 8 distribution CD using a local CD-ROM drive. However, software can be installed over the network if the appropriate systems are set up. These systems are:

- *Install server*—A server created by copying the contents of the Solaris 8 distribution CD to its disk drive or that has the distribution CD available in its CD-ROM drive.
- *Boot server*—A server used for booting clients that are located on a different subnet than the install server. The boot server should be located on the same subnet as the clients.

You set up systems to be installed over the network either by using Solstice Host Manager to add (preconfigure) information about the systems to NIS/NIS+ or by adding the information to configuration files of an install server or boot server.

# Software Package Administration

Both Sun Microsystems and third-party vendors deliver software as easily manipulated collections of files and executable installation/removal procedures referred to as *packages*.

Software packages can be installed on or removed from standalone systems or servers in a fairly straightforward manner, because both the root and /usr file systems are local.

## Package Tools

Solaris 8 package tools provide a convenient mechanism for installing and removing packaged software. These are standard Unix commands and are accessible through the shell command-line interface. In addition, the system administration tool, **admintool**(1M), provides a graphical user interface (GUI) for installing and removing packages.

The most commonly used command-line package tools are:

- **pkgadd**(1M)—Installs packages
- **pkginfo**(1) *and* **pkgparam**(1) —Displays information about packages

- **pkgrm**(1M)—Removes a package
- **pkgchk**(1M)—Checks the proper installation of a package

## Installing a Package Using the pkgadd Command

The **pkgadd** command can install a package from disk or CD-ROM. Typically, software obtained through the network or from magnetic tape or diskette is copied into a spool directory on the system before installation. The default package spool directory is /var/spool/pkg, but you can use any location with adequate free space.

To install one or more packages located in the default spool directory using the **pkgadd** command, only the package names need to be specified as command-line arguments. For example, to install the SUNWast package, you use the following command:

```
# pkgadd SUNWast

Processing package instance <SUNWast> from </var/spool/pkg>

Automated Security Enhancement Tools
(i386) 11.8.0,REV=2000.01.08.18.17
Copyright 2000 Sun Microsystems, Inc. All rights reserved.
Using </> as the package base directory.
## Processing package information.
## Processing system information.
   1 package pathname is already properly installed.
## Verifying package dependencies.
## Verifying disk space requirements.
## Checking for conflicts with packages already installed.
## Checking for setuid/setgid programs.

This package contains scripts which will be executed with
super-user permission during the process of installing this
package.

Do you want to continue with the installation of <SUNWast> [y,n,?]
y

Installing Automated Security Enhancement Tools as <SUNWast>
## Installing part 1 of 1.
Installation of <SUNWast> was successful.
#
```

If a package was spooled onto the system into a different directory, you specify the alternate spool directory using the **-d** command-line argument. For example, if the /tmp directory was used to spool the SUNWast package onto the system, use the following command to install the package:

```
pkgadd -d /tmp SUNWast
```

To install a package located on CD-ROM, use the **-d** command-line argument to specify the pathname to the CD-ROM drive. For example, you can use the **pkgadd** command to install the SUNWast package from a CD-ROM mounted at /cdrom/cdrom0:

```
pkgadd -d /cdrom/cdrom0 SUNWast
```

Actually, the **pkgadd** command does not require the name of a package. If no package name is specified, the **pkgadd** command will prompt you with a list of packages that are available in the specified spool directory or on the CD-ROM.

You use the **-s** command-line argument to spool a package into a spool directory instead of installing it. The following command will spool the SUNWast package in from the second CD-ROM of the Solaris distribution to the /var/spool/pkg directory (long lines are wrapped):

```
# pkgadd -s /var/spool/pkg
  -d /cdrom/sol_8_600_ia_2/Solaris_8/Product SUNWast
Transferring <SUNWast> package instance
#
```

When you're using the default spool directory, just the word *spool* can be specified with the -s command-line argument.

## Installing a Package Using admintool

After you start the **admintool** command, select Software from the Browse menu. The Software window is displayed, as shown in Figure 3.1.

To install a package, select Add from the Edit menu. The Set Source Media window is displayed, in which you can select either CD-ROM or Hard Disk. Figure 3.2 shows the Set Source Media Software Location set to CD With Volume Management. The other choices are CD Without Volume Management and Hard Disk. If you're using a CD-ROM, fill in the appropriate CD Path.

If the package has been spooled onto disk, change the Software Location selection to Hard Disk (as shown in Figure 3.3) and specify the spool directory if necessary.

After selecting the appropriate source media, click OK. The Add Software window opens, as shown in Figure 3.4.

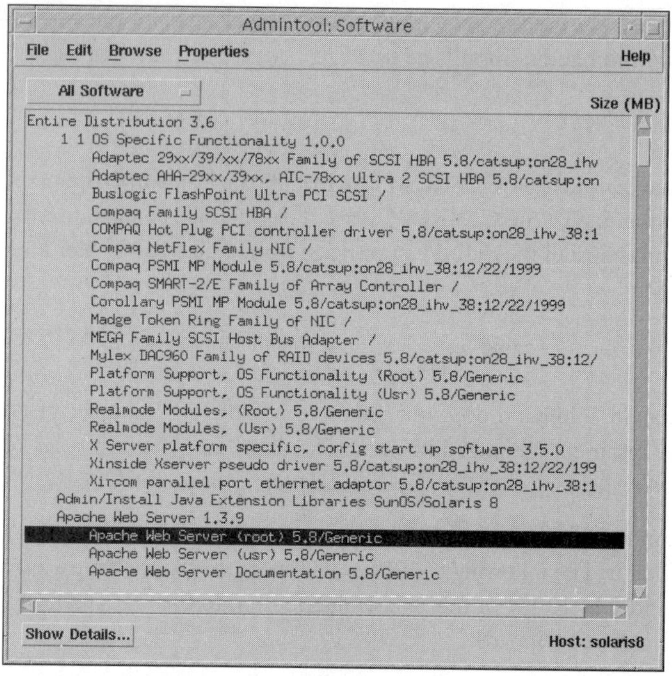


**Figure 3.1** The Admintool: Software window.

**Figure 3.2** The Admintool: Set Source Media (CD-ROM) window.

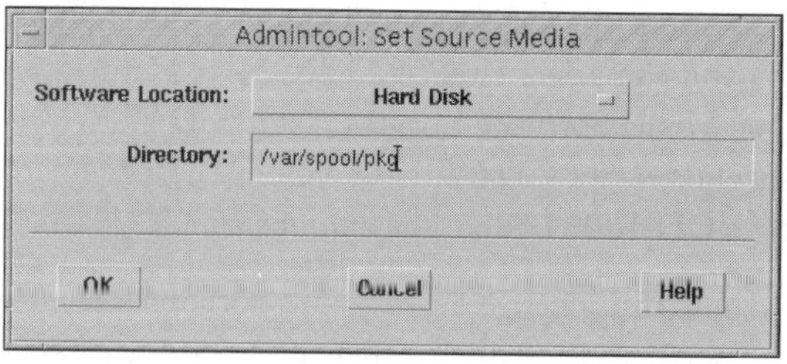


**Figure 3.3** The Admintool: Set Source Media (Hard Disk) window.

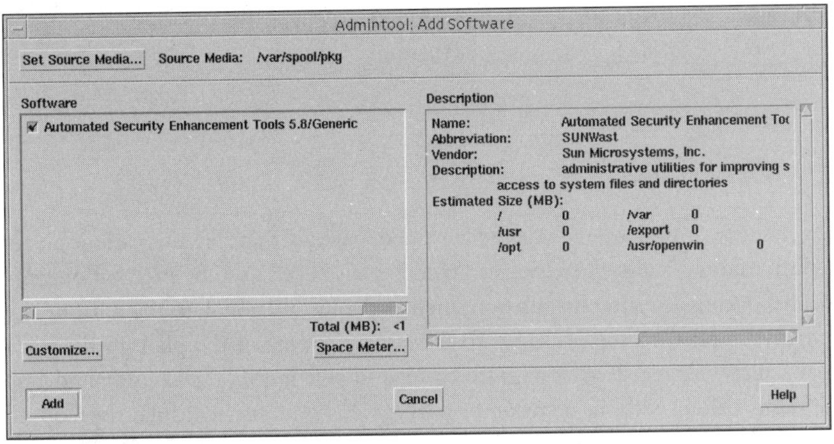


**Figure 3.4** The Admintool: Add Software window.

The available packages on the CD-ROM or in the spool directory are listed. Figure 3.4 shows one package in the /var/spool/pkg directory, the Automated Security Enhancement Tools package. To install the package, select the checkbox to the left of the package title and click the Add button. The **admintool** command calls the **pkgadd** command and opens a window to display the results.

## Obtaining Package Information Using the pkginfo Command

The **pkginfo** command with no command-line arguments displays a list of installed packages. The following example shows a partial listing of installed packages:

```
# pkginfo
system      AMImega       MEGA Family SCSI Host Bus Adapter
system      CPQcnft       Compaq NetFlex Family NIC
system      CPQncr        Compaq Family SCSI HBA
system      CPQsmii       Compaq SMART-2/E Array Controller
system      MADGFmt       Madge Token Ring Family of NIC
system      MYLXflp       Buslogic FlashPoint Ultra PCI SCSI
.
.
.
system      SUNWapchu     Apache Web Server (usr)
system      SUNWarc       Archive Libraries
system      SUNWarrf      X11 Arabic required fonts
system      SUNWast       Automated Security Enhancement Tools
system      SUNWatfsr     AutoFS, (Root)
system      SUNWatfsu     AutoFS, (Usr)
system      SUNWaudd      Audio Drivers
```

```
system      SUNWaudh       Audio Header Files
system      SUNWaudio      Audio applications
.
.
.
#
```

Each software package includes a file named "*pkginfo*" that contains various pieces of information about the package. This file is also used to store information generated during and after installation, such as the installation date and a list of any patches applied to the package. To view the contents of the pkginfo file for a particular package, use the **pkginfo** command and specify the **-l** command-line argument along with the name of the package. For example, to display the pkginfo file for the SUNWast package, use the following **pkginfo** command:

```
# pkginfo -l SUNWast
   PKGINST:  SUNWast
      NAME:  Automated Security Enhancement Tools
  CATEGORY:  system
      ARCH:  i386
   VERSION:  11.8.0,REV=2000.01.08.18.17
   BASEDIR:  /
    VENDOR:  Sun Microsystems, Inc.
      DESC:  administrative utilities for improving system
             security by monitoring or restricting access to
             system files and directories

    PSTAMP:  catsup20000108183522
  INSTDATE:  Jan 13 2001 21:31
   HOTLINE:  Please contact your local service provider
    STATUS:  completely installed
     FILES:     41 installed pathnames
                 1 shared pathnames
                 8 directories
                29 executables
               232 blocks used (approx)
#
```

## Obtaining Package Information Using admintool

The same information obtained from the **pkginfo** command can also be obtained using the **admintool** command. To display a list of installed packages, select Software from the Browse menu. For a sample list, see Figure 3.1.

To view selected contents of the pkginfo file for a particular package, highlight the package name in the list and click the Show Details button. The Software Details window is displayed, as shown in Figure 3.5.

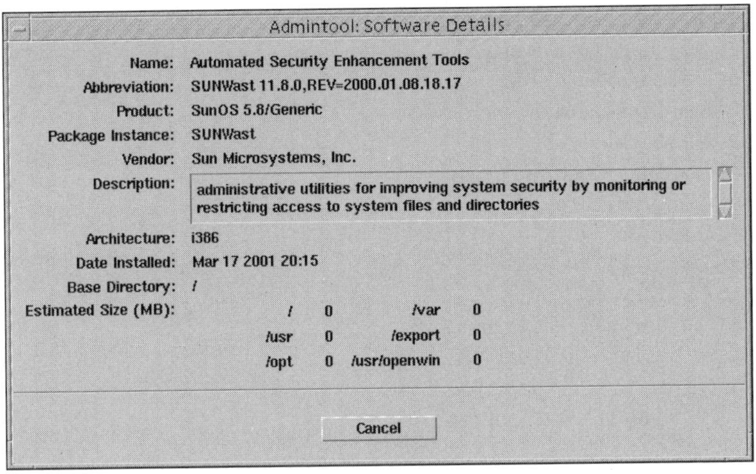


**Figure 3.5** The Admintool: Software Details window.

> **TIP:** The pkginfo file for each installed package, along with other package-related files, is located under the /var/sadm/pkg directory in a subdirectory with the same name as the package.

## Removing a Package Using the **pkgrm** Command

The **pkgrm** command is used to remove installed packages. To remove one or more packages, only the package names need to be specified as command-line arguments. For example, to remove the SUNWast package, use the following command:

```
# pkgrm SUNWast

The following package is currently installed:
   SUNWast          Automated Security Enhancement Tools
                    (i386) 11.8.0,REV=2000.01.08.18.17

Do you want to remove this package? y
# Removing installed package instance <SUNWast>
## Verifying package dependencies.
## Processing package information.
## Removing pathnames in class <none>
/usr/aset/util/taskstat
/usr/aset/util/str_to_mode
.
.
.
```

```
/usr/aset/masters/uid_aliases
/usr/aset/masters/tune.med
/usr/aset/masters/tune.low
/usr/aset/masters/tune.high
/usr/aset/masters
/usr/aset/asetenv
/usr/aset/aset.restore
/usr/aset/aset
/usr/aset/archives
/usr/aset
/usr <shared pathname not removed>
## Updating system information.

Removal of <SUNWast> was successful.
#
```

### Removing a Package Using **admintool**

You can also remove an installed package using the **admintool** command. First, to display a list of installed packages, select Software from the Browse menu. For a sample list, see Figure 3.1.

To delete a package, highlight its name in the list and select Delete from the Edit menu. A Warning window opens to confirm removal of the package, as shown in Figure 3.6. Click Delete to delete the package. The **admintool** command calls the **pkgrm** command and opens a window to display the results.

## Patch Administration

A *patch* is a collection of files intended to update or fix problems with installed software. For example, a patch might be required to fix a problem with a system command or address a security issue. Because most system and application software is installed as packages, patches are applied against one or more packages. Actually, patches are special packages that are used to update other packages. Like packages, a collection of patches can be grouped together into a *patch cluster*.

The ability to obtain and install patches, keep track of installed patches, and occasionally remove patches are key skills of a competent system administrator.

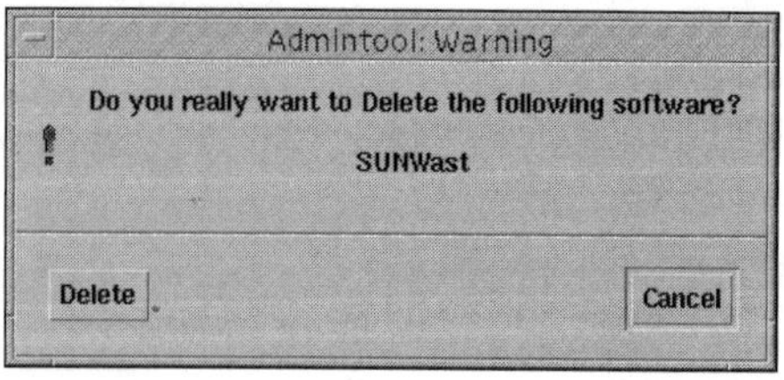


**Figure 3.6** The Admintool: Warning window.

## Obtaining Patches and Patch Information

You can obtain patches from Sun Microsystems in several ways. The two most common methods are purchasing a service contract from Sun or downloading the patches yourself from Sun's Web or FTP site.

Sun Service customers have access to an online patch database and an extended set of patches. The patches can be downloaded from Sun's Web site or FTP site. In addition, Sun Service customers receive a CD-ROM of patches every six to eight weeks.

Everyone else can obtain recommended and security patches for supported systems on the Web at **sunsolve.sun.com** or through anonymous FTP from **sunsolve1.sun.com/pubs/patches**. An alternate site to obtain Solaris patches is **www.ibiblio.org/pub/sun-info/sun-patches**.

> **TIP** Sun provides a bimonthly report that summarizes recommended and security patches for each supported system. Like the patches, the information is available at **sunsolve.sun.com** along with other system support information.

Patches are identified with an eight-digit number. The first six digits identify the base patch, and the last two digits identify the revision. For example, patch number 110906-01 is the update for the x86 version of the Solaris 8 **find**(1) command.

## Installing a Patch

You install patches using the **patchadd** command. The appropriate type of system configuration must be specified using a **patchadd** command-line argument. You also may need to specify a target directory. In addition, you can use a single **patchadd** command to install more than one patch.

Regardless of the type of system configuration being patched, the **patchadd** command is typically executed locally on the system where the software being patched resides (the *target directory*). However, you can install patches remotely over the network if the target directory can be accessed through Network File System (NFS) services.

If the patch is on a CD-ROM, you can install it directly from the CD-ROM. A patch downloaded from the Sun Web or FTP site must reside on a system hard disk. The area where patches are stored before they are installed is referred to as the *spool directory*.

> **TIP** Although patches have no required spool directory, the most commonly used location is the /var/spool/patch directory. However, you can use any location on the system that has adequate free space.

If a patch was obtained via download, chances are good that it is *zipped* (compressed) to make it easier and quicker to download. Some patches (mainly for SPARC platforms) are compressed using the **gzip**(1) command and have file names that end with the .gz suffix. Others are compressed using the **zip**(1) command and have file names that end with the .zip suffix. The **zip** command is used for both SPARC and Intel x86 platforms. To uncompress or *unzip* the x86 find patch (110906-01), which is located in the current directory, use the **unzip**(1) command as shown in the following listing:

```
# unzip 110906-01.zip
Archive:  110906-01.zip
   creating: 110906-01/
  inflating: 110906-01/.diPatch
   creating: 110906-01/SUNWcsu/
  inflating: 110906-01/SUNWcsu/pkgmap
  inflating: 110906-01/SUNWcsu/pkginfo
   creating: 110906-01/SUNWcsu/install/
  inflating: 110906-01/SUNWcsu/install/checkinstall
  inflating: 110906-01/SUNWcsu/install/copyright
  inflating: 110906-01/SUNWcsu/install/i.none
  inflating: 110906-01/SUNWcsu/install/patch_checkinstall
  inflating: 110906-01/SUNWcsu/install/patch_postinstall
  inflating: 110906-01/SUNWcsu/install/postinstall
  inflating: 110906-01/SUNWcsu/install/preinstall
   creating: 110906-01/SUNWcsu/reloc/
   creating: 110906-01/SUNWcsu/reloc/usr/
   creating: 110906-01/SUNWcsu/reloc/usr/bin/
  inflating: 110906-01/SUNWcsu/reloc/usr/bin/find
  inflating: 110906-01/README.110906-01
#
```

A subdirectory with the same name as the patch will be created under the current directory, and the unzipped files will be placed in this subdirectory.

You then use the **patchadd** command to install the patch. Because patches have no default spool directory, you must specify the full pathname to the patch as a command-line argument. The following example shows the installation of the x86 **find** command patch on a standalone system:

```
# patchadd 110906-01

Checking installed patches...
Verifying sufficient filesystem capacity (dry run method)...
Installing patch packages...

Patch number 110906-01 has been successfully installed.
See /var/sadm/patch/110906-01/log for details
```

```
Patch packages installed:
  SUNWcsu

#
```

Note that the patch modified the SUNWcsu package (core Solaris software). The **patchadd** command is actually a ksh script that calls the **pkgadd** command to install the patch.

To apply a patch to the bootable root image of a diskless client or AutoClient, use the -**R** command-line argument and specify the path to the client's root image. For example, applying the Solaris 8 x86 **find** command patch to a diskless client that uses a root image stored under the /export/root/client directory on the current system requires the following command:

```
patchadd -R /export/root/client /var/spool/patch/110906-01
```

To apply a patch to an operating system (OS) service, use the -**S** command-line argument and specify the service (see Chapter 13 for information about OS servers). For example, applying the Solaris 8 **find** command patch to an x86 Solaris 8 OS service named Solaris_8x86 on the OS server requires the following command:

```
patchadd -S Solaris_8x86 /var/spool/patch/110906-01
```

To apply a patch to the mini root of a net install image (the image used to install a system over the network), use the -**C** command-line argument and specify the pathname to the net install image. For example, applying the Solaris 8 **find** command patch to an x86 Solaris 8 image on a net install server named Solaris_8x86 on an install server requires the following command:

```
patchadd -C /export/Solaris_8x86/Tools/Boot
/var/spool/patch/110906-01
```

Multiple patches can be installed using the **patchadd** command with the -M command-line argument and by specifying a directory where all the patches are located along with a list of the patch numbers. For example, to install patches 108529-05, 108653-23, and 108876-07, which are all located in the /var/spool/patch directory, you can use the following command:

```
patchadd -M /var/spool/patch 108529-05 108653-23 108876-07
```

Instead of listing a large number of patches on the command line, you can create a text file that contains a list of patches. Then, specify the name of the text file on the command line in place of all the individual patch names.

For example, to install the 108529-05, 108653-23, and 108876-07 patches located in the /var/spool/patch directory, create a text file with the name /var/spool/patch/patchlist that contains the name of the three patches (separated by spaces or returns). Then, use the following command to install the patches:

```
patchadd -M /var/spool/patch /var/spool/patch/patchlist
```

The **-M** command-line argument can be used to install multiple patches for client, services, or install servers by specifying the previously described **-R**, **-S**, or **-C** command-line argument. This argument should be specified after the **-M** patch spool directory and patch names or patch list command-line arguments. See the previous examples of the **patchadd** command for use of all these arguments.

By default, any files that will be changed as a result of the patch's installation are copied to one or more backup directories. If necessary, you can then remove the patch and return the system to its state before the patch was installed. However, if you specify the **-d** command-line argument on the **patchadd** command, the files are not backed up, and the patch cannot be removed.

The default backup directories are located under /var/sadm/pkg and are based on the installed package or packages being modified by the patch and the patch number. For example, the x86 **find** command patch (110906-01) modified the SUNWcsu package. Any files changed by installing this patch will be saved under the /var/sadm/pkg/SUNWcsu/110906-01 directory. You can specify a different backup directory by using the **-B** command-line argument.

The **patchadd** command will fail if any of the following occur:

- A package being patched is not installed or is only partially installed.
- The patch requires another patch that is not installed.
- The patch is incompatible with another patch already installed.
- The current version or a higher version of the patch is already installed.
- The architecture of the patch and the system do not match.

TIP

After you unzip a patch, you can delete the zip file to save space. Likewise, after you install a patch, you can delete the files associated with the patch in the patch spool directory to save space.

## Determining Which Patches Are Installed

Two commands can be used to generate a list of installed patches for a standalone system:

- **showrev -p**
- **patchadd -p**

Both commands generate almost identical lists. The following example illustrates the use of the **showrev**(1M) command (the output is formatted for readability):

```
$ showrev -p
Patch: 110906-01
Obsoletes:
Requires:
Incompatibles:
Packages: SUNWcsu
Patch: 108632-06
Obsoletes:
Requires: 109000-01, 109038-01, 109067-02, 108994-01, 108969-01
Incompatibles:
Packages: SUNWcsr, SUNWnisr, SUNWncar
$
```

When a patch is installed, information regarding the patch is added to the pkginfo file of each package updated by the patch. The pkginfo files are located in subdirectories under the /var/sadm/pkg directory. The **showrev** and **patchadd** commands extract and format information from the pkginfo files. In addition to the patch number and the package(s) that the patch updates, the commands list any appropriate dependency information, such as other required patches or incompatible patches.

You can use the **patchadd** command to display a list of installed patches for other system configurations using the **-C**, **-R**, and **-S** command-line arguments, as previously described. For example, to display the patches applied to an OS service named Solaris8x86, you can use the following **patchadd** command:

```
patchadd -S solaris8x86 -p
```

To display a list of patches applied to a particular package, use the **pkgparam** command. The following example lists the patches applied to the SUNWcsu package:

```
$ pkgparam SUNWcsu PATCHLIST
108529-01 108826-01 108900-01 108980-04 108986-01 108990-02
109010-01 109020-01 109028-01 109044-02 109046-02 109092-01
109138-01 109146-01 109148-01 109150-01 109278-01 108965-02
```

```
108976-02 109004-01 109006-01 109008-01 109012-01 109016-01
109018-01 109022-01 109024-01 109032-01
109034-01 109036-01
110906-01
$
```

## Removing a Patch

The **patchrm** command is used to remove or back out a patch by specifying the patch number as a command-line argument. The system configurations supported by the **patchadd** command are also supported by the **patchrm** command. You also use the same **-C**, **-R**, and **-S** command-line arguments, as previously described. For example, to remove patch 110906-01 from the bootable root image of a diskless client named client5, you can use the following **patchrm** command:

```
patchrm -R /export/root/client5 110906-01
```

Because the default backup directory could have been changed during installation using the **-B** command-line argument to the **patchadd** command, the **patchrm** command also supports the **-B** argument.

In addition, you can force the **patchrm** command to remove a patch that has been superseded by another patch by using the **-f** command-line argument.

You can remove installed patches and return the system to the state it was in before the patch was installed as long as the following conditions are met:

- The patch is not required by another patch or has been made obsolete by a later patch.
- The patch was not installed using **patchadd -d**, which informs **patchadd** not to save a copy of files before they are updated or replaced.

# Practice Questions

## Question 1

Which of the following can be used to install multiple patches? [Select all that apply]

- ❑ a. **patchadd -M /var/spool/patch 104567-03 106583-10 103276-04**
- ❑ b. Use **patchadd** to install each patch separately.
- ❑ c. **patchadd -M /var/spool/patch patchlist**

Answers a, b, and c are correct. All the answers can be used to install multiple patches. The command in answer a installs three patches located in the /var/spool/patch directory. The command in answer c uses a file named patchlist that contains a list of patches to install. Of course, the **pkgadd** command can be used to installs several patches, one at a time (answer b).

## Question 2

Which of the following can be used to install packages? [Select all that apply]

- ❑ a. **admintool**
- ❑ b. **pkgtool**
- ❑ c. **pkgadd**
- ❑ d. **pkgrm**
- ❑ e. **pkginfo**

Answers a and c are correct. You can use **admintool** and **pkgadd** to install packages. **pkgtool** does not exist. Therefore, answer b is incorrect. **pkgrm** is used to remove packages, and **pkginfo** is used to display information about packages. Therefore, answers d and e are incorrect.

## Question 3

What are the two most commonly used methods for installing Solaris 8? [Select all that apply]

- ❑ a. Tape
- ❑ b. CD-ROM
- ❑ c. Over-the-network
- ❑ d. Diskette
- ❑ e. Web

Answers b and c are correct. Solaris 8 is most commonly installed via CD-ROM or over-the-network. Tape and diskettes are valid boot devices but are not used for installation. Therefore, answers a and d are incorrect. Answer e, the Web, is not feasible.

## Question 4

Which of the following is the default spool directory for packages?

- ❍ a. /var/spool
- ❍ b. /var/sadm/pkg
- ❍ c. /tmp
- ❍ d. /var/spool/pkg

Answer d is correct. /var/spool/pkg is the default spool directory for packages. The system spool directory is /var/spool. Therefore, answer a is incorrect. The directory that contains information about installed packages is /var/sadm/pkg. Therefore, answer b is incorrect. The temporary directory is /tmp. Therefore, answer c is incorrect.

## Question 5

Solaris 8 cannot be installed on which of the following?

- ❍ a. Macintosh system
- ❍ b. Sun SPARC
- ❍ c. Intel Pentium
- ❍ d. AMD or Cyrix (Intel-compatibles)

Answer a is correct. Solaris 8 cannot be installed on a Macintosh system. Solaris 8 can be installed on Sun SPARC, Intel Pentium, or Intel-compatibles (AMD and Cyrix). Therefore, answers b, c, and d are incorrect.

## Question 6

Which commands will display selected information from the SUNWast pkginfo file? [Select all that apply]

- ❑ a. **pkginfo SUNWast**
- ❑ b. **pkginfo -l SUNWast**
- ❑ c. **display pkginfo SUNWast**
- ❑ d. Highlight SUNWast in the Admintool Software window and click Show Details.

Answers a, b, and d are correct. You can display selected information from the SUNWast pkginfo file using the **pkginfo SUNWast** or **pkginfo -l SUNWast** command, or by highlighting SUNWast in the Admintool Software window and clicking Show Details. Although the command in answer a provides only the package title and type of software, the pkginfo file is the only place you can obtain this information. The command in answer c does not exist.

## Question 7

Which of the following commands can be used to remove a patch?

- ❍ a. **rmpatch**
- ❍ b. **patchrm**
- ❍ c. **pkgrm -p**
- ❍ d. **patchadd -d**

Answer b is correct. You can use the **patchrm** command to remove a patch. Answer a (**rmpatch**) is not a valid command. The **pkgrm** command is used to remove packages, and no **-p** command-line argument exists. Therefore, answer c is incorrect. The **patchadd -d** command is used to add a patch without saving files before they are updated or replaced. Therefore, answer d is incorrect.

## Question 8

Which of the following commands can be used to list all installed patches? [Select all that apply]

- ❑ a. **showrev -p**
- ❑ b. **patchinfo**
- ❑ c. **patchlist all**
- ❑ d. **patchadd -p**

Answers a and d are correct. You can use the **showrev -p** and **patchadd -p** commands to list all installed patches. The commands in answers b and c do not exist.

## Question 9

During an upgrade, the disk space needs to be reallocated. Which of the following can be used as the backup medium? [Select all that apply]

- ❑ a. Unused system disk
- ❑ b. Tape
- ❑ c. Diskette
- ❑ d. CD-ROM
- ❑ e. Remote file system

Answers a, b, c, and e are correct. An unused system disk, tape, diskette, or remote file system can be used as the backup medium during an upgrade, assuming it provides enough storage space. A CD-ROM, as the name implies, is read only (Compact Disk - Read Only Media). Read-only media cannot be used for backup. Therefore, answer d is incorrect. A writable CD could probably be used, but that option was not provided as a choice.

## Question 10

Which of the following items can be selected during a custom installation using Web Start? [Select all that apply]

- ❑ a. File system layout
- ❑ b. Software localizations
- ❑ c. Additional software products
- ❑ d. System locale
- ❑ e. Software group or cluster

Answers a, b, c, d, and e are correct. The file system layout lets you add file systems and/or adjust the size of file systems. Software localizations can be used to select a geographical region (such as North America), and the system locale further defines the system language (for North America, you can select one of several English variations). The software group and additional products also can be selected. These items are available only when you choose Custom Installation.

# Need to Know More?

Mulligan, John P., *Solaris 8 Essential Reference* (New Riders, Indianapolis, IN, 2001), ISBN 0-7357-1007-4.

Sun Microsystems, *Solaris 8 (Intel Platform Edition) Hardware Compatibility List*. Available in printed form (part number 806-1054-11), on the Web at **docs.sun.com**, and from the online documentation, AnswerBook2, provided with the Solaris 8 operating system.

Sun Microsystems, *Solaris 8 (Intel Platform Edition) Installation Guide*. Available in printed form (part number 806-0956-10), on the Web at **docs.sun.com**, and from the online documentation, AnswerBook2, provided with the Solaris 8 operating system.

Sun Microsystems, *Solaris 8 (SPARC Platform Edition) Installation Guide*. Available in printed form (part number 806-0955-10), on the Web at **docs.sun.com**, and from the online documentation, AnswerBook2, provided with the Solaris 8 operating system.

Sun Microsystems, *Solaris 8 1/01 Sun Hardware Platform Guide*. Available in printed form (part number 806-6513-10), on the Web at **docs.sun.com**, and from the online documentation, AnswerBook2, provided with the Solaris 8 operating system.

Sun Microsystems, *System Administration Guide, Volume 1*. Available in printed form (part number 805-7228-10), on the Web at **docs.sun.com**, and from the online documentation, AnswerBook2, provided with the Solaris 8 operating system.

Sun Microsystems, *System Reference Manual, Section 1 - User Commands*. Available in printed form (part number 806-0624-10), on the Web at **docs.sun.com**, and from the online documentation, AnswerBook2, provided with the Solaris 8 operating system.

Sun Microsystems, *System Reference Manual, Section 1M - System Administration Commands*. Available in printed form (part number 806-0625-10), on the Web at **docs.sun.com**, and from the online documentation, AnswerBook2, provided with the Solaris 8 operating system.

4

# Booting and Shutting Down the System

**Terms you'll need to understand:**

- ✓ OpenBoot
- ✓ Nonvolatile RAM (NVRAM)
- ✓ Device aliases
- ✓ The boot process
- ✓ Kernel modules
- ✓ init program
- ✓ System run levels
- ✓ rc scripts

**Techniques you'll need to master:**

- ✓ Creating and deleting a device alias
- ✓ Troubleshooting boot problems
- ✓ Changing system run levels
- ✓ Adding system services using rc scripts

This chapter addresses topics related to booting and shutting down the system. The first section covers key aspects of the system firmware on Sun SPARC platforms, including the *Boot PROM* test objectives. The second section summarizes the boot process for both SPARC and Intel x86 platforms. This section covers the *Boot Process* test objectives. The third section describes system run levels, the services available at the different run levels, and how to change between the run levels. Also included is a description of how to add custom services at a selected run level. This section includes the *Initialization and Shutdown* test objectives.

# Boot PROM Firmware (OpenBoot)

The boot Programmable Read-Only Memory (PROM) of a system is used to store the firmware that is executed immediately after the system hardware finishes the Power On SelfTest (POST). This firmware is called OpenBoot, and it's the standard firmware for Sun Systems. OpenBoot firmware pertains only to SPARC platforms, but some limited functionality is available on Intel x86 platforms.

OpenBoot is used to boot the operating system, run diagnostics, modify boot-related parameters stored in nonvolatile RAM (NVRAM), and provide a *Forth* interpreter.

Currently, two supported versions of OpenBoot are available: version 2.x and version 3.x. OpenBoot 2.x was introduced with SPARCstation 2 and SPARCstation IPX systems. OpenBoot 3.x is an enhanced version of OpenBoot 2.x; it's based on Institute of Electrical and Electronics Engineers (IEEE) Standard 1275-1994, "Standard for Boot Firmware." OpenBoot 3.x is used on Sun Ultra series and newer SPARC platforms.

OpenBoot provides a command-line interface for the system console. The command-line interface has two modes:

- *Restricted Monitor*—Allows the administrator to boot the operating system, continue a suspended operation, or start the Forth Monitor. The prompt for the Restricted Monitor is the > symbol.

- *Forth Monitor*—Allows the administrator to boot the operating system, run diagnostics, and modify system configuration parameters. The prompt for the Forth Monitor is the word *ok*, which is typically referred to as the *OpenBoot prompt*.

System configuration parameters are stored in the system NVRAM. These parameters determine the initial configuration and related communication characteristics of the system and retain their value even if the power to the system is shut off.

You can view the value of these parameters using the OpenBoot **printenv** command. To modify them, use the OpenBoot **setenv** command.

## Important OpenBoot Commands

Some of the more important OpenBoot commands are used to display system configuration information, perform hardware testing, and control system booting. All these commands are entered at the Forth Monitor or OpenBoot **ok** prompt.

Table 4.1 lists the OpenBoot commands that display system configuration data, and Table 4.2 lists the OpenBoot commands that you use to perform basic hardware testing. Table 4.3 lists the variations of the OpenBoot **boot** command that you can use to select different boot devices.

**Table 4.1 OpenBoot commands for displaying system configuration data.**

| Command | Description |
|---|---|
| **banner** | Displays the power-on banner |
| **devalias** | Lists all device aliases |
| **.enet-addr** | Displays an Ethernet address |
| **.idprom** | Displays formatted ID PROM contents |
| **module-info** | Displays the CPU speed (2.x only) |
| **printenv** | Lists all NVRAM parameters and default values |
| **show-devs** | Lists all installed devices |
| **.speed** | Displays CPU and bus speeds (3.x only) |
| **.traps** | Lists types of SPARC traps |
| **.version** | Displays the boot PROM's version and data |

**Table 4.2 OpenBoot commands for performing hardware testing.**

| Command | Description |
|---|---|
| **pcia-probe-list** | Tests the Peripheral Component Interconnect (PCI) bus |
| **probe-scsi** | Tests the built-in Small Computer System Interface (SCSI) bus for connected devices |
| **probe-scsi-all** | Tests all SCSI buses |
| **test-all** | Tests a group of installed devices |
| **test floppy** | Tests the diskette drive |
| **test /memory** | Tests system memory |
| **test net** | Tests the on-board Ethernet interface |
| **watch-clock** | Monitors the system clock |
| **watch-net** | Monitors the network connection |

**Table 4.3 OpenBoot commands for selecting different boot devices.**

| Command | Description |
|---|---|
| **boot cdrom** | Boots from the local CD-ROM |
| **boot disk** | Boots from the default hard disk |
| **boot floppy** | Boots from the diskette drive |
| **boot net** | Boots from the network |
| **boot tape** | Boots from the SCSI tape drive |

The **boot** command supports a couple of options that you may find useful. The **-a** option requests an interactive boot so that OpenBoot will prompt for information when needed. In addition, the **-s** option causes OpenBoot to boot to single-user mode instead of the default system run level. When you're booting from the hard disk, the default device is specified by the boot-device NVRAM configuration parameter. From the OpenBoot **ok** prompt, use the following command to display the default device:

```
ok printenv boot-device
boot-device = disk
ok
```

The default device can be changed as required. For example, to change the default boot device to a device with the alias disk2, use the following command. Then, use **reset** to save the new value and reboot:

```
ok setenv boot-device disk2
ok reset
```

## Device Aliases

OpenBoot identifies system hardware using a full device pathname that represents the type of device and its location in the system. A device pathname consists of system buses, addresses, and possibly driver names. The following is an example of a full device name for a partition of a SCSI disk drive:

```
/sbus@1f,0/SUNW,fas@e,8800000/sd@3,0:a
```

For more details on device names, see Chapter 8. Because device names are typically long, complex, and awkward to enter, OpenBoot lets you assign a *device alias* to a full device name; this alias is a name that's short and easy to remember and type.

## Creating a Device Alias

You can create a device alias two ways. The first method uses the **devalias** command. Aliases created with this command are lost when the system is rebooted. The second method uses the **nvalias** command. Aliases created with this command are stored in nonvolatile memory and remain there until you remove them using other OpenBoot commands. Both commands use the same syntax.

For example, both of the following commands, entered at the OpenBoot **ok** prompt, will assign the alias disk2 to the device named /sbus/esp/sd@2,0 (a SCSI disk):

```
ok devalias disk2 /sbus/esp/sd@2,0
ok nvalias disk2 /sbus/esp/sd@2,0
ok
```

Whenever the device name is required in the OpenBoot environment, you can use the alias instead. When you enter the **nvalias** command, it's stored in nonvolatile memory. This portion of memory is treated as an OpenBoot parameter called the **nvramrc** parameter. The contents of the **nvramrc** parameter are called the *script*. In addition to storing user-defined commands, this parameter is used by device drivers to save startup configuration variables, to patch device driver code, and to store bug patches or other installation-specific device configuration information.

If the OpenBoot **use-nvramrc** parameter is set to **true**, the script is executed during system boot. Any aliases defined in **nvramrc** using the **nvalias** command will be set, and then the aliases can be used in a later part of the script or as the value of one or more other OpenBoot parameters.

## Displaying a Device Alias

You can also use the **devalias** command to display defined device aliases. If you enter the command without any command-line arguments, all defined device aliases are listed. If you list a device alias as a command-line argument, the **devalias** command will display only the named device alias. The following example shows using the **devalias** command from the OpenBoot **ok** prompt of a SPARC 20 workstation:

```
ok devalias
screen      /iommu@f,e000000/sbus@f,e001000/cgsix@2,0
ttyb        /obio/zs@0,100000:b
ttya        /obio/zs@0,100000:a
keyboard    /obio/zs@0,0
floppy      /obio/SUNW,fdtwo
scsi        /iommu/sbus/espdma@f,400000/esp@f,800000
net-aui     /iommu/sbus/ledma@f,400010:aui/le@f,c0000
```

```
net-tpe      /iommu/sbus/ledma@f,400010:tpe/le@f,c0000
net          /iommu/sbus/ledma@f,400010/le@f,c0000
disk         /iommu/sbus/espdma@f,400000/esp@f,800000/sd@3,0
cdrom        /iommu/sbus/espdma@f,400000/esp@f,800000/sd@6,0:d
tape         /iommu/sbus/espdma@f,400000/esp@f,800000/st@4,0
tape1        /iommu/sbus/espdma@f,400000/esp@f,800000/st@5,0
tape0        /iommu/sbus/espdma@f,400000/esp@f,800000/st@4,0
disk3        /iommu/sbus/espdma@f,400000/esp@f,800000/sd@3,0
disk2        /iommu/sbus/espdma@f,400000/esp@f,800000/sd@2,0
disk1        /iommu/sbus/espdma@f,400000/esp@f,800000/sd@1,0
disk0        /iommu/sbus/espdma@f,400000/esp@f,800000/sd@0,0

ok devalias disk
disk         /iommu/sbus/espdma@f,400000/esp@f,800000/sd@3,0
ok
```

### Deleting a Device Alias

An alias defined by the **nvalias** command is stored in the script and remains there until you remove it using the **nvunalias** command, or until you restore the system configuration to its original defaults using the **set-defaults** command. Keep in mind that an alias defined using the **devalias** command is *not* stored in the script and is lost when the system reboots.

To delete the nonvolatile device alias (an alias stored in the script) disk2, enter the following command at the OpenBoot **ok** prompt:

```
ok nvunalias disk2
ok
```

**TIP:** When you're deleting an alias, be certain that the alias is not used anywhere; otherwise, a possibly critical system parameter might become undefined.

## Viewing and Modifying NVRAM Parameters from Solaris

Typically, you view and modify the NVRAM parameters using OpenBoot commands. It is possible to view and modify the NVRAM parameters from the Solaris 8 environment using the **eeprom**(1M) command. However, only the superuser can modify NVRAM parameters using the **eeprom** command.

To view the value of the **auto-boot?** NVRAM parameter, enter the following **eeprom** command at the system prompt:

```
$ /usr/sbin/eeprom auto-boot?
auto-boot?=true
$
```

To view all NVRAM parameters, enter the **eeprom** command without any command-line arguments.

You can also use the **eeprom** command to modify a NVRAM parameter. To set the value of **auto-boot?** to **false**, enter the following command at the system prompt:

```
# eeprom auto-boot?=false
#
```

## Troubleshooting Boot Problems

When reset or powered on, a SPARC system typically runs the POST. After this, the system boots automatically (if **auto-boot?** is **true**) or enters the Forth Monitor.

The boot process or OpenBoot initialization sequence performs various checks and loads the appropriate modules. You can view status messages regarding this initialization sequence in the /var/adm/messages file after the system has successfully loaded and started the operating system.

However, if a boot problem occurs, the Solaris 8 system will not be started, and you can't view the messages. To get around this situation, OpenBoot has the ability to send the initialization sequence messages to tty serial port A (TTYA). You accomplish this by setting the **diag-switch?** OpenBoot parameter to **true** and using the **setenv** command before starting the system boot, as in the following example:

```
ok setenv diag-switch? true
ok
```

By attaching a terminal or PC to TTYA, you can observe the messages generated by the OpenBoot initialization sequence and identify the boot problem.

## Emergency Commands (SPARC Only)

Sometimes you need to take control over a system, regardless of its state. From the keyboard of a SPARC system, you can immediately enter the Forth Monitor. Table 4.4 lists the emergency keyboard commands supported by OpenBoot. All make use of the stop function key on the SPARC keyboard.

EXAM ALERT

When you need to recover a system that has stopped responding, after the stop+a sequence, be sure to enter the OpenBoot **sync** command to synchronize the system disks and write a crash dump before issuing the appropriate boot command.

**Table 4.4 Emergency keyboard commands (SPARC only).**

| Sequence | System Response |
|---|---|
| stop | Bypasses the POST |
| stop+a | Aborts the operating system or boot process (returns to the OpenBoot **ok** prompt) |
| stop+d | Enters diagnostic mode |
| stop+f | Enters the Forth Monitor on TTYA (instead of the system console) |
| stop+n | Resets the NVRAM contents to default values |

The stop+a sequence can be enabled or disabled using the **kbd**(1) command. You can also set the keyboard characteristics by modifying the /etc/default/kbd file and then executing the **kbd -i** command. For example, the following **kbd** command will disable the keyboard abort sequence:

```
# kbd -a disable
```

To accomplish the same task, place the *KEYBOARD_ABORT=disable* entry in /etc/default/kbd and execute

```
# kbd -i
```

# The Boot Process

The boot PROM stores firmware that is responsible for booting the operating system. Because the SPARC boot process is somewhat different than the Intel x86 boot process, they are covered separately here.

## The SPARC Boot Process

The SPARC boot process consists of the following phases:

1. *Boot PROM*—This phase displays system information and then runs the POST diagnostics. After the diagnostics are complete, the primary boot program, bootblk, is loaded. Its function is to locate the secondary boot program, ufsboot, on the boot device.

2. *Boot Programs*—In this phase, bootblk loads the ufsboot program into memory and executes it.

3. *Kernel Initialization*—In this phase, the ufsboot program loads the core kernel into memory and causes it to execute. The kernel initializes its data structures and begins loading other kernel modules on the basis of the /etc/system

file using the ufsboot program. After all the necessary modules are loaded and initialized, the kernel starts the /sbin/init program.

4. *init*—In the init phase, the init program starts other processes on the basis of the information contained in the /etc/inittab file. These processes include a program that calls the run control (rc) scripts that set up various system services.

## Intel x86 Boot Process

The Intel x86 boot process consists of the following phases:

1. *BIOS*—During this phase, the POST diagnostics are executed. Then, the master boot record, mboot, is read from disk to locate the active partition that contains the pboot program.

2. *Boot Programs*—In this phase, the pboot program is loaded and in turn locates and loads the primary boot program, bootblk. Then, the secondary boot program, either boot.bin or ufsboot, is located in the root file system and loaded.

3. *Kernel Initialization*—In this phase, the boot.bin or ufsboot program loads the core kernel into memory and causes it to execute. The kernel initializes its data structures and begins loading other kernel modules. After all the necessary modules are loaded and initialized, the kernel starts the /sbin/init program.

4. *init*—In the init phase, the init program starts other processes on the basis of the information contained in the /etc/inittab file. These processes include a program that calls the rc scripts that set up various system services.

## Kernel Modules

Kernel software is divided into groups of related functions called *modules*. Some modules are part of a small, common core of the operating system. Some modules provide platform-specific operations, whereas other modules are device drivers. This architecture allows portions of the kernel to be included or excluded on the basis of the desired functionality or allows portions of the kernel to be updated without replacing the entire kernel. Device drivers are dynamic kernel modules that are loaded when the device is accessed.

The kernel modules are stored in three directories—two under the root file system and one endeb the /usr file system:

- */platform/sparc/kernel for SPARC platforms or /platform/i86pc/kernel for x86 platforms*—Modules that are specific to the platform

- *Ikernel*—Common kernel modules required for booting
- */usr/kernel*—Common kernel modules used by platforms with a particular instruction set

The /etc/system file is used to determine which kernel modules are loaded and to define various kernel parameters. This file takes the form of one or more keywords followed by one or more parameters. The supported keywords are:

- *exclude*—Prevents modules from loading
- *forceload*—Forces a module to load
- *moddir*—Changes the common kernel module directories
- *rootdev*—Sets the physical pathname to the root device
- *rootfs*—Defines the type of root file system
- *set*—Sets kernel or module variables

## The init Program

The last phase of the boot process is the init program. The init program is used to control system processes and services. Its primary purpose is to create or stop processes on the basis of the current state of the system. The system state is referred to as a *system run level*. Several run levels are defined on the basis of the type of activities that the system should be supporting while at a particular run level, such as maintenance, a single user, multiple users, and so on. Information regarding which processes and services should be running at a particular run level is stored in the /etc/inittab file.

The default run level is defined in /etc/inittab by the initdefault entry. The following example shows run level 3 as the default run level:

```
is:3:initdefault:
```

Every run level (except 4) has an entry in the /etc/inittab file that identifies an rc program to execute. In addition, each run level has a directory associated with it, which contains rc scripts that should be executed by the rc program to start or stop processes and services when that run level becomes the current run level.

The init program also sets the default environment variables as defined in /etc/default/init. These include local variables and system parameters based on location, such as the time zone.

# System Run Levels

To provide a convenient way for the system administrator to shut down or reboot the system and control system services and resources, eight system run levels (also referred to as *init states*) are defined and assigned specific functionality. Table 4.5 describes the eight run levels.

**Table 4.5 The eight system run levels.**

| Run Level | init State | Functionality |
|---|---|---|
| 0 | Power Down | The system is being shut down. All users are forced off the system. All operating system services are stopped in an orderly manner. When this process is complete, the system is at firmware mode. For SPARC platforms, firmware mode is the **ok** OpenBoot prompt. It is safe to turn off the power to the system and peripherals. |
| s or S | Single User | The system is prepared for maintenance. Any users are logged off the system. Any services except the most basic operating system services are stopped in an orderly manner. Any mounted file systems remain mounted. A command-line interface (with superuser privileges) is started and associated with the system console, so the system administrator can perform maintenance (such as system backup) without interference from users or applications. |
| 1 | Administrative | Any logged-on users are not affected. Multiple users can log on and use available system resources. All services except the most basic operating system services are stopped in an orderly manner. Any mounted file systems remain mounted. A command-line interface (with superuser privileges) is started and associated with the system console, so the system administrator can perform maintenance while allowing users to access the system. |
| 2 | Multiuser | The system is set up for normal operations. Multiple users can log on and use the system resources. All services, except the Network File System (NFS) server, are started. All default file systems are mounted. |
| 3 | Multiuser with NFS | The system is set up for normal operations. This is typically the default system state. Multiple users can access and use the system resources. All services, including resource sharing (the NFS server), are started. All default file systems are mounted. |
| 4 | Alternative Multiuser | Currently, this state is not used and is unavailable. |

*(continued)*

**Table 4.5 The eight system run levels *(continued)*.**

| Run Level | init State | Functionality |
|---|---|---|
| 5 | Power Down | The system is shut down. All users are logged off the system. All operating system services are stopped in an orderly manner. When this process is complete, it is safe to turn off the power to the system and peripherals. If supported by the system hardware, the power to the system is automatically turned off. |
| 6 | Reboot | The system is shut down (run level 0) and then restarted and brought back up to the default run level (as defined in the /etc/inittab file, typically 3). |

EXAM ALERT

Solaris has eight run levels, of which seven are used. Even though no functionality is defined for run level 4, it is still considered a valid run level. Also note that the NFS client is started at run level 2, whereas the NFS server is started at run level 3.

## Changing the System Run Level

Occasionally, you'll need to change the system run level—for example, when you shut down the system to add or remove hardware, perform backups, prepare for an expected power outage, or prepare to physically move the system to another location. Table 4.6 lists the commands you use to change the system run level from the command line.

**Table 4.6 Commands used to change the system run level.**

| Command | Path | Run Level(s) | Description |
|---|---|---|---|
| **halt** | /usr/sbin | 0 | Stops the processor(s) |
| **init** | /sbin | 0,1,2,3,4,5,6,s | Processes control initialization |
| **poweroff** | /usr/sbin | 5 | Stops the processor(s) and powers off the system (if possible) |
| **reboot** | /usr/sbin | 6 | Reboots the system |
| **shutdown** | /etc | 0,1,5,6,s | Used for compatibility (symbolically linked to /usr/sbin/shutdown) |
| **shutdown** | /usr/sbin | 0,1,5,6,s | Changes the system run level |
| **telinit** | /etc | 0,1,2,3,4,5,6,s | Used for compatibility (symbolically linked to /usr/sbin/init) |
| **uadmin** | /sbin | 0,5,6 | Used for administrative control |

The **halt**(1M) command normally logs the shutdown to the system log, writes a shutdown record to the system accounting file, performs a call to the **sync**(1M) command to write any pending information to the disks, and halts the processor(s). You can prevent the system and account logging, along with disk syncing, by using command-line arguments. The **halt** command changes to run level 0 but does not execute the rc scripts associated with run level 0 as the **shutdown**(1M) and **init**(1M) commands do.

You can use the **init**(1M) and **telinit**(1M) commands to change to any of the eight run levels. The commands identified in the /etc/inittab file for each run level are executed, and any running process not in /etc/inittab is sent a SIGTERM signal or possibly a SIGKILL signal (see Chapter 7) to cause it to terminate. For each run level, an entry in /etc/inittab runs the appropriate rc scripts to start and stop processes.

The **init** command is unique in that it is the only command that can be used to change to any system run level. Although all the commands listed in Table 4.6 can shut down/reboot the system (run levels 0, 1, 5, 6, s), only the **init** command can bring a system up from run level s or 1 to run level 2 or 3.

The **poweroff**(1M) command changes the system to run level 5. Normally, it logs the shutdown to the system log, writes a shutdown record to the system accounting file, performs a call to **sync**(1M) to write any pending information to the disks, halts the processor(s), and, if possible, shuts off the power. The **poweroff** command is equivalent to the **init 5** command.

The **reboot**(1M) command changes the system to run level 6. Normally, it logs the reboot to the system log, writes a shutdown record to the system accounting file, performs a call to **sync** to write any pending information to the disks, and initiates a multiuser reboot.

The **reboot** command is unique in that it can pass arguments to the OpenBoot **boot** command using the **--** argument. For example, the command **reboot -- -rv** passes the **-rv** command-line arguments to the OpenBoot **boot** command; they are then passed to the kernel. In this case, the **r** causes a reconfigure (probes all devices and build nodes) and the **v** enables verbose mode.

The **shutdown** command (under both the /usr/sbin and /etc directories) provides a grace period and warning message capability and also executes the appropriate rc scripts. You can use the **shutdown** command to change to run levels 0, 1, 5, 6, and s.

The **shutdown** command without any command-line arguments will result in a one-minute grace period with warning messages at 1 minute, 30 seconds, and now. The **shutdown** command will prompt for confirmation to continue before the *shutdown now* message is broadcast and the run level change continues. The system is then changed to run level s.

The **uadmin**(1M) command provides basic administrative functions, such as shutting down or rebooting a system. Typically, it is called by various system administration procedures and is not intended for general use.

EXAM ALERT

You can use the **who -r** command to determine the current run level of the system and the date on which the change to that run level occurred.

## Run Control (rc) Scripts

As previously stated, every run level (except 4) has an entry in the /etc/inittab file that identifies an rc program to execute. In addition, each run level has a directory associated with it.

The directory contains rc scripts that should be executed by the rc program to start or stop processes and services when that run level becomes the current run level. These rc programs and rc script directories use a standard naming convention based on the run level.

For run level 0, the rc program is /etc/rc0, and /etc/rc0.d is the rc script directory. Likewise, for run level 1, the rc program is /etc/rc1, and /etc/rc1.d is the rc script directory. The same naming convention is applied for run levels 2, 3, and s. Run levels 5 and 6 do not have separate rc directories but rather use the run level 0 rc directory.

Typically, both the rc program and the scripts under the rc script directories are referred to as *rc scripts*. Referring to the script called directly from the /etc/inittab as the *rc program* helps avoid confusion.

The rc scripts are shell scripts (typically Bourne) written to start and stop various processes and services. An rc script is usually written in two portions: a start portion and a stop portion. As the name implies, the start portion is executed to start a service, whereas the stop portion is called to stop a service. Thus, a single script can control the service. When the rc program calls the rc script, the program provides either a **start** or a **stop** command-line argument to the rc script, depending on whether the service should be started or stopped at a particular run level. The decision to start or stop a particular service is based on the name of the rc script in the appropriate rc directory.

For example, the standard Unix utility to execute maintenance commands automatically is the **cron** program. It is usually started at run level 2 and stopped at run levels 0, 1, 5, 6, and s. To start **cron** at run level 2, you can copy (or link) the cron rc script into /etc/rc2.d and name it S75cron. The *S* at the beginning of an rc script causes the rc program to start the service at the particular run level (in this example, run level 2) by calling the rc script with the **start** argument.

Likewise, you can copy (or link) the same cron rc script into the /etc/rc0.d, /etc/rc1.d, and /etc/rcS.d directories and name it K40cron. The *K* at the beginning of an rc script causes the rc program to stop the service at the particular run level by calling the rc script with the **stop** argument.

Note that the numbers included in the names of the cron rc script files are different. The numbers provide a method for the rc program to start or stop services in a particular, consistent order. The rc scripts with lower numbers are executed before the rc scripts with higher numbers. This order is necessary, because some services require the presence of other services to operate properly.

For example, a networking application requires that the networking services be available. So, the rc script to start the application should have a higher number than the rc script to start the networking. In addition, services should be stopped in reverse order. In the case of a networking application, the rc script to stop the application should have a lower number than the rc script to stop the networking.

Copies of all rc scripts are placed in the /etc/init.d directory. To start or stop a particular service, the system administrator only has to locate the appropriate rc script in a single directory.

## Adding rc Scripts

Use the following procedure to add rc scripts for a new service:

1. Write a shell script that accepts the command-line arguments **start** and **stop** along with the appropriate actions to perform those functions.

2. As superuser, copy the new rc script to the /etc/init.d directory.

3. Determine the run level at which to start the service (typically 2).

4. Determine the two-digit number to control the start sequence (00 through 99). Look at the other startup rc scripts in the appropriate rc directory and choose a number that is not being used: one that is greater than any required services but less than any services that will use the new service.

5. Copy or link the new script from the /etc/init.d directory to the appropriate rc directory, giving it a name starting with *S* followed by the selected two-digit number and then the service name.

6. Determine the run level(s) at which the service should stop (typically, 0, 1, and s), meaning that the script needs to be linked to one or more of the rc directories.
7. Determine the two-digit number to control the stop sequence (00 through 99). Look at the other stop rc scripts in the appropriate rc directories and choose a number that is not being used: one that is less than any required services but greater than any services that were using the service.
8. Copy or link the new script from the /etc/init.d directory to the appropriate rc directories, giving it a name starting with *K* followed by the selected two-digit number and then the service name.

# Practice Questions

## Question 1

Which of the following versions of OpenBoot are currently supported by Sun Microsystems? [Select all that apply]

- ❑ a. 1.x
- ❑ b. 2.x
- ❑ c. 3.x
- ❑ d. 4.x

Answers b and c are correct. OpenBoot versions 2.x and 3.x currently are supported by Sun Microsystems. Version 1.x is no longer supported. Therefore, answer a is incorrect. Version 4.x does not exist. Therefore, answer d is incorrect.

## Question 2

Which OpenBoot command can be used to view system configuration information?

- ❍ a. **env**
- ❍ b. **display**
- ❍ c. **banner**
- ❍ d. **list**
- ❍ e. **show**

Answer c is correct. You can use the **banner** command to view system configuration information. The Solaris 8 **env** command lists shell variables in the current environment. Therefore, answer a is incorrect. The commands in answers b, d, and e do not exist, although a **show-dev** OpenBoot command does.

## Question 3

Which of the following OpenBoot commands are used to test hardware? [Select all that apply]

- ❑ a. **probe-scsi**
- ❑ b. **test floppy**
- ❑ c. **test net**
- ❑ d. **watch-clock**
- ❑ e. **test memory**

Answers a, b, c, and d are correct. The **probe-scsi**, **test floppy**, **test net**, and **watch-clock** commands test the SCSI controller, floppy diskette drive, network interface, and system clock, respectively. The correct command to test memory is **test /memory** (note the / before **memory**) . Therefore, answer e is incorrect.

## Question 4

Name the OpenBoot command used to delete a nonvolatile device alias.

________________________________

The correct answer is either **nvunalias** or **set-defaults.**

## Question 5

Which emergency keyboard command is used to abort the boot process?

- ❍ a. stop
- ❍ b. stop+a
- ❍ c. stop+b
- ❍ d. stop+s
- ❍ e. stop+!

Answer b is correct. The stop+a emergency keyboard command aborts the boot process. The stop keyboard command bypasses the POST. Therefore, answer a is incorrect. The keyboard commands in answers c, d, and e do not exist.

## Question 6

Provide the OpenBoot command to boot a system from the CD-ROM.

______________________

The correct answer is **boot cdrom**.

## Question 7

Which of the following is the last phase in the Solaris boot process?

- ❍ a. init
- ❍ b. Boot PROM
- ❍ c. BIOS
- ❍ d. Kernel Initialization
- ❍ e. Boot Programs

Answer a is correct. The init phase is the last in the Solaris boot process. All the answers are phases of either the SPARC or Intel x86 boot process. The Boot PROM and BIOS phases test hardware, the Boot Programs phase locates and loads boot programs, and then the Kernel Initialization phase loads the kernel. Only then can the init phase occur to initialize the operating system services. Therefore, answers b, c, d, and e are incorrect.

## Question 8

Give the full path name of the file that determines whether the keyboard abort sequence is enabled or disabled.

______________________

The correct answer is **/etc/default/kbd.**

## Question 9

Which of the following default directories are used to store kernel modules? [Select all that apply]

- ❑ a. /kernel
- ❑ b. /usr/kernel
- ❑ c. /var/kernel
- ❑ d. /etc/system
- ❑ e. /etc/kernel

Answers a and b are correct. The /kernel and /usr/kernel default directories are used to store kernel modules. The directories in answers c and e do not exist. The /etc/system directory is used to configure the system kernel. Therefore, answer d is incorrect.

## Question 10

Which of the following commands can be used to change to system run level 2 or 3?

- ❍ a. **init**
- ❍ b. **reboot**
- ❍ c. **shutdown**
- ❍ d. **poweroff**
- ❍ e. **uadmin**
- ❍ f. **halt**

Answer a is correct. The **init** command can be used to change to system run level 2 or 3. The **reboot** command can be used only to change to system run level 6. Therefore, answer b is incorrect. The **shutdown** command can be used only to change to system run levels 0, 1, 5, 6, and s. Therefore, answer c is incorrect. The **poweroff** command can be used only to change to system run level 5. Therefore, answer d is incorrect. The **uadmin** command can be used only to change to run levels 0, 5, and 6. In addition, this command is not intended for direct use. Therefore, answer e is incorrect. The **halt** command can be used only to change to system run level 0. Therefore, answer f is incorrect.

## Question 11

How many run levels are there in Solaris 8?

- ❍ a. 6
- ❍ b. 7
- ❍ c. 8
- ❍ d. 9

Answer c is correct. Solaris 8 has eight run levels. Answers a and d are not feasible. You might think that Solaris 8 has seven levels, because run level 4 is not used, but run level 4 is still counted. Therefore, answer b is incorrect.

## Question 12

Name the OpenBoot command used to list or create device aliases.

________________________________

The correct answer is **devalias.**

# Need to Know More?

Mulligan, John P., *Solaris 8 Essential Reference* (New Riders, Indianapolis, IN, 2001), ISBN 0-7357-1007-4.

Sun Microsystems, *OpenBoot 2.x Command Reference Manual.* Available in printed form (part number 806-2906-10), on the Web at **docs.sun.com**, and from the online documentation, AnswerBook2, provided with the Solaris 8 operating system.

Sun Microsystems, *OpenBoot 3.x Command Reference Manual.* Available in printed form (part number 806-1377-10), on the Web at **docs.sun.com**, and from the online documentation, AnswerBook2, provided with the Solaris 8 operating system.

Sun Microsystems, *System Administration Guide, Volume 1.* Available in printed form (part number 805-7228-10), on the Web at **docs.sun.com**, and from the online documentation, AnswerBook2, provided with the Solaris 8 operating system.

Sun Microsystems, *System Reference Manual, Section 1M - System Administration Commands.* Available in printed form (part number 806-0625-10), on the Web at **docs.sun.com**, and from the online documentation, AnswerBook2, provided with the Solaris 8 operating system.

# 5

# System Security and File Permissions

**Terms you'll need to understand:**

- ✓ Superuser account
- ✓ User and group accounts
- ✓ /etc/passwd, /etc/shadow, and /etc/group file formats
- ✓ Absolute and symbolic access modes
- ✓ Access Control List (ACL)

**Techniques you'll need to master:**

- ✓ Restricting and monitoring the superuser account
- ✓ Changing default and existing file permissions
- ✓ Setting and displaying Access Control Lists
- ✓ Changing file ownership

This chapter covers system security and file permissions. System security involves controlling access to the system by use of passwords and restricting/monitoring the use of the administrative user accounts. The file permissions portion of the chapter addresses controlling access to the data in files by using both basic and extended access controls. Most of the *Security* test objectives are covered in this chapter.

# System Security

Unix system security is based on controlling access to files (programs and data). You control access by defining user and group accounts and granting these accounts different levels of file access. The user accounts are protected by passwords.

Administrative accounts are given access to system data and tools that allow them to perform system maintenance. These accounts include root, sys, bin, and adm.

Several account administration files are used to store the information associated with user and group accounts, such as account names and passwords.

## The Superuser (Root) Account

The root, or superuser, account is a special administrative account that provides the ultimate in access to data and services, because it can override any file permissions on the system. To enforce good system security, you must restrict access to the superuser account and monitor it as closely as possible. Solaris 8 provides several ways to restrict and monitor the superuser account, as discussed in the following sections.

### Restricting and Monitoring the Superuser Account

You can restrict the root account so that it cannot log in to the system remotely; instead, it must log in from the system console. This restriction can be enforced by the following entry in the /etc/default/login file:

```
CONSOLE=/dev/console
```

By default, the root account is restricted. To disable this feature, edit the /etc/default/login file and put the shell comment character (#) at the beginning of the entry.

Restricting the root login to the console forces anyone accessing the superuser account remotely to log in with a regular system account and then use the **su**(1M) command to become the superuser. You can monitor and log the use of the **su** command in several ways. The /etc/default/su file controls this monitoring and logging.

To display use of the **su** command on the system console, add the following entry to the /etc/default/su file:

```
CONSOLE=/dev/console
```

Both failed and successful attempts to use the **su** command are displayed on the console. By default, the use of the **su** command is not displayed on the console. To enable this feature, edit the /etc/default/su file and remove the shell comment character (#) at the beginning of the entry. Note that this entry is identical to the entry used in the /etc/default/login file to restrict root login to the system console.

The following examples show the messages displayed on the console for two uses of the **su** command. The first shows an unsuccessful attempt to become root on the system named solaris8 from the login dla. The second shows a successful attempt to become the root. The messages that begin with a date are displayed regardless of the CONSOLE entry in the /etc/default/su file. The message beginning with *SU* is displayed because the CONSOLE entry in the /etc/default/su file is uncommented:

```
Mar 29 02:46:01 solaris8 su: 'su root' failed for dla
on /dev/pts/5

SU 03/29 02:49 + pts/5 dla-root
Mar 29 02:49:16 solaris8 su: 'su root' succeeded for dla
on /dev/pts/5
```

The use of the **su** command can be logged to a file dedicated for **su** logging by adding the following entry in the /etc/default/su file (although the default is shown here, you can use any file for the sulog):

```
SULOG=/var/adm/sulog
```

Both failed and successful attempts to use the **su** command are logged. By default, use of the **su** command is logged to the sulog. To disable this feature, edit the /etc/default/su file and add the shell comment character (#) at the beginning of the entry.

The following lines show the contents of a /var/adm/sulog file:

```
SU 03/18 01:46 + console root-daemon
SU 03/22 00:58 + pts/5 dla-root
SU 03/29 02:42 + pts/5 dla-guest
SU 03/29 02:43 + pts/5 dla-root
```

```
SU 03/29 02:46 - pts/5 dla-root
SU 03/29 02:49 + pts/5 dla-root
```

The plus (+) or minus (-) sign following the date and time indicates success or failure, respectively. The next field indicates where the command was entered, and the last field lists the from and to user accounts.

You can also log use of the **su** command using the system logging (syslog) facility. To enable it, add the following entry to the /etc/default/su file:

```
SYSLOG=YES
```

The syslog facility must be properly configured to capture and log these messages. The syslog facility is an objective for Part II (Exam 310-012) and is covered in Chapter 14.

By default, use of the **su** command is logged to the syslog facility. To disable this feature, edit the /etc/default/su file and add the shell comment character (#) at the beginning of the SYSLOG entry.

### The sysadmin Group

A user account that is a member of the sysadmin group (numerical group 14) can perform some selected system administration activities using **admintool** (1M) without being granted full superuser privileges. As a result, more than one person can perform basic system administration (adding and deleting users, printers, software, and so on) without compromising system security. To enable this ability, configure the setuid to root permission for **admintool** and specify membership in the sysadmin group as a requirement for using **admintool**. Additional information about groups and the setuid permission is provided later in this chapter.

## User and Group Account Administration Files

Three administrative files are used to define and manage user and group accounts:

- /etc/passwd
- /etc/shadow
- /etc/group

### /etc/passwd

The /etc/passwd file is an ASCII file that defines user accounts on the local system. Each line in the file represents a user account and consists of seven colon-delimited fields. Table 5.1 lists the fields of an entry in the /etc/passwd file.

**Table 5.1 /etc/passwd fields.**

| Field | Purpose |
|---|---|
| User name | The unique name assigned to the user account. |
| Password | In earlier versions of Unix, the password field contained the encrypted account password. For security reasons, the passwords have been moved to the /etc/shadow file. The letter *x* is typically placed in this field to indicate that the password is in /etc/shadow. |
| UID | A unique numeric identification assigned to the user account. Any processes or files created by the user account will be owned by this UID. The system administrator account, root, is assigned the UID of 0. This is the UID of a superuser account. System maintenance accounts are usually assigned a UID of less than 100, whereas user accounts typically start at 1001. |
| GID | The numeric identification of the default group that the user account has been assigned to as a member. Groups are defined in the /etc/group file. |
| Comment | Information about the owner of the user account, such as real name, phone number, mailing address, and so on. An ampersand (&) in this field is interpreted as the contents of the user name field. |
| Home directory | The full path to the directory where the user is initially located after logging in. |
| Login shell | The full pathname of the initial shell used as a command interpreter. If this field is empty, the default is /usr/bin/sh. |

The following listing shows the default contents of a Solaris 8 /etc/password file:

```
root:x:0:1:Super-User:/:/sbin/sh
daemon:x:1:1::/:
bin:x:2:2::/usr/bin:
sys:x:3:3::/:
adm:x:4:4:Admin:/var/adm:
lp:x:71:8:Line Printer Admin:/usr/spool/lp:
uucp:x:5:5:uucp Admin:/usr/lib/uucp:
nuucp:x:9:9:uucp Admin:/var/spool/uucppublic:/usr/lib/uucp/uucico
listen:x:37:4:Network Admin:/usr/net/nls:
nobody:x:60001:60001:Nobody:/:
noaccess:x:60002:60002:No Access User:/:
nobody4:x:65534:65534:SunOS 4.x Nobody:/:
```

## /ctc/shadow

The /etc/shadow file is an ASCII file that stores passwords for local user accounts along with any password restrictions or aging. Access is restricted to superusers to protect the passwords. Each line represents the password of a user

**Table 5.2 /etc/shadow fields.**

| Field | Purpose |
|---|---|
| User account | Relates the /etc/shadow entry to a user account defined in the /etc/passwd file. |
| Password | A 13-character encrypted password for the associated user account. If the field contains NP, this account is used only to own processes or files (setuid) and cannot be used to log in to the system. If the field contains *LK*, the account is locked and cannot be used to access the system. If the field is empty, no password exists, and the user is forced to enter a password the first time the account is used. |
| Last changed | The number of days between January 1, 1970, and the last date the password was changed. |
| Minimum | The minimum number of days required to pass before the user is allowed to change the password. |
| Maximum | The maximum number of days the password is valid. |
| Warning | The number of days the user is warned before the password expires. |
| Inactivity | The number of days the account can be inactive before the password must be changed. |
| Expiration | The number of days between January 1, 1970, and the date on which the account expires. |
| Flag | Reserved for future use. |

account and consists of nine colon-delimited fields. Table 5.2 lists the fields of an entry in the /etc/shadow file.

The following line shows the guest entry from a Solaris 8 /etc/shadow file that uses all the fields except the flag field:

```
guest:on7GbE18yYAek:10688:5:30:5:20:10844:
```

## /etc/group

The /etc/group file is an ASCII file that stores information about groups on the local system. Each line represents a group and consists of four colon-delimited fields. Table 5.3 lists the fields of an entry in the /etc/group file.

The following listing shows the partial default contents of a Solaris 8 /etc/group file:

```
root::0:root
other::1:
bin::2:root,bin,daemon
sys::3:root,bin,sys,adm
adm::4:root,adm,daemon
uucp::5:root,uucp
mail::6:root
```

**Table 5.3 /etc/group fields.**

| Field | Purpose |
|---|---|
| Group name | The unique name of the group. |
| Password | The password associated with the group. If a password is present, the **newgrp**(1) command prompts users to enter it. |
| GID | The unique numeric group identification. |
| Users | A comma-separated list of user accounts that belong to the group. |

# File Permissions and Ownership

File permissions determine the operations that can be performed on files and directories along with who can perform these operations. Solaris 8 provides two types of file permissions: standard, which provides basic security; and extended, which expands the standard permissions.

## Standard File Permissions

Files and directories can have read, write, and execution permissions. You can assign permissions to three classes of system accounts: the user account that owns the file, the group account that has group permissions, and everyone else. These are referred to as *user*, *group*, and *other* permissions. The read, write, and execution permissions for user, group, and other can be set independently of one another.

You use two types of notation to specify file permissions (also known as the *file access mode*): absolute mode and symbolic mode. *Absolute mode* (also referred to as *octal mode*) is a numeric value assigned to each permission per account class. Table 5.4 lists the absolute modes.

**Table 5.4 Absolute file permission modes.**

| Absolute Mode | Description |
|---|---|
| 001 | Other execution |
| 002 | Other write |
| 004 | Other read |
| 010 | Group execution |
| 020 | Group write |
| 040 | Group read |
| 100 | User execution |
| 200 | User write |
| 400 | User read |

The access mode of a file is determined by adding these absolute modes (user permissions + group permissions + other permissions). For example, a file that has user read (400) and user write (200) permissions but no other permissions for group or other will have an access mode of 400 + 200, or 600. Adding group read (040) and group write (020) to this file results in an access mode of 600 + 060, or 660. Adding other read (004) and other write (002) results in 666. Adding user execution (100) results in a file access mode of 766.

The other type of notation is symbolic mode. Using this mode, read access is represented by the letter *r*, write by the letter *w*, and execution by the letter *x*. The letters *u*, *g*, and *o* are used to represent user, group, and other permissions, respectively. Symbolic mode supports adding permissions (+), removing permissions (-), and setting only the specified permissions (=).

Using *u+x* adds execution permission to user, *g-w* removes write permission from group, and *o=r* sets only read access to other (that is, it removes any other permissions).

The **ls**(1) command uses something similar to symbolic mode to represent file access modes. The following listing shows the output of an **ls** command:

```
# ls -l
total 2
-rw-rw-rw-   1 sarah    other        384 Jan 24 11:53 file1
-rwxrw-rw-   1 sarah    other       1237 Jan 24 11:53 file2
-rw-r--r--   1 sarah    other      23678 Jan 24 11:53 file3
#
```

The **ls** command lists three sets of *rwx* permissions: one for user, one for group, and one for other. In the absence of a permission, the hyphen (-) character is displayed. In the previous listing, the file named file1 has read/write access for user, group, and other (absolute mode of 666). The file named file2 has read/write/execute for user and read/write for group and other (absolute mode of 766). The file named file3 has read/write for user and read only for group and other (absolute mode of 644). Use of the **ls** command to list file permissions is discussed in detail later in this chapter.

## Default File Permissions

When a file is created, a set of default permissions are assigned to it. The default permissions are defined using the **umask**(1) command. The **umask** command sets a mask of the permissions that should *not* be included in the file access mode by default.

For example, to allow full permission for owner and to remove write permission for group and other, the umask value is 022. That is, a file created with an access mode of 666 will have the umask of 022 subtracted from its access mode (666 – 022 = 644), removing write for group and other. You should add the **umask** command to the contents of the user's login initialization file to provide a consistent permission mask.

The following listing shows the impact of the **umask** command on created files and directories:

```
# umask 022
# >file1
# mkdir dir1
# ls -l
total 2
drwxr-xr-x   2 root     other           512 Mar 30 02:28 dir1
-rw-r--r--   1 root     other             0 Mar 30 02:28 file1
```

A umask of 022 removes group and other write permissions for newly created directories and files. In the previous example, file1 is created with the default mode 666. Subtracting the umask of 022 results in 644, or *rw-r--r--*. The directory dir1 is created with a default mode of 777. Subtracting the umask of 022 results in 755, or *rwxr-xr-x*.

Remember that directories *are* created with execution permission (777) and files *are not* created with execution permission (666). Specifying an umask that contains execution permission (values of 1,3, 5, or 7) will only affect directories.

The following listing shows using the **umask** command to modify the default umask:

```
# umask 111
# >file2
# mkdir dir2
# ls -l
total 2
drw-rw-rw-   2 root     other           512 Mar 30 02:29 dir2
-rw-rw-rw-   1 root     other             0 Mar 30 02:29 file2
#
# umask 027
# >file3
# mkdir dir3
# ls -l
total 2
drwxr-x--    2 root     other           512 Mar 30 02:48 dir3
-rw-r----    1 root     other             0 Mar 30 02:48 file3
#
```

### Changing File Permissions

You can modify the access mode of existing files and directories using the **chmod**(1) command. The **chmod** command can use either absolute mode or symbolic mode.

Absolute mode is straightforward, as shown in the following listing:

```
# ls -l file1
-rwxrwxrw-   1 dla      other          636 Jan 24 12:39 file1
 # chmod 645 file1
# ls -l file1
-rw-r--r-x   1 dla      other          636 Jan 24 12:39 file1
#
```

When you use symbolic mode, the class of system account (user, group, or other) is defined using the letters *u*, *g*, and *o*. Permissions are added using the plus (+) character, whereas permissions are removed using the minus (-) character. To specify multiple changes, separate them with commas. The following listing shows using the **chmod** command with symbolic mode:

```
# ls -l file1
-rwxrwxrw-   1 dla      other          636 Jan 24 12:40 file1
# chmod u-x,g-w,g-x,o-w,o+x file1
# ls -l file1
-rw-r---r-x  1 dla      other          636 Jan 24 12:40 file1
#
```

## Special Permissions

Several special permissions can be set on files and directories. These are as follows:

- *Set User ID (setuid)*—Sets the effective UID to owner on execution
- *Set Group ID (setgid)*—Sets the effective GID to group on execution
- *Mandatory locking*—Prevents reading or writing a file while a program has the file open
- *Sticky bit*—Allows only the owner to remove files or directories under a specific directory

The setuid and setgid permissions impact security and allow a user account or group account to temporarily become another user account or group account during the execution of a program. You control these permissions using the **chmod** command like the read, write, and execute file permissions.

The setuid permission has an absolute mode of 4000 and a symbolic mode of *s* when used with the **chmod** command.

> The user execution permission must be set in order for setuid to be effective. This permission is shown as *s* in the user account execution permission field in the output of an **ls** command. If setuid is added to a file without execution permission, it is an undefined state. This state is shown as *S* in the user execution permission field of an **ls** command.

The following listing shows the **chmod** command using absolute mode to add the setuid permission to a file and then using symbolic mode to remove the setuid permission from the file:

```
# ls -l file1
-rwxr--r--   1 dla      other        636 Jan 24 12:41 file1
# chmod 4744 file1
# ls -l file1
-rwsr--r--   1 dla      other        636 Jan 24 12:41 file1
# chmod u-s file1
# ls -l file1
-rwxr--r--   1 dla      other        636 Jan 24 12:41 file1
#
```

The setgid permission has an absolute mode of 2000 and a symbolic mode of *s* when used with the **chmod** command.

> The group execution permission must be set in order for the setgid to be effective. This permission is shown as *s* in the group account execution permission field in the output of an **ls** command. If setgid is added to a file without group execution permission, mandatory locking is enabled on the file. This locking is shown as *l* in the group execution permission field of an **ls** command.

The following listing shows using the **chmod** command to add and remove the setgid permission from a file. Note in the third **chmod** example that if setgid is added (*g+s*) to a file that does not have group execution permission, mandatory locking permission is enable instead of setgid:

```
# ls -l file1
-rwxr-xr--   1 dla      other        636 Jan 24 12:42 file1
# chmod g+s file1
# ls -l list
-rwxr-sr--   1 dla      other        636 Jan 24 12:42 file1
# chmod 764 file1
# ls -l
-rwxrw-r--   1 dla      other        636 Jan 24 12:42 file1
# chmod g+s file1
# ls -l
-rwxrwlr--   1 dla      other        636 Jan 24 12:42 file1
#
```

Another special file permission is the sticky bit. Originally, it was used to indicate programs that should be left in memory after execution. When set for frequently used programs, the sticky bit saved time and CPU cycles by using the image left in memory instead of loading it from disk again.

When the sticky bit is set on a directory that allows write permission for everyone, only the user account that created files and subdirectories under the directory can remove those files and subdirectories. This restriction is especially useful for the /tmp directory, which is available from any user account.

The sticky bit permission has an absolute mode of 1000 and a symbolic mode of *t* when used with the **chmod** command. This permission is shown as *t* in the other account execution permission field in the output of an **ls** command, but it is considered a user account (owner) permission. The following listing shows using the **chmod** command to remove the sticky bit permission from and then add it to a directory:

```
# ls -ld /tmp
drwxrwxrwt   7 sys      sys          410 Jan 28 03:30 /tmp
# chmod u-t /tmp
# ls -ld /tmp
drwxrwxrwx   7 sys      sys          410 Jan 28 03:30 /tmp
# chmod 1777 /tmp
# ls -ld /tmp
drwxrwxrwt   7 sys      sys          410 Jan 28 03:30 /tmp
#
```

## Extended File Permissions: Access Control Lists

Solaris 8 extends the standard Unix file permissions by adding an Access Control List (ACL) capability. ACLs let you add permissions for specific users and groups along with a default permission (mask).

In addition to supporting the standard read/write/execute permissions for the standard file user account (owner), ACLs can be used to set read/write/execute permissions for additional user accounts. Likewise, ACLs support read/write/execute permissions for the standard file group account and allow read/write/execution permissions for additional group accounts. In addition, ACLs support read/write/execution permissions for the standard others (everyone else).

ACLs also include a mask capability that controls the maximum allowed permissions given to user and group accounts other than the standard file user account and the standard file group account.

For example, suppose root owns a file and sets its ACL mask to read/execute. Later, root adds read/write/execute permission to the file ACL for the guest user account. Because of the mask, the write permission is overridden, and the effective permissions for the guest account are read/execute.

The ACL for a directory includes default entries that determine the permissions assigned to files and subdirectories created under the directory. Default permissions can be defined for the standard Unix user, group, and other along with a default mask and default permissions for specific users or groups.

Two commands are used to manage ACLs: The **setfacl** command sets ACLs, and the **getfacl** command displays ACLs.

Use of the **setfacl** command to add, modify, and delete ACLs on files and directories is a capability that is a stated test objective.

### Setting ACLs Using `setfacl`

You use the **setfacl**(1) command to set and modify ACLs. It supports three command-line arguments:

- **-d**—Deletes the specified ACL entries
- **-m**—Adds/changes the specified ACL entries
- **-s**—Replaces the whole ACL with the specified entries

ACL entries for the standard user and group permissions are specified using the format *entry*::*permissions* (note the two colons), where *entry* is the keyword **user** or **group** (or the single-letter abbreviation **u** or **g**), and *permissions* is the appropriate combination of **r**, **w**, **x**, and - needed to define the permission.

ACL entries for the standard other permission and the mask used for maximum permissions use a slightly different syntax. The format is *entry*:*permissions* (note the single colon), where *entry* is the keyword **other** or **mask** (or the single-letter abbreviation **o** or **m**), and *permissions* is the appropriate combination of **r**, **w**, **x**, and - needed to define the permission.

The following line shows the **setfacl** command used to set the user permission to read/write, and to set the group and other permissions to read-only:

```
# setfacl -s u::rw-,g::r--,o:r-- file1
```

ACL entries for other users and groups are specified using the format *entry*:*id*:*permissions*, where *entry* is the keyword **user** or **group** (or the single-letter abbreviation **u** or **g**); *id* is a user name, UID, group name, or GID; and *permissions* is the appropriate combination of **r**, **w**, **x**, and - needed to define the permission.

The following line shows the **setfacl** command used to add read/write permission for user account guest and read-only permission for group account staff:

```
# setfacl -m u:guest:rw-,g:staff:r-- file1
```

In addition to all the previously described ACL entries, you can define additional entries for directories. These entries specify the default ACL entries for files and subdirectories created under the directory. To establish defaults, use the previously described formats and add *d:* at the beginning of the *entry* field. All the standard user, group, and other defaults, along with the default mask, must be defined initially at the same time.

For example, to define the default ACL entries for the directory shlog, you can use the following **setfacl** command:

```
# setfacl -m d:u::rw-,d:g::rw-,d:o:r--,d:m:r-- shlog
```

The **-d** command-line argument is used to delete ACL entries. The remainder of the mask and file command-line arguments are identical to those used with the -s and **-m** command-line arguments.

## Displaying ACLs Using getfacl

To display the ACLs for a file or directory, use the **getfacl** command. The following listing displays the ACLs for the shlog directory using the **getfacl** command:

```
# getfacl shlog

# file: shlog
# owner: shlog
# group: staff
user::rwx
group::r-x                #effective:r-x
mask:r-x
other:r-x
default:user::rw-
default:group::rw-
default:mask:r--
default:other:r--
#
```

When you use the **ls** command, files that have ACLs are shown with a "+" in front of the file entry.

## Changing File Ownership

Two commands are used to control file ownership:

- **chown**(1M)—Changes file user account ownership
- **chgrp**(1M)—Changes file group account ownership

### Changing the File User Account

The **chown** command is used to change the file user account that is the owner of a file or directory. You specify the user account name or associated UID along with the name of one or more files that should be owned by the specified user account. The following listing uses the **chown** command to change the ownership of several files to the guest user account, which has a UID of 1001. Each **chown** command is preceded and followed by the **ls** command, which lists the ownership and permissions of files:

```
# ls -l
total 18
-rw-rw-rw-   1 root    other      120 Feb 28 07:38 data
-rw-rw-rw-   1 root    other     6528 Feb 28 07:38 junk
-rw-r--r--   1 root    other      636 Feb 28 07:39 list
# chown guest junk
# ls -l
total 18
-rw-rw-rw-   1 root    other      120 Feb 28 07:38 data
-rw-rw-rw-   1 guest   other     6528 Feb 28 07:38 junk
-rw-r--r--   1 root    other      636 Feb 28 07:39 list
# chown 1001 data list
# ls -l
total 18
-rw-rw-rw-   1 guest   other      120 Feb 28 07:38 data
-rw-rw-rw-   1 guest   other     6528 Feb 28 07:38 junk
-rw-r--r--   1 guest   other      636 Feb 28 07:39 list
#
```

The **chown** command supports a recursive command line argument, -R. When you use it to change the owner of a directory, the ownership of any files or subdirectories under the directory also changes.

Even though a separate command exists to change file group account ownership, you can use the **chown** command to change group ownership at the same time by following the user account name or UID with a colon (:) and a group account name or GID. The following example uses the **chown** command to change both user account ownership and group account ownership:

```
# ls -l
total 18
-rw-rw-rw-   1 guest    other        120 Feb 28 07:38 data
-rw-rw-rw-   1 guest    other       6528 Feb 28 07:38 junk
-rw-r--r--   1 guest    other        636 Feb 28 07:39 list
# chown sys:staff data junk list
# ls -l
total 18
-rw-rw-rw-   1 sys      staff        120 Feb 28 07:38 data
-rw-rw-rw-   1 sys      staff       6528 Feb 28 07:38 junk
-rw-r--r--   1 sys      staff        636 Feb 28 07:39 list
#
```

If the **chown** command is used by anyone other than root to change the ownership of a file that has the setuid special permission, then setuid is cleared. This action prevents a user from setting up a setuid file, changing the ownership to someone else, and then using the file to gain access to another user account.

As an enhanced security feature of Solaris 8, use of the **chown** command is restricted to the superuser account. You can remove this restriction by clearing the following kernel parameter in the /etc/system file and rebooting the system:

```
set rstchown = 0
```

Setting **rstchown** to 1 and rebooting the system will enforce the restriction again.

## Changing the File Group Account

The **chgrp** command changes the file group account associated with a file or directory. Only the user account that currently owns the file or the superuser account (root) can change file ownership. By default, the owner of a file can change only a group account to which the user belongs.

You specify the group account name or associated GID along with the name of one or more files that should be owned by the specified group account. The following listing shows the **chgrp** command being used to change the ownership of several files to the other group account, which has a GID of 1. Each **chgrp** command is preceded and followed by the **ls** command, which lists the ownership and permissions of files:

```
# ls -l
total 18
-rw-rw-rw-   1 sys      staff        120 Feb 28 07:38 data
-rw-rw-rw-   1 sys      staff       6528 Feb 28 07:38 junk
-rw-r--r--   1 sys      staff        636 Feb 28 07:39 list
# chgrp other junk
```

```
# ls -l
total 18
-rw-rw-rw-   1 sys     staff        120 Feb 28 07:38 data
-rw-rw-rw-   1 sys     other       6528 Feb 28 07:38 junk
-rw-r--r--   1 sys     staff        636 Feb 28 07:39 list
# chgrp 1 data list
# ls -l
total 18
-rw-rw-rw-   1 sys     other        120 Feb 28 07:38 data
-rw-rw-rw-   1 sys     other       6528 Feb 28 07:38 junk
-rw-r--r--   1 sys     other        636 Feb 28 07:39 list
#
```

Like the **chown** command, the **chgrp** command supports a recursive command line argument, -**R**. When you use it to change the group ownership of a directory, the group ownership of any files or subdirectories under the directory also changes.

If the **chgrp** command is used by an account other than root that does not have the appropriate permissions and the file has the setuid special permission and/or the setgid special permission, the setuid and/or getuid special permission is cleared. This action prevents a user from setting up a setuid and/or setgid file, changing the ownership to someone else, and then using the file to gain access to another user account and/or group account.

As an enhanced security feature of Solaris 8, use of the **chgrp** command is restricted by requiring the user account attempting to change group ownership to be a member of the new group. You can remove this restriction by clearing the following kernel parameter in the /etc/system file and rebooting the system:

```
set rstchown = 0
```

Setting **rstchown** to 1 and rebooting the system will enforce the restriction again.

## Displaying File Permissons and Ownership

The **ls**(1) command displays file permissions and ownership. The **ls** command supports the command-line arguments described in Table 5.5.

The **ls** command supports a wide variety of command-line arguments to display and sort almost everything anyone would want to know about directories and files.

EXAM ALERT

The more important command-line options are **-a**, **-d**, **-F**, **-l**, **-r**, **-R**, **-t**, and **-1**. Be certain to understand the affect of these command-line arguments on the information displayed by the **ls** command.

**Table 5.5 Command-line arguments for the ls command.**

| Argument | Description |
|---|---|
| **name** | The name of a directory or file to display information about. To specify more than one name, separate them with spaces and/or use metacharacters (see Chapter 10). If one or more *names* are directories, then the contents of those directories are listed. If no *names* are specified, then all directories/files in the current directory are listed. |
| **-a** | Lists all directories and files, including those that begin with a dot (which are normally not displayed). |
| **-A** | Lists all directories and files, including those that begin with a dot (except the current directory (.) and the parent directory (..). |
| **-b** | Displays non-printable characters in file/directory names using octal *ddd* notation. |
| **-c** | Uses the time of the last i-node modification for sorting or listing. |
| **-C** | Generates multicolumn output sorted down columns (default). |
| **-d** | Lists the names of directories instead of the directory contents. |
| **-f** | Interprets all *names* as directories. |
| **-F** | Indicates the type of files by marking them with a trailing character. Marks directories with a forward slash (/), doors with a greater-than sign (>), executable files with an asterisk (*), FIFOs with a vertical bar (\|), symbolic links with an ampersand (@), and sockets with an equals sign (=). |
| **-g** | Lists file permissions, ACL indication, number of links, group, byte size, and last modification time stamp. Same as **-l** but does not list the owner. |
| **-i** | Lists the i-node. |
| **-l** | Lists file permissions, ACL indication, number of links, owner, group, byte size, and last modification time stamp. |
| **-L** | For symbolic links, lists the referenced directory/file instead of the link. |
| **-m** | Lists information across the page, separated by columns. |
| **-n** | Lists file permissions, ACL indication, number of links, UID of the owner, GID of the group, byte size, and last modification time stamp. Same as **-l** but lists the UID and GID instead of the owner and group. |
| **-o** | Lists file permissions, ACL indication, number of links, owner, byte size, and last modification time stamp. Same as **-l** but does not list the group. |
| **-p** | Marks directories with a trailing forward slash (/). |
| **-q** | Uses a question mark (?) for any non-printing characters in directory/file names. |
| **-r** | Reverses the order of the sort (*zyx...* instead of *abc...* or oldest instead of newest). |
| **-R** | Recursively lists the contents of subdirectories. |
| **-s** | Lists the size in blocks (including indirect blocks). |

*(continued)*

**Table 5.5 Command-line arguments for the ls command *(continued)*.**

| Argument | Description |
|---|---|
| **-t** | Sorts by modification time instead of alphabetically by directory/file. When combined with **-u**, sorts by access time; when combined with **-c**, sorts by i-node modification time. |
| **-u** | Uses the last access time for sorting and displaying. |
| **-x** | Displays multiple columns sorted across the page instead of down. |
| **-1** | Displays one directory/file per line. |

When you're using one of the long listing formats (**-g**, **-l**, **-n**, or **-o**), the file permissions and additional information are displayed in the first 11 characters of each directory/file. Table 5.6 lists the characters used in the first character of this file permission field.

Table 5.7 lists the characters that are used in positions 2 through 10 of the file permission field.

**Table 5.6 First character used in the file permisison field of the ls command display.**

| Character | Description |
|---|---|
| b | Block special file |
| c | Character special file |
| d | Directory |
| D | Door |
| l | Symbolic link |
| p | FIFO or named pipe |
| s | Socket |
| - | Ordinary file |

**Table 5.7 Characters in positions 2 through 10 used in the file permisison field of the ls command display.**

| Character | Description |
|---|---|
| l | Mandatory locking |
| r | Read permission |
| s | Set UID (when in fourth position) or set GID (when in seventh position) |
| S | Undefined state |

*(continued)*

**Table 5.7 Characters in positions 2 through 10 used in the file permisison field of the ls command display *(continued).***

| | |
|---|---|
| t | Sticky bit |
| T | Undefined state |
| w | Write permission |
| x | Execution permission |
| - | No permission granted |

Position 11 normally is a space, except when an ACL has been defined on the directory/file. In this case, a plus sign (+) appears in the eleventh position. The following listing shows examples of the permission field portion of the output generated by the **ls** command:

```
# ls -l
total 2
drwxrwxrwt   2 sarah    other         512 Jan 24 13:49 dir1
-rwsrwxr-x   1 sarah    other        1112 Jan 24 13:53 file1
lrwxrwsr-x   1 sarah    other        1112 Jan 24 13:53 file2
-rwxrwlrwx+  1 sarah    other        1112 Jan 24 13:53 file3
```

The listing for dir1 shows that it is a directory with mode 1777 (sticky bit plus read, write, execute permissions for owner, group, and others). The listing for file1 shows that it is a file with mode 4775 (setuid; read, write, execute for owner; read, write, execute for group; and read, execute for others). The listing for file2 shows that it is a symbolic link with mode 2775 (setgid; read, write, execute for owner; read, write, execute for group; and read, execute for others). The listing for file3 shows that it is a file with mode 2777 (mandatory locking; read, write, execute for owner; read, write for group; and read, write, execute for others). The "+" indicates that an ACL has been defined for file3.

# Practice Questions

## Question 1

Which command is used to determine the default access mode for files when they are created?

- ❍ a. **setfacl**
- ❍ b. **chmod**
- ❍ c. **umask**
- ❍ d. **getfacl**
- ❍ e. **ls**

Answer c is correct. The **umask** command determines the default access mode for files when they are created. The **setfacl** and **chmod** commands set access modes of existing files. Therefore, answers a and b are incorrect. The **getfacl** and **ls** commands display access modes of existing files. Therefore, answers d and e are incorrect.

## Question 2

Which of the following are true about the listing produced by executing the **ls -F** command? [Select all that apply]

- ❑ a. The names of directories are followed by a forward slash (/).
- ❑ b. The names of symbolic links are followed by an asterisk (*).
- ❑ c. The names of directories are followed by a plus sign (+).
- ❑ d. The names of executable files are followed by an asterisk (*).
- ❑ e. The names of symbolic links are followed by an ampersand (@).

Answers a, d, and e are correct. In the listing that results from the **ls** -F command, directory names are followed by a forward slash, executable file names are followed by an asterisk, and symbolic link names are followed by an ampersand. Symbolic links are not followed by an asterisk. Therefore, answer b is incorrect. Directory names are not followed by a plus sign. Therefore, answer c is incorrect.

## Question 3

Give the command (without command-line arguments) used to add read/write permission for user account fred to a file owned by user account george.

____________________________

The correct answer is **setfacl**.

## Question 4

To restrict logging in directly as root to the system console, which file needs to be modified?

- ❍ a. /dev/console
- ❍ b. /etc/passwd
- ❍ c. /etc/default/login
- ❍ d. /etc/default/su

Answer c is correct. To restrict root login to the system console, you must modify the /etc/default/login file. /dev/console is the pathname for the console. Therefore, answer a is incorrect. /etc/passwd is the password file. Therefore, answer b is incorrect. /etc/default/su is the file that controls the behavior of the **su** command. Therefore, answer d is incorrect.

## Question 5

Where are user account passwords stored?

____________________________

The correct answer is /etc/shadow.

## Question 6

The file test currently has the access mode 644. Which of the following will add mandatory locking? [Select all that apply]

- ❑ a. **chmod 2664 test**
- ❑ b. **chmod 2674 test**
- ❑ c. **chmod g+s test**
- ❑ d. **chmod g+l test**
- ❑ e. **setfacl -s u::rw-,g::rws,o:r-- test**

Answers a, c, and d are correct. The **chmod** commands in those answers will add mandatory locking. The command **chmod 2674 test** also adds group execution, which results in setgid permission, not mandatory locking. Therefore, answer b is incorrect. The **setfacl** command cannot be used to add or remove mandatory locking. Therefore, answer e is incorrect.

## Question 7

The file /etc/default/su controls the behavior of the **su** command, which includes which of the following? [Select all that apply]

- ❑ a. Displaying **su** usage on the system console
- ❑ b. Restricting superuser usage to the system console
- ❑ c. Logging failed **su** attempts
- ❑ d. Enabling logging of **su** usage through syslog
- ❑ e. Logging successful **su** attempts

Answers a, c, d, and e are correct. You can use /etc/default/su to control **su** behavior by displaying **su** usage on the system console, logging failed **su** attempts, enabling logging of **su** usage through syslog, and logging successful **su** attempts. You restrict superuser usage to the system console by editing the /etc/default/login file. Therefore, answer b is incorrect.

## Question 8

Which of the following shows the access mode of a file that has setuid enabled?

- ❍ a. **srwxrwxrwx**
- ❍ b. **-rwsrwxrwx**
- ❍ c. **-rwxrwsrwx**
- ❍ d. **-rwxrwxrws**
- ❍ e. **-rwxrwxrwt**

Answer b is correct. The file access mode of **-rwsrwxrwx** shows the file has setuid enabled. **srwxrwxrwx** and **-rwxrwxrws** are not valid file access modes. Therefore, answers a and d are incorrect. **-rwxrwsrwx** shows setgid, and **-rwxrwxrwt** shows the sticky bit set. Therefore, answers c and e are incorrect.

## Question 9

The file test currently has the access mode 644. Which of the following will add write access for the group owner? [Select all that apply]

- ❑ a. **chmod test 664**
- ❑ b. **chmod 664 test**
- ❑ c. **chmod test g+w**
- ❑ d. **chmod g+w test**
- ❑ e. **setfacl -s u::rw-,g::rw-,o:r-- test**

Answers b, d, and e are correct. Each of those commands will add write access for the group owner. Even though the **setfacl -s** command replaces the existing ACLs, the original access mode is reinstated along with the added group write access. Using **setfacl -m** would also have worked, but was not specified as an answer. The commands **chmod test 664** and **chmod test g+w** do not follow the correct syntax. Therefore, answers a and c are incorrect.

## Question 10

Match each of the following **ls** command-line arguments with its function.

| | |
|---|---|
| a. **-R** | 1. Displays directory names instead of directory contents |
| b. **-l** | 2. Identifies file types using /, >, *, @, and other characters |
| c. **-a** | 3. Recursively lists the contents of subdirectories |
| d. **-F** | 4. Lists file permissions, owner, group, size, and so on |
| e. **-d** | 5. Lists directory/file names that begin with a dot (.) |

Answers a-3, b-4, c-5, d-2, and e-1 are correct. **-R** recursively lists directory contents; **-l** lists permissions, owner, and so on; **-a** lists names beginning with a dot; **-F** identifies file types; and **-d** lists directory names.

# Need to Know More?

Mulligan, John P., *Solaris 8 Essential Reference* (New Riders, Indianapolis, IN, 2001), ISBN 0-7357-1007-4.

Sun Microsystems, *System Administration Guide, Volume 2.* Available in printed form (part number 805-7229-10), on the Web at **docs.sun.com**, and from the online documentation, AnswerBook2, provided with the Solaris 8 operating system.

Sun Microsystems, *System Reference Manual, Section 1 - User Commands.* Available in printed form (part number 806-0624-10), on the Web at **docs.sun.com**, and from the online documentation, AnswerBook2, provided with the Solaris 8 operating system.

Sun Microsystems, *System Reference Manual, Section 1M - System Administration Commands.* Available in printed form (part number 806-0625-10), on the Web at **docs.sun.com**, and from the online documentation, AnswerBook2, provided with the Solaris 8 operating system.

Sun Microsystems, *System Reference Manual, Section 4 - File Formats.* Available in printed form (part number 806-0633-10), on the Web at **docs.sun.com**, and from the online documentation, AnswerBook2, provided with the Solaris 8 operating system.

6

# The User Environment

**Terms you'll need to understand:**

- ✓ User and group accounts
- ✓ **admintool** command
- ✓ Password aging
- ✓ Initialization files and templates
- ✓ System profile

**Techniques you'll need to master:**

- ✓ Creating and deleting user accounts
- ✓ Administering passwords
- ✓ Creating and deleting group accounts
- ✓ Using the **admintool** command
- ✓ Customizing initialization files and templates
- ✓ Logging in and out of the system
- ✓ Identifying and monitoring users

This chapter covers the Part I exam objectives that address *User Administration*. We'll discuss administering user and group accounts, the initialization files associated with user accounts, logging in and out of a system, and identifying the users currently logged in to the system.

# Account Administration

The Solaris 8 system controls access to data and resources by means of user and group accounts. The administration of user accounts and group accounts, along with the passwords associated with these accounts, is a key system administration activity.

## User Accounts

You can add, modify, or delete user accounts using command-line utilities or the **admintool**(1M) command. Using the **admintool** command reduces or eliminates the possible introduction of typos and other errors that might affect all the user accounts.

However, the **admintool** command requires a graphical interface, and using it is more time consuming than using the command-line utilities manually. These command-line utilities are:

- **useradd**(1M)
- **usermod**(1M)
- **userdel**(1M)

Both the **admintool** command and the command-line utilities are described in the following sections.

### Creating an Account Using the admintool Command

When you start the **admintool** command, the Users window is displayed, as shown in Figure 6.1. To display the Add User window, select Add from the Edit pull-down menu. The Add User window, shown in Figure 6.2, consists of three portions: User Identity, Account Security, and Home Directory.

The User Identity portion provides the information that you must define in order to add a user account. All this information is stored in the /etc/passwd file except secondary groups information, which is stored in the /etc/group file. Table 6.1 lists the fields of the User Identity section.

The Account Security portion provides the information used to determine how the password should be defined and to set up password aging. All this information is stored in the /etc/shadow file. Table 6.2 lists the fields of the Account Security section.

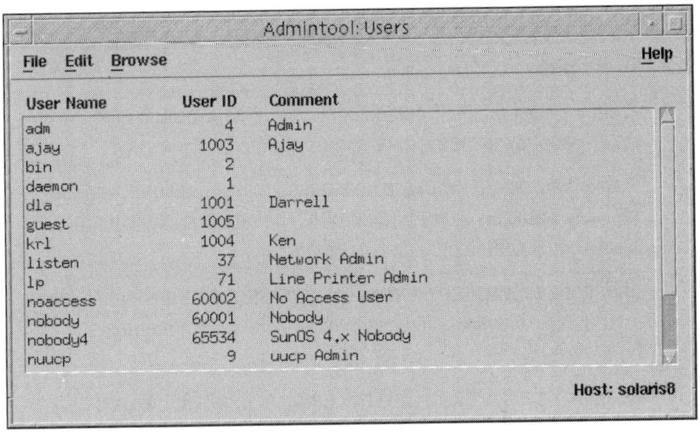


**Figure 6.1** The Admintool: Users window.

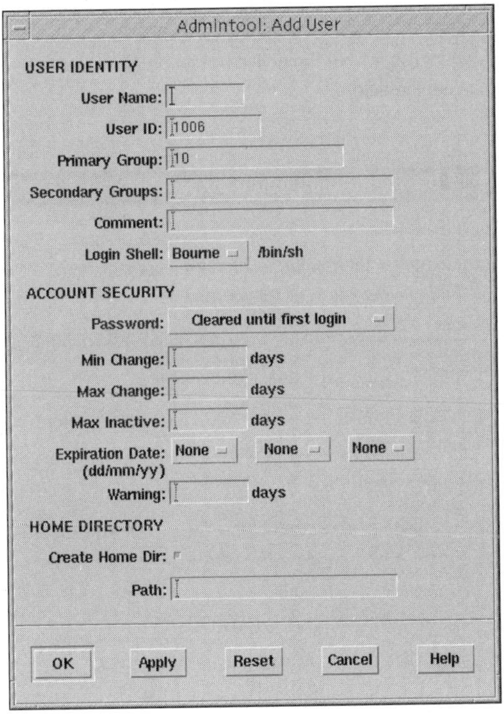


**Figure 6.2** The Admintool: Add User window.

The Home Directory portion is used to define the home directory of the account and to create it if necessary. This path is stored in the /etc/passwd file. The appropriate initialization files are created in the home directory based on the type of login shell selected.

**Table 6.1 User Identity fields of the Admintool: Add User window.**

| Field | Description |
|---|---|
| User Name | A unique user account name consisting of a maximum of eight upper- and lowercase letters and/or numbers. |
| User ID | The UID associated with the user account. It is a unique number, typically between 1,000 and 60,000. The next available number starting at 1,000 is provided automatically. |
| Primary Group | The group to which the user should be assigned. The default value is 10 (staff). Any specified group must exist before members can be added. |
| Secondary Groups | Additional groups (separated by commas) to which the user should be assigned. Specified groups must exist before members can be added. |
| Comment | Any text that should be placed in the /etc/passwd gcos field. |
| Login Shell | The Bourne (default), C, or Korn shell can be selected. To specify another shell, select Other from the pull-down menu and enter the name of the shell in the field. |

**Table 6.2 Account Security fields of the Admintool: Add User window.**

| Field | Description |
|---|---|
| Password | The choices are Cleared until first login, Account is locked, No password — setuid only, or Normal Password. |
| Min Change | The minimum number of days required between password changes. |
| Max Change | The maximum number of days the password is valid. |
| Max Inactive | The maximum number of days the account can be inactive before the password must be changed. |
| Expiration Date | The date the account expires. |
| Warning | The number of days the user is warned before the password expires. |

## Modifying an Account Using the **admintool** Command

To modify a user account, start the **admintool** command if it is not already active. Display the Users window by selecting Users from the Browse pull-down menu (see Figure 6.1).

Click the desired account entry to highlight it, and then select Modify from the Edit pull-down menu. The Modify User window is displayed. The fields of the window are filled in with information about the selected user. The Modify User window is similar to the Add User window (see Figure 6.2). Change the fields as appropriate and click Apply to save the changes.

## Deleting an Account Using the admintool Command

To delete a user account, start the **admintool** command if it is not already active. Display the Users window by selecting Users from the Browse pull-down menu (see Figure 6.1).

Click the desired account entry to highlight it, and then select Delete from the Edit pull-down menu. The Warning window will be displayed, as shown in Figure 6.3. Click Delete to delete the user account.

> **EXAM ALERT:** Because using the **admintool** command makes creating, modifying, and deleting user accounts very easy and intuitive, Exam 310-011 concentrates on using the **useradd**, **usermod**, and **userdel** commands for administering user accounts.

## Creating an Account Using the useradd Command

The **useradd**(1M) command provides a quick method to add a new user account. At a minimum, you must specify the account name as a command-line argument. Table 6.3 lists the command-line arguments supported by the **useradd** command.

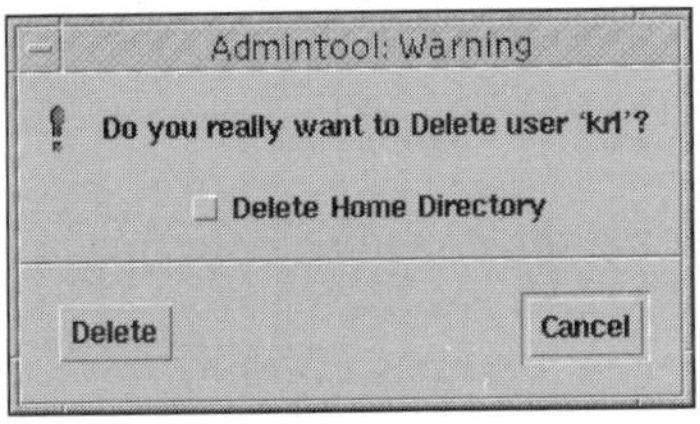


**Figure 6.3** The Admintool: Warning window.

**Table 6.3 Command-line arguments for the useradd command.**

| Argument | Description |
|---|---|
| ***account*** | Specifies the name of the new user account (required). |
| **-A *authorizations*** | Specifies one or more authorizations. |
| **-b *base*** | Defines a base directory. If a home directory (**-d**) is not specified, the ***account*** name is added to ***base*** and used as the home directory. |
| **-c *comment*** | Specifies a comment that is placed in the comment (gcos) field of the /etc/passwd file. |
| **-d *directory*** | Defines the home directory of the account. |
| **-e *date*** | Specifies an expiration date for the account. After the specified date, the account is disabled. |
| **-f *days*** | Specifies the maximum number of days the account can be inactive before it is disabled. |

*(continued)*

**Table 6.3 Command-line arguments for the useradd command *(continued).***

| Argument | Description |
|---|---|
| **-g *group*** | Defines the GID or name of an existing group that will be the primary group for the user account. |
| **-G *group*** | Defines a GID or name of an existing group that will be a secondary group for the user account. |
| **-k *template_dir*** | Specifies the directory that contains a template (default) .profile used for the user account. |
| **-m** | Creates the home directory if it doesn't exist. The home directory is defined by **-b** and the ***account*** name or **-d**. |
| **-o** | Allows you to specify an existing UID. That is, you can create an account with a duplicate UID (see **-u**). |
| **-p *profiles*** | Specifies one or more execution profiles. |
| **-R *roles*** | Specifies one or more user roles. |
| **-s *shell*** | Specifies the login shell; the default is the Bourne shell (/bin/sh). |
| **-u *uid*** | Specifies the UID of the user account. It must be a decimal integer. If *uid* is not specified, the next highest available UID is assigned. |

The following example creates a user account using the **useradd** command:

```
# useradd -d /export/home/user1 -m -g other -u 1050 user1
6 blocks
#
```

This command creates the user1 user account, assigns it UID 1050, makes it a member of the group other, and creates its home directory /export/home/user1.

To make life a little easier, the **useradd** command also supports the **-D** command-line argument, which lets you assign default values to authorizations (**-A**), the base directory (**-b**), the group (**-g**), the expiration date (**-e**), the maximum inactivity (**-f**), execution profiles (**-P**), and roles (**-R**). Subsequent uses of the **useradd** command will use these default values if they are not specified. For example:

```
# useradd -D -b /export/home -g other
group=other,1  project=,3  basedir=/export/home
skel=/etc/skel  shell=/bin/sh  inactive=0
expire=  auths=  profiles=  roles=
#
# useradd -m -u 1051 user2
6 blocks
#
```

Because a default base and group were defined, the user2 account is a member of the other group and has a home directory of /export/home/user2.

> **EXAM ALERT:** User accounts created with the **useradd** command do not have a password. These accounts are locked and cannot be used until a password is defined for the account using the **passwd**(1) command.

## Modifying an Account Using the usermod Command

The **usermod**(1M) command is used to modify an existing user account. The command-line arguments are identical to the **useradd** command-line arguments, with the following exceptions:

- The base directory (**-b**) is not available. Use **-d** to specify a new directory. Don't forget to include **-m** if the specified directory doesn't exist.
- Set defaults (**-D**) is not available.
- The template directory (**-k**) is not available.
- You specify a new user account name using **-l** ***account*** if the account name is being modified.

Keep in mind that if the account name is changed, the name of the home directory does not change unless you use the **-d** and **-m** command-line arguments. The following example uses the **usermod** command to change the name of the user1 account to user3:

```
# ls -l
total 22
drwx------   2 root     root         8192 Jan 13 21:05 lost+found
drwxr-x--   2 user3    other        512 Mar 31 13:23 user1
drwxr-x--   2 user2    other        512 Mar 31 13:45 user2
#
# usermod -l user3 -d /export/home/user3 -m user1
6 blocks
#
# ls -l
total 22
drwx------   2 root     root         8192 Jan 13 21:05 lost+found
drwxr-x--   2 user2    other        512 Mar 31 13:45 user2
drwxr-x--   2 user3    other        512 Mar 31 13:23 user3
#
```

### Deleting an Account Using the **userdel** Command

The **userdel**(1M) command is used to delete a user account. You specify the user account as a command-line argument. Only one other command-line argument, **-r**, is supported—it's used to remove the home directory:

```
# userdel -r user3
#
```

## Group Accounts

You can add, modify, or delete group accounts using command-line utilities or the **admintool**(1M) command. Using the **admintool** command reduces or eliminates the possible introduction of typos and other errors that might affect all the group accounts.

However, the **admintool** command requires a graphical interface, and using it is more time consuming than using the command-line utilities manually. These command-line utilities are:

- **groupadd**(1M)
- **groupmod**(1M)
- **groupdel**(1M)

Both the **admintool** command and the command-line utilities are described in the following sections.

### Creating a Group Using the **admintool** Command

To create a group account, start the **admintool** command if it is not already active. Display the Groups window by selecting Groups from the Browse pull-down menu. The Groups window is shown in Figure 6.4.

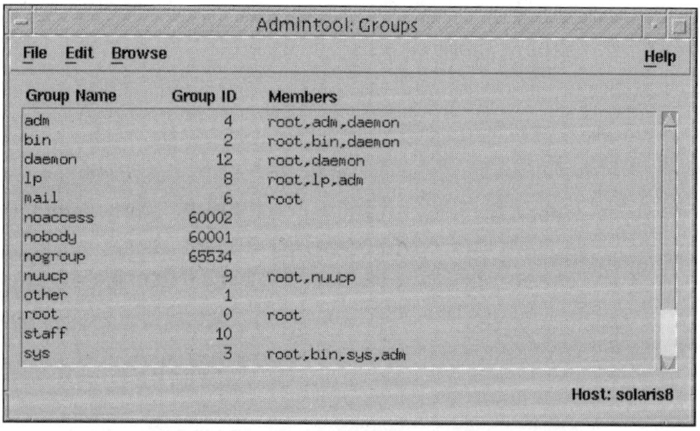


**Figure 6.4** The Admintool: Groups window.

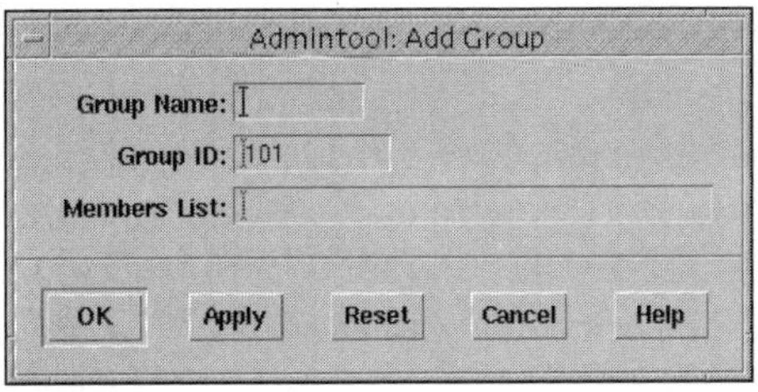


**Figure 6.5** The Admintool: Add Group window.

Then, display the Add Group window by selecting Add from the Edit pull down menu. The Add Group window is shown in Figure 6.5.

Enter a unique group name in the Group Name field. Use the next available GID number or enter a unique GID in the Group ID field. In the Members List field, enter one or more user account names separated by commas. Click OK, and the new group is displayed in the Groups window.

### Modifying a Group Using the **admintool** Command

To modify a group account, start the **admintool** command if it is not already active. Display the Group window by selecting Groups from the Browse pull-down menu (see Figure 6.4).

Click the desired account entry to highlight it, and then select Modify from the Edit pull-down menu. The Modify Group window is displayed. The fields of the window are filled in with information about the selected group. The Modify Group window is similar to the Add Group window (see Figure 6.5). Change the fields as appropriate and click Apply to save the changes.

### Deleting a Group Using the **admintool** Command

To delete a group account, start the **admintool** command if it is not already active. Display the Groups window by selecting Groups from the Browse pull-down menu (see Figure 6.4).

Click the desired account entry to highlight it, and then select Delete from the Edit pull-down menu. A Warning window similar to the one shown in Figure 6.3 will be displayed, but it will list a group instead of a user. Click Delete to delete the group account.

> EXAM ALERT: Because using the **admintool** command makes creating, modifying, and deleting group accounts very easy and intuitive, Exam 310-011 concentrates on using the **groupadd**, **groupmod**, and **groupdel** commands for administering group accounts.

### Creating a Group Using the **groupadd** Command

The **groupadd**(1M) command provides a quick method to add a new group account. At a minimum, you must specify the group account name as a command-line argument. The **groupadd** command supports two other command-line arguments. The first is **-g** *gid*, which specifies the unique GID that should be associated with the group. It must be a decimal integer. If you don't specify a GID, the next highest available GID is assigned. The other command-line argument is **-o**, which lets you assign a duplicate GID to the group.

The following example creates a group using the **groupadd** command:

```
#
# groupadd -g 1000 newgroup
#
```

### Modifying a Group Using the **groupmod** Command

The **groupmod**(1M) command is used to modify an existing group account. The command-line arguments are identical to the **groupadd** command-line arguments, except that you specify the new group account name using **-n** *name* if the group account name is being modified. The following example uses **groupmod** to change the group newgroup to ngroup:

```
# groupmod -n ngroup newgroup
#
```

### Deleting a Group Using the **groupdel** Command

The **groupdel**(1M) command is used to delete a group account. The group account is specified as a command-line argument:

```
# groupdel ngroup
#
```

## Password Administration

Password administration involves setting parameters to control password aging, changing a user's password as needed, and possibly locking a user account to prevent its use.

### Password Aging

The parameters of the /etc/shadow file, which you set through the Account Security fields of the **admintool** command's Add or Modify User Account window, determine the password aging policy. These parameters include how long a password is valid (Max Change), how often it can be changed (Min Change), and how long an account can be inactive before the password must be changed (Max Inactive). They enforce a policy for protecting the integrity of passwords.

Note that of these three password-aging parameters, only Max Inactive can be specified using the **useradd** command and modified using the **usermod** command.

## Password Requirements

Unless specified by a superuser account such as root, passwords must meet the following requirements:

- A password must contain at least the number of characters specified by the PASSLENGTH parameter contained in the /etc/default/passwd file. The default is six.
- A password must contain at least two alphabetic characters and at least one numeric character (within the first PASSLENGTH characters).
- A password cannot be the same as the user account name, the reverse of the user account name, or a circular shift of the user account name. Any uppercase letters are mapped to lowercase letters for requirement checking. As a result, the password for the guest user account cannot be *guest*, *tseug*, *uestg*, *estgu*, *GUEST*, and so on.
- A new password must differ by at least three characters from the old password. Once again, uppercase and lowercase letters are equivalent for requirement checking.

> **EXAM ALERT** Passwords can be any length, but only the first eight characters are significant. For example, if a password is defined as *25administration*, the characters *25admini* can be used to log in to the system.

Keep in mind that these requirements do not apply when root or some other superuser account defines its own password or the password of another user account.

## Changing Passwords Using the admintool Command

To change the password of a user account, start the **admintool** command if it is not already active. Display the Users window by selecting Users from the Browse pull-down menu.

You can select the user account in two ways: by double-clicking the account entry or by clicking the account entry to highlight it and then selecting Modify from the Edit pull-down menu. Using either method, the Modify User window is displayed, as shown in Figure 6.6. Note that the current password setting for the user account is shown in the Password field. In Figure 6.6, the user account has a Normal Password currently set.

To modify the account password, position the mouse cursor over the Password field and hold down the left button. Then, move the mouse cursor over the Nor-

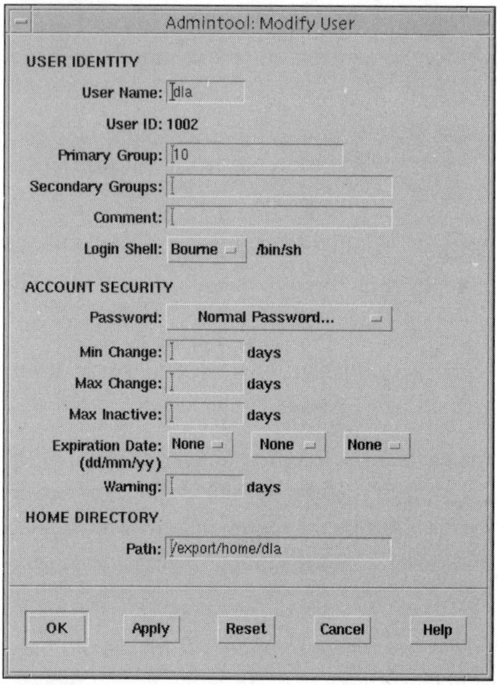


**Figure 6.6** The Admintool: Modify User (Normal Password) window.

**Figure 6.7** The Set User Password window.

mal Password item and release the mouse button. The Set User Password window is displayed, as shown in Figure 6.7.

Enter the same password in both the Enter Password and Verify Password fields. Asterisks are displayed in the place of each character entered. Click OK. To save the password, click OK in the Modify User window.

## Changing Passwords Using the passwd Command

Other than the **admintool** command, the **passwd**(1) command is the only way to change the password for a user account. When used without any command-line arguments, the **passwd** command changes the password of the current user account. For example:

```
$ passwd
passwd:  Changing password for dla
Enter login password:
New password:
Re-enter new password:
passwd (SYSTEM): passwd successfully changed for dla
$
```

Note that the current password must be entered before a new password can be specified. When a superuser account, such as root, uses the **passwd** command, the current password is not required.

A variety of command-line arguments are provided to support changing passwords. Table 6.4 lists the more significant command-line arguments.

A superuser account can change the password for another user account. The user account is specified as a command-line argument. For example:

```
# passwd dla
New password:
Re-enter new password:
passwd (SYSTEM): passwd successfully changed for dla
#
```

## Locking a User Account Using the **admintool** Command

An account can be locked to prevent it from being used. To do so, start the **admintool** command if it is not already active. Display the Users window by selecting Users from the Browse pull-down menu.

You can select the user account in two ways: by double-clicking the account entry or by clicking the account entry to highlight it and then selecting Modify from the Edit pull-down menu. Using either method, the Modify User window is displayed.

**Table 6.4 Selected command-line arguments for the passwd command.**

| Argument | Description |
|---|---|
| ***account*** | Specifies the name of the user account for which the password will be changed |
| **-as** | Lists password attributes for all user accounts (displays *LK* for locked, *PS* for password, and so on) |
| **-d** | Deletes the password for the specified account |
| **-l** | Locks the specified account so it cannot be accessed |

To lock the account, position the mouse cursor over the Password field and hold down the left button. Then, move the mouse cursor over the Account Is Locked item and release the mouse button. The Account Is Locked item is displayed in the Password field, as shown in Figure 6.8. To save the change, click OK in the Modify User window.

# Initialization Files

Several initialization (or startup) files are associated with each user account home directory. These files specify commands to be executed when the associated event occurs. Depending on the login shell being used, a login initialization file, a shell startup file, or a logout file may exist. Table 6.5 lists the various initialization files.

**Table 6.5 Initialization files.**

| File | sh | csh | ksh |
|---|---|---|---|
| Login initialization file | .profile | .login | .profile |
| Shell startup file | N/A | .cshrc | User-defined |
| Logout file | N/A | .logout | N/A |

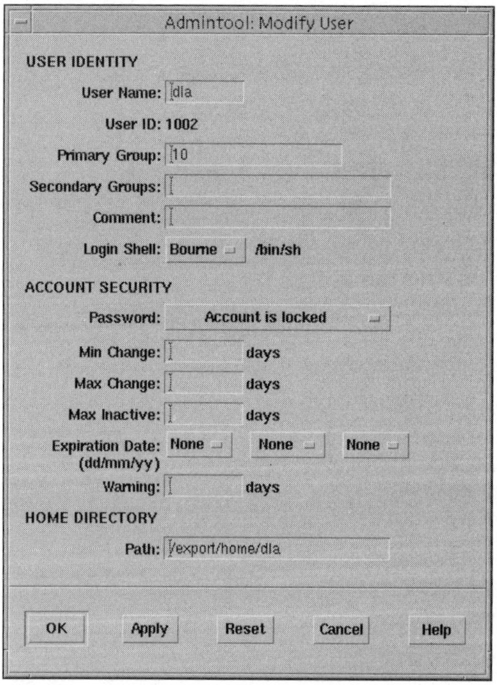


**Figure 6.8** The Admintool: Modify User (Account Is Locked) window.

Commands in the login initialization file are executed when the user logs in. All three common shells provide a login initialization file. Commands in the shell startup file are executed whenever the logged-in user starts a shell. Both csh and ksh provide this capability. The ENV parameter is used to define the name of the ksh shell startup initialization file. Only csh provides a file for automatic execution of commands when a user logs out.

EXAM ALERT: It is important to know the names of the initialization files and their uses, for the Bourne shell and also the C and Korn shells.

## The System Profile

For user accounts that use the Bourne shell (sh) or Korn shell (ksh) as a login shell, commands in the system profile are executed before the user's login initialization file. This file is named /etc/profile and, when executed, it sets a default terminal type (TERM) and then calls **umask**(1) to set the default file permission mask to 022. If the user's home directory does not include a file named .hushlogin, the user's storage quota is displayed using **quot**(1M), the message of the day (if any) is displayed, and a notification message is displayed if new email has arrived for the user.

The following listing shows the default contents of /etc/profile for a Solaris 8 system:

```
# The profile that all logins get before using their own .profile.

trap ""  2 3
export LOGNAME PATH
if [ "$TERM" = "" ]
then
        if /bin/i386
        then
                TERM=sun-color
        else
                TERM=sun
        fi
        export TERM
fi
# Login and -su shells get /etc/profile services.
# -rsh is given its environment in its .profile.
case "$0" in
-sh | -ksh | -jsh)
        if [ ! -f .hushlogin ]
```

```
        then
                /usr/sbin/quota
                # Allow the user to break the Message-Of-The-Day only.
                trap "trap '' 2"  2
                /bin/cat -s /etc/motd
                trap "" 2
                /bin/mail -E
                case $? in
                0)
                        echo "You have new mail."
                        ;;
                2)
                        echo "You have mail."
                        ;;
                esac
        fi
esac
umask 022
trap  2 3
```

## Initialization File Templates

When you create a user account and specify a home directory, setting up the user account includes copying the appropriate default initialization files to the user's home directory. These initial files or templates are stored in the /etc/skel directory.

For user accounts that use sh or ksh as the login shell, the /etc/skel/local.profile file is copied to the .profile file in the user's home directory. The following listing shows the default contents of the /etc/skel/local.profile file:

```
stty istrip
PATH=/usr/bin:/usr/ucb:/etc:.
export PATH
#
# If possible, start the windows system
#
if [ "`tty`" = "/dev/console" ] ; then
        if [ "$TERM" = "sun" -o "$TERM" = "sun-color"
        -o "$TERM" = "AT386" ]
        then
                if [ ${OPENWINHOME:-""} = "" ] ; then
                        OPENWINHOME=/usr/openwin
                        export OPENWINHOME
                fi
                echo ""
                echo "Starting OpenWindows in 5 seconds"
                sleep 5
                echo ""
```

```
            $OPENWINHOME/bin/openwin
            clear # get rid of annoying cursor rectangle
            exit # logout after leaving windows system
      fi
fi
```

For user accounts that use the C shell (csh) as the login shell, the /etc/skel/local.login file is copied to the .login file in the user's home directory. The following listing shows the default contents of the /etc/skel/local.login file:

```
stty -istrip
# setenv TERM 'tset -Q -'
#
# if possible, start the windows system.
#
if ( "`tty`" == "/dev/console" ) then
      if ( "$TERM" == "sun" || "$TERM" == "sun-color"
           || "$TERM" == "AT386" ) then
            if ( ${?OPENWINHOME} == 0 ) then
            setenv OPENWINHOME /usr/openwin
            endif
            echo ""
            echo -n "Starting OpenWindows in 5 seconds"
            sleep 5
            echo ""
            $OPENWINHOME/bin/openwin
            clear # get rid of annoying cursor rectangle
            logout # logout after leaving windows system
      endif
endif
```

In addition, for user accounts that use csh as the login shell, the /etc/skel/local.cshrc file is copied to the .cshrc file in the user's home directory. The following listing shows the default contents of the /etc/skel/local.cshrc file:

```
umask 022
set path=(/bin /usr/bin /usr/ucb /etc .)
if ( $?prompt ) then
      set history=32
endif
```

The /etc/skel directory also contains a simple .profile that can be used as a default:

```
# This is the default standard profile provided to a user.
# They are expected to edit it to meet their own needs.
MAIL=/usr/mail/${LOGNAME:?}
```

When you create an account using the **admintool** command, the appropriate /etc/skel file is copied to the home directory of the user account based on the selected login shell. When you use the **useradd** command, all the /etc/skel files (.profile, local.cshrc, local.login, and local.profile) are copied to the home directory. The appropriate file(s) must be set up manually.

## Customizing the User Environment

You can modify the initialization file templates to provide a custom environment for new user accounts. In addition, you can modify the system profile (/etc/profile) to customize the environment for all users during login initialization.

EXAM ALERT

Keep in mind that the system profile, /etc/profile, is executed before the user's profile. This execution order gives you the ability to control and restrict the user environment before the user has an opportunity to make any modifications.

To customize individual user accounts, you can modify the initialization files in the user's home directories. For the most part, this change will consist of adding commands to be executed automatically or defining shell parameters.

### Defining Shell Variables in .profile

Variables defined and exported in the .profile become part of the user's environment. These variables are available to programs and shells executed by the user.

A common shell variable defined in the .profile is **LPDEST**, which is used to specify a default printer. To define the printer HPLaser as the default printer, include the following in the .profile for a user account:

```
LPDEST=HPLaser
export LPDEST
```

Alternatively, you can specify both commands on the same line and separate them with a semicolon:

```
LPDEST=HPLaser; export LPDEST
```

A similar syntax can be used for a user account that uses ksh as a login shell:

```
export LPDEST=HPLaser
```

Although defining variables for csh user accounts is not a certification requirement, the syntax for two csh methods of defining variables is shown here:

```
set LPDEST=HPlaser
setenv LPDEST HPlaser
```

> Changes made to the user's login initialization file do not take effect until the user logs in again or the .profile is executed by preceding it with a dot followed by a space. This technique executes the .profile and makes it part of the current environment.

### Sourcing .profile

For user accounts that use the Solaris Common Desktop Environment (CDE), you can configure the /usr/dt/bin/Xsession command that starts the desktop to read and process the .login (csh) or .profile (sh and ksh) login initialization file in the user's home directory as part of the startup process.

The first user-specific file that Xsession calls is the .dtprofile file located in the user's home directory. The last line of the default .dtprofile file is

```
DTSOURCEPROFILE=true
```

This line will cause the .login or .profile file to be executed (or sourced) automatically. To change this default behavior and prevent the login initialization file from being sourced, change **true** to **false**.

# Login and Logout Procedures

This section covers command-line login and logout procedures. Keep in mind that from the system console a Graphical User Interface (GUI) can be used to login to the Solaris CDE.

## Logging In to a Solaris 8 System

The **login**(1) command is used to log *in* (or *into* or *on to*) a system. When connection is made to a system via the network or tty device, the **login** command typically is used to interact with the user to prompt for and obtain a user account name and password. These are then compared to the entries in the /etc/passwd and /etc/shadow files to determine if the user should be given access to the system. If so, the login shell specified in the /etc/passwd file is started to provide the user an interface to the system. If not, the **login** command tries several more times to obtain a valid user account and password. If all these attempts fail, then the connection to the system is dropped.

### Failed Login Attempts

Failed login attempts are saved in the /var/adm/loginlog file after five unsuccessful attempts. This logging is enabled by creating the loginlog file and disabled by deleting it. The file should be created with read/write permissions for root only.

## Logging Out of a Solaris 8 System

In most situations, you can use the **exit**(1) command to log out of (or, in some circles, *off of*) a system. All three shells recognize this command. For csh, the **logout**(1) command can also be used to log off a system.

# Identifying and Monitoring Users

You can use several commands to identify and monitor users:

- **id**(1M)—Displays the real and effective UID and GID
- **finger**(1)—Displays information about local and remote users
- **last**(1)—Displays login and logout information
- **who**(1)—Displays the users currently logged in to the system
- **whodo**(1M)—Displays who is doing what

### The id Command

The **id** command displays the real and effective UID and GID for the invoking process or specified user account. If you invoke **id** with **-a** as an option, all groups in which the user ID is a member will be returned. The following lines show the results of executing the **id** command:

```
# id -a
uid=0(root) gid=1(other)groups=1(other),0(root),2(bin),
3(sys),4(adm),5(uucp),6(mail),7(tty),8(lp),9(nuucp),12(daemon)
#
```

### The finger Command

The **finger** command displays information about users logged in either to the local system or to a specified remote system. The **-l** command-line argument causes the detailed information to be displayed. You can also specify the user account name of a logged-in user as a command-line argument to limit the information displayed to a single user. The following listing shows the results of the **finger** command:

```
$ finger
Login    Name              TTY        Idle  When       Where
root     Super-User        console    36    Sun 01:47  :0
dla      Darrell           pts/7      1:35  Sat 20:37  winnt40
$
$ finger -l
Login name: root                          In real life: Super-User
Directory: /                              Shell: /sbin/sh
```

```
On since Mar 18 01:47:03 on console from :0
36 minutes Idle Time
No unread mail
No Plan.

Login name: dla                         In real life: Darrell
Directory: /export/home/dla             Shell: /bin/sh
On since Mar 31 20:37:53 on pts/7 from winnt40
1 hour 36 minutes Idle Time
Unread mail since Fri Feb  9 13:53:42 2001
No Plan.
$
$ finger dla
Login name: dla                         In real life: Darrell
Directory: /export/home/dla             Shell: /bin/sh
On since Mar 31 22:14:03 on pts/5 from winnt40
Unread mail since Fri Feb  9 13:53:42 2001
No Plan.

Login name: dla                         In real life: Darrell
Directory: /export/home/dla             Shell: /bin/sh
On since Mar 31 20:37:53 on pts/7 from winnt40
1 hour 43 minutes Idle Time
$
```

You can also use the **finger** command to display information about users logged in to a remote system by specifying a host name preceded by the at (@) character. For example, to display information about users logged in to the system sparc20, use the following command:

```
$ finger @sparc20
[sparc20]
Login    Name               TTY         Idle      When    Where
root     Super-User         console     7d Tue    21:25   :0
$
```

## The last Command

The **last** command displays login and logout activity. This command is useful because it can identify users that are on the system currently and those that have been on the system recently. The following listing shows the results of the **last** command:

```
$ last
root    console      :0       Sun Mar 18 01:47   still logged in
reboot  system boot           Sun Mar 18 01:45
root    console      :0       Sun Mar 18 01:02 - 01:44  (00:41)
```

```
reboot   system boot                Sun Mar 18 00:55
dla      ftp          winnt40   Sat Mar 17 21:14 - 21:16  (00:02)
root     console      :0        Sat Mar 17 20:53 - 00:43  (03:49)
reboot   system boot                Mon Mar  5 01:54
dla      ftp          winnt40   Sun Feb 18 20:23 - 00:05 (1+03:42)
root     console      :0        Sat Feb 10 12:17 - down  (22+13:36)
reboot   system boot                Fri Feb  9 13:51
dla      pts/8        solaris8 Sun Feb  4 21:29 - 23:38 (1+02:08)
dla      pts/7        winnt40   Fri Feb  2 23:50 - down  (6+14:00)
root     console      :0        Sat Jan 27 18:41 - down  (12+19:10)
reboot   system boot                Sat Jan 27 18:34
dla      ftp          solaris8 Fri Jan 19 01:46 - 01:59  (00:13)
root     console      :0        Sat Jan 13 21:44 - down  (13+20:50)
reboot   system boot                Sat Jan 13 21:42

wtmp begins Sat Jan 13 21:42
$
```

## The who Command

The **who** command displays the users currently logged in to the system and, optionally, information about processes, system reboots, and so on. The following listing shows the results of two **who** commands. The second command uses the **-a** command-line argument that provides additional information such as last reboot, current run level, and other details:

```
# who
root       console      Mar 18 01:47    (:0)
root       pts/4        Mar 18 01:49    (:0.0)
dla        pts/5        Mar 20 03:34    (winnt40)
root       pts/6        Mar 29 02:42    (:0.0)
# who -a
   .       system boot  Mar 18 01:45
   .       run-level 3  Mar 18 01:46      3      0  S
rc2             .       Mar 18 01:46  old      78  id=  s2 term=0
     exit=0
rc3             .       Mar 18 01:46  old     279  id=  s3 term=0
     exit=0
sac             .       Mar 18 01:46  old     306  id=  sc
LOGIN      console      Mar 18 01:46  0:15    307
zsmon           .       Mar 18 01:46  old     309
root     + console      Mar 18 01:47  0:15    330       (:0)
root     + pts/4        Mar 18 01:49  old     428       (:0.0)
dla      + pts/5        Mar 20 03:34   .     1712       (winnt40)
root     + pts/6        Mar 29 02:42  0:14   7099       (:0.0)
#
```

### The **whodo** Command

The **whodo** command allows the system administrator to combine the information from **who** with process information to produce a list of what users are doing. The following listing shows the results of a **whodo** command:

```
# whodo
Thu Mar 29 04:15:13 EST 2001
solaris8

console      root        1:47
      ?            330     0:00 Xsession
    pts/3          374     0:00 sdt_shell
    pts/3          390     0:06 dtsession
    pts/6         7099     0:00 sh
    pts/4          428     0:00 sh
pts/5        dla         3:34
    pts/5         1712     0:00 sh
    pts/5         7124     0:00 sh
    pts/5         7179     0:00 whodo
```

# Practice Questions

## Question 1

Where are the user account initialization file templates stored?

❍ a. Under the user account home directories

❍ b. In the /etc/skel directory

❍ c. In the /usr/skel directory

❍ d. In the /skel directory

Answer b is correct. The user account initialization file templates are stored in the /etc/skel directory. The user's copies of the templates (not the templates themselves) are stored under the home directories. Therefore, answer a is incorrect. The /usr/skel and /skel directories do not exist. Therefore, answers c and d are incorrect.

## Question 2

Which of the following are valid settings for the **admintool** command's Password field? [Select all that apply]

❑ a. Normal Password

❑ b. Account is locked

❑ c. Cleared until first login

❑ d. No password — setuid only

❑ e. One-time Password

Answers a, b, c, and d are correct. Normal Password, Account is locked, Cleared until first login, and No password — setuid only are valid settings for the **admintool** command's Password field. Solaris 8 does not provide a one-time password capability. Therefore, answer e is incorrect.

## Question 3

Enter the command used to add a user-defined Bourne shell variable to the user environment so that other programs can use the variable.

________________________

The correct answer is **export**.

## Question 4

Which of the following command-line arguments can be specified when using the **useradd** or **usermod** command? [Select all that apply]

- ❑ a. **-u *uid***
- ❑ b. **-g *gid***
- ❑ c. **-d *home_directory***
- ❑ d. **-l *account***

Answers a, b, and c are correct. The UID, GID, and home directory can be defined using the specified **useradd** command-line arguments and modified using the same **usermod** command-line arguments. The **-l** command-line argument is used only with the **usermod** command to specify a new account name. The account name for the **useradd** command does not use the **-l** command-line argument. Therefore, answer d is incorrect.

## Question 5

Which command can be used to change the members (that is, the user accounts) assigned to an existing group?

- ❍ a. **usermod**
- ❍ b. **groupmod**
- ❍ c. **groupadd**
- ❍ d. **groupmem**

Answer a is correct. The **usermod** command is used once for each user account that is to be added or deleted from a group. The **groupmod** command and the **groupadd** command do not affect group membership. Therefore, answers b and c are incorrect. The **groupmem** command does not exist. Therefore, answer d is incorrect.

## Question 6

Enter the full pathname of the system profile.

____________________________

The correct answer is /etc/profile.

## Question 7

What does the **-P** command-line argument of the **useradd** command specify?

❍ a. Account password

❍ b. Execution profile

❍ c. Initialization file (profile) template

❍ d. Primary group

Answer b is correct. The **-P** command-line argument of the **useradd** command specifies the execution profile. A password cannot be specified using the **useradd** command; all accounts created using **useradd** are locked until a password is defined using the **passwd** or **admintool** command. Therefore, answer a is incorrect. A template cannot be specified; however, a profile template directory can be specified using the **-k** command-line argument. Therefore, answer c is incorrect. The primary group in specified by the **-g** command-line argument. Therefore, answer d is incorrect.

## Question 8

What is the /var/adm/loginlog file used to log?

❍ a. Logins

❍ b. Logouts

❍ c. Failed logins

❍ d. Successful logins

❍ e. All logins and logouts

Answer c is correct. The /var/adm/loginlog file logs failed login attempts. The **last** command is used to determine logins, logouts, and both logins and logouts. Therefore, answers a, b, d, and e are incorrect. In addition, the **who** command can be used to identify users currently logged in to the system.

## Question 9

When used with the **usermod** command, what effect does the **-o** command-line option have?

- ❍ a. The existing user information is overwritten.
- ❍ b. A duplicate UID can be specified.
- ❍ c. The information about the specified user is displayed.
- ❍ d. A duplicate GID can be specified.
- ❍ e. The user account is deleted.

Answer b is correct. The **-o** command-line option of the **usermod** command lets you specify a duplicate UID. The actions listed in the other answers are not supported by the **usermod** command. Therefore, answers a, c, d, and e are incorrect.

## Question 10

When using the **admintool** command to create a user account, which of the following can be specified as the login shell? [Select all that apply]

- ❑ a. Bourne (/bin/sh)
- ❑ b. C (/bin/csh)
- ❑ c. Korn (/bin/ksh)
- ❑ d. Other (specify path)

Answers a, b, c, and d are correct. When you're using the **admintool** command to create a user account, you can choose Bourne, C, or Korn as the login shell, or you can specify another login shell.

## Question 11

Which commands can be used by root to change a password? [Select all that apply]

- ❑ a. **admintool**
- ❑ b. **passmgmt**
- ❑ c. **usermod**
- ❑ d. **passwd**

Answers a and d are correct. Root can use the **admintool** and **passwd** commands to change a password. The **passmgmt** and **usermod** commands do not provide any facility to specify a password. Therefore, answers b and c are incorrect.

## Question 12

Which command shows all the users that are currently logged in to the system? [Select all that apply]

- ❑ a. **who**
- ❑ b. **last**
- ❑ c. **whodo**
- ❑ d. **id**

Answers a, b, and c are correct. The **who, last**, and **whodo** commands show all the users currently logged in to the system. The **id** command shows the real and effective UID, GID, and groups for a specified user account. Therefore, answer d is incorrect.

# Need to Know More?

Mulligan, John P., *Solaris 8 Essential Reference* (New Riders, Indianapolis, IN, 2001), ISBN 0-7357-1007-4.

Sorbell, Mark G., *A Practical Guide to Solaris* (Addison-Wesley, Reading, MA, 1999), ISBN 0-201-89548-X.

Sun Microsystems, *System Administration Guide, Volume 1.* Available in printed form (part number 805-7228-10), on the Web at **docs.sun.com**, and from the online documentation, AnswerBook2, provided with the Solaris 8 operating system.

Sun Microsystems, *System Administration Guide, Volume 2.* Available in printed form (part number 805-7229-10), on the Web at **docs.sun.com**, and from the online documentation, AnswerBook2, provided with the Solaris 8 operating system.

Sun Microsystems, *System Reference Manual, Section 1 - User Commands.* Available in printed form (part number 806-0624-10), on the Web at **docs.sun.com**, and from the online documentation, AnswerBook2, provided with the Solaris 8 operating system.

Sun Microsystems, *System Reference Manual, Section 1M - System Administration Commands.* Available in printed form (part number 806-0625-10), on the Web at **docs.sun.com**, and from the online documentation, AnswerBook2, provided with the Solaris 8 operating system.

7

# Controlling Processes

### Terms you'll need to understand:

✓ Process attributes

✓ The **ps**, **prstat**, and **pgrep** commands

✓ Signals

✓ The **kill** and **pkill** commands

✓ The **cron** and **crontab** commands

✓ Crontab files

### Techniques you'll need to master:

✓ Viewing process attributes using the **ps**, **prstat**, and **pgrep** commands

✓ Terminating processes using the **kill** and **pkill** commands

✓ Scheduling processes using the **cron** and **at** commands

✓ Controlling use of the **cron** and **at** commands

This chapter covers controlling programs or processes running on the system. This control consists of viewing the status of processes, killing processes as needed, and scheduling the automatic starting of processes. The *Process Control* test objectives are covered in this chapter.

# Viewing and Terminating Processes

The **ps**(1), **prstat**(1M), and **pgrep**(1) commands are used to view attributes of processes, whereas the **kill**(1) and **pkill**(1) commands are used to terminate processes.

## The ps Command

The **ps** command is used to display information about active processes. Without any command-line arguments, the **ps** command displays processes that have the same effective user ID (UID) of the user account that executed the command. Table 7.1 lists the command-line arguments supported by the **ps** command.

A considerable amount of information on processes is available through the **ps** command and its several display formats.

The default information displayed for a process consists of its process ID (PID), the terminal device it is associated with (TTY), its accumulated execution time (TIME), and the program or command name (CMD). This information is included in all formats unless specifically omitted.

**Table 7.1 The ps command-line arguments.**

| Argument | Description |
| --- | --- |
| **-a** | Displays all processes except process group leaders and processes not associated with terminals |
| **-A** | Displays all processes (identical to **-e**) |
| **-c** | Displays alternate columns |
| **-d** | Displays all processes except process session leaders |
| **-e** | Displays all processes |
| **-f** | Uses the full listing display format |
| **-g *Process Group ID*** | Displays processes with the specified process group ID |
| **-G *Group ID*** | Displays processes with the specified group ID (GID) |
| **-j** | Displays the session and process group ID |
| **-l** | Uses the long listing display format |
| **-L** | Displays information about each lightweight process (LWP) |
| **-n *Name*** | Uses an alternate name list file (ignored) |

*(continued)*

**Table 7.1 The ps command-line arguments *(continued)*.**

| Argument | Description |
|---|---|
| **-o *Format*** | Uses an alternate display format |
| **-p *Process ID*** | Displays the process with the specified process ID (PID) |
| **-P** | Displays the number of the processor executing the process (only meaningful on a multiprocessor system) |
| **-s *Process Session ID*** | Displays processes with the specified process session ID |
| **-t *Terminal Device Path*** | Displays processes associated with the specified terminal device path |
| **-u *Effective User ID*** | Displays processes with the specified effective user ID |
| **-U *Real User ID*** | Displays processes with the specified real user ID |
| **-Y** | Displays alternate columns in long listing |

All the command-line arguments used to specify an ID—such as process group ID, real group ID, PID, process session ID, effective UID, and real UID—accept multiple IDs (separated by commas). For the real and effective user IDs and the real group ID, you can specify either the numeric IDs or the account names.

The following listing uses the **ps** command with several different command-line arguments:

```
$ ps -udla
   PID TTY      TIME CMD
   781 ?        0:19 xterm
   782 pts/5    0:00 sh
   910 pts/5    0:10 telnet
   913 pts/6    0:01 sh
$ ps -tpts/5
   PID TTY      TIME CMD
   782 pts/5    0:00 sh
   910 pts/5    0:10 telnet
$ ps -f -udla
      UID   PID  PPID  C    STIME TTY      TIME CMD
      dla   781     1  0   Aug 28 ?        0:19 xterm -display
      dla   782   781  0   Aug 28 pts/5    0:00 sh
      dla   910   782  0   Aug 28 pts/5    0:10 telnet solaris
      dla   913   911  0   Aug 28 pts/6    0:01 -sh
$
```

The PPID column lists the parent PID of the process, the C column lists processor utilization (obsolete), and the STIME shows the start date.

## The prstat Command

The **prstat**(1M) command generates a statistics report on active processes. If you use it with no command-line arguments, information on all active processes is displayed, sorted by CPU usage. The report is updated approximately every three seconds until it is killed. The following listing shows the use of the **prstat** command:

```
$ prstat
 PID USER   SIZE    RSS STATE  PRI NICE    TIME    CPU  PROCESS/NLWP
 793 dla   1032K  844K cpu0     58    0   0:00.00 0.1% prstat/1
 789 dla   2960K 2132K sleep    58    0   0:00.00 0.1% xterm/1
 217 root 1908K 1100K sleep    53    0   0:00.00 0.1% nscd/7
 312 root 1936K  660K sleep    48    0   0:00.00 0.1% mibiisa/12
 397 root    64M   47M sleep    59    0   0:00.07 0.0% perfmeter/1
 790 dla    808K  628K sleep    41    0   0:00.00 0.0% sh/1
 177 root 1576K     0K sleep    30    0   0:00.00 0.0% lockd/1
 229 root 2692K     0K sleep    48    0   0:00.00 0.0% lpsched/1
 165 root 1940K  696K sleep    58    0   0:00.00 0.0% in.named/1
 250 root   804K  480K sleep    58    0   0:00.00 0.0% utmpd/1
 188 root 2720K  664K sleep    58    0   0:00.00 0.0% automountd/5
 143 root 2144K  672K sleep    58    0   0:00.00 0.0% rpcbind/1
 129 root 1552K  300K sleep    59    0   0:00.00 0.0% in.ndpd/1
 122 root 1304K  220K sleep    58    0   0:00.00 0.0% in.routed/1
Total: 64 processes, 146 lwps, load averages: 0.11, 0.04, 0.05
$
```

The **prstat** command-line arguments let you select processes to monitor based on PID, the UID of the owner, the CPU being used, and so on. Table 7.2 lists the **prstat** command-line arguments.

**Table 7.2 The prstat command-line arguments.**

| Argument | Description |
|---|---|
| **-a** | Displays separate reports on processes and users. |
| **-c** | Prints new reports instead of overprinting the initial report. |
| **-C *sets*** | Reports only processes bound to the specified processor sets. |
| **-L** | Reports on each LWP. |
| **-m** | Reports microstate information. |
| **-n *number*** | Restricts the report to ***number*** lines in the window or on the terminal. The default is to use the entire display. |
| **-p *pids*** | Reports only processes whose PIDs are listed by ***pids***. |
| **-P *cpus*** | Reports only processes executing on the CPUs listed by ***cpus***. |

*(continued)*

**Table 7.2 The prstat command-line arguments *(continued)*.**

| Argument | Description |
|---|---|
| -R | Executes **prstat** in realtime mode. |
| -s *key* | Sorts the report in descending order based on key (cpu, time, size, rss, or pri). |
| -S *key* | Sorts the report in ascending order based on key (cpu, time, size, rss, or pri). |
| -t | Reports a total usage summary for each user. |
| -u *euids* | Reports only processes whose effective UID is listed in ***euids***. |
| -U *uids* | Reports only processes whose real UID is listed in ***uids***. |
| -v | Reports using verbose mode, which includes the percentage of time in user mode and system mode. |

The following example uses the **prstat** command to list the processes associated with the dla user account:

```
$ prstat -c -u dla
PID USER  SIZE   RSS STATE PRI NICE  TIME    CPU  PROCESS/NLWP
9830 dla  812K  696K cpu0   48   0   0:00.00 0.2% prstat/1
9789 dla 2960K 2136K sleep  59   0   0:00.00 0.1% xterm/1
9790 dla  808K  628K sleep  48   0   0:00.00 0.0% sh/1
Total: 3 processes, 3 lwps, load averages: 0.00, 0.00, 0.01
$
```

Be sure you understand that both **ps** and **prstat** provide information about active processes. The **ps** command provides more user-oriented information (parent PID, TTY, start date, and so on), whereas the **prstat** command provides more system-oriented information (process size, priority, CPU utilization, and so on).

## The kill Command

The **kill**(1) command terminates a process by sending a signal to it that will cause it to exit. Many different types of signals exist. The signals that are typically used to terminate a process are listed in Table 7.3, and a complete listing of base signals can be found in **signal**(3HEAD).

The default response of processes that receive these signals is to terminate, but this behavior can be changed on a process-by-process basis.

You can specify the signal using either its symbolic name (excluding the *SIG* prefix) or its numeric value. If a signal is not specified, SIGTERM (15) is sent by

**Table 7.3 Signals used to terminate processes.**

| Symbolic Name | Value | Description |
|---|---|---|
| SIGHUP | 1 | Hangup |
| SIGINT | 2 | Interrupt |
| SIGKILL | 9 | Kill |
| SIGTERM | 15 | Terminate (default signal for the **kill** and **pkill** commands) |
| SIGUSR1 | 16 | User signal 1 |
| SIGUSR2 | 17 | User signal 2 |

default. The PIDs of the processes to be terminated must be known. The following listing sends the KILL signal (9) to several processes using the **kill** command:

```
# kill -KILL 4220 4224 4229
#
4229 Killed
4224 Killed
4220 Killed
# kill -9 4247
#
4247 Killed
```

A PID preceded by a minus sign is interpreted as a process group ID, and the signal is sent to all processes in that process group.

## The pgrep and pkill Commands

The **pgrep**(1) and **pkill**(1) commands support viewing and terminating processes by name or other attributes, such as UID, GID, and so on. Table 7.4 lists the command-line arguments supported by both the **pgrep** and the **pkill** commands.

The ***pattern*** is a regular expression that is used to select processes based on the program name. The following lines show the difference between obtaining the PID of the **admintool** command using the **ps** and **grep**(1) commands versus the **pgrep** command:

```
$ ps -eaf|grep admintool
root  2898  1096  0   Sep 04 pts/7    0:02 admintool
$ pgrep adm*
2898
$
```

When you specify the -f command-line argument along with the ***pattern***, the ***pattern*** is compared against the program arguments instead of the program name.

**Table 7.4 Common pgrep and pkill command-line arguments.**

| Argument | Description |
|---|---|
| *pattern* | Regular expression to match against the program name and/or arguments |
| -f | Matches the pattern against full arguments instead of the program name |
| -g *Process Group ID* | Matches processes with the specified process group ID |
| -G *Real Group ID* | Matches processes with the specified real group ID |
| -n | Matches only the newest process that meets the specified criteria |
| -P *Parent Process ID* | Matches processes with the specified parent process ID |
| -s *Process Session ID* | Matches processes with the specified process session ID |
| -t *Terminal Device Path* | Matches processes associated with the specified terminal device path |
| -u *Effective User ID* | Matches processes with the specified effective user ID |
| -U *Real User ID* | Matches processes with the specified real user ID |
| -v | Matches all processes except those that meet specified criteria |
| -x | Matches only processes that exactly match the pattern |

In addition, if you specify the **-x** command-line argument, the regular expression interpretation of ***pattern*** is disabled, and ***pattern*** must match the program name or program arguments exactly.

All the ID types of command-line arguments accept multiple IDs (separated by commas). In the case of real and effective user IDs and real group ID (**-G**), either the numeric IDs or the account names can be specified.

The **pgrep** command supports two additional command-line arguments. The **-d** command-line argument specifies a delimiter for separating PIDs when the specified **pgrep** criteria match more than one PID. By default, this delimiter is the newline character. The following listing shows using the **pgrep** command to list the processes owned by the dla user account and the effect of specifying the space character as the delimiter:

```
$ pgrep -u dla
781
782
910
913
$ pgrep -d' ' -u dla
781 782 910 913
$
```

The delimiter command-line argument allows the output of the **pgrep** command to be used as the input to other commands or shell scripts.

The other command-line argument is **-l**, which includes the name of the program with the PIDs of matched processes. The following listing shows the use of the **-l** command-line argument:

```
$ pgrep -l -u dla
  781 xterm
  782 sh
  910 telnet
  913 sh
$
```

The **pkill** command is similar to the **pgrep** command, but instead of displaying information on matched processes, the matched processes are terminated using the SIGTERM (15) signal.

All the command-line arguments listed in Table 7.4 are supported, allowing processes to be selected on the basis of regular expression pattern matching and/or various IDs. In addition, the **pkill** command supports a command-line argument to specify a signal to be used instead of SIGTERM. This command-line argument is the minus sign followed by a symbolic name (not including the *SIG* prefix) or the signal number. The following lines use the SIGKILL signal to terminate all processes associated with the dla user account:

```
# pkill -KILL -u dla
#
```

Be familiar with the signals used to terminate processes. You should know how to specify them using the both signal numbers and names along with the default signal used by the **kill** and **pkill** commands: (SIGTERM).

# Scheduling Processes

Two commands are available for scheduling automatic execution of processes: **cron**(1M) and **at**(1).

## The cron Command

The **cron** command is a daemon started during system boot. It is responsible for executing commands at a future time and perhaps periodically on a scheduled basis. The commands to be executed are specified in a standardized tabular format and stored in files referred to as *crontab files*. These files are located under the /var/spool/cron/crontabs directory.

Commands that are executed automatically by being placed in a crontab file are referred to as *cron jobs*. Commands to be executed only once at a future time can be submitted using the **at** command instead of modifying the crontabs. The **at** command is described in the next section.

The two general classes of crontabs are system crontabs, which are owned by system accounts such as root, lp, and so on, and user crontabs, which are created and maintained by nonadministrative user accounts.

### Default cron Settings

As with other system utilities, you can set parameters to control the behavior of the **cron** command. These settings are listed in the /etc/default/cron file.

The **cron** command will log its activities in the /var/cron/log file if the following entry is contained in the /etc/default/cron file:

```
CRONLOG=YES
```

This is the default. To disable logging, change **YES** to **NO** and reboot the system or restart cron using the /etc/init.d/cron run control (rc) script.

You can add two other entries to /etc/default/cron: **PATH**, which sets the **PATH** shell environment parameter for user cron jobs, and **SUPATH**, which sets the **PATH** shell environment variable for root cron jobs. The following lines shows the **PATH** and **SUPATH** settings:

```
PATH=/usr/bin:/usr/ucb:
SUPATH=/usr/sbin:/usr/bin:
```

### Crontab Files

The /var/spool/cron/crontabs directory contains both the system and the user crontab files. These files have the same name as the account name of the owner. For example, the crontab for the guest user account is named guest.

The crontab file contains entries that specify a command to execute along with a time and frequency of execution. Commands can be executed daily, weekly, or monthly at any time of the day.

A crontab entry consists of six fields separated by spaces or tabs. An asterisk (*) is used as a placeholder in a field that is not used. Table 7.5 lists the fields of a crontab entry.

**Table 7.5 The fields of a crontab entry.**

| Field | Values | Description |
|---|---|---|
| minute | 0 through 59 | Minute of the hour |
| hour | 0 through 23 | Hour of the day |
| day | 1 through 31 | Day of the month |
| month | 1 through 12 | Month of the year |
| weekday | 0 through 6 | Day of the week (0 = Sunday) |
| command | N/A | The command to execute |

The following listing shows the contents of a typical root crontab file:

```
10 3 * * 0,4 /etc/cron.d/logchecker
10 3 * * 0   /usr/lib/newsyslog
15 3 * * 0 /usr/lib/fs/nfs/nfsfind
1 2 * * * [ -x /usr/sbin/rtc ] && /usr/sbin/rtc -c
30 3 * * * [ -x /usr/lib/clean ] && /usr/lib/clean
```

Note that you can specify multiple values in a field by separating them with a comma, as shown in the weekday field in the crontab entry for logchecker. In this example, logchecker will be executed at 3:10 A.M. every Sunday and Thursday morning.

A critical skill for system administrators is the ability to understand and use crontabs to schedule log maintenance, system backups, and other routine maintenance.

## Manipulating Crontabs

You can use the **crontab**(1) command to create, list, edit, and delete crontabs. One capability of the **crontab** command (the ability to edit the crontab files of other users) is available only to the superuser.

When **crontab** is executed without any command-line arguments, it reads the standard input (typically the keyboard). When the command is terminated with Ctrl+D, the entered data is used to create the crontab (or overwrite an existing crontab) for the user account that executed the **crontab** command. When a file name is specified as a command-line argument, the contents of the specified file are used to create/overwrite the user crontab.

When you execute **crontab** with a **-e** command-line argument, the editor specified by the shell environment parameter **EDITOR** is invoked on the user crontab. If the **EDITOR** parameter is not set, the **ed**(1) text editor is used. This mechanism allows editing of the crontab associated with the invoking user account.

The **crontab -l** command displays the contents of the user's crontab, and the **crontab -r** command deletes the user's crontab.

> When the **cron** daemon starts, it reads all existing crontabs. Because it normally does not reread the crontabs, it will not be aware of any changes unless they are made using the **crontab** command. The **crontab** command notifies the **cron** daemon that a crontab has changed or been added. The **cron** daemon then updates its information.

The superuser can specify a user account name to control the crontab of another user account. This account name can be used with the **-l** or **-r** command-line argument to list or delete the crontab of another user account; however, do not specify a user account name with the **-e** command-line argument.

> If the superuser attempts to modify the crontab of another user account by using the **crontab -e** command and specifying the user account name as a command-line argument, the results will be unpredictable. Instead, use the **su**(1) command to become the other user account and then use the **crontab -e** command.

### Access Control

Access to the **crontab** command is controlled by two files, cron.allow and cron.deny, both of which reside under the /etc/cron.d directory. These text files contain lists of user account names (one per line) that are allowed or denied access to the command.

Users are allowed access to the **crontab** command if their user account name is listed in the /etc/cron.d/cron.allow file. If the cron.allow file does not exist, users will be allowed access if their user account name is not listed in the /etc/cron.d/cron.deny file. In addition, users will be denied access if neither file exists.

These access rules also apply to the root account if either the cron.allow or the cron.deny file exists. By default, the /etc/cron.d/cron.deny file is created and contains all initial nonadministrative user accounts. If neither file exists, only the superuser can submit jobs.

Note that the /usr/lib/cron directory is symbolically linked to the /etc/cron.d directory. Therefore, the crontab control files can be accessed using either path name. That is, either /etc/cron.d/cron.allow or /usr/lib/cron/cron.allow and /etc/cron.d/cron.deny or /usr/lib/cron/cron.deny.

## The at Command

A simple way to execute one or more commands once without modifying a crontab is to use the **at**(1) command. Commands submitted for later execution are grouped together as an at-job and are assigned an at-job ID.

The basic format of the **at** command is **at *time***, where ***time*** specifies the time at which the command(s) should be executed. You can specify the time using any combination of A.M./P.M. or 24-hour format, plus month and day in conjunction with the keywords **now, today, tomorrow,** and so on. The following listing shows several types of time specifications:

```
at now
at 10am
at 2pm
at noon
at 3pm + 1 week
at 3pm next week
at 2am jan 24
at 1400 tomorrow
```

You can enter the command(s) to be executed from the standard input and end them with Ctrl+D, or you can use the **-f*file*** command-line argument to specify a file they should be read from. The at-jobs are stored under the /var/spool/cron/atjobs directory.

The **at** command supports other command-line arguments to specify that the commands should be executed using the Bourne shell (**-b**), the C shell (**-c**), or the Korn shell (**-k**) and whether the user should be notified by mail when the command is executed (**-m**). Like the **crontab** command, the **at** command supports the **-l** and **-r** command-line arguments and allows at-jobs to be listed and removed by at-job ID.

The **batch**(1) command is equivalent to **at -m now** and allows a batch job to be entered by means of the standard input.

Use of the **at** and **batch** commands is controlled by the /etc/cron.d/at.allow and /etc/cron.d/at.deny files. These files function similarly to the **cron** access control files except that an empty at.deny file allows access to everyone.

Note that the /usr/lib/cron directory is symbolically linked to the /etc/cron.d directory. Therefore, the **at** control files can be accessed using either path name. That is, either /etc/cron.d/at.allow or /usr/lib/cron/at.allow and /etc/cron.d/at.deny or /usr/lib/cron/at.deny.

# Practice Questions

## Question 1

Which of the following criteria can be specified to select processes using the **pkill** command? [Select all that apply]

- ❑ a. Program name
- ❑ b. Start time
- ❑ c. Real or effective UID
- ❑ d. Associated terminal device

Answers a, c, and d are correct. The program name, real or effective UID, and associated terminal device can be used to select processes using the **pkill** command. The start time is not supported as a criterion for either the **pkill** or the **pgrep** command. Therefore, answer b is incorrect.

## Question 2

Enter the command that can be used to list, edit, and delete crontab files.

________________________

The correct answer is **crontab**.

## Question 3

If a signal is not specified when using the **kill** command, by default, which signal is sent to the specified processes?

- ❍ a. SIGHUP
- ❍ b. SIGINT
- ❍ c. SIGKILL
- ❍ d. SIGTERM

Answer d is correct. All of these signals can typically be used to terminate processes, but SIGTERM is the default signal used by the **kill** and **pkill** commands. Therefore, answers a, b, and c are incorrect.

## Question 4

What is the order of the fields in a crontab file?

- ❍ a. month, day, hour, minute, weekday, command
- ❍ b. command, weekday, minute, hour, day, month
- ❍ c. minute, hour, day, month, weekday, command
- ❍ d. second, minute, hour, day, month, weekday, command

Answer c is correct. The field order in a crontab file is minute, hour, day, month, weekday, command. Answers a and b contain all the correct fields, but the fields are not in the correct order. Therefore, answers a and b are incorrect. Answer d lists an extra field (second) that is not valid in a crontab file. Therefore, answer d is incorrect.

## Question 5

Which command can be used to schedule command execution using A.M./P.M. time notation?

________________________

The correct answer is **at**.

## Question 6

Which of the following criteria can be specified to select processes using the **pgrep** command? [Select all that apply]

- ❑ a. Program name
- ❑ b. Process ID (PID)
- ❑ c. Real or effective UID
- ❑ d. Associated terminal device

Answers a, c, and d are correct. You can specify the program name, real or effective UID, and associated terminal device to select processes using **pgrep**. The PID cannot be specified as a criterion because the **pgrep** command is used to determine process IDs. Therefore, answer b is incorrect.

## Question 7

The /etc/cron.d/cron.deny file exists, but the /etc/cron.d/cron.allow file does not. Which of the following statements are true regarding access to the cron capability? [Select all that apply]

- ❑ a. Without a cron.allow file, no one, including root, is allowed to create, edit, or delete crontab files.
- ❑ b. Without a cron.allow file, only root is allowed to create, edit, or delete crontab files.
- ❑ c. Any user account not listed in the cron.deny file can create, edit, or delete their crontab file.
- ❑ d. Any user account listed in the cron.deny file cannot create, edit, or delete their crontab file.

Answers c and d are correct. User accounts not listed in the cron.deny file can create, edit, or delete their crontab files, and user accounts listed in the cron.deny file cannot create, edit, or delete their crontab files. If a cron.deny exists and a cron.allow does not exist, any account not listed in the cron.deny file can use the cron facility. Therefore, answers a and b are incorrect.

## Question 8

Other than the **ps** command, what command can be used to view information about active processes?

________________________________

The correct answer is **prstat**.

# Need to Know More?

Mulligan, John P., *Solaris 8 Essential Reference* (New Riders, Indianapolis, IN, 2001), ISBN 0-7357-1007-4.

Sun Microsystems, *System Administration Guide, Volume 2.* Available in printed form (part number 805-7229-10), on the Web at **docs.sun.com**, and from the online documentation, AnswerBook2, provided with the Solaris 8 operating system.

Sun Microsystems, *System Reference Manual, Section 1 - User Commands.* Available in printed form (part number 806-0624-10), on the Web at **docs.sun.com**, and from the online documentation, AnswerBook2, provided with the Solaris 8 operating system.

Sun Microsystems, *System Reference Manual, Section 1M-Administration Commands.* Available in printed form (part number 806-0625-10), on the Web at **docs.sun.com**, and from the online documentation, AnswerBook2, provided with the Solaris 8 operating system.

Sun Microsystems, *System Reference Manual, Section 3-Library Interfaces and Headers.* Available in printed form (part number 806-0632-10), on the Web at **docs.sun.com**, and from the online documentation, AnswerBook2, provided with the Solaris 8 operating system.

8

# Disk Administration

### Terms you'll need to understand:

- ✓ Physical device name
- ✓ Logical device name (raw and block disk devices)
- ✓ Raw and block logical device names
- ✓ Instance name
- ✓ /etc/path_to_inst file
- ✓ **devfsadm**, **df**, **dmesg**, **format**, **mount**, **prtconf**, **prtvtoc**, and **sysdef** commands
- ✓ Hot-plugging device
- ✓ Disk label (volume table of contents)
- ✓ Partitions and the partition table

### Techniques you'll need to master:

- ✓ Displaying physical, logical, and instance names
- ✓ Partitioning disks
- ✓ Displaying the partition table
- ✓ Using raw and block logical device names
- ✓ Managing hot-plugging devices
- ✓ Using the **format** command

The first part of this chapter describes the three naming conventions used to identify system devices. It then focuses on the device names associated with disks and the commands used to display these names. The second part of the chapter provides a brief introduction to hot-plugging devices and their management. The third part defines the logical structure of a disk, referred to as a *partition*, and describes how to create and display partition-related data. The last section describes the use of the **format** command. This chapter covers the *Disk Configuration* and *Format* test objectives.

# Disk Device Names

Disks, like other devices of the Solaris 8 operating system, can be referenced using three naming conventions:

- Physical device name
- Logical device name
- Instance name

## Physical Device Names

When the system is booted, the kernel builds a device hierarchy, referred to as the *device tree*, to represent the devices attached to the system. This tree is a hierarchy of interconnected buses; the devices attached to the buses are nodes. The root node is the main physical address bus.

Each device node can have attributes such as properties, methods, and data. In addition, each node typically has a parent node and might have children nodes. A node with children is typically another bus, whereas a node without children is a device attached to a bus.

The *full device pathname* identifies a device in terms of its location in the device tree by listing a series of *node names* separated by slashes; the root is indicated by a leading slash. Each node name in the full device pathname has the following form:

```
driver-name@unit-address:device arguments
```

***driver-name*** identifies the device name, ***@unit-address*** is the physical address of the device in the address space of the parent, and ***:device arguments*** defines additional information regarding the device software. For example, the following full device address represents a slice (or partition) of a small computer system interface (SCSI) disk drive on a SPARC system:

```
/sbus@1f,0/esp@0,4000/sd@3,0:a
```

This address identifies a device attached to the sbus with a main system bus address of 1f,0; an esp device (SCSI bus) attached at SBus slot 0, offset 4000; and an sd device (SCSI disk) with a SCSI bus target of 3, a logical unit of 0, and an argument of a, which represents slice a of the disk.

Devices can also be referenced using physical device names. These names are located under the /devices directory. Although these physical names define the exact location of devices within the system, they are difficult to remember and use.

## Logical Device Names

Logical device names are easier to use. They identify disk, tape, and CD-ROM devices and provide either *raw (character) access* (one character at a time) or *block access* (via a buffer for accessing large blocks of data).

The logical name of a SCSI disk device on a SPARC system identifies the SCSI controller (bus), SCSI target (location on the bus), drive (almost always 0), and slice (partition), as in the following logical device name:

```
/dev/dsk/c0t3d0sa
```

All logical device names reside under the /dev directory, and the dsk subdirectory identifies the device as a block disk device (the rdsk subdirectory indicates a raw disk device). This block disk device is addressed as SCSI controller 0, SCSI bus target 3, drive 0, and slice (partition) a. Note the similarities (and differences) between this logical device name and its physical device name as described in the previous section. Devices that have direct controllers as opposed to bus-oriented controllers (such as IDE drives) do not include the t# (bus target) portion of the logical device name.

Some commands, such as the **format**(1M) command used to format a disk, the **newfs**(1M) command used to create a file system, and the **fsck**(1M) command used to check a file system, expect raw (character) device names (/dev/rdsk). Other commands, such as the **mount**(1M) command used to make a file system available for use and the **df**(1M) command used to display free file system space, expect block device names (/dev/dsk). A few commands, such as **prtvtoc**(1M), accept either raw or block logical device names.

EXAM ALERT: Of the three types of disk device names used in the Solaris environment, logical devices names are used most frequently.

## Instance Names

Instance names are abbreviated names that are mapped to or associated with the physical device names of devices. These names allow devices to be quickly and easily identified without requiring the use of the long and typically complicated physical device names. An instance name typically consists of a short driver binding name, such as sd, and an instance number. For example, sd0 could be the instance name of the first SCSI disk or fd0 could be the instance name of the first diskette drive.

You map physical device names (also known as full device pathnames) with instance names using the /etc/path_to_inst file. This file is rebuilt automatically when you reconfigure the system using the **touch /reconfigure** command or the **boot -r** command. The format of the /etc/path_to_inst file consists of three fields separated by tab characters. The fields are described in Table 8.1.

The following listing shows the /etc/path_to_inst file for an x86 Solaris 8 Operating System. The tab between each field has been replaced with an appropriate number of spaces to improve readability:

```
"/pci@0,0"                                 0   "pci"
"/pci@0,0/pci-ide@0,1"                     0   "pci-ide"
"/pci@0,0/pci-ide@0,1/ide@1"               1   "ata"
"/pci@0,0/pci-ide@0,1/ide@1/sd@1,0"        0   "sd"
"/pci@0,0/pci-ide@0,1/ide@1/st@1,0"        0   "st"
"/pci@0,0/pci-ide@0,1/ide@0"               0   "ata"
"/pci@0,0/pci-ide@0,1/ide@0/cmdk@1,0"      1   "cmdk"
"/pci@0,0/pci-ide@0,1/ide@0/cmdk@0,0"      0   "cmdk"
"/pci@0,0/pci1039,1@2"                     0   "pci_pci"
"/pci@0,0/pci1039,1@2/display@0"           1   "vgatext"
"/pci@0,0/display@a"                       0   "vgatext"
"/isa"                                     0   "isa"
"/isa/lp@1,378"                            0    "lp"
"/isa/i8042@1,60"                          0    "i8042"
"/isa/i8042@1,60/keyboard@0"               0    "kb8042"
"/isa/i8042@1,60/mouse@1"                  0    "mouse8042"
"/isa/pnpTCM,5090@pnpTCM,5090,240c3297"    0    "elx"
"/isa/asy@1,3f8"                           0    "asy"
"/isa/fdc@1,3f0"                           0    "fdc"
"/isa/fdc@1,3f0/fd@0,1"                    1    "fd"
"/isa/fdc@1,3f0/fd@0,0"                    0    "fd"
"/options"                                 0    "options"
"/objmgr"                                  0    "objmgr"
"/pseudo"                                  0    "pseudo"
```

| Table 8.1 Fields of the /etc/path_to_inst file. | |
|---|---|
| **Field** | **Description** |
| Physical Name | Full physical device name or full path device name |
| Instance Number | The unique number (typically starting with 0) |
| Driver Binding Name | Name assigned to the device driver |

## The **devfsadm** and **devfsadmd** Commands

The **devfsadm**(1M) command and its daemon version **devfsadmd**(1M) are used to maintain the /dev/ and /devices directories. As device drivers are loaded into the kernel, the **devfsadm** program creates the appropriate /devices special files and /dev links to provide access to the devices. The **devfsadmd** program is started during the later stages of the system boot and handles any /devices and /dev modifications required to support reconfigurations and hot-plugging (dynamic reconfiguration) activities. **devfsadm** also maintains the path_to_inst file. The **devfsadm** command can be used to manually manage the /dev and /devices files as required.

## Determining Disk Device Names

You can use several commands to identify disk device names. They include the following:

- **df**(1M)
- **dmesg**(1M)
- **format**(1M)
- **mount**(1M)
- **prtconf**(1M)
- **sysdef**(1M)

See the appropriate System Referece Manual page of each command for more details.

### The **df** Command

The **df** command lists free blocks (available storage space) and files (number of additional files that can be created) on a file system basis. The file systems are identified using logical block disk device names as shown in the following listing:

```
# df
/            (/dev/dsk/c0d0s0    ): 28658862 blocks 1862425 files
/boot        (/dev/dsk/c0d0p0:boot):   17722 blocks       -1 files
/proc        (/proc              ):        0 blocks     1868 files
/dev/fd      (fd                 ):        0 blocks        0 files
```

```
/etc/mnttab  (mnttab            ):       0 blocks      0 files
/var/run     (swap              ): 1135576 blocks  21076 files
/tmp         (swap              ): 1135576 blocks  21076 files
/export/home (/dev/dsk/c0d0s7   ):  384784 blocks  98147 files
```

## The dmesg Command

The **dmesg** command collects and displays diagnostic messages from the syslog (typically /var/adm/messages). These messages are generated during system boot and use instance names (and physical names) to identify devices. The following listing shows a partial output from the **dmesg** command:

```
# dmesg
Apr  3 21:39:05 solaris8 genunix:
SunOS Release 5.8 Version Generic_108529-01 32-bit
Apr  3 21:39:05 solaris8 genunix:
Copyright 1983-2000 Sun Microsystems, Inc.  All rights reserved.
Apr  3 21:39:05 solaris8 unix: ACPI detected: -1 0 0 0
Apr  3 21:39:05 solaris8 unix: mem = 130620K (0x7f8f000)
Apr  3 21:39:05 solaris8 unix: avail mem = 117542912
Apr  3 21:39:05 solaris8 rootnex: root nexus = i86pc
Apr  3 21:39:05 solaris8 rootnex: pci0 at root: space 0 offset 0
Apr  3 21:39:05 solaris8 genunix: pci0 is /pci@0,0
Apr  3 21:39:05 solaris8 ata: IDE device at targ 0, lun 0
Apr  3 21:39:05 solaris8 ata: model WDC WD200BB-00AUA1, stat 50
```

## The format Command

The **format** command supports menu selection of disk devices. Both logical device names (minus the /dev/rdsk prefix) and physical device names are displayed:

```
# format
Searching for disks...done
AVAILABLE DISK SELECTIONS:
       0. c0d0 <DEFAULT cyl 38767 alt 2 hd 16 sec 63>
          /pci@0,0/pci-ide@0,1/ide@0/cmdk@0,0
       1. c0d1 <DEFAULT cyl 1019 alt 2 hd 255 sec 63>
          /pci@0,0/pci-ide@0,1/ide@0/cmdk@1,0
Specify disk (enter its number):
```

Note that in the case of the **format** command, the logical device name does not include the slice/partition portion, because this information is not required to identify the disk drive.

## The mount Command

The **mount** command lists mounted file systems. The file systems are identified using logical block disk device names as shown in the following listing:

```
# mount
/ on /dev/dsk/c0d0s0 read/write on Tue Apr  3 21:39:11 2001
/boot on /dev/dsk/c0d0p0:boot read/write on
     Tue Apr  3 21:39:09 2001
/proc on /proc read/write on Tue Apr  3 21:39:10 2001
/dev/fd on fd read/write on Tue Apr  3 21:39:12 2001
/etc/mnttab on mnttab read/write on Tue Apr  3 21:39:17 2001
/var/run on swap read/write on Tue Apr  3 21:39:17 2001
/tmp on swap read/write on Tue Apr  3 21:39:19 2001
/export/home on /dev/dsk/c0d0s7 read/write on
     Tue Apr  3 21:39:19 2001

#
```

### The **prtconf** Command

The **prtconf** command displays system configuration information. Devices are identified using the driver binding name and instance number, which compose the instance name. The following listing shows the output from the **prtconf** command on an x86 Solaris 8 system:

```
# prtconf
System Configuration:  Sun Microsystems  i86pc
Memory size: 128 Megabytes
System Peripherals (Software Nodes):

i86pc
    +boot (driver not attached)
        memory (driver not attached)
    aliases (driver not attached)
    chosen (driver not attached)
    i86pc-memory (driver not attached)
    i86pc-mmu (driver not attached)
    openprom (driver not attached)
    options, instance #0
    packages (driver not attached)
    delayed-writes (driver not attached)
    itu-props (driver not attached)
    isa, instance #0
        motherboard (driver not attached)
        asy, instance #0
        lp, instance #0 (driver not attached)
        fdc, instance #0
            fd, instance #0
            fd, instance #1 (driver not attached)
        i8042, instance #0
            keyboard, instance #0
            mouse, instance #0
```

```
        bios (driver not attached)
        bios (driver not attached)
        pnpTCM,5090, instance #0
```

### The sysdef Command

The **sysdef** command displays the system configuration or definition that lists all hardware devices, including pseudo and system devices, loadable modules, and tunable kernel parameters. Like the **prtconf** command, **sysdef** identifies devices using the driver binding name and instance number, which compose the instance name. The following listing shows the partial output of the **sysdef** command:

```
# sysdef
*
* Hostid
*
  3093740b
*
* i86pc Configuration
*
*
* Devices
*
+boot (driver not attached)
        memory (driver not attached)
aliases (driver not attached)
chosen (driver not attached)
i86pc-memory (driver not attached)
i86pc-mmu (driver not attached)
openprom (driver not attached)
options, instance #0
packages (driver not attached)
delayed-writes (driver not attached)
itu-props (driver not attached)
isa, instance #0
```

## Hot-Plugging and Dynamic Reconfiguration

Typically, adding, removing, or replacing system components such as SCSI drives and PCI adapter cards requires that the system be shut down, the components changed, and then the system reconfigured during the next system boot. *Hot-plugging* lets you change these types of hardware system components without shutting down the system. *Dynamic reconfiguration* supports hot-plugging by allowing the system to recognize the new hardware (or even software) configuration.

Not all SCSI and PCI devices are hot-plugging capable. It is a feature of the latest generation of system components and associated device drivers that support high availability computer configurations. Also keep in mind that not all devices that are hot-plugging capable are supported in the Solaris environment. Check the Solaris 8 Sun Platform Guide or the Solaris 8 (Intel Platform Edition) Hardware Compatibility List for a list of hot-plugging devices supported by the Solaris 8 Operating System.

The **cfgadm**(1M) command provides the dynamic reconfiguration capability in the Solaris 8 environment. You can use this command to change system component configurations, test system components, and display system component status. The **cfgadm** command supports hot-plugging SCSI devices on SPARC and Intel-compatible platforms and PCI adapter cards on Intel-compatible platforms.

The components in the system that support hot-plugging and require dynamic reconfiguration are referred to as *attachment points*. An attachment point consists of an *occupant* (a device that can be added to or removed from the system) and a *receptacle* (a location such as a slot or connector that accepts the occupant). Receptacles have three states:

- *Empty*—No occupant.
- *Disconnected*—The occupant is isolated from the system (typically used for testing the occupant or when the occupant is unconfigured).
- *Connected*—The occupant is configured and accessible by the system (this is the normal state).

Occupants are typically in the unconfigured state or in the configured state. Configured is the normal operational state.

The overall status condition of the attachment point (receptacle and occupant) can be ok, failing, failed, unusable, or unknown. The status condition of an attachment point is the result of errors that occur during operation or diagnostic tests run to identify and isolate faulty components.

## Hot-Plugging SCSI Controllers and Devices

The **cfgadm** command displays information about hot-plugging configurations, connects and disconnects SCSI controllers, and configures or unconfigures SCSI devices.

Attachment points are represented using *attachment point IDs* (AP_Ids). For example, SCSI controllers are represented using IDs such as c0 and c1. A SCSI device such as disk /dev/dsk/c1t3d0 that is attached to controller c1 has an AP_Id of c1::dsk/c1t3d0, whereas a tape drive such as /dev/rmt/0 attached to controller c0 has an AP_Id of c0::rmt/0. Refer to the **cfgadm**(1M) manual page for more information on attachment point IDs.

You can use the **-al** command-line argument to display information about SCSI controllers and devices. The following **cfgadm** command displays this information:

```
# cfgadm -al
AP_Id          Type       Receptacle   Occupant     Condition
c0             scsi-bus   connected    configured   unknown
c0::rmt/0      tape       connected    configured   unknown
c1             scsi-bus   connected    configured   unknown
c1::dsk/c1t3d0 disk       connected    configured   unknown
#
```

You can disconnect a SCSI controller using the **cfgadm -c disconnect** ***AP_Id*** command. For example, to disconnect the c1 controller, use the following command:

```
# cfgadm -c disconnect c1
#
```

Likewise, to connect the c1 controller, use the following command:

```
# cfgadm -c connect c1
#
```

Adding a SCSI device (such as a disk) requires the **cfgadm -x insert_device** ***AP_Id*** command. For example, to add a disk to the c0 controller on a SPARC system, use this command:

```
# cfgadm -x insert_device c0
Adding device to SCSI HBA: /devices/sbus@1f,0/SUNW:fas@0,8800000
This operation will suspend activity on SCSI bus: c0
Continue (yes/no)? y
SCSI bus quiesced successfully.
It is now safe to proceed with hotplug operation.
Enter y if operation is complete or n to abort (yes/no)? y
#
```

You can use similar **cfgadm** commands to replace (**cfgadm -x replace_device** ***AP_Id***), remove (**cfgadm -x remove_device** ***AP_Id***), configure (**cfgadm -c configure** ***AP_Id***), or unconfigure (**cfgadm -c unconfigure** ***AP_Id***) SCSI devices as needed. In addition, diagnostic tests can be performed on an attachment point using the **cfgadm -t** ***AP_Id*** command.

## Hot-Plugging PCI Adapter Cards

The **cfgadm** command displays information about hot-plugging configurations, connects, disconnects, configures, and unconfigures PCI adapter cards.

Attachment point IDs (AP_Ids) for PCI devices are based on the PCI bus and slot. For example, slot 0 of PCI bus 1 has an AP_Id of pci1:hpc0_slot0. Refer to the **cfgadm**(1M) manual page for more information on attachment point IDs.

The **cfgadm** command (without any command-line arguments) displays information about PCI devices. You can use the following **cfgadm** command to display this information:

```
# cfgadm
AP_Id             Type      Receptacle   Occupant      Condition
pci1:hpc0_slot0   unknown   empty        unconfigured  unknown
pci1:hpc0_slot1   ethernet  connected    configured    ok
pci1:hpc0_slot2   unknown   empty        unconfigured  unknown
pci1:hpc0_slot3   unknown   empty        unconfigured  unknown
```

A PCI device can be disconnected (**cfgadm -c disconnect** *AP_Id*), connected (**cfgadm -c connect** *AP_Id*), configured (**cfgadm -c configure** *AP_Id*) or unconfigured (**cfgadm -c unconfigure** *AP_Id*) as needed. In addition, you can perform diagnostic tests on an attachment point using the **cfgadm -t** *AP_Id* command.

# Partitioning Disks

The Solaris 8 operating system requires that disk drives support a logical structure in order to use its storage space. The logical structure consists of a small *disk label*, also called a *volume table of contents (VTOC)*, with the remainder of the disk being divided into *slices* or *partitions*. Once a partition is defined, a file system can be created within the partition. The physical and logical device name associated with a file system is actually the name of the partition in which it resides.

## The Disk Label, or VTOC

The disk label, or VTOC, contains various geometry data about the disk, such as sectors per track, tracks per cylinder, available cylinders, and so on. In addition, the disk label contains the *partition table*.

## Partitions

A partition, or disk slice, is a contiguous collection of disk sectors as defined by the partition table. Once a partition is defined in the partition table, a file system can be created within the partition. The partition table contains an entry for each partition on the disk. Table 8.2 describes the fields of the partition table.

**Table 8.2 Fields of the partition table.**

| Field | Description |
|---|---|
| Partition Name | A single hexadecimal character used as a name for the partition (0 through f). |
| Tag | The intended use of the partition (obsolete; see Table 8.3). |
| Flags | 1 if the partition is not mountable; 10 if the partition is read-only (obsolete). |
| First Sector | The number of the first sector in the partition. |
| Sector Count | The number of sectors in the partition. |
| Last Sector | The number of the last sector assigned to the partition. |
| Mount Directory | The directory where the partition (actually file system) was last mounted. |

When you define partitions, you can assign them a hexadecimal tag that identifies the intended use of the partition. These tags can be used during system maintenance to quickly identify and select partitions. The tags are stored in the tag field of the partition table. Table 8.3 provides a list of partition tags.

You can create the partition table using either the **format** command or the **fmthard**(1M) command. To display it, use the **format** command or the **prtvtoc**(1M) command.

Once the partition table has been populated with the appropriate information (the disk partitions have been defined), you can create file systems within the partitions; however, not all partitions are intended to hold a file system.

**Table 8.3 Partition tags.**

| Partition Type | Tag Value |
|---|---|
| unassigned | 0 |
| boot | 1 |
| root | 2 |
| swap | 3 |
| usr | 4 |
| backup | 5 |
| stand | 6 |
| var | 7 |
| home | 8 |
| altsctr | 9 |
| cache | a |

## Using the **format** Command to Partition a Disk

You can use the **format** command to create or modify a partition table. After you select a disk, the Format Menu is displayed. From this menu, select Partition to display the Partition Menu, as shown in the following listing:

```
PARTITION MENU:
        0      - change '0' partition
        1      - change '1' partition
        2      - change '2' partition
        3      - change '3' partition
        4      - change '4' partition
        5      - change '5' partition
        6      - change '6' partition
        7      - change '7' partition
        select - select a predefined table
        modify - modify a predefined partition table
        name   - name the current table
        print  - display the current table
        label  - write partition map and label to the disk
        !<cmd> - execute <cmd>, then return
        quit
```

To modify existing partitions, select the partition number (0 through 7) and then enter the tag, flags, starting cylinder, and partition size in bytes or cylinders. A predefined table can be selected and used. Alternatively, you can use an existing partition table as a starting point to create a custom table. To save custom tables, choose the Save item of the Format Menu.

## Using the **prtvtoc** Command to Display the VTOC

The **prtvtoc** command displays the VTOC of a physical disk drive. In addition to displaying the partition table, it displays the disk geometry. The following listing shows the output of the **prtvtoc** command for an x86 IDE disk drive:

```
# prtvtoc /dev/rdsk/c0d0s0
# prtvtoc /dev/rdsk/c0d0s0
* /dev/rdsk/c0d0s0 partition map
*
* Dimensions:
*     512 bytes/sector
*      63 sectors/track
*      16 tracks/cylinder
*    1008 sectors/cylinder
*   38769 cylinders
*   38767 accessible cylinders
*
```

```
* Flags:
*   1: unmountable
*  10: read-only
*
* Unallocated space:
*        First      Sector        Last
*        Sector      Count       Sector
*      32183424    6893712     39077135
*
*                          First     Sector       Last
* Partition  Tag Flags    Sector      Count      Sector  Mount Directory
       0      2   00    1052352   30720816   31773167  /
       1      3   01       3024    1049328    1052351
       2      5   00          0   39078144   39078143
       7      8   00   31773168     410256   32183423  /export/home
       8      1   01          0       1008       1007
       9      9   01       1008       2016       3023
#
```

# The format Command

The **format**(1M) command supports the ability to format, analyze, repair, label, and partition disk drives. The **format** command provides an interactive menu from which subcommands and submenus can be selected. Table 8.4 describes these **format** subcommands and submenus.

**Table 8.4 Subcommands and submenus of the format command.**

| Subcommand or Submenu | Description |
|---|---|
| **disk** | Selects a disk |
| **type** | Defines a disk type |
| **partition** | Creates/modifies a partition table for the selected disk (submenu) |
| **current** | Displays information on the selected disk |
| **format** | Formats and analyzes the selected disk |
| **fdisk** | Runs the **fdisk**(1M) program for the selected disk (Intel-compatible only) |
| **repair** | Repairs a defective sector on the selected disk |
| **show** | Translates a disk address (Intel-compatible only) |
| **label** | Writes a label to the selected disk |
| **analyze** | Performs surface analysis on the selected disk (submenu) |

*(continued)*

**Table 8.4 Subcommands and submenus of the format command *(continued).***

| Subcommand or Submenu | Description |
|---|---|
| **defect** | Displays a defect lists for the selected disk (submenu) |
| **backup** | Searches for backup labels |
| **verify** | Displays the label for the selected disk |
| **save** | Saves new disk/partition definitions |
| **inquiry** | Displays the vendor, model, and revision of the selected disk (SPARC only) |
| **volname** | Defines an eight-character volume name for the selected disk |
| **!*cmd*** | Executes ***cmd*** using the user's shell, and then returns to the **format** command |
| **quit** | Exits the **format** command |

When the **format** command starts, it lists the available disk drives, and you select one. The *format>* string is used as a command prompt.

The following listing shows starting the **format** command:

```
# format
Searching for disks...done


AVAILABLE DISK SELECTIONS:
       0. c0d0 <DEFAULT cyl 38767 alt 2 hd 16 sec 63>
          /pci@0,0/pci-ide@0,1/ide@0/cmdk@0,0
       1. c0d1 <DEFAULT cyl 1019 alt 2 hd 255 sec 63>
          /pci@0,0/pci-ide@0,1/ide@0/cmdk@1,0
Specify disk (enter its number): 0
selecting c0d0
Controller working list found
[disk formatted, defect list found]
Warning: Current Disk has mounted partitions.


FORMAT MENU:
        disk       - select a disk
        type       - select (define) a disk type
        partition  - select (define) a partition table
        current    - describe the current disk
        format     - format and analyze the disk
        fdisk      - run the fdisk program
        repair     - repair a defective sector
```

```
        show        - translate a disk address
        label       - write label to the disk
        analyze     - surface analysis
        defect      - defect list management
        backup      - search for backup labels
        verify      - read and display labels
        save        - save new disk/partition definitions
        volname     - set 8-character volume name
        !<cmd>      - execute <cmd>, then return
        quit
format>
```

Basic understanding and general use of the **format** command is a test objective. Be familiar with the **format** subcommands and submenus along with their use.

The following listing uses several of the **format** subcommands: **disk, volname, verify,** and **current**. Consult the **format**(1M) manual page for more information:

```
format> disk

AVAILABLE DISK SELECTIONS:
       0. c0d0 <DEFAULT cyl 38767 alt 2 hd 16 sec 63>
          /pci@0,0/pci-ide@0,1/ide@0/cmdk@0,0
       1. c0d1 <DEFAULT cyl 1019 alt 2 hd 255 sec 63>  solaris7
          /pci@0,0/pci-ide@0,1/ide@0/cmdk@1,0
Specify disk (enter its number)[0]: 0
selecting c0d0
Controller working list found
[disk formatted, defect list found]
Warning: Current Disk has mounted partitions.

format> volname
Enter 8-character volume name (remember quotes)[""]:"solaris8"
Ready to label disk, continue? y

format> verify

Primary label contents:

Volume name = <solaris8>
ascii name  = <DEFAULT cyl 38767 alt 2 hd 16 sec 63>
pcyl        = 38769
ncyl        = 38767
acyl        =    2
bcyl        =    0
```

```
nhead       =   16
nsect       =   63
Part      Tag  Flag   Cylinders      Size      Blocks
  0       root  wm    1044 - 31520  14.65GB   (30477/0/0) 30720816
  1       swap  wu       3 -  1043  512.37MB  (1041/0/0)   1049328
  2     backup  wm       0 - 38767  18.63GB   (38768/0/0) 39078144
  3 unassigned  wm       0              0     (0/0/0)            0
  4 unassigned  wm       0              0     (0/0/0)            0
  5 unassigned  wm       0              0     (0/0/0)            0
  6 unassigned  wm       0              0     (0/0/0)            0
  7       home  wm   31521 - 31927 200.32MB   (407/0/0)     410256
  8       boot  wu       0 -     0   0.49MB   (1/0/0)         1008
  9 alternates  wu       1 -     2   0.98MB   (2/0/0)         2016

format> current
Current Disk = c0d0: solaris8
<DEFAULT cyl 38767 alt 2 hd 16 sec 63>
/pci@0,0/pci-ide@0,1/ide@0/cmdk@0,0

format>
```

## The Partition Submenu

Of the three **format** submenus (Partition, Analyze, and Defect), Partition is the most frequently used. You can use the Partition submenu not only to view and modify the partition table of the selected disk, but also to create new partition tables.

> Basic understanding and general use of the **format** Partition submenu is a test objective. Be familiar with the Partition submenu commands and their intended use.

Table 8.5 describes the subcommands available on the Partition submenu.

**Table 8.5 Subcommands of the format Partition submenu.**

| Subcommand | Description |
|---|---|
| **0** through **7** | Modifies the tag, flags, starting cylinder, and size associated with partitions 0 through 7. |
| **select** | Selects a partition table. |
| **modify** | Modifies a partition table. Starts with the current partition table or all disk space in an unassigned partition (a large unassigned partition is referred to as "free hog"). |
| **name** | Assigns a name to the current partition table. |

*(continued)*

**Table 8.5 Subcommands of the format Partition submenu *(continued).***

| Subcommand | Description |
|---|---|
| **print** | Displays the current partition table. |
| **label** | Writes the current partition table and label to disk. |
| **!*cmd*** | Executes ***cmd*** using the user's shell, and then returns to the **format** command. |
| **quit** | Returns to the **format** menu. |

The following listing uses the Partition submenu to name the partition table, select a partition table, and display the current selected table:

```
format> partition


PARTITION MENU:
        0      - change '0' partition
        1      - change '1' partition
        2      - change '2' partition
        3      - change '3' partition
        4      - change '4' partition
        5      - change '5' partition
        6      - change '6' partition
        7      - change '7' partition
        select - select a predefined table
        modify - modify a predefined partition table
        name   - name the current table
        print  - display the current table
        label  - write partition map and label to the disk
        !<cmd> - execute <cmd>, then return
        quit

partition> name
Enter table name (remember quotes): "solaris 8"

partition> select
        0. solaris 8
Specify table (enter its number)[0]: 0

partition> print
Volume:  solaris8
Current partition table (solaris 8):
Total disk cylinders available: 1019 + 2 (reserved cylinders)
```

```
Part      Tag    Flag   Cylinders       Size                Blocks
  0       root    wm      3 -  283      2.15GB  (281/0/0)    4514265
  1        usr    wm    284 -  326    337.30MB  (43/0/0)      690795
  2     backup    wm      0 - 1018      7.81GB  (1019/0/0) 16370235
  3        var    wm    327 -  454   1004.06MB  (128/0/0)    2056320
  4       swap    wu    455 -  474    156.88MB  (20/0/0)      321300
  5 unassigned    wm    475 -  755      2.15GB  (281/0/0)    4514265
  6        usr    wm    756 -  890      1.03GB  (135/0/0)    2168775
  7       home    wm    891 - 1018   1004.06MB  (128/0/0)    2056320
  8       boot    wu      0 -    0      7.84MB  (1/0/0)        16065
  9 alternates    wu      1 -    2     15.69MB  (2/0/0)        32130

partition>
```

# Practice Questions

## Question 1

Which of the following activities can be performed using the **format** command? [Select all that apply]

- ❑ a. Display a partition table.
- ❑ b. Modify a single partition in a partition table.
- ❑ c. Replace the entire partition table.
- ❑ d. Copy the partition table from one disk to another.

Answers a, b, and c are correct. Using the **format** command, you can display a partition table, modify a single partition in a partition table, and replace the entire partition table. Although a partition table can be created, saved, and used on another disk, the **format** command does not provide a method for copying a table from one disk to another. Therefore, answer d is incorrect.

## Question 2

Enter the command that can be used to display the date and time the file systems were mounted.

______________________________

The correct answer is **mount**.

## Question 3

Which command supports dynamic reconfiguration for hot-plugging?

- ❍ a. **reconfig**
- ❍ b. **configadm**
- ❍ c. **cfgadm**

Answer c is correct. The **cfgadm** command supports dynamic reconfiguration for hot-plugging. The commands in answers a and b do not exist.

## Question 4

Enter the full pathname of the file used to map between physical device names and instance name (driver binding name and instance number).

______________________________

The correct answer is /etc/path_to_inst.

## Question 5

What command can be used to display both the physical device name and the (partial) logical device name of disks?

______________________________

The correct answer is **format**.

## Question 6

Devices can be addressed using physical device names. Under which directory are these?

- ❍ a. /dev
- ❍ b. /etc
- ❍ c. /devices
- ❍ d. /phy

Answer c is correct. Physical device names are listed under the /devices directory. The /dev directory is used for logical device names. Therefore, answer a is incorrect. The /etc directory is not used for devices. Therefore, answer b is incorrect. The /phy directory does not exist. Therefore, answer d is incorrect.

## Question 7

Which of the following use logical device names? [Select all that apply]

- ❑ a. **format**
- ❑ b. **newfs**
- ❑ c. **fsck**
- ❑ d. **mount**
- ❑ e. **df**
- ❑ f. **prtvtoc**

Answers a, b, c, d, e, and f are correct. All of these commands either display or expect logical device names.

## Question 8

Files under the /dev and /devices directories are maintained by which of the following programs?

- ❍ a. **devadm**
- ❍ b. **devfsadm**
- ❍ c. **devfsadmin**
- ❍ d. **devicesadm**

Answer b is correct. The **devfsadm** program maintains files under the /dev and /devices directories. The commands in answers a, c, and d do not exist.

## Question 9

Enter the command used to display a list of free blocks and number of files on a file system basis.

____________________________

The correct answer is **df**.

## Question 10

Which of the following are fields of a partition table? [Select all that apply]

- ❑ a. Partition name
- ❑ b. Partition tag
- ❑ c. Disk label
- ❑ d. Volume table of contents
- ❑ e. Number of sectors in partition

Answers a, b, and e are correct. Partition name, partition tag, and number of sectors in the partition are fields of a partition table. The disk label is the portion of the disk that contains the partition table. Therefore, answer c is incorrect. The volume table of contents is another name for the disk label. Therefore, answer d is incorrect.

## Question 11

Which of the following information is displayed by the **prtvtoc** command? [Select all that apply]

- ❑ a. Disk dimensions (geometry)
- ❑ b. Partition table
- ❑ c. Disk label
- ❑ d. Volume table of contents

Answers a, b, c, and d are correct. The **prtvtoc** command displays the disk label (otherwise known as the volume table of contents), which consists of the disk geometry and the partition table.

## Question 12

Which of the following can be performed by the **cfgadm** command? [Select all that apply]

❑ a. Display the receptacle state, occupant state, and attachment point condition

❑ b. Configure and unconfigure EDI disk drives

❑ c. Connect and disconnect SCSI controllers

❑ d. Test attachment points

Answers a, c, and d are correct. The **cfgadm** command can display the receptacle state, occupant state, and attachment point condition; connect and disconnect SCSI controllers; and test attachment points. Only SCSI devices and PCI adapter cards are supported by the **cfgadm** command. Therefore, answer b is incorrect.

## Question 13

Which of the following is the **format** Partition submenu command used to display the current partition table?

❍ a. **display**

❍ b. **verify**

❍ c. **print**

❍ d. **select**

❍ e. **show**

Answer c is correct. The Partition submenu **print** command displays the current partition table. The **display** command does not exist. Therefore, answer a is incorrect. The **verify** command displays the partition table from the main **format** menu, not the Partition submenu. Therefore, answer b is incorrect. The **select** command lets you select a new partition table from a list of partition tables, but none are displayed by this submenu command. Therefore, answer d is incorrect. The **show** command is a **format** menu command used to translate a disk address. Therefore, answer e is incorrect.

# Need to Know More?

Mulligan, John P., *Solaris 8 Essential Reference* (New Riders, Indianapolis, IN, 2001), ISBN 0-7357-1007-4.

Sorbell, Mark G., *A Practical Guide to Solaris* (Addison-Wesley, Reading, MA, 1999), ISBN 0-201-89548-X.

Sun Microsystems, *System Administration Guide, Volume 1.* Available in printed form (part number 805-7228-10), on the Web at **docs.sun.com**, and from the online documentation, AnswerBook2, provided with the Solaris 8 operating system.

Sun Microsystems, *System Reference Manual, Section 1-User Commands.* Available in printed form (part number 806-0624-10), on the Web at **docs.sun.com**, and from the online documentation, AnswerBook2, provided with the Solaris 8 operating system.

Sun Microsystems, *System Reference Manual, Section 1M-Administration Commands.* Available in printed form (part number 806-0625-10), on the Web at **docs.sun.com**, and from the online documentation, AnswerBook2, provided with the Solaris 8 operating system.

Sun Microsystems, *System Reference Manual, Section 4-File Formats.* Available in printed form (part number 806-0633-10), on the Web at **docs.sun.com**, and from the online documentation, AnswerBook2, provided with the Solaris 8 operating system.

9

# File System Administration

**Terms you'll need to understand:**

- ✓ File system
- ✓ Types of file systems
- ✓ Default Solaris 8 file systems
- ✓ **mkfs**, **mkfs_ufs**, and **newfs** commands
- ✓ **fsck** command
- ✓ /etc/mnttab and /etc/vfstab files
- ✓ **mount** and **umount** commands
- ✓ **mountall** and **umountall** commands
- ✓ **df**, **du**, and **quot** commands
- ✓ Types of files (regular, directory, and special)
- ✓ Types of links (symbolic and hard)
- ✓ **compress**, **gzip**, and **zip** commands
- ✓ **mt** command
- ✓ **ufsdump** and **ufsrestore** commands
- ✓ **tar**, **cpio**, and **find** commands

**Techniques you'll need to master:**

- ✓ Creating (making) file systems
- ✓ Checking and repairing file systems
- ✓ Mounting and unmounting file systems
- ✓ Monitoring file system usage
- ✓ Backing up and restoring file systems, directories, and files
- ✓ Recovering the root or /usr file system
- ✓ Identifying different types of files and links
- ✓ Compressing files and directories

The first part of this chapter reviews some basic information about file systems, including creating, checking, repairing, monitoring, mounting, unmounting, and monitoring usage. The second part provides an overview of some file and directory concepts and commands that you can use to save storage space. The third portion describes the commands used to back up and restore files, directories, and file systems. This chapter covers the *File Systems*, *Files and Directories,* and *Backup and Recovery* test objectives.

# File System Basics

A *file system* is a logical collection of files and directories contained in a partition. It can be treated as a single entity when you're making it available for use (mounting), checking it, and repairing it.

The three types of file systems supported by the Solaris 8 environment are disk based, memory based (pseudo), and network based. The Part I exam concentrates on disk-based files systems. The Part II exam covers pseudo file systems (Chapter 16) and network-based file systems (Chapter 18).

Disk-based file systems are stored on physical disks, CD-ROMs, and diskettes on the local system. Table 9.1 lists the disk-based file system formats.

Pseudo file systems are memory based and provide access to special system information, such as processes. Several pseudo file system formats are used, including CacheFS for system cache, Lookback File System (LOFS) to provide alternate path names, the Temporary File System (TMPFS), and the Process File System (PROCFS).

## Default Solaris 8 File Systems

The disk space available for use with a Solaris 8 operating system is a collection of mounted file systems. The top directory is the location where the root file system is mounted. The locations where other file systems are mounted, called *mount points*, are typically subdirectories of the root file system, and normally are

**Table 9.1 Disk-based file systems.**

| Format | Description |
|---|---|
| High Sierra File System (HSFS) | The default format for CD-ROM file systems |
| PC File System (PCFS) | The default format for diskette file systems; same as the DOS disk format |
| Universal Disk Format (UDF) | Format for optical media referred to as Digital Versatile Disc (DVD) |
| Unix File System (UFS) | The default format for hard disk file systems |

**Table 9.2 Default file systems.**

| File System | Use |
|---|---|
| root (/) | The top of the hierarchical file system tree. Contains critical system files, such as the kernel and device drivers. |
| /usr | System files, such as commands and programs, used to administer and use the system. |
| /home | User home directories. On some systems, it might be /export/home or a network-based file system. |
| /var | System files that change or grow, such as logs, queues, and spooling areas. |
| /opt | Third-party software and applications. |
| /tmp | Temporary files cleared each time the system boots. |
| /proc | Information on active processes. |

used to refer to the file systems themselves. For example, the file system mounted at /usr normally is referred to as the *usr file system*. Table 9.2 lists the default file systems of a Solaris 8 operating system.

All the disk-based file systems are UFS. The two memory-based file systems (/tmp and /proc) are type TMPFS and PROCFS, respectively.

Because kernel files reside in the root file system and system files reside in the /usr file system, these two file systems are required to boot a usable system.

## Creating UFS File Systems

You can use the **mkfs**(1M), **mkfs_ufs**(1M), and **newfs**(1M) commands to create a UFS file system. The **mkfs_ufs** command is typically not used directly. It is called by the **mkfs** command when **mkfs** is used to create a UFS file system. The **newfs** command is the preferred method for creating a UFS file system, because it provides a user-friendly interface to the **mkfs** command.

The **newfs** command calculates the appropriate parameters and calls the **mkfs** command to create the file system. You can specify command-line arguments to override the calculated parameters. The only required command-line argument is the raw logical device name of the partition in which the file system should be created. The following listing uses the **newfs** command to create a UFS in a 1GB partition. The **-v** command-line argument specifies *verbose mode*, which causes the **newfs** command to display its actions:

```
# newfs -v /dev/rdsk/c0d1s7
newfs: construct a new file system /dev/rdsk/c0d1s7: (y/n)? y
mkfs -F ufs /dev/rdsk/c0d1s7 2104515 63 240 8192 1024 . . . 8 7
Warning: 12286 sector(s) in last cylinder unallocated
/dev/rdsk/c0d1s7: 2104514 sectors in 140 cylinders of 240 tracks,
        63 sectors
        1027.6MB in 24 cyl groups (6 c/g, 44.30MB/g, 10688 i/g)
super-block backups (for fsck -F ufs -o b=#) at:
 32, 90816, 181600, 272384, 363168, 453952, 544736, 635520,
 726304, 817088, 907872, 998656, 1089440, 1180224, 1271008,
 1361792, 1452576, 1543360, 1634144, 1724928, 1815712,
 1906496, 1997280, 2088064,
#
```

Another useful **newfs** command-line option is **-N**, which causes the **newfs** command to calculate the parameters that will be used to call the **mkfs** command; however, the **mkfs** command is not actually called, and the file system is not created. The **-v** command-line argument is used to preview the file system parameters. In addition, most of the **mkfs** command-line arguments can be specified as **newfs** command-line arguments. If any of these are specified, then they will override any calculated parameters and be passed to the **mkfs** command. See the **newfs**(1M) and **mkfs**(1M) manual pages for details.

If you're using the **mkfs** command directly, you should include the **-F** command-line argument to identify the type of file system to create. If you don't specify a file system type, then the type listed in the /etc/default/fs file is used by default. The default type for local (disk-based) file systems is UFS. Additional parameters, such as block size and disk geometry (sectors per track, tracks per cylinder, and so on) can also be specified.

> **EXAM ALERT** The commands used to create file systems expect raw (character) logical device names. In addition, the only type of disk-based file system that can be created on a standard Solaris 8 operating system is UFS. However, when a diskette is formatted, the PCFS is created on the diskette automatically, because the PCFS format is the DOS disk format.

## Checking and Repairing File Systems

File systems are damaged when the data that defines the file systems is corrupted. This corruption can be caused either by software errors or by failures of the underlying physical disk hardware. The **fsck**(1M) command checks (audits) the logical consistency of a file system and attempts to make the repairs necessary to eliminate any inconsistency. The **fsck** command checks the superblock, inodes, indirect blocks, and directory data block.

The **fsck** command is typically executed when a file system is mounted automatically as part of system boot. It can also be executed manually on one or more file systems. Only unmounted file systems should be checked and repaired, because changes can affect programs accessing the file system and in turn cause even more damage. One or more raw logical device names (partitions) can be specified as command-line arguments. As with the **mkfs** command, you should use the **-F** command-line argument to specify the type of file system being checked. The following listing shows using the **fsck** command to check the 1GB file system previously created:

```
# fsck -F ufs /dev/rdsk/c0d1s7
** /dev/rdsk/c0d1s7
** Last Mounted on
** Phase 1 - Check Blocks and Sizes
** Phase 2 - Check Pathnames
** Phase 3 - Check Connectivity
** Phase 4 - Check Reference Counts
** Phase 5 - Check Cyl groups
2 files, 9 used, 1019783 free
#
```

If you don't specify the **-F** command-line argument, the type of file system defined in the /etc/default/fs file is used by default. In addition, if no partitions (raw logical device names) are specified, all the file systems listed in the /etc/vfstab file are checked.

EXAM ALERT

Like the commands used to create file systems, the **fsck** command expects raw logical device names. You can use the **fsck** command to check and repair CacheFS, UDF, and UFS file systems. Remember to unmount the file system first.

## Mounting and Unmounting File Systems

File systems are made accessible using the **mount**(1M) command. This command associates the file system with a subdirectory of a currently mounted file system.

The **mount** command typically is called with two command-line arguments: a logical block device name (partition) associated with a file system and a mount point where the file system should be mounted. If only one command-line argument is specified (either device name or mount point), the /etc/vfstab file is searched for an entry that matches the argument, and if found will mount the file system using the information from the /etc/vfstab file entry. In addition, the **-F** command-line can be specified to identify the type of file system being mounted. Mounted file systems are listed in the /etc/mnttab file (unless the **-m** command-line argument is specified). If the **mount** command is used with no command-line arguments, all mounted file systems listed in the /etc/mnttab file are displayed.

The **mount** command supports several options specified as command-line arguments. One significant option is UFS large file support. By default, UFS file systems support large files (greater than 2GB in size). This default is the same as specifying **-o largefiles** as a command-line argument. To disable large file support, specify **-o nolargefiles** as a command-line argument to the **mount** command. If this option is specified and a large file exists on the file system, the mount will fail.

Table 9.3 lists the commonly used command-line arguments for the **mount** command.

Multiple file-system-specific options (**-o**) can be specified separated by commas. Some of the frequently used UFS options are:

- **atime**—Use normal access time recording (default).
- **intr**—Allow keyboard interrupts to kill processes waiting on file system I/O (default).
- **largefiles**—Allow files larger than 2GB (default).
- **noatime**—Reduce file system activity by not updating file access times.
- **nointr**—Do not allow keyboard interrupts to kill processes waiting on file system I/O.
- **nolargefiles**—Do not allow files larger than 2GB. If any exist in the file system, the mount will fail.
- **nosuid**—Disallow **setuid** execution on files.
- **suid**—Allow **setuid** execution on files (default).

The following (abbreviated) listing shows the use of the **mount** command:

```
# mount
/proc on /proc read/write
/ on /dev/dsk/c0d0s0 read/write/largefiles
/usr on /dev/dsk/c0d0s6 read/write/largefiles
/var on /dev/dsk/c0d0s3 read/write/largefiles
/opt on /dev/dsk/c0d0s5 read/write/largefiles
/tmp on swap read/write
# mount -F ufs -o nolargefiles,noatime /dev/dsk/c0d1s7 /usr2
# mount
/proc on /proc read/write
/ on /dev/dsk/c0d0s0 read/write/largefiles
/usr on /dev/dsk/c0d0s6 read/write/largefiles
/var on /dev/dsk/c0d0s3 read/write/largefiles
/opt on /dev/dsk/c0d0s5 read/write/largefiles
/tmp on swap read/write
/usr2 on /dev/dsk/c0d1s7 read/write/nolargefiles/noatime
#
```

**Table 9.3 Selected mount command-line arguments.**

| Argument | Use |
|---|---|
| **-F *type*** | Specify the type of file system (NFS, UFS, and so on) |
| **-m** | Mount the file system without making an entry in /etc/mnttab |
| **-o** | Specify file-system-specific options |
| **-p** | List the mounted file systems (abbreviated listing) |
| **-r** | Mount the file system as read-only |
| **-v** | List the mounted file systems (verbose listing) |

EXAM ALERT

You can use the **mount** command to mount CacheFS, HSFS, NFS, PCFS, TMPFS, UDF, and UFS file systems. Unlike the other file system commands, the **mount** command expects a logical block device name of a partition in which the file system resides.

The **umount**(1M) command is used to unmount a file system. The file system cannot be unmounted if it is busy (a program that resides on the file system is being executed or the current directory of a logged-in user account is within the file system). Either the logical block device name or the mount point can be specified as a command-line argument.

The **mountall**(1M) command mounts all file systems listed in the /etc/vfstab file. This file is also used to determine the file systems to automatically mount during system boot. You can add or remove file systems in the /etc/vfstab file with any standard text editor. Table 9.4 lists the (tab-separated) fields of an entry in the /etc/vfstab file. A hyphen (-) is used to indicate no entry in a field.

**Table 9.4 Fields of the /etc/vfstab file.**

| Field | Description |
|---|---|
| Device To Mount | Logical block device name of the file system partition to mount |
| Device To fsck | Logical raw device name used for the **fsck** command |
| Mount Point | Subdirectory where the file system should be mounted |
| FS Type | File system type |
| fsck Pass | Flag used to indicate whether the **fsck** command should be executed automatically (a nonzero numeric value indicates yes) |
| Mount At Boot | A "yes" indicates that the file system should be mounted at boot or when the **mountall** command is executed; otherwise, "no" |
| Mount Options | Any mount options that are desired and appropriate for the file system |

The **umountall**(1M) command unmounts all the file systems listed in the /etc/mnttab file, except root, /proc, /var, and /usr.

> Keep in mind the purpose of the /etc/mnttab and /etc/vfstab files. The /etc/mnttab file lists currently mounted file systems (unless the **-m** command-line argument is used with the **mount** command). The /etc/vfstab file provides a list of files systems that should be mounted automatically at system boot or when the **mountall** command is used.

## Accessing Data on CD-ROMs and Diskettes

Properly formatted diskettes and CD-ROMs can be mounted using the **mount** command and accessed like any other file system. The **umount** command also is used to unmount a diskette or CD-ROM. However, in the Solaris environment, mounting these types of media has been made easier by use of *Volume Management*. Volume Management provides automatic mounting of removable volumes (diskettes and CD-ROMs). This service is provided by the Volume Management daemon, **vold**(1M). By default, **vold** is enabled.

### Using CD-ROMs

When a CD-ROM is inserted into a CD-ROM drive, the **vold** program recognizes a properly formatted CD-ROM and automatically mounts it under the /cdrom directory. The first CD-ROM is mounted at /cdrom/cdrom0, the second at /cdrom/cdrom1, and so on. If the CD-ROM is partitioned (which it probably is), each slice or partition is mounted. For example, if the CD-ROM volume contains six slices (s0 through s5), then each is mounted (/cdrom/cdrom0/s0 through /cdrom/cdrom0/s5). Once mounted, the partitions can be used like any other read-only disk drive.

When the CD-ROM is no longer needed, all the partitions associated with it can be automatically unmounted and the CD-ROM ejected from the CD-ROM drive using the **eject cdrom** command. If more than one CD-ROM is mounted, you specify the mount point: for example, **eject cdrom0**. See the **eject**(1) manual page for more details.

### Using Diskettes

Unlike CD-ROMs, diskettes are not automatically mounted by the **vold** program. Instead, you can use the **volcheck**(1) command to instruct **vold** to scan all floppy disk drives and mount any diskettes found. The diskettes are mounted under the /floppy directory. The first diskette is mounted at /floppy/floppy0, the second at /floppy/floppy1, and so on. Once mounted, the diskette can be used like any (small) read/write disk drive.

When the diskette is longer needed, it can be unmounted using the **eject** command without any command-line arguments. Or, if more than one diskette is mounted, you provide the name of the mount point as a command-line argument: for example, **eject floppy0**.

## Monitoring File System Usage

Several commands can be used to monitor file system usage. These are the **df**(1), **du**(1), and **quot**(1M) commands.

The **df** command (without command-line arguments) displays the mount point, logical block device name, number of free 512-byte blocks, and number of files that can be created for each file system. (The **-k** command-line argument lists sizes in 1,024-byte blocks or kilobytes instead of 512-byte blocks.) The command can also be used to display the disk space used by file systems. The following listing shows the use of the **df** command:

```
# df
/proc        (/proc             ):       0 blocks      948 files
/            (/dev/dsk/c0d0s0 ):   56098 blocks    35834 files
/usr         (/dev/dsk/c0d0s6 ):  181578 blocks   168053 files
/var         (/dev/dsk/c0d0s3 ):  307080 blocks   147835 files
/export/home (/dev/dsk/c0d0s7 ): 1854626 blocks   488828 files
/opt         (/dev/dsk/c0d0s5 ):   15272 blocks   109653 files
/tmp         (swap             ):  311360 blocks     9985 files
/usr2        (/dev/dsk/c0d1s7 ): 2039566 blocks   256508 files
#
```

The **du** command lists the number of 512-byte blocks allocated to each subdirectory and the total for the current directory. Several frequently used command-line arguments include **-a** to list all nondirectory files, **-k** to list sizes in terms of 1,024-byte blocks (kilobytes) instead of 512-byte blocks, and **-s** to report only the total sum of the specified files. The following listing uses the **du** command to determine the amount of storage space allocated to the /etc/openwin directory and its contents:

```
# cd /etc/openwin
# du
4       ./etc/devdata/SUNWaccel/monitors/pnp
6       ./etc/devdata/SUNWaccel/monitors
8       ./etc/devdata/SUNWaccel
10      ./etc/devdata
12      ./etc
10      ./server/etc
12      ./server
```

```
2       ./devdata/profiles
4       ./devdata
30      .
#
```

The **quot** command lists the number of 1,024-byte blocks of a file system owned by each user. You must specify either a file system (mount point) or **-a** (all mounted file systems) as a command-line argument. Another useful command-line argument is **-f**, which displays the number of files in addition to the amount of space available. The following listing shows the **quot** command:

```
# quot /export/home
/dev/rdsk/c0d0s7:
17627   root
  133   dla
    2   guest
    1   sys
#
```

# File and Directory Concepts

Data stored on file systems consists of directories and files. Directories serve as folders to arrange the files into some organized, user-defined structure. In reality, all the files and directories are stored more or less randomly on the disk. The files and (other) directories are then referenced or *linked* into directories to provide the organization. In addition, several types of special files are used.

Sometimes files and directories are not needed frequently or use up more space than desired. To address this issue, Solaris 8 provides several utilities to *compress* files and directories so they take up less space; they can be *uncompressed* as needed.

This portion of the chapter provides an overview of these file/directory concepts and file/directory compression.

## Types of Files

The allocated space on file systems is in the form of either directories or files. Only one type of directory exists. However, there are several types of files. The files used to store data or executables are referred to as *regular* or *ordinary* files. Other files are used for special purposes. Table 9.5 lists all supported files types. You can identify a file's type by a single character ID produced by the **ls -l** command.

EXAM ALERT

Be familiar with the types of files supported in the Solaris environment and the character IDs used by the **ls** command to identify the types of files.

**Table 9.5 File types.**

| Type | ls -l ID | Description |
|---|---|---|
| Regular | - | An ordinary or regular file. Used for data and executables. |
| Directory | **d** | A directory. Used to organize files and other directories. |
| Link | **l** | A symbolic link. Used to provide an alternate path to a file or directory (see the next section). |
| Block special | **b** | A file that provides an interface to a block-oriented peripheral device. These files typically are located under the /dev or /device directory. Also referred to as device files. |
| Character special | **c** | A file that provides an interface to a character-oriented peripheral device. These files typically are located under the /dev or /device directory. Also referred to as device files. |
| Door | **D** | A file that provides an Remote Procedure Call (RPC) mechanism interface between programs and between the kernel and a user space process. |
| FIFO | **p** | A First-In-First-Out or named pipe data structure that provides a mechanism for two cooperating programs to communicate. |
| Socket | **s** | A network (AF_UNIX) socket data structure used to communicate via a network interface. |

## Types of Links

As previously mentioned, files and directories are *linked* into a directory. This link is stored as an entry in the directory and provides a reference by which the file or directory can be located and accessed.

The directory entry is actually a pointer to the location of the file or directory within the file system and is referred to as a *hard link*. Because links point to files or directories based on their location in the file system, links cannot be used to point to files or directories in a different file system. Thus a hard link implies the file or directory is located in the current file system.

A *soft link* or *symbolic link* provides a mechanism to reference a file or directory on another file system. Instead of pointing to a location in the file system, the directory entry contains the full path name of another file or directory. Using symbolic links lets you create multiple pathnames and filenames on different file systems that all point to the same file or directory.

You can use the **link**(1M) and **ln**(1) commands to create hard links. However, only the **ln** command can be used to create symbolic links (using the **-s** command-line argument). The **unlink**(1M) command deletes hard or soft links. When all hard links to a file or directory are deleted, the file or directory is removed. You can also use the **rm**(1) and **rmdir**(1) commands to delete hard or soft links.

## File and Directory Compression

Directories and files can be compressed to use less space on disk drives and, more importantly, on backup devices such as magnetic tape and optical media. Solaris supports three types of utilities to compress and uncompress (that is, expand) data:

- **compress**(1) and **uncompress**(1)
- **gzip**(1) and **gunzip**(1)
- **zip**(1) and **unzip**(1)

### The compress and uncompress Commands

The **compress** command uses the adaptive Lempel-Ziv coding algorithm to compress one or more files specified as command-line arguments (separated by spaces). Files compressed using the **compress** command are given a .Z extension. You can uncompress files using the **uncompress** command, specifying the file names as command-line arguments (separated by spaces). Note that the **compress** command can only be used on regular files, and each file is compressed separately. The following listing shows the use of these commands:

```
# ls -l
total 3
-rw-r--r--   1 root     other     103306 Apr  6 02:27 file4

# compress file4

# ls -l
total 3
-rw-r--r--   1 root     other      41280 Apr  6 02:27 file4.Z

# uncompress file4

# ls -l
total 3
-rw-r--r--   1 root     other     103306 Apr  6 02:27 file4
#
```

You can use the **zcat**(1) command to view the contents of a file compressed with the **compress** command. However, the **zcat** command does not generate an uncompressed file or remove the compressed file like the **uncompress** command.

### The **gzip** and **gunzip** Commands

The **gzip** command uses the using adaptive Lempel-Ziv coding (LZ77) algorithm to compress one or more files specified as command-line arguments (separated by spaces). Files compressed using the **gzip** command are given a .gz extension. You can uncompress files using the **gunzip** command, specifying the file names as command-line arguments (separated by spaces). Note that the **gzip** command can only be used on regular files, and each file is compressed separately. The following listing shows the use of these commands:

```
# ls -l
total 3
-rw-r--r--    1 root     other      103306 Apr  6 02:27 file4

# gzip file4

# ls -l
total 70
-rw-r--r--    1 root     other       32757 Apr  6 02:27 file4.gz

# gunzip file4

# ls -l
-rw-r--r--    1 root     other      103306 Apr  6 02:27 file4
#
```

You can use the **gzcat**(1) command to view the contents of a file compressed by the **gzip** command. However, the **gzcat** command does not generate an uncompressed file or remove the compressed file like the **gunzip** command.

### The **zip** and **unzip** Commands

The **zip** command compresses one or more files and/or directories specified as command-line arguments into a single archive. Archives created by the **zip** command are given a .zip extension. You can uncompress the archive using the **unzip** command, specifying the archive as a command-line argument. The following listing shows the use of these commands:

```
# ls -lR
total 2
drwxr-xr-x    2 root     other         512 Apr  6 03:15 dir1

./dir1:
total 296
-rw-r--r--    1 root     other          27 Apr  6 03:04 file1
-rw-r--r--    1 root     other         389 Apr  6 03:04 file2
 rw-r-----    1 root     other       34341 Apr  6 03:04 file3
-rw-r--r--    1 root     other      103306 Apr  6 03:04 file4
```

```
# zip dir1.zip dir1/*
  adding: dir1/file1 (deflated 33%)
  adding: dir1/file2 (deflated 59%)
  adding: dir1/file3 (deflated 68%)
  adding: dir1/file4 (deflated 68%)

# rm -r dir1

# ls -l
total 88
-rw-r--r--   1 root     other      44284 Apr  6 03:15 dir1.zip

# unzip dir1.zip
Archive:  dir1.zip
  inflating: dir1/file1
  inflating: dir1/file2
  inflating: dir1/file3
  inflating: dir1/file4

# ls -lR
total 90
drwxr-xr-x   2 root     other        512 Apr  6 03:16 dir1
-rw-r--r--   1 root     other      44284 Apr  6 03:15 dir1.zip

./dir1:
total 296
-rw-r--r--   1 root     other         27 Apr  6 03:04 file1
-rw-r--r--   1 root     other        389 Apr  6 03:04 file2
-rw-r-----   1 root     other      34341 Apr  6 03:04 file3
-rw-r--r--   1 root     other     103306 Apr  6 03:04 file4
#
```

# Backing Up and Restoring

Solaris 8 provides utilities to back up and restore not only entire file systems but also directories and even selected files. A magnetic tape is typically used to back up data, but other media, such as hard disks, writable CDs, and even diskettes, can be used.

A magnetic tape can contain more than one grouping of data, or *data set*. In some cases a data set might be a single file. Usually, the data set is a collection of files written to a tape as a single unit. The data sets are separated by an End Of File (EOF) mark and are composed of any number of records or blocks. The size of the block is determined by the command used to store the data on the tape.

## The mt Command

The **mt**(1) command is used to control magnetic tape operations, including positioning the tape to the beginning of a data set, rewinding the tape, and even erasing the tape. Table 9.6 lists the **mt** operations you can specify as command-line arguments. Most operations expect a value as another command-line argument that specifies the number of times the operation should be repeated (shown in the table as ***count***). If ***count*** is not specified, the operation is performed once.

If a raw tape device is not specified following the **-f** command-line argument, the default tape device /dev/rmt/0n is assumed. The following listing positions a tape to the fifth data set (that is, skips over four EOF marks):

```
# mt -f /dev/rmt/0n fsf 4
#
```

## The ufsdump and ufsrestore Commands

The **ufsdump**(1M) and **ufsrestore**(1M) commands are used to back up and restore UFS file systems or specified files/directories. These commands can perform incremental backup and restore using the file modification date as the selection criterion.

### Dumping a File System Using the ufsdump Command

The **ufsdump** command provides several command-line arguments. Most of them relate to changing the default characteristics of the backup media. Table 9.7 lists the more significant command-line arguments of the **ufsdump** command.

**Table 9.6 The mt operations.**

| Command | Description |
|---|---|
| **asf *count*** | Positions the tape after the ***count***–1 EOF mark |
| **bsf *count*** | Skips backward over ***count*** EOF marks |
| **bsr *count*** | Skips backward over ***count*** records |
| **eof *count*** | Writes ***count*** EOF marks |
| **eom** | Skips forward to a position after the last data set |
| **erase** | Erases the entire tape |
| **fsf *count*** | Skips forward over ***count*** EOF marks |
| **fsr *count*** | Skips forward over ***count*** records |
| **rewind** | Rewinds the tape |
| **status** | Displays status of tape drive |

**Table 9.7 The ufsdump command-line arguments.**

| Argument | Description |
|---|---|
| **0** through **9** | Dump level (**0** is the entire file system) |
| **a** ***archive_file*** | Uses ***archive_file*** to store a dump table of the contents |
| **c** | Uses cartridge tape instead of standard half-inch reel tape |
| **f** ***dump_file*** | Uses ***dump_file*** instead of /dev/rmt/0 |
| **u** | Records the dump level and date in /etc/dumpdates |
| **v** | Verifies the dump media after backup |

You specify these single-character arguments together as a single group followed by the files (*archive_file*, *dump_file*, and so on) in the same order as the single-character arguments. Along with the appropriate command-line arguments, you must specify the files to dump (typically a logical raw device name of a file system).

> To ensure a usable backup, the file system should be unmounted or the system should be in the single-user run level before the backup is performed.

If no command-line arguments other than the files are specified to dump, the default is **9uf /dev/rmt/0**. This command creates a dump level 9 backup using /dev/rmt/0 as the dump file and records the backup in the /etc/dumpdates file.

The dump level determines which files are backed up. If **0** is specified, the entire file system is backed up; otherwise, all files that have changed since the backup using a lower-numbered dump level are backed up. The following line uses **ufsdump** to back up the entire file system identified by its logical raw device name, /dev/rdsk/c0t1d0s5, to the default tape device (/dev/rmt/0). The backup is verified:

```
# ufsdump 0vu /dev/rdsk/c0t1d0s5
```

## Restoring a File System Using the ufsrestore Command

The **ufsrestore** command restores a file system backed up using the **ufsdump** command. Like the **ufsdump** command, the **ufsrestore** command supports an f *dump_file* command-line argument for identifying the media that contains the backup. If this argument is not specified, the /dev/rmt/0 device is used by default. The following line uses the **ufsrestore** command to restore a file system backup from the /dev/rmt/1 device to the current directory:

```
# ufsrestore f /dev/rmt/1
```

The **ufsrestore** command also supports an interactive restore capability that is enabled using the **i** command-line argument.

### Restoring Selected Files Using the ufsrestore Command

You can use the **ufsrestore** command's extract (**x**) command-line argument to restore selected files from a backup instead of the entire file system. The files or directories to be restored from the backup are also listed as command-line arguments on the **ufsrestore** command. The following line extracts the /etc/passwd file and the /etc/default directory (and its contents) from a backup of the root file system on the /dev/rmt/1 device and restores them to the /etc directory:

```
# ufsrestore xf /dev/rmt/1 /etc/passwd /etc/default
```

## The tar Command

The **tar**(1) command creates a tape archive and adds or extracts files from the archive. Table 9.8 lists the five basic functions of the **tar** command.

Along with these functions, the **f** ***tar_file*** command-line argument specifies a backup device. If this command-line argument is not used, either the backup device specified by the **TAPE** environmental variable or the backup device identified in the /etc/default/tar file is used. The files or directories to be backed up are listed as command-line arguments after the function and argument. You can use the **v** option to display the names of files as they are added to or extracted from the archive.

In some situations, using the **tar** command to create a single archive of directories and files will result in an archive that uses less space than all the original files and directories. Thus, using the **tar** command can reduce storage space requirements.

### Backing Up a Directory Using the tar Command

The following line uses the **tar** command to back up the /export/home directory to the /dev/rmt/0 tape drive:

```
# tar cf /dev/rmt/0 /export/home
```

**Table 9.8 The tar functions.**

| Function | Description |
|---|---|
| c | Creates (overwrites) a tape archive |
| r | Replaces the named files in a tape archive |
| t | Lists the files in a tape archive |
| u | Updates the named files in a tape archive |
| x | Extracts all the named files from a tape archive |

### Restoring a Directory Using the tar Command

The following line uses the **tar** command to restore the /export/home directory from the /dev/rmt/0 tape drive:

```
# tar xf /dev/rmt/0 /export/home
```

## The cpio Command

You can also use the **cpio**(1) command to create an archive of directories and files. The **cpio** command operates in three modes:

- *Copy out (-o command-line argument)*—Reads a list of directory and file names and then copies their contents and control information to an archive format
- *Copy in (-i command-line argument)*—Reads an archive to extract the directories and files and re-creates them at a specified location on the system
- *Pass (-p command-line argument)*—Reads a list of directories/files (along with their contents) and reproduces them at a specified location on the system

Table 9.9 lists the most commonly used **cpio** command-line arguments. See the **cpio**(1) manual page for details.

The following listing shows some typical uses of the **cpio** command. The first **cpio** command uses the output of the **ls** command to generate a list of files to

**Table 9.9 Selected cpio command-line arguments.**

| Argument | Description |
|---|---|
| -a | Resets file access times (used with **-i**) |
| -A | Appends to an archive (used with **-o**) |
| -d | Creates directories as needed (used with **-i** and **-p**) |
| -i | Copies in (extracts from an archive) |
| -I *file* | Reads the contents of ***file*** as an input archive (used with **-i**) |
| -L | Follows symbolic links (used with **-o** and **-p**) |
| -m | Retains modification times (used with **-i** and **-p**) |
| -o | Copies out (creates an archive) |
| -O *file* | Uses ***file*** as an output archive (used with **-o**) |
| -p | Passes input to output |
| -t | Prints an archive table of contents; no files are created (used with **-i**) |
| -u | Copies files unconditionally; older files will overwrite newer files (used with **-i** and **-p**) |
| -v | Prints file names (verbose mode) |

place in the file named archive. The second **cpio** command lists the contents of archive. The third **cpio** command extracts files from archive:

```
# ls
file1  file2  file3  file4

# ls | cpio -ov -O archive
file1
file2
file3
file4
272 blocks

# cpio -ivt -I archive
-rw-r--r--    1 root     other          27 Apr  6 03:04 2001, file1
-rw-r--r--    1 root     other         389 Apr  6 03:04 2001, file2
-rw-r-----    1 root     other       34341 Apr  6 03:04 2001, file3
-rw-r--r--    1 root     other      103306 Apr  6 03:04 2001, file4
272 blocks

# cpio -ivum -I archive
file1
file2
file3
file4
272 blocks
#
```

## The find Command

You can use the **find**(1) command to generate a list of files (that is, their names) under a particular directory or a list of file names that meet specified criteria. The **find** command is especially useful when combined with the **cpio** command.

At a minimum, one command-line argument is required: the name of the directory. By default, the directory and all files and directories under it are also listed. The **find** command provides a variety of command-line arguments. Table 9.10 lists some of the more useful ones.

To make the **find** command even more powerful (and harder to figure out), these command-line arguments can be combined into complex expressions using the *and* (**-a**) and *or* (**-o**) operators. For example, the expression **-type p -a -user dla** will cause **find** to list only plain (ordinary) files owned by the user account dla.

The following listing uses the **find** command to generate a list of files. The first **find** command lists all files under the /export/home/sarah directory. This list of files is used to generate the sarah.cpio archive. The second **cpio** command lists the

**Table 9.10 Selected find command-line arguments.**

| Argument | Description |
|---|---|
| **-atime *n*** | List only files accessed ***-n*** (less than ***n*** days ago) or ***+n*** (more than ***n*** days ago). |
| **-ctime *n*** | List only files whose status changed ***-n*** (less than ***n*** days ago) or ***+n*** (more than ***n*** days ago). |
| **-exec *cmd*** | Execute ***cmd*** for each listed file. |
| **-group *grp*** | List only files that belong to the group name of GID ***grp***. |
| **-mtime *n*** | List only files modified ***-n*** (less than ***n*** days ago) or ***+n*** (more than ***n*** days ago). |
| **-name *pattern*** | List only files whose name matches ***pattern***. |
| **-newer *file*** | List only files that are newer than ***file***. |
| **-print** | Print the selected files (always true even if not specified). |
| **-type *c*** | List only the specified type of file (***b***lock, ***c***haracter, ***d***irectory, ***D***oor, ***f***ifo, ***l***ink, ***p***lain, or ***s***ocket. |
| **-user *usr*** | List only files owned by user name or UID *usr*. |

files under /etc that have been modified in the last two days. The same command is repeated and used as input for the **cpio** command to create the etc.cpio archive:

```
# find /export/home/sarah | cpio -o -O sarah.cpio
544 blocks

# find /etc -mtime -2
/etc/saf/zsmon/_pmpipe
/etc/saf/_sacpipe
/etc/mnttab
/etc/utmppipe

# find /etc/ -mtime -2 | cpio -o -O etc.cpio
16 blocks
#
```

## Recovering the root or /usr File System

Occasionally, the root or /usr file system needs to be recovered. Assuming that the file system has been backed up and that the backup is available, you can use the following procedure:

1. Select an available partition or, if additional hardware is required, install the new disk in the system and then format and create an appropriately sized partition.

2. Create a file system using the **newfs** command or another command (such as the **mkfs** command).
3. Mount the new file system on a temporary mount point. Change the directory to the temporary mount point.
4. Use the **ufsrestore** command to restore the root or /usr backup to the new file system.
5. Remove the restoresymtable file created by the **ufsrestore** command.
6. Unmount the new file system.
7. Use the **fsck** command to check the new file system. Modify /etc/vfstab to identify the new root or /usr partition.
8. If you're recovering the root file system, use the **installboot**(1M) command to create a boot block on the new file system.
9. Reboot the system.

# Practice Questions

## Question 1

Which of the following can be backed up using the **ufsdump** command? [Select all that apply]

- ❑ a. File systems on hard disks
- ❑ b. Files on hard disks
- ❑ c. File systems on CD-ROMs
- ❑ d. Directories on hard disks

Answers a, b, and d are correct. You can back up file systems, files, and directories on hard disks using the **ufsdump** command. File systems on CD-ROMs are not UFS file systems and cannot be backed up using the **ufsdump** command. Therefore, answer c is incorrect.

## Question 2

Enter the command that can be used to instruct the Volume Manager daemon to mount a diskette.

______________________________

The correct answer is **volcheck**.

## Question 3

Which command-line argument is used to disable support for files larger than 2GB in size?

- ❍ a. **-o no2gfiles**
- ❍ b. **-o nobigfiles**
- ❍ c. **-o largefiles**
- ❍ d. **-o nolargefiles**

Answer d is correct. The **-o nolargefiles** command-line argument disables support for files larger than 2GB in size. **-o no2gfiles** and **-o nobigfiles** are not valid command-line arguments. Therefore, answers a and b are incorrect. **-o largefiles** would enable (not disable) large file support. Therefore, answer c is incorrect.

## Question 4

Which of the following file systems is typically used for user-accessible commands?

- ❍ a. root
- ❍ b. /usr
- ❍ c. /var
- ❍ d. /home

Answer b is correct. The /usr file system is typically used for system commands. The root file system is used for the kernel and device drivers. Therefore, answer a is incorrect. The /var file system is used for logging and spooling. Therefore, answer c is incorrect. The /home file system is used for user home directories. Therefore, answer d is incorrect.

## Question 5

Which of the following commands can be used to create a UFS file system?

- ❍ a. **newfs /dev/rdsk/c0d1s7**
- ❍ b. **mkfs -t UFS /dev/rdsk/c0d1s7**
- ❍ c. **newfs /dev/dsk/c0d1s7**
- ❍ d. **newfs /dev/dsk/c0t1d1s7**

Answer a is correct. The **newfs /dev/rdsk/c0d1s7** creates a UFS file system. The correct command-line argument to specify a UFS file system is **-F**. Therefore, answer b is incorrect. **newfs /dev/dsk/c0d1s7** and **newfs /dev/dsk/c0t1d1s7** use logical *block* device names, but the **newfs** command requires logical *raw* device names. Therefore, answers c and d are incorrect.

## Question 6

Which of the following commands use logical block device names? [Select all that apply]

- ❑ a. **mount**
- ❑ b. **umount**
- ❑ c. **fsck**
- ❑ d. **newfs**

Answers a and b are correct. The **mount** and **umount** commands use logical block device names. **umount** can also use a mount point. **fsck** and **newfs** both use logical raw device names. Therefore, answers c and d are incorrect.

## Question 7

Which of the following types of file systems can be mounted using the **mount** command? [Select all that apply]

- ❑ a. UDF
- ❑ b. UFS
- ❑ c. TMPFS
- ❑ d. HSFS

Answers a, b, c, and d are correct. UDF, UFS, TMPFS, and HSFS file systems all can be mounted using the **mount** command.

## Question 8

Which of the following **tar** commands can be used to back up the /etc directory?

- ❍ a. **tar cvf /dev/rmt/0 /etc**
- ❍ b. **tar cvf /etc /dev/rmt/0**
- ❍ c. **tar -cvf /dev/rmt/0 /etc**
- ❍ d. **tar -cvf /etc/ dev/rmt/0**

Answer a is correct. **tar cvf /dev/rmt/0 /etc** can be used to back up the /etc directory. The proper order of command-line arguments is function, followed by backup device, followed by the files to back up. Therefore, answer b is incorrect. No hyphen is required before **c**. Therefore, answers c and d are incorrect.

## Question 9

Which of the following functions can be performed by the **fsck** command? [Select all that apply]

- ❑ a. Mounting file systems
- ❑ b. Repairing corrupted file systems
- ❑ c. Checking for file system damage
- ❑ d. Displaying the amount of space used by each user

Answers b and c are correct. The **fsck** command can repair corrupted file systems and check for file system damage. Mounting file systems is the function of the **mount** and **mountall** commands. Therefore, answer a is incorrect. Displaying the amount of space used by each user is the function of the **quot** command. Therefore, answer d is incorrect.

## Question 10

Which of the following statements is true about the command **find / -mtime +7 -print | cpio -o -O 7days.cpio**?

- ❍ a. All files and directories under the / directory that were modified seven or more days ago will be used to create the 7days.cpio archive.
- ❍ b. Only files under the / directory that were modified seven or more days ago will be used to create the 7days.cpio archive.
- ❍ c. The command will fail because the **find** command-line arguments are incorrect.
- ❍ d. All files and directories under the / directory that were modified seven or fewer days ago will be used to create the 7days.cpio archive.
- ❍ e. The command will fail because the **cpio** command-line arguments are incorrect.

Answer a is correct. All files and directories under the / directory that were modified seven or more days ago will be used to create the 7days.cpio archive. The specified **find** command will list directories also. Therefore, answer b is incorrect. Nothing is wrong with either the **find** or **cpio** command-line arguments. Therefore, answers c and e are incorrect. The plus (+) that precedes the number of days associated with the **-mtime** command-line argument means *or more*; a minus (-) would imply *or less*. Therefore, answer d is incorrect.

## Question 11

Which of the following commands can be used to create a single archive of one or directories and files? [Select all that apply]

- ❑ a. **compress**
- ❑ b. **tar**
- ❑ c. **gzip**
- ❑ d. **zip**

Answers b and d are correct. Both **tar** and **zip** can be used to create archives of multiple files and directories. The **zip** command will typically reduce the size of files using a data compression algorithm, whereas the **tar** command may or may not reduce storage requirements. The **compress** and **gzip** commands can only compress a single file at a time (no directories). Therefore, answers a and c are incorrect.

## Question 12

Which file contains a list of file systems to mount during system boot or when the **mountall** command is used?

- ❍ a. /etc/vfstab
- ❍ b. /etc/default/fs
- ❍ c. /etc/mnttab
- ❍ d. /etc/autofs

Answer a is correct. The /etc/vfstab file system contains a list of file systems to mount during system boot or when **mountall** is used. /etc/default/fs contains the default file system type. Therefore, answer b is incorrect. /etc/mnttab contains the list of currently mounted file systems. Therefore, answer c is incorrect. The answer /etc/autofs does not exist. Therefore, answer d is incorrect.

## Question 13

Which of the following commands can be used to position a tape loaded in device /dev/rmt/0n to the third data set after the tape has been rewound? [Select all that apply]

- ❑ a. **mt -f /dev/rmt/0n fsf 2**
- ❑ b. **mt fsf 2**
- ❑ c. **mt -f /dev/rmt/0n fsf 3**
- ❑ d. **mt fsf 3**
- ❑ e. **mt asf 3**

Answers a, b, and e are correct. The **mt -f /dev/rmt/0n fsf 2, mt fsf 2,** and **mt asf 3** commands can be used to position a tape loaded in device /dev/rmt/0n to the third data set after the tape has been rewound. The **mt -f /dev/rmt/0n fsf 3** and **mt fsf 3** commands would position the tape to the beginning of the fourth data set. Therefore, answers c and d are incorrect.

## Question 14

Which of the following can be used to link a file across file systems?

- ❍ a. Hard
- ❍ b. Symbolic
- ❍ c. Character special
- ❍ d. Door

Answer b is correct. A symbolic link can be used to link a file across file systems. Hard links reference a file based on its position on the current disk, so it cannot reference a file on another disk. Therefore, answer a is incorrect. Character special and door are types of files, not links. Therefore, answers c and d are incorrect.

## Need to Know More?

Mulligan, John P., *Solaris 8 Essential Reference* (New Riders, Indianapolis, IN, 2001), ISBN 0-7357-1007-4.

Sun Microsystems, *System Administration Guide, Volume* 1. Available in printed form (part number 805-7228-10), on the Web at **docs.sun.com**, and from the online documentation, AnswerBook2, provided with the Solaris 8 operating system.

Sun Microsystems, *System Reference Manual, Section 1 - User Commands*. Available in printed form (part number 806-0624-10), on the Web at **docs.sun.com**, and from the online documentation, AnswerBook2, provided with the Solaris 8 operating system.

Sun Microsystems, *System Reference Manual, Section 1M - Administration Commands*. Available in printed form (part number 806-0625-10), on the Web at **docs.sun.com**, and from the online documentation, AnswerBook2, provided with the Solaris 8 operating system.

10

# System Basics

**Terms you'll need to understand:**

- ✓ The directory tree
- ✓ Metacharacters
- ✓ Absolute and relative pathnames

**Techniques you'll need to master:**

- ✓ Navigating the directory tree using absolute and relative pathnames
- ✓ Selecting directories and files using metacharacters
- ✓ Creating and deleting directories
- ✓ Creating, copying, renaming, and deleting files
- ✓ Using the **vi** text editor
- ✓ Transferring data between systems
- ✓ Executing programs on remote systems

This chapter covers some system basics, including navigating the Unix directory tree, using the **vi** editor, and accessing remote systems. This chapter covers the *Basic Command Syntax, Editor*, and *Remote Connection* test objectives.

# The Unix Directory Tree

The Unix data storage facility is a collection of directories that contain files and other directories. These files and directories are organized in a hierarchical structure with the root (/) directory as the starting point. Thus the Unix data storage is organized in the form of an inverted tree with directories as branches and files as leaves.

## Metacharacters

*Metacharacters* are characters or combinations of characters that can be used to represent all or portions of directory or file names. Metacharacters allow a short phrase to represent a longer directory/file name or even a series of directory/file names. The three standard shells (Bourne, C, and Korn) support the metacharacters listed in Table 10.1.

An example will best illustrate the use of metacharacters. Given a set of files filea, fileb, through filez, you can specify the following metacharacter expressions as an argument to the **ls** command to represent all 26 of these files:

```
ls file[abcdefghijklmnopqrstuvwxzy]
ls file[a-ef-jk-op-tu-z]
ls file[a-mn-z]
ls file[a-z]
ls file*
ls file?
```

Thus metacharacters can be used to reference files that have a common prefix or a common suffix. For example, given a set of C language source code files that all end with the .c extension, you can reference all these files using the ***.c** metacharacter expression.

**Table 10.1 Directory/File name metacharacters.**

| Metacharacter | Description |
|---|---|
| ? | Matches any single character. |
| * | Matches zero or more occurrences of any character. |
| [...] | Represents a set of characters of which any one character can match. Commonly used character sets can be represented as ranges. For example, lowercase letters (**[a-z]**), uppercase letters (**[A-Z]**), and numbers (**[0-9]**) are frequently used. |

## Directory Tree Navigation

When a user logs in to the system, the user is positioned somewhere in the Unix directory tree—typically in the home directory of the user account. The current directory, referred to as the *current working directory*, can be displayed using the **pwd**(1) command.

The user can move around the directory tree using the **cd**(1) command. When used without any command-line arguments, **cd** relocates the user to the directory specified by the **HOME** environmental parameter (typically the home directory of the user account). A new directory can be specified as a command-line argument. If the directory exists and the user has execution permission for that directory, then the user is relocated to that directory. The new directory can be specified using a complete directory name, a partial directory name and metacharacters, or (in a few cases) all metacharacters.

The new directory also can be specified as a *full* or *absolute path name* starting with the root (/) directory, or a *partial* or *relative path name* starting at the current working directory. You can reference the current directory using a single dot (.) and the directory above the current directory (the *parent directory*) using two dots (..). For example:

```
$ pwd
/export/home/dla
$ cd ..
$ pwd
/export/home
$ cd .
$ pwd
/export/home
$ cd /export/home
$ pwd
/export/home
$ cd dla
$ pwd
/export/home/dla
$
```

You can also reference multiple parents in the same path using (..). For example:

```
$ pwd
/export/home/dla
$ cd ../..
$ pwd
/export
$
```

The metacharacters ? and * can also specify directory names. Remember that ? can represent any single character and * can represent any number of any character. Assuming that the home directory dla is the only directory under /export/home that matches all the metacharacter expressions, then all the following commands will result in changing the current working directory to /export/home/dla:

```
cd /export/home/dla
cd /export/home/dl?
cd /export/home/d?a
cd /export/home/d??
cd /export/home/?la
cd /export/home/?l?
cd /export/home/??a
cd /export/home/???
cd /export/home/*
cd /export/home/d*
cd /export/home/*a
cd /export/home/*l*
cd /export/home/?l*
```

EXAM ALERT: Be certain you understand the meaning and use of the *****, **?** and **[ ]** metacharacters used to construct directory paths and file names. Used separately or in combinations, they can simplify specifying long, complex path names or large sets of files.

## Directories

Several commands let you create, move, and delete directories:

- **mkdir**(1)—Creates a directory.
- **mv**(1)—Moves a file or directory.
- **rmdir**(1) or **rm**(1)—Removes a directory.

### Creating Directories Using the mkdir Command

The **mkdir**(1) command creates the directory specified as a command-line argument. The command-line argument can be an absolute (from /) path name or a path name relative to the current directory. The directory will be owned by the user account used to create the directory and by the owner's group. It will be created with access permissions based on the current **umask** or the access permissions specified by the **-m** ***mode*** command-line argument, where ***mode*** is a set of permissions defined using absolute mode format. To create multiple directories, specify them as command-line arguments (separated by spaces).

Normally, the directory in which the new directory is to be created must already exist. However, if you specify the **-p** command-line argument, any necessary parent directories are created first. The following examples show several uses of the **mkdir** command. The first creates a directory using the **umask** permissions. The second creates a directory with specified permissions. The third fails, because a necessary parent directory does not exist. The fourth **mkdir** command uses the **-p** command-line argument to create the parent directory:

```
# mkdir exam

# ls -l exam
total 0

# ls -ld exam
drwxr-xr-x   2 root     other        512 Apr 13 17:32 exam

# mkdir -m 777 test2

# ls -ld test*
drwxr-xr-x   2 root     other        512 Apr 13 17:32 exam
drwxrwxrwx   2 root     other        512 Apr 13 17:33 test2

# mkdir /exam/Solaris/8
mkdir: Failed to make directory "/exam/Solaris/8";
No such file or directory

# mkdir -p /exam/Solaris/8

# ls -lR /exam
/exam:
total 2
drwxr-xr-x   3 root     other        512 Apr 13 17:33 Solaris

/exam/Solaris:
total 2
drwxr-xr-x   2 root     other        512 Apr 13 17:33 8

/exam/Solaris/8:
total 0
#
```

## Moving Directories Using the **mv** Command

The **mv**(1) command moves a directory and its contents just like an ordinary file:

```
# mv /exam /test

# ls -lR /test
/test:
total 2
drwxr-xr-x   3 root     other          512 Apr 13 17:33 Solaris

/test/Solaris:
total 2
drwxr-xr-x   2 root     other          512 Apr 13 17:33 8

/test/Solaris/8:
total 0
```

## Removing Directories Using the rmdir or rm Command

Either the **rmdir**(1) or **rm**(1) command can be used to remove directories. The **rmdir** command removes the directories specified as one or more command-line arguments (separated by spaces). If a directory contains files or other directories, then the remove will fail. If the **-p** command-line argument is specified, then all parent directories that are empty also will be removed. The **-s** command-line argument is used to suppress error messages. For example:

```
# rmdir /test/Solaris/8
# ls -lR /test
/test:
total 2
drwxr-xr-x   2 root     other          512 Apr 13 19:15 Solaris

/test/Solaris:
total 0

# rmdir -p /test/Solaris

# ls -lr /test
/test: No such file or directory
#
```

The **rm**(1) command also removes one or more directories specified as command-line arguments (separated by spaces). Directories can be removed only if the **-R** or **-r** command-line argument is specified. Either of these command-line arguments will recursively remove all files and directories *under* the directory being removed. Note that you can use the **rmdir** command to remove parent directories (directories *above* the directory being removed). For example:

```
# mkdir -p /test/Solaris/8
```

```
# rm /test
rm: /test is a directory

# rm -r /test

# ls -lr /test
/test: No such file or directory
#
```

The **-i** command-line argument provides interactive control over the remove command:

```
# mkdir -p /test/Solaris/8

# rm -r -i /test
rm: examine files in directory /test (yes/no)? y
rm: examine files in directory /test/Solaris (yes/no)? y
rm: examine files in directory /test/Solaris/8 (yes/no)? y
rm: remove /test/Solaris/8: (yes/no)? y
rm: remove /test/Solaris: (yes/no)? y
rm: remove /test: (yes/no)? y
#
```

Normally, if the **rm** command encounters a write-protected file, it will prompt to confirm the file's removal. However, if you specify the **-f** command-line argument, write-protected files are removed without confirmation. The -f command-line argument cannot be specified with **-i** command-line argument.

# Files

Typically, system programs and applications create files. These files can be copied, moved (or renamed), and deleted as required. These operation are performed by the following commands:

- **cp**(1)—Copies one or more files.
- **mv**(1)—Moves or rename files.
- **rm**(1)—Removes one or more files.

## Copying Files Using the cp Command

The **cp**(1) command copies one or more files to another directory or creates a copy of an existing file with a different name. Note that when you're copying multiple files, they cannot be renamed.

When you're copying one or more files to another directory, the last command-line argument is the target directory and all preceding command-line arguments are the files to be copied. The files to be copied can be complete file names, multiple files selected using metacharacters, or any combination. Multiple file names are separated by spaces. In the following examples, the first two **cp** commands copy one file to a different file name. The third command copies several files into another directory:

```
# ls -l
total 224
-rw-r--r--   1 root     other     103306 Apr 13 20:48 file1

# cp file1 file2

# ls -l
total 448
-rw-r--r--   1 root     other     103306 Apr 13 20:48 file1
-rw-r--r--   1 root     other     103306 Apr 13 20:48 file2

# cp file2 xfile

# ls -l
total 672
-rw-r--r--   1 root     other     103306 Apr 13 20:48 file1
-rw-r--r--   1 root     other     103306 Apr 13 20:48 file2
-rw-r--r--   1 root     other     103306 Apr 13 20:48 xfile

# cp xfile file* /tmp

# ls -l /tmp
total 1496
-rw-r--r-- 1 daemon other   19521 Apr  6 00:52 ab2.socat.cache
-rw-r--r-- 1 root   other  103306 Apr  6 02:10 comp
-rw------- 1 root   other  307892 Apr  4 18:57 dtdbcache_:0
-rw-r--r-- 1 root   other  103306 Apr 13 20:49 file1
-rw-r--r-- 1 root   other  103306 Apr 13 20:49 file2
-rw-rw-r-- 1 root   sys      5032 Apr  4 18:56 ps_data
-rw-r--r-- 1 root   other       0 Apr  9 00:45 sdtvolcheck390
-rw-r--r-- 1 root   other  103306 Apr 13 20:49 xfile
#
```

## Moving and Renaming Files Using the mv Command

The **mv**(1) command can be used to:

- Move one or more files to another directory.
- Rename a file in the current directory.
- Move a file to another directory and rename it in the process.

When you're moving one or more files, the last command-line argument is the target directory and all preceding command-line arguments are the files to be moved. The files to be moved can be complete file names, multiple files selected using metacharacters, or any combination. The file names must be separated by spaces. For example:

```
# ls - R /test
/test:
Solaris

/test/Solaris:
8

/test/Solaris/8:
310-011   310-012   sysadmin

# mv /test/Solaris/8/310* /test/Solaris/8/sysadmin

# ls -R /test
/test:
Solaris

/test/Solaris:
8

/test/Solaris/8:
sysadmin

/test/Solaris/8/sysadmin:
310-011  310-012
#
```

A single file can be renamed in the current directory or moved to another directory and renamed at the same time. In the following example, the first **mv** command renames the 310-011 file. The second command moves it to another directory (the parent or .. directory). The third command moves the 310-012 file to the parent directory and renames it at the same time:

```
# ls
310-011  310-012

# mv 310-011 part1

# mv part1 ..

# mv 310-012 ../part2
#
```

### Deleting Files Using the rm Command

The **rm**(1) command deletes one or more files specified as command-line arguments. The files to be deleted can be complete file names, multiple files selected using metacharacters, or any combination. Multiple file names must be separated by spaces. The **-i** command-line argument provides interactive control over the remove command. Normally, if the **rm** command encounters a write-protected file, it will prompt to confirm the file's removal. However, if you specify the **-f** command-line argument, write-protected files are removed with confirmation. The **-f** command-line argument cannot be specified with **-i** command-line argument. For example:

```
# ls
file1  file2  xfile

# rm xfile file*

# ls
#
```

File and directory names that begin with a dot character, such as .profile, are not included in multiple file/directory specifications using metacharacters. For example, ***profile** does not include .profile. A file that begins with a dot must be specified separately using a preceding dot, as in **.p***.

## The vi Editor

The **vi**(1) command is a screen-oriented text editor. In this section, we will cover the three modes of operation, controlling the cursor position, manipulating text (add, delete, copy, and move), and search/replace functions.

*Note: In this description of the* **vi** *text editor, we use the symbols < and > to define a key that you should press on the keyboard. For example,* **<a>** *indicates that you should press the key labeled "a", and* **<Enter>** *indicates that you should press the key labeled "Enter" or "Return".*

### Modes of Operation

The **vi** editor has three modes of operation:

- Command
- Input
- Last Line

Command mode is the initial and default mode of operation. In this mode, file navigation is supported so that you can view different parts of the file. You control the view by using commands to scroll the file forward or backward (vertically on the screen) and to move between the left and right side of the display. Character, word, and line deletion is also supported in Command mode.

Input mode allows text to be added, deleted or modified. This mode provides a variety of commands to manipulate the text contents of a file.

Last Line mode supports the input of commands to save changes, perform searches, and execute other **ex**(1) and **ed**(1) commands.

## Command Mode

The main functions of Command mode are navigation and deletion. Navigation allows you to position the cursor at a desired location within the file. You can then perform deletion or Input mode operations (add or modify) on the file contents.

### Cursor Positioning

Table 10.2 lists the commonly used cursor-positioning keyboard sequences. See the **vi**(1) manual page for additional commands.

Note that there are two sets of single character/line cursor positioning commands. One set uses the dedicated cursor (arrow) keys and the other uses the lowercase alphabet keys. These dual commands allow the **vi** text editor to be used with

**Table 10.2 Cursor-positioning (Command mode) keyboard sequences for the vi editor.**

| Sequence | Description |
|---|---|
| **<up arrow>** | Moves the cursor up one line. |
| **<down arrow>** | Moves the cursor down one line. |
| **<left arrow>** | Moves the cursor left one character. |
| **<right arrow>** | Moves the cursor right one character. |
| **<h>** | Moves the cursor left one character. |
| **<j>** | Moves the cursor down one line. |
| **<k>** | Moves the cursor up one line. |
| **<l>** | Moves the cursor right one character. |
| **<Ctrl><f>** | Moves forward an entire screen. |
| **<Ctrl><b>** | Moves backward an entire screen. |
| **<Ctrl><d>** | Moves forward half a screen. |
| **<Ctrl><u>** | Moves backward half a screen. |

keyboards that do not have the cursor keys or that for some reason the cursor keys are not recognized by the **vi** text editor. Also note that you can enter a number before each of these cursor-positioning commands to position the cursor by multiple lines or characters at a time. For example, **20j** moves the cursor down 20 lines and **10<right arrow>** moves the cursor 10 characters to the right.

### Text Deletion

Deletion is also supported in Command mode. Table 10.3 lists the commonly used text-deletion keyboard sequences.

As with the cursor-positioning commands, you can enter a number before each of these text-deletion commands to delete characters, words, or lines at a time. For example, **5x** deletes the next five characters and **10dd** deletes the next 10 lines.

Know the purpose of Command mode along with the cursor-positioning and text-deletion keyboard sequences. Also keep in mind that Command mode is the default mode.

## Input Mode

Input mode provides the ability to manipulate text. That is, you can insert (before the cursor), append (after the cursor), change, and replace text. Table 10.4 lists the Input mode keyboard sequences used to manipulate text. You enter Input mode from Command mode, and it remains in effect until you terminate it by pressing the <Esc> key (except **r**, which is in affect for only one character). Then, the **vi** editor is returned to Command mode.

You can combine the <**c**> keystroke with <**w**> to change the current word (**cw**) or with <**$**> to change the rest of the current line (**c$**).

Know the purpose of Input mode along with the text-manipulation keyboard sequences. Also keep in mind that **<Esc>** terminates Input mode and returns the **vi** editor to Command mode.

**Table 10.3 Text-deletion (Command mode) keyboard sequences for the vi editor.**

| Sequence | Description |
|---|---|
| **<x>** | Deletes the current character. |
| **<d><w>** | Deletes the current word. |
| **<d><d>** | Deletes the current line. |

**Table 10.4 Text-manipulation (Input mode) keyboard sequences for the vi editor.**

| Key | Description |
|---|---|
| <a> | Appends after the cursor. |
| <A> | Appends to the end of the file. |
| <i> | Inserts before the cursor. |
| <I> | Inserts before the first non-blank. |
| <c> | Changes the line. |
| <C> | Changes the rest of the line. |
| <o> | Inserts a new line below the current line. |
| <O> | Inserts a new line above the current line. |
| <r> | Replaces a character. |
| <R> | Replaces text. |
| <s> | Substitutes a character. |
| <S> | Substitutes a line. |

Last Line mode is used to perform searches and enter commands associated with the **ed** and **ex** line-oriented text editors. You enter Last Line mode from Command mode by pressing any of the following three keyboard characters:

- *Colon* <:>—Specifies **ed** or **ex** commands; mainly file control commands (such as writing the file) or executing a shell command.
- *Forward slash* </>—Performs a search for a text pattern in the file starting from the current position and searching toward the end of the file.
- *Question mark* <?>—Performs a search for a text pattern in the file starting from the current position and searching toward the beginning of the file.

Once you're in Last Line mode, you can specify the desired operation. When you press <Enter>, the specified operation is performed and the **vi** editor returns to Command mode.

### File Control and Execution

Table 10.5 lists some of the common Last Line mode keyboard sequences used for file control and command execution. See the **vi**(1) manual page for more information.

### Text Search

Table 10.6 lists some of the common Last Line mode keyboard sequences used to perform test searches. See the **vi**(1) manual page for more information.

**Table 10.5 File-control and -execution (Last Line mode) keyboard sequences for the vi editor.**

| Sequence | Description |
|---|---|
| **<:><e>*name*** | Edits the ***name*** file. |
| **<:><e><!>** | Discards changes and re-edits. |
| **<:><w>** | Writes changes to a file. |
| **<:><w><!>** | Writes changes regardless of file permission. |
| **<:><q>** | Quits. |
| **<:>q><!>** | Discards changes and quits. |
| **<:><!>*cmd*** | Executes the specified ed or ex ***cmd*** command. |

**Table 10.6 Text search (Last Line mode) keyboard sequences for the vi editor.**

| Sequence | Description |
|---|---|
| **</>*text*</>** | Searches forward for ***text*** (trailing slash optional). |
| **<?>*text*<?>** | Searches backward for ***text*** (trailing question mark optional). |

If the text is found, the cursor is positioned at the beginning of the specified text. When the end (or beginning) of the file in encountered, the search continues at the beginning (or end) of the file contents. Press </> or <?> followed by **<Enter>** repeats the last search.

## Text Search and Replace

The **vi** editor supports text search-and-replace functions. They combine the ability to search-and-replace the located text into a single operation. Table 10.7 lists the text search and replace keyboard sequences.

Note that **g** is used to denote a global search and that there are two meanings of "global". The first refers to the current line. A global replacement affects all occurrences on the current line as opposed to just the first occurrence. Thus the **g** at the end of the keyboard sequence refers to all occurrences on the current line. The second meaning of "global" refers to all lines.

Two mechanisms address all lines. The first uses the **1,$** sequence to indicate all lines. When this sequence is used with the **s///** sequence, **vi** attempts search and replace on all lines in the file. The second mechanism uses the **g/*old*/** sequence to locate all lines that contain the phrase ***old***. When this sequence is used with the **s///** sequence to perform a replacement, the ***old*** text does not need to be specified within the first field of the **s///** sequence. Although both **1,$s/*old*/*new*/** and **g/*old*/s//*new*/** use different approaches, the results are the same. That is, the first

**Table 10.7 Text search and replace (Last Line mode) keyboard sequences for the vi editor.**

| Sequence | Description |
|---|---|
| **<:><s></>*old*</>*new*</>** | Searches the current line for the first occurrence of ***old*** and replaces it with ***new*** (trailing slash optional). |
| **<:><s></>*old*</>*new*</><g>** | Searches the current line for all occurrences of ***old*** and replaces them with ***new***. |
| **<:><1><,><$><s></>*old*</>*new*</>** | Searches for the first occurrence of ***old*** on all lines and replaces them with ***new*** (trailing slash optional). |
| **<:><1><,><$><s></>*old*</>*new*</><g>** | Searches for all occurrences of ***old*** on all lines and replaces them with ***new***. |
| **<:><g></>old</><s></></>*new*</>** | Searches for the first occurrence of ***old*** on all lines and replaces them with ***new*** (trailing slash optional). |
| **<:><g></>*old*</><s></></>*new*</><g>** | Searches for all occurrences of ***old*** on all lines and replaces them with ***new***. |

occurrence of *old* in every line is replaced with *new*. Note that you can add a <g> to the end of both these command to affect all occurrences of *old*.

EXAM ALERT: Know the purpose of Last Line mode along with the file control, search, and search-and-replace keyboard sequences. Also keep in mind that **<Enter>** terminates Last Line mode and returns the **vi** editor to Command mode.

# Accessing Remote Systems

Solaris 8 provides several commands to perform remote login, remote copy, and remote execution of commands:

- **telnet**(1)—Remote Network Terminal utility
- **ftp**(1)—File Transfer Protocol utility
- **rlogin**(1)—Remote login
- **rcp**(1)—Remote copy
- **rsh**(1)—Remote shell execution

The **ftp** and **telnet** commands both require the user to log in to the remote system using a valid user account name and password setup on the remote system. The **rlogin**, **rcp**, and **rsh** commands are collectively referred to as the "r commands" and all can use the remote authentication database in place of requiring a user account name and password to validate the user.

## Remote Login

Two commands provide the ability to log in to a remote system as a local user over the network. These are the **telnet** command and the **rlogin** command.

### The telnet Command

The **telnet** command is used to log in remotely to a system over the network. The user must provide a valid user account name and password as defined on the remote system, because the **telnet** command uses standard Unix login/password authentication.

The hostname or IP address of the remote system is typically specified as a command-line argument. If this address is not specified, then the **telnet** command is placed in an interactive mode. The remote system prompts for a user account name and password. The following example uses the **telnet** command to log in to the remote system solaris8 using the dla user account name:

```
$ telnet solaris8
Trying 192.168.99.8...
Connected to solaris8.
Escape character is '^]'.


SunOS 5.8

login: dla
Password:
Last login: Sat Feb  3 22:34:56 from winnt40
Sun Microsystems Inc.   SunOS 5.8       Generic February 2000
$
```

### The rlogin Command

The **rlogin** command also can be used to log in remotely to a system over the network. If the remote authentication database has been set up properly, the user might be able to log in without providing a valid user account name and password. This capability is described later in this chapter.

If this database has not been set up properly, the user must, as with the **telnet** command, provide a valid user account name and password as defined on the remote system. If the user account name executing the **rlogin** command on the local system exists on the remote system, then the user account name is not required (it is assumed to be the same as the user account name of the local system). If another user account is to be used on the remote system, then the user account name must be specified with the **rlogin** command-line using the **-l** command-line argument.

The following listing shows three examples of using the **rlogin** command to log in to the remote system solaris8. In the first example, the database has been set up to allow the local user account (dla) to log in to the same user account on the remote system. In the second example, the database has not been set up. The user account name dla is assumed and a prompt is issued for a password. In the third example, a different user account is used (sarah) and the user account name is specified as the **rlogin -l** command-line argument:

```
$ rlogin solaris8
Last login: Sun Feb  4 21:32:12 from solaris8
Sun Microsystems Inc.   SunOS 5.8       Generic February 2000
$

$ rlogin solaris8
Password:
Last login: Sun Feb  4 21:33:45 from solaris8
Sun Microsystems Inc.   SunOS 5.8       Generic February 2000
$

$ rlogin -l sarah solaris8
Password:
Last login: Sun Feb  4 21:28:44 from solaris8
Sun Microsystems Inc.   SunOS 5.8       Generic February 2000
$
```

## Remote Copy

Two commands are available to copy files between systems. These are the **ftp**(1) command and the **rcp**(1) command.

### The **ftp** Command

The **ftp** command copies one or more files between a local system and a remote system over the network. The user must provide a valid user account name and password as defined on the remote system, because the **ftp** command uses standard Unix login/password authentication.

The hostname or IP address of the remote system is typically specified as a command-line argument. If this address is not specified, then the **ftp** command is placed in an interactive mode. The remote system will prompt for a user account name and password.

Once you've logged in to the remote system, you can transfer files between the systems by issuing the appropriate **ftp** subcommand. To copy a file from the local system to the remote system, use the **put** subcommand. To copy a file from the remote system to the local system, use the **get** subcommand. Table 10.8 lists the commonly used **ftp** subcommands.

**Table 10.8 Commonly used ftp subcommands.**

| Subcommand | Description |
|---|---|
| **?** | Lists **ftp** subcommands. |
| **ascii** | Sets the transfer mode to ASCII (performs end-of-line character mapping). ASCII is the default mode. |
| **binary** | Sets the transfer to binary (does not perform end-of-line character mapping). |
| **cd** ***path*** | Changes the remote current directory to ***path***. |
| **get** ***remote local*** | Copies the file ***remote*** from the remote system to the file ***local*** on the local system. If ***local*** is not specified, the file is given the same name on the local system. |
| **hash** | Prints a pound (#) character for every 8,912 bytes sent or received. |
| **help** ***subcommand*** | Displays a short description of ***subcommand***. |
| **lcd** ***path*** | Changes the local current directory to ***path***. |
| **ls** | Lists the contents of the remote current directory. |
| **mget** ***meta*** | Copies multiple files from the remote system to the local system. A set of files is specified by ***meta***, which is an expression with one or more metacharacters. |
| **mput** ***meta*** | Copies multiple files from the local system to the remote system. A set of files is specified by ***meta***, which is an expression with one or more metacharacters. |
| **put** ***local remote*** | Copies the file ***local*** from the local system to the file ***remote*** on the remote system. If ***remote*** is not specified, the file is given the same name on the remote system. |
| **quit** | Exits the **ftp** command. |

The following example uses the **ftp** command to access the remote system solaris8 using the dla user account name. Various subcommands (in italics) are used to transfer files between systems:

```
$ ftp solaris8
Connected to solaris8.
220 solaris8 FTP server (SunOS 5.8) ready.
Name (solaris8:dla): dla
331 Password required for dla.
Password:
230 User dla logged in.
ftp> cd /tmp
250 CWD command successful.
ftp> ls
200 PORT command successful.
```

```
150 ASCII data connection for /bin/ls (0 bytes).
ab2.socat.cache
dtdbcache_:0
file.txt
mp5eaaNc
mpfnaOFc
mpjAaWMc
mpqvaOMc
ps_data
sdtvolcheck388
226 ASCII Transfer complete.
100 bytes received in 0.0032 seconds (30.14 Kbytes/s)
ftp> lcd /export/home/dla
Local directory now /export/home/dla
ftp> get file.txt
200 PORT command successful.
150 ASCII data connection for xx  (3448 bytes).
226 ASCII Transfer complete.
local: file.txt remote: file.txt
3529 bytes received in 0.0044 seconds (776.02 Kbytes/s)
ftp> binary
200 Type set to I.
ftp> mget mp*
mget mp5eaaNc? n
mget mpfnaOFc? y
200 PORT command successful.
150 ASCII data connection for mpfnaOFc  (16198 bytes).
226 ASCII Transfer complete.
local: mpfnaOFc remote: mpfnaOFc
16726 bytes received in 0.0074 seconds (2219.89 Kbytes/s)
mget mpjAaWMc? y
200 PORT command successful.
150 ASCII data connection for mpjAaWMc  (0 bytes).
226 ASCII Transfer complete.
mget mpqvaOMc? n
ftp> quit
221 Goodbye.
```

## The rcp Command

You can also use the **rcp**(1) command to copy a specified file from the local system to the specified remote system. The destination is specified as ***host*:*path*** where ***host*** is the name of the remote system and ***path*** is the full path to either a directory or a file. If a different user account is being used on the remote system, then it is specified before the ***host*** separated by a @ symbol. The **rcp** command uses the remote authentication database.

The following listing shows the dla user account on the local system attempting to copy a file to the home directories of two different user accounts on the remote "system solaris 8". Note that the second attempt fails, because the remote authentication database on the remote system does not allow the local dla user account to access the remote sarah user account:

```
$ rcp /tmp/file.txt solaris8:/export/home/dla/file.txt
$ rcp /tmp/file.txt sarah@solaris8:/export/home/sarah/file.txt
permission denied
$
```

## Remote Shell Execution

The **rsh**(1) command can be used to execute a command on a remote system. The **remsh** command is a symbolic link to the **rsh** command.

### The rsh Command

The **rsh** command executes a command on a remote system. At a minimum, two command-line arguments are required: the name of the remote host and the command to be executed. As with the other r commands, the remote authentication database is used. If the desired remote user account is not the same as the local user account, then it is identified using the **-l** command-line argument. In the following examples, the **ls** command is executed for the /tmp directory on the remote system solaris8:

```
$ rsh solaris8 "ls /tmp"
ab2.socat.cache
dtdbcache_:0
file.txt
mp5eaaNc
mpfnaOFc
mpjAaWMc
mpqvaOMc
ps_data
sdtvolcheck388
$
```

## The Remote Authentication Database

The remote authentication database is used to determine which remote hosts and users are considered "trusted". The **rlogin**, **rsh**, and **rcp** commands (collectively known as the "r commands") use the remote authentication database. This database consists of two types of files: the /etc/host.equiv file, which applies to the entire system, and the .rhosts files, which apply to individual user accounts and are located in the home directories of user accounts.

You use the remote authentication database to determine whether a user on a remote system can access the local system using the same user account. For example, if the "guest" account on a remote system is authorized to access the local system and then does so using the **rlogin** command, the user is automatically logged in to the local system as "guest" without providing a user account name and a password.

The remote authentication procedure first checks to determine whether the hostname of the remote system is listed in the /etc/hosts.equiv file. If it is listed, remote authentication succeeds and the user is granted access.

If the hostname of the remote system is not listed, the remote authentication continues. The home directory of the local user account name (that matches the user account name of the remote user) is checked to determine whether the hostname of the remote system is listed in the .rhosts file. If it is listed, remote authentication succeeds and the user is granted access to the local system. If it is not listed, remote authentication fails and the user is prompted for a local user account name and password.

Both files consist of a list of hostnames (one per line). A hostname by itself or preceded by a plus sign (+) is considered a trusted host and allowed access. If a hostname is preceded by a minus sign (-), the host is considered untrusted and denied access.

Optionally, a hostname can be followed by a user account name. If this form is used in the /etc/hosts.equiv file and the remote user account matches the specified user account name, the user is given access as any user. If the user is allowed to access the system using any user account, then the user either provides the user account as a command-line option to the **rlogin** command or is prompted for it. If the optional form is used in the .rhosts file, the remote user is given access as the specified user account.

# Practice Questions

## Question 1

Which of the following commands use the remote authentication database to validate users? [Select all that apply]

❑ a. **telnet**

❑ b. **rlogin**

❑ c. **rcp**

❑ d. **ftp**

❑ e. **rsh**

Answers b, c, and e are correct. The r commands (**rlogin**, **rcp**, and **rsh**) use the remote authentication database. The **telnet** and **ftp** commands use only the Unix account name and password for authentication. Therefore, answers a and d are incorrect.

## Question 2

Which **mkdir** command-line argument creates any parent directories as needed?

❍ a. **-P**

❍ b. **-c**

❍ c. **-p**

❍ d. **-m**

Answer c is correct. The **-p** command-line argument of **mkdir** will create any parent directories as needed. **-P**, **-c**, and **-m** are not valid command-line arguments for the **mkdir** command. Therefore, answers a, b, and d are incorrect.

## Question 3

Which of the following **vi** commands will replace all occurrences of the text string ***old*** with the text string ***new***?

❍ a. **:g/*old*/s//*new*/**

❍ b. **:!/*old*/*new*/g**

❍ c. **:s/*old*/*new*/g**

❍ d. **:1,$s/*old*/*new*/**

❍ e. **:1,$s/*old*/*new*/g**

Answer e is correct. The **:1,$s/*old*/*new*/g** command replaces all occurrences of the text string *old* with the text string *new*. The :g/*old*/s//*new*/ and **:1,$s/*old*/*new*/** commands replace the first occurrence of *old* in each line with *new*. Therefore, answers a and d are incorrect. :!/*old*/*new*/g will not work because the ! is used to execute a shell command. Therefore, answer b is incorrect. :s/*old*/*new*/g will replace all occurrences of *old* with *new*, but only for the current line. Therefore, answer c is incorrect.

## Question 4

Match each of the following **ftp** subcommands with its description.

| | |
|---|---|
| a. **binary** | 1. Transfers multiple files to the remote system. |
| b. **hash** | 2. Transfers multiple files to the local system. |
| c. **ascii** | 3. Doesn't map newline characters during transfer. |
| d. **mput** | 4. Maps newline characters during transfer. |
| e. **mget** | 5. Changes the working directory on the local system. |
| f. **lcd** | 6. Prints a "#" for every 8,192 characters transferred. |

Answers a-3, b-6, c-4, d-1, e-2, and f-5 are correct. **binary** mode does not map newlines in transferred data. The **hash** subcommmand marks every 8,192 characters transferred with a "#" character. **ascii** mode maps newlines in transferred data. The **mput** subcommand transfers multiple files to the remote system. The **mget** subcommand transfers multiple files to the local system. The **lcd** subcommand changes the local working directory.

## Question 5

Which of the following is the correct syntax for the **rsh** command?

❍ a. **rsh -c *command* -s *system***

❍ b. **rsh -s *system* -c *command***

❍ c. **rsh *system command***

❍ d. **rsh *command system***

❍ e. **rsh *system:command***

Answer c is correct. The system name should be specified before the command. A space separates the system and the command. The other syntax choices are not valid. Therefore, answers a, b, d, and e are incorrect.

## Question 6

Given the list of files abc, abc123, and 123abc, which of the following metacharacter expressions will select one or more of these files? [Select all that apply]

❑ a. **abc***

❑ b. **?*123**

❑ c. ***2***

❑ d. **??2***

Answers a, b, and c are correct. **abc*** will select abc and abc123. **?*123** will select abc123. ***2*** will select abc123 and 123abc. **??2*** will not select any of the specified files because 2 does not occur as the third character. Therefore, answer d is incorrect.

## Question 7

Which of the following **vi** modes return to Command mode when terminated? [Select all that apply]

❑ a. Input

❑ b. Last Line

❑ c. Search

❑ d. Replace

❑ e. File control

Answers a and b are correct. The Input and Last Line **vi** modes return to Command mode when terminated. Although search, replace, and file control are capabilities, they are not **vi** modes. Therefore, answers c, d, and e are incorrect.

## Question 8

Which of the following is the correct format for the target file of the **rcp** command?

- ❍ a. ***system:file***
- ❍ b. ***system@file***
- ❍ c. ***system!file***
- ❍ d. ***file@system***

Answer a is correct. *system:file* is the correct format for the target file of the **rcp** command. An alternate format is *user@system:file*, where *user* specifies the user that should be the owner of the file. The other formats are not valid. Therefore, answers b, c, and d are incorrect.

# Need to Know More?

Lamb, Linda, *Learning vi* (O'Reilly & Associates, Englewood Cliffs, NJ, 1994), ISBN 0-937175-67-6.

Mulligan, John P., *Solaris 8 Essential Reference* (New Riders, Indianapolis, IN, 2001), ISBN 0-7357-1007-4.

Peek, Jerry, Grace Todino, and John Strang, *Learning the UNIX Operating System* (O'Reilly & Associates, Englewood Cliffs, NJ, 1998), ISBN 1-56592-390-1.

Sorbell, Mark G., *A Practical Guide to Solaris* (Addison-Wesley, Reading, MA, 1999), ISBN 0-201-89548-X.

Sun Microsystems, *System Reference Manual, Section 1 - User Commands.* Available in printed form (part number 806-0624-10), on the Web at **docs.sun.com**, and from the online documentation, AnswerBook2, provided with the Solaris 8 operating system.

11

# Sample Test I

This chapter provides pointers to help you develop a successful test-taking strategy, including how to choose proper answers, how to decode ambiguity, how to work within the Solaris testing framework, how to decide what you need to memorize, and how to prepare for the test. At the end of the chapter are 57 questions on the topics that pertain to Exam 310-011, "Sun Certified System Administrator for Solaris 8, Part I."

Keep in mind that to become certified, you must pass this exam and a second exam (310-012). The sample test for the second exam is in Chapter 22.

## Questions, Questions, Questions

There should be no doubt in your mind that you're facing a test full of specific and pointed questions. The Part I exam is a fixed-length exam; it will include 57 questions, and you'll be allotted 90 minutes to complete it. You'll be required to achieve a score of 66 percent or better to pass the exam.

For this exam, questions belong to one of four types:

- Multiple choice (with a single answer)
- Multiple choice (with multiple answers)
- Multiple match (drag and drop)
- Fill in the blank (free choice)

Always take the time to read a question at least twice before selecting an answer, and always look for an Exhibit button as you examine each question. Exhibits include graphics information related to a question. An exhibit is usually a screen capture of program output or GUI information that you must examine to analyze the question's contents and to formulate an answer. The Exhibit button brings up graphics and charts used to help explain a question, provide additional data, or illustrate program behavior.

Not every question has only one answer; many questions require multiple answers. If you don't select all the correct answers, you will not get credit for answering the question correctly. Therefore, you need to read each question carefully to determine how many answers are necessary or possible and to look for additional hints or instructions when selecting answers. Such instructions often occur in brackets immediately following the question itself (as they do for all multiple-choice, multiple-answer questions). Unfortunately, some questions do not have any straightforward correct answers and you're forced to find the "most correct" choice.

The multiple-match (drag and drop) questions are new to the Solaris exams and require you to match, for example, terms with definitions. On the real exam, you'll use the mouse to drag and drop one part (such as the term) so that it is in front of its definition. These questions will be easy if know all or all but one of the matches. But if you don't know two or more, this type of question could be a problem. We've included several multiple-match questions (more than you'll see on the exam). Because you can't use a mouse on the questions in this book, you'll need to match the a, b, c, ... items with the 1, 2, 3, ... items.

# Picking Proper Answers

Obviously, the only way to pass any exam is to select enough of the correct answers to obtain a passing score. However, the exams are not standardized like the SAT and GRE exams; in some cases, questions are strangely worded, and deciphering them can be a real challenge. In those cases, you might need to rely on answer-elimination skills. You can almost always immediately eliminate at least one answer out of the possible choices for a question because it matches one of these conditions:

- The answer does not apply to the situation.
- The answer describes a nonexistent issue, an invalid option, or an imaginary state.
- The answer can be eliminated because of the question itself.

After you eliminate all answers that are obviously incorrect, you can apply your retained knowledge to eliminate further answers. Look for items that sound correct but that refer to actions, commands, or features that are not present or not available in the situation that the question describes.

If you're still faced with a blind guess among two or more potentially correct answers, reread the question. Try to picture how each of the possible remaining answers would alter the situation. Be especially sensitive to terminology; sometimes the choice of words (*print* instead of *display*) can make the difference between a right answer and a wrong one.

Only when you've exhausted your ability to eliminate answers, but remain unclear about which of the remaining possibilities is correct, should you guess at an answer. An unanswered question offers you no points, but guessing gives you at least some chance of getting a question right; just don't be too hasty when making a blind guess.

**EXAM ALERT** Because you're taking a fixed-length test, you can wait until the last round of reviewing marked questions (just as you're about to run out of time or out of unanswered questions) before you start making guesses. Guessing should be your technique of last resort!

# Decoding Ambiguity

You'll discover that many exam questions test your knowledge of things that are not directly related to the issue that a question raises. This means that the answers you must choose from—even incorrect ones—are just as much a part of the skill assessment as the question itself. If you don't know something about a variety of system administration topics, you might not be able to eliminate obviously wrong answers because they relate to a different area of system administration than the area the question at hand is addressing. In other words, the more you know about Solaris system administration, the easier it will be for you to tell a right answer from a wrong one.

Questions often give away their answers, but you have to be alert to see the clues. Often, subtle hints appear in the question's text in such a way that they seem almost irrelevant to the situation. You must realize that each question is a test unto itself and that you need to inspect and successfully navigate each question to pass the exam. Look for small clues, such as a reference to *raw* as opposed to *block* device names and invalid commands. Little things like these can point at the right answer if you properly understand the question; if missed, they can leave you facing a blind guess.

Another common difficulty with certification exams is vocabulary. Be sure to brush up on the key terms presented at the beginning of each chapter.

## Working within the Framework

The test questions appear in random order, and many elements or issues mentioned in one question might also crop up in other questions. It's not uncommon to find that an incorrect answer to one question is the correct answer to another question and vice versa. Take the time to read every answer to each question, even if you recognize the correct answer to a question immediately. That extra reading might spark a memory or remind you about a function or command that helps you on another question elsewhere in the exam.

Because you're taking a fixed-length test, you can revisit any question as many times as you like. If you're uncertain of the answer to a question, check the box that's provided to mark it for easy return later on. You should also mark questions that you think offer information that you can use to answer other questions. The testing software is designed to let you mark every question if you choose; use this framework to your advantage. Everything you'll want to see again should be marked; the testing software can then help you return to marked questions quickly and easily.

## Deciding What to Memorize

The amount of memorization that you must undertake for an exam depends on how well you remember what you've read and how well you know Solaris system administration by heart. The tests will stretch your recollection of system administration commands and functions.

At a minimum, you'll want to memorize the following kinds of information for Part 1:

- File system administration and maintenance (creating, mounting, backing up, and restoring)
- Commands related to file Access Control Lists (ACLs) and standard access permissions
- Commands related to user administration (creating, modifying, and deleting user/group accounts)
- The basic command syntax and use of metacharacters.

For the Part II exam, be sure to memorize information about:

- NFS
- NIS
- JumpStart

If you work your way through this book while logged in as root to a Solaris 8 system and try to manipulate this environment's features and functions as they're discussed, you should have little or no difficulty mastering this material. In addition, don't forget that the Cram Sheet at the front of the book is designed to capture the material that's most important to memorize; use this to guide your studies as well.

## Preparing for the Test

The best way to prepare for the test—after you've studied—is to take at least one practice exam. One is included in this chapter for that reason; the test questions are located in the pages that follow (and, unlike the preceding chapters in this book, the answers don't follow the questions immediately; you'll have to flip to Chapter 12 to review the answers separately).

Give yourself 90 minutes to take the exam, keep yourself on the honor system, and don't look back at the text in the book or jump ahead to the answer key. When your time is up or you've finished the questions, you can check your work in Chapter 12. Pay special attention to the explanations for the incorrect answers; they can also help reinforce your knowledge of the material. Knowing how to recognize correct answers is good, but understanding why incorrect answers are wrong can be equally valuable.

Also, review all the questions at the end of each chapter. They cover the topics from a different point of view than the questions in this sample test. This review should help you better understand the similarities and differences between related topics.

## Taking the Test

Relax. Once you're sitting in front of the testing computer, there's nothing more you can do to increase your knowledge or preparation. Take a deep breath, stretch, and start reading that first question.

There's no need to rush; you have plenty of time to complete each question and return to those questions that you skip or mark for return. If you read a question twice and remain clueless, you can mark it. Both easy and difficult questions are intermixed throughout the test in random order. Don't cheat yourself by spending too much time on a difficult question early on in the test, thereby depriving yourself of the time you need to answer the questions at the end of the test.

On a fixed-length test, you can read through the entire test and, before returning to marked questions for a second visit, figure out how much time you have to answer each question. As you answer each question, remove its mark. Continue to review the remaining marked questions until you run out of time or you complete the test.

That's it for pointers. Here are some questions for you to practice on.

# Sample Test

## Question 1

Enter the directory where group account membership is stored.

____________________________

## Question 2

Which of the following can be backed up using the **ufsdump** command? [Select all that apply]

- ❑ a. File systems
- ❑ b. Files
- ❑ c. Volume table of contents
- ❑ d. Directories

## Question 3

Match the items of the **format** command Partition submenu with their function.

| | |
|---|---|
| a. **select** | 1. Writes the current partition table to disk. |
| b. **label** | 2. Displays the current partition table. |
| c. **name** | 3. Assigns a label to the current partition table. |
| d. **print** | 4. Selects a partition table. |

## Question 4

Enter the type of file link that references a file based on location in the local file system and that cannot be used to point a file on another file system.

____________________________

## Question 5

Which of the following commands is used to manage the dynamic configuration of hot-plugging devices?

❍ a. **hpadmin**

❍ b. **cfgadm**

❍ c. **attach**

## Question 6

Enter the command used to terminate a process on the basis of its program name.

________________________________

## Question 7

Match the following default file systems with their intended use:

| | |
|---|---|
| a. / (root) | 1. Systems files that change or grow, such as logs or spool areas |
| b. /usr | 2. User home directories |
| c. /home | 3. Kernel and device files |
| d. /var | 4. Third-party software and applications |
| e. /opt | 5. User-accessible system commands and programs |

## Question 8

Which of the following are **-o** command-line arguments for the **mount** command? [Select all that apply]

❑ a. **nosuid**

❑ b. **atime**

❑ c. **nolargefiles**

❑ d. **nomnttab**

## Question 9

Identify the metacharacter used by the shell to match any single character.

______________________________

## Question 10

Which of the following commands can be used to compress files and directories?

❍ a. **compress**

❍ b. **zip**

❍ c. **gzip**

❍ d. **shrink**

## Question 11

Which of the following commands can be used to unmount a CD-ROM and eject it from the CD-ROM drive?

❍ a. **eject cdrom**

❍ b. **eject**

❍ c. **eject -m cd**

❍ d. **eject cd**

❍ e. **eject /cdrom/cdrom0**

## Question 12

Match the **vi** cursor positioning keys based on their direction of cursor movement.

| | |
|---|---|
| a. **h** | 1. **<up arrow>** |
| b. **j** | 2. **<right arrow>** |
| c. **k** | 3. **<left arrow>** |
| d. **l** | 4. **<down arrow>** |

## Question 13

Which of the following files will match the metacharacter expression **[abc][123]**?

❍ a. abc123

❍ b. b2

❍ c. ab2

❍ d. a23

❍ e. ab3

## Question 14

What must be specified when using the **kill** command to terminate a process?

❍ a. The signal to send to the process.

❍ b. The process ID (PID) of the process.

❍ c. The owner (UID) of the process.

❍ d. The name of the process.

## Question 15

Which of the following commands can be used to create a UFS file system? [Select all that apply]

❑ a. **mkfs**

❑ b. **mkfs -F ufs**

❑ c. **mkfs_ufs**

❑ d. **newfs**

## Question 16

When the **mount** command is entered without any command-line arguments, what happens? (Assume that none of the currently mounted files systems was mounted with the **-m mount** command-line argument.) [Select all that apply]

❑ a. All file systems in /etc/vfstab are mounted.

❑ b. All mounted file systems are displayed.

❑ c. All file systems in /etc/vfstab are displayed.

❑ d. All file systems listed in /etc/mnttab are displayed.

## Question 17

What does /dev/dsk/c0t3d0s6 identify?

❍ a. The logical raw device addressed as Controller 0 Target 3 Disk 0 Partition 6.

❍ b. The logical block device addressed as Controller 0 Target 3 Disk 0 Partition 6.

❍ c. The physical raw device addressed as Controller 0 Target 3 Disk 0 Partition 6.

❍ d. The physical block device addressed as Controller 0 Target 3 Disk 0 Partition 6.

## Question 18

Three different characters can be used to enter **vi** Last Line mode. Two are colon (:) and slash (/). What is the third character?

❍ a. %

❍ b. $

❍ c. #

❍ d. ?

## Question 19

Match each of the following types of file systems with its associated hardware device.

| | |
|---|---|
| a. PCFS | 1. DVD |
| b. UFS | 2. CD-ROM |
| c. UDF | 3. Floppy diskette |
| d. HSFS | 4. Disk drive |

## Question 20

Which of the following commands either display or can use logical raw device names? [Select all that apply]

- ❑ a. **format**
- ❑ b. **newfs**
- ❑ c. **fsck**
- ❑ d. **mount**
- ❑ e. **df**
- ❑ f. **prtvtoc**

## Question 21

Which of the following functions can be performed using OpenBoot commands? [Select all that apply]

- ❑ a. Boot the operating system.
- ❑ b. Change the root password.
- ❑ c. View and modify NVRAM parameters.
- ❑ d. Set the system time.
- ❑ e. Run diagnostics.

## Question 22

Enter the command used to display only the PID of a process if only the program name is known.

______________________________

## Question 23

Which of the following commands can be used to log in to a remote system? [Select all that apply]

- ❑ a. **rlogin**
- ❑ b. **login**
- ❑ c. **telnet**
- ❑ d. **rsh**

## Question 24

What information is provided on all process listings generated by the **ps** command? [Select all that apply]

- ❑ a. Program or command name
- ❑ b. Parent process ID
- ❑ c. Process ID
- ❑ d. Associated terminal device

## Question 25

The logical structure of a disk consists of a disk label (volume table of contents) and what?

______________________________

## Question 26

Enter the command used to change file access modes.

______________________________

## Question 27

At which run level is Network File System (NFS) server typically started?

❍ a. 2

❍ b. 3

❍ c. 4

❍ d. 5

## Question 28

Enter the command used to identify the parent process ID of a process.

______________________________

## Question 29

Which command can be used by the guest account to change its password?

❍ a. **admintool**

❍ b. **passmgmt**

❍ c. **usermod**

❍ d. **passwd**

## Question 30

Which of the following files are associated with the remote authentication database? [Select all that apply]

❑ a. /etc/hosts

❑ b. /etc/hosts.equiv

❑ c. .rhosts

❑ d. /etc/system

## Question 31

When a user account is created, the .profile is copied from which file?

❍ a. /etc/skel/default.profile

❍ b. /etc/profile

❍ c. /etc/skel/local.profile

❍ d. /.profile

## Question 32

Which is the preferred method to temporarily prevent a user account from being used?

❍ a. Delete the user account and all files in the home directory of the user account.

❍ b. Lock the account using **admintool**.

❍ c. Modify the user account .profile to change the user environment.

❍ d. Use **admintool** to change the UID and GID associated with the user account.

## Question 33

What is the access mode of a file created with the umask set to 123?

❍ a. **321**

❍ b. **-rwxrwxrwx**

❍ c. **345**

❍ d. **rw-r--r--**

## Question 34

Which of the following can be used to remove packages? [Select all that apply]

- ❑ a. **admintool**
- ❑ b. **pkgtool**
- ❑ c. **pkgadd**
- ❑ d. **pkgrm**
- ❑ e. **pkginfo**

## Question 35

Which of the following shows the access mode of a file that has the setgid enabled?

- ❍ a. **srwxrwxrwx**
- ❍ b. **-rwsrwxrwx**
- ❍ c. **-rwxrwsrwx**
- ❍ d. **-rwxrwxrws**
- ❍ e. **-rwxrwxrwt**

## Question 36

Enter the full pathname to the file used to modify the configuration of the kernel.

_______________________________

## Question 37

Which commands can be used to install a package from CD-ROM? [Select all that apply]

- ❑ a. **admintool** with Source Media set to CD with Volume Management
- ❑ b. **pkgadd -d /cdrom/cdrom0**
- ❑ c. **admintool** with Source Media set to CD without Volume Management
- ❑ d. **pkgadd -s /cdrom/cdrom0**

## Question 38

Which command shows the users that have logged off the system?

❍ a. **who**

❍ b. **last**

❍ c. **whodo**

❍ d. **id**

## Question 39

Which of the following situations will allow a user account to execute **admintool**? [Select all that apply]

❑ a. The account is a member of the sysadmin group.

❑ b. The account is root.

❑ c. The account is logged in at the console.

❑ d. The account is a member of the sys group.

❑ e. The account is a member of the adm group.

## Question 40

Enter the command used to rewind a magnetic tape.

______________________________

## Question 41

Which command is used to change the system boot device?

❍ a. **use disk2 as boot-device**

❍ b. **set boot-device disk2**

❍ c. **setenv boot-device disk2**

❍ d. **set boot-dev disk2**

❍ e. **setdev boot disk2**

## Question 42

Enter the command used to delete an existing group account.

______________________________

## Question 43

Enter a command that can be used to generate a list of installed packages.

______________________________

## Question 44

What is the result of the following command?

```
setfacl -s u::rw-,g::r--,o:r--file1
```

❍ a. Access mode 644 is added to the existing ACLs for file1.

❍ b. Access mode 644 is deleted from the existing ACLs for file1.

❍ c. Access mode 644 replaces the existing ACLs for file1.

❍ d. Access mode 622 is added to the existing ACLs for file1.

❍ e. Access mode 622 replaces the existing ACLs for file1.

## Question 45

Which of the following Solaris 8 commands can be used to modify a NVRAM parameter?

❍ a. **setenv**

❍ b. **set**

❍ c. **setnvram**

❍ d. **eeprom**

❍ e. **setprom**

## Question 46

Which of the following can be used to remove multiple patches?

❍ a. **patchrm -M /var/spool/patch 104567-03 106583-10 103276-04**

❍ b. Use **patchrm** to remove each patch separately.

❍ c. **patchrm -M /var/spool/patch patchlist**

## Question 47

Enter the command that provides the ability to issue a warning message before the system run level is changed.

______________________________

## Question 48

How can the system be configured to allow using a keyboard sequence to abort the system operation?

❍ a. Add **KEYBOARD_ABORT=enable** to the /etc/default/kbd file.

❍ b. Execute the **no_abort** command.

❍ c. Create the /etc/default/kbd_abort file.

❍ d. Execute the **kbd abort enable** command.

## Question 49

Enter a command that can be used to remove an installed package.

______________________________

## Question 50

You enter the **patchrm 108577-03** command, and it fails. Which of the following situations will cause the command to fail? [Select all that apply]

❑ a. You are not logged in as root.

❑ b. Patch 108577-03 is not installed on the system.

❑ c. Patch 108577-04 is installed on the system.

❑ d. The patch was installed using **patchadd -d**.

## Question 51

A patch obtained from Sun Microsystems can be installed using which of the following commands? [Select all that apply]

❑ a. **pkgadd -patch 107588-01**

❑ b. **patchadd 107588-01**

❑ c. **patchadd /var/spool/patch/107588-01**

❑ d. **patch SUNWaccu 107588-01**

## Question 52

When is the system profile executed?

❍ a. After the .profile in the home directory of the user account.

❍ b. Before the .profile in the home directory of the user account.

❍ c. Instead of the .profile in the home directory of the user account.

## Question 53

Which of the following is the first phase in the Solaris boot process?

❍ a. init

❍ b. Boot PROM or BIOS

❍ c. Boot programs

❍ d. Kernel initialization

## Question 54

Which of the following statements are true about the command **newfs -v /dev/dsk/c0d1s7**? [Select all that apply]

- ❑ a. Verbose mode is enabled.
- ❑ b. It will create a new S5 type of file system.
- ❑ c. It will fail—a raw (character) device must be specified instead.
- ❑ d. It will calculate all the necessary **mkfs** command-line arguments.

## Question 55

Enter the command-line argument used with the **man** command to display a man page from Section 4.

______________________________

## Question 56

Which of the following commands can be used to back up the entire file system located on the disk drive identified by c0t1d0s5?

- ❍ a. **ufsdump 0u /dev/dsk/c0t1d0s5**
- ❍ b. **ufsdump 0u /dev/rdsk/c0t1d0s5**
- ❍ c. **ufsdump 9u /dev/rdsk/c0t1d0s5**
- ❍ d. **ufsdump 9u /dev/dsk/c0t1d0s5**

## Question 57

Three types of naming conventions can be used to reference disks. Two of the conventions are physical device names and logical device names. Enter the third type of naming convention.

______________________________

# 12

# Answer Key I

1. /etc/group
2. a, b, d
3. a-4, b-1, c-3, d-2
4. hard
5. b
6. **pkill**
7. a-3, b-5, c-2, d-1, e-4
8. a, b, c
9. ?
10. b
11. a
12. a-3, b-4, c-1, d-2
13. b
14. b
15. a, b, c, d
16. b, d
17. b
18. d
19. a-3, b-4, c-1, d-2
20. a, b, c, f
21. a, c, e
22. **pgrep**
23. a, c
24. a, c, d
25. slices or partitions
26. **setfacl** or **chmod**
27. b
28. **ps**
29. d
30. b, c
31. c
32. b
33. d
34. a, d
35. c
36. /etc/system
37. a, b, c
38. b
39. a, b
40. **mt**
41. c
42. **groupdel** or **admintool**
43. **admintool** or **pkginfo**
44. c
45. d
46. b
47. **shutdown**
48. a
49. **admintool** or **pkgrm**
50. a, b, c, d
51. b, c
52. b
53. b
54. a, c, d
55. **-s 4**
56. b
57. instance

## Question 1

The correct answer is */etc/group*.

## Question 2

Answers a, b, and d are correct. The **ufsdump** command can back up files and directories within a UFS file system, including the entire file system. The volume table of contents is part of the disk layout and does not physically reside within a file system. Therefore, answer c is incorrect.

## Question 3

Answers a-4, b-1, c-3, and d-2 are correct. This question is meant to be misleading. **Select** is used to select a partition table. **Print** displays the current partition table. Answers 2 and 3 were vaguely worded—keep in mind that **label** writes a partition table *and label* to disk, whereas **name** only assigns a label or name to a partition table.

## Question 4

The correct answer is *hard*. The other type of link, soft or symbolic, references by name and can be used to point to a file on another file system.

## Question 5

Answer b is correct. The **cfgadm** command is used to manage the dynamic configuration of hot-plugging devices. **hpadmin** and **attach** are not valid commands. Therefore, answers a and c are incorrect.

## Question 6

The correct answer is **pkill**.

## Question 7

Answers a-3, b-5, c-2, d-1, and e-4 are correct. Root (/) is used for critical system files such as kernel and device drivers, /usr is used for user-accessible system commands and programs, /home is used for user home directories, /var is used for logs and spool areas, and /opt is used for applications.

## Question 8

Answers a, b, and c are correct. **nosuid, atime,** and **nolargefiles** are all **-o** command-line arguments. **-o nosuid** disables setuid permissions any files (**-o suid** allows it). **-o atime** allows access times on files to be updated (**-o noatime** prevents it). **-o nolargefiles** will cause the **mount** command to fail if any of the files on the file system are 2GB in size or larger (**-o largefiles** allows large files). **nomnttab** does not exist. Therefore, answer d is incorrect. To prevent a mounted file from being added to the/etc/mnttab file, use the **-m** command-line argument.

## Question 9

The correct answer is the question mark (?).

## Question 10

Answer b is correct. The **zip** command can be used to compress files and directories. **compress** and **gzip** can only compress files, not directories. Therefore, answers a and c are incorrect. **shrink** does not exist. Therefore, answer d is incorrect.

## Question 11

Answer a is correct. The **eject cdrom** command can be used to unmount a CD-ROM and eject it from the CD-ROM drive. The **eject** command without a command-line argument is used to unmount and eject a floppy diskette. Therefore, answer b is incorrect. Answers c, d, and e all use incorrect command-line arguments.

## Question 12

Answers a-3, b-4, c-1, and d-2 are correct. Both **h** and **<left arrow>** move the cursor to the left. **j** and **<down arrow>** both move the cursor down. **k** and **<up arrow>** both move the cursor up. **l** and **<right arrow>** both move the cursor to the right.

## Question 13

Answer b is correct. The file b2 will match the metacharacter expression **[abc][123]**. The metacharacter expression will match only a two-character file name. The first character must be *a*, *b*, or *c*, and the second character must be *1*, *2*, or *3*. Answers a, c, d, and e consist of three or more characters; therefore, they are incorrect.

## Question 14

Answer b is correct. The PID of the process must be specified when you use the **kill** command to terminate a process. The system uses the PID to identify a specific process. The signal to send to the process is not required because the SIGTERM signal is used by default if a signal is not specified. Therefore, answer a is incorrect. The UID and name could refer to more than one process; something more unique is required to identify a particular process. Therefore, answers c and d are incorrect.

## Question 15

Answers a, b, c, and d are correct. Because a file system type is not specified with **mkfs**, the default file system type as specified in the /etc/default/fs file, which is UFS, is assumed. All the other commands specify file system type UFS or are intended for UFS file systems.

## Question 16

Answers b and d are correct. Since the **-m** command-line argument was not used, all mounted file systems are listed in the /etc/mnttab file. The **mount** command without command-line arguments displays all file system listed in the /etc/vfstab file. Answer a is a description of the **mountall** command, not the **mount** command. The **mountall** command mounts all file systems in /etc/vfstab. Therefore, answer a is incorrect. The **mount** command displays the contents of the /etc/mnttab, not the /etc/vfstab file. Therefore, answer c is incorrect.

## Question 17

Answer b is correct. The path is /dev/dsk instead of /dev/rdsk, which identifies a raw device. Therefore, answer a is incorrect. Physical device names are located under the /devices directory, not the /dev directory. Therefore, answers c and d are incorrect.

## Question 18

Answer d is correct. The question mark (?) can be used to enter **vi** Last Line mode. The "%", "$", and "#" characters are not used to change **vi** modes. Therefore, answers a, b, and c are incorrect.

## Question 19

Answers a-3, b-4, c-1, and d-2 are correct. PCFS is used for floppy diskettes, UFS is used for disk drives; UDF is used for DVDs, and HSFS is used for CD-ROMs.

## Question 20

Answers a, b, c, and f are correct. The **format, newfs, fsck,** and **prtvtoc** commands either display or can use logical raw device names. The **mount** and **df** commands display or expect logical block devices. Therefore, answers d and e are incorrect.

## Question 21

Answers a, c, and e are correct. You can boot the operating system, view and modify NVRAM parameters, and run diagnostics using OpenBoot commands. You can change the root password and set the system time only from the Solaris 8 operating system. Therefore, answers b and d are incorrect.

## Question 22

The correct answer is **pgrep**. The **ps** command could be used, but it would list more than just the PID of the process.

## Question 23

Answers a and c are correct. You can use **rlogin** and **telnet** to log in to a remote system. **login** is used to log in to a local system. Therefore, answer b is incorrect. **rsh** is used to execute a command on a remote system without logging in to the system. Therefore, answer d is incorrect.

## Question 24

Answers a, c, and d are correct. The purpose of the **ps** command is to identify processes and who owns the processes. The program/command name allows the human user to determine the PID of a process that requires some attention (such as termination using the **kill** command). The process ID (PID) uniquely identifies the process. More than one process of the same name might be listed. To uniquely identify who owns a process, either a username (not a choice) or the terminal device associated with the process is needed. The parent process ID is only displayed on selected formats such as the those generated by the **-l** command-line argument.

## Question 25

Either *slices* or *partitions* is correct.

## Question 26

Either **setfacl** or **chmod** is correct.

## Question 27

Answer b is correct. NFS server services typically start at run level 3. Run level 2 is multiuser without server capabilities enabled. Therefore, answer a is incorrect. Run level 4 is not used. Therefore, answer c is incorrect. Run level 5 is used to shut down the system. Therefore, answer d is incorrect.

## Question 28

The correct answer is **ps**.

## Question 29

Answer d is correct. The **passwd** command can be used by the guest account to change its password. The guest account is not and should not be a member of the sysadmin group. Therefore, answer a is incorrect. The **passmgmt** and **usermod** commands do not support changing passwords. Therefore, answers b and c are incorrect.

## Question 30

Answers b and c are correct. /etc/hosts.equiv and .rhosts are associated with the remote authentication database. /etc/hosts is used to resolve host names to IP addresses and is not part of the remote authentication database. Therefore, answer a is incorrect. /etc/system is used to configure the Solaris kernel. Therefore, answer d is incorrect.

## Question 31

Answer c is correct. The .profile is copied from /etc/skel/local.profile. /etc/skel/default.profile does not exist. Therefore, answer a is incorrect. /etc/profile is the system profile. Therefore, answer b is incorrect. /.profile is the profile for the root account. Therefore, answer d is incorrect.

## Question 32

Answer b is correct. Locking the account using **admintool** is the preferred method to temporarily prevent a user account from being used. All the other choices would cause problems or not prevent the user account from being used. Therefore, answers a, c, and d are incorrect.

## Question 33

Answer d is correct. Execute permissions in the umask do not affect files (only directories). The umask equivalent of 123 for files is 022. This results in 666 – 022 = 644, which translates to **rw-** for user, **r--** for group, and **r--** for others. Answers a, b, and c are incorrect.

## Question 34

Answers a and d are correct. **admintool** and **pkgrm** can be used to remove packages. **pkgtool** does not exist. Therefore, answer b is incorrect. The **pkgadd** command is used to install packages. Therefore, answer c is incorrect. The **pkginfo** command is used to display information about packages. Therefore, answer e is incorrect.

## Question 35

Answer c is correct. **-rwxrwsrwx** shows the access mode of a file that has the setgid enabled. **srwxrwxrwx** and **-rwxrwxrws** are not valid file access modes. Therefore, answers a and d are incorrect. **-rwsrwxrwx** shows setuid enabled, and **-rwxrwxrwt** shows the sticky bit set. Therefore, answers b and e are incorrect.

## Question 36

The correct answer is */etc/system*.

## Question 37

Answers a, b, and c are correct. To install a package from CD-ROM, you can use **admintool** with Source Media set to CD with Volume Management, **pkgadd -d /cdrom/cdrom0**, or **admintool** with Source Media set to CD without Volume Management. The **-s** command-line argument is used to spool a package, not install it. Therefore, answer d is incorrect.

## Question 38

Answer b is correct. The **last** command shows users that have logged off the system. The **who** and **whodo** commands show who is currently logged in to the system. Therefore, answers a and c are incorrect. **id** shows the real and effective UID, GID, and groups for a user account. Therefore, answer d is incorrect.

## Question 39

Answers a and b are correct. To execute **admintool**, the account must be root or a member of the sysadmin group. The device used to log in to the system does not affect access. Therefore, answer c is incorrect. The sys group and the adm group do not enable access to the **admintool**. Therefore, answers d and e are incorrect.

## Question 40

The correct answer is **mt**.

## Question 41

Answer c is correct. You use the **setenv boot-device disk2** command to change the system boot device. None of the other answers provided lists valid OpenBoot commands.

## Question 42

The correct answer is **groupdel** or **admintool**.

## Question 43

Either **admintool** or **pkginfo** is correct.

## Question 44

Answer c is correct. The **-s** command-line argument to **setfacl** causes the ACLs to be replaced as opposed to being added (**-m**) or deleted (**-d**). Therefore answers a, b, and d are incorrect. The specified access mode, **rw-r--r--** is 644, not 622. Therefore answer e is incorrect.

## Question 45

Answer d is correct. The **eeprom** command can be used to modify a NVRAM parameter. The **setenv** and **set** commands are used to set shell parameters. Therefore, answers a and b are incorrect. The commands in answers c and e do not exist.

## Question 46

Answer b is correct. You must use **patchrm** to remove each patch separately. The **patchrm** command does not support the **-M** command-line argument as the **patchadd** command does. Therefore, answers a and c are incorrect.

## Question 47

The correct answer is **shutdown**.

## Question 48

Answer a is correct. Adding **KEYBOARD_ABORT=enable** to the /etc/default/kbd file will configure the system to let you use a keyboard sequence to abort the system operation. The options in answers b, c, and d do not yield meaningful results.

## Question 49

Either **admintool** or **pkgrm** is correct.

## Question 50

Answers a, b, c, and d are correct. Any of these situations will cause the **patchrm** command to fail.

## Question 51

Answers b and c are correct. If your current working directory is /var/spool/patch, a full pathname is not required. The **pkgadd** command can be used to install only packages, not patches. Therefore, answer a is incorrect. The **patch** command is a user command for updating text files and has nothing to do with system patches. Therefore, answer d is incorrect.

## Question 52

Answer b is correct. The system profile, /etc/profile, is executed before the .profile in the user's home directory. Answers a and c are incorrect.

## Question 53

Answer b is correct. All other phases occur after the Boot PROM (SPARC) or BIOS (x86) phase. Therefore, answers a, c, and d are incorrect.

## Question 54

Answers a, c, and d are correct. **-v** enables verbose mode. The device specified must be a raw device. And, the primary advantage of using the **newfs** command is that it calculates all necessary **mkfs** command-line arguments The **newfs** command can only be used to create UFS file systems. Therefore, answer b is incorrect.

## Question 55

The correct answer is **-s 4**.

## Question 56

Answer b is correct. The command **ufsdump 0u /dev/rdsk/c0t1d0s5** backs up the entire file system located on the disk drive identified by c0t1d0s5. **ufsdump 0u /dev/dsk/c0t1d0s5** uses the block device name (/dev/dsk) instead of a raw device name (/dev/rdsk). Therefore, answer a is incorrect. **ufsdump 9u /dev/rdsk/c0t1d0s5** uses dump level 9 instead of dump level 0. Therefore, answer c is incorrect. In the command **ufsdump 9u /dev/dsk/c0t1d0s5**, both the dump level and the device name are incorrect. Therefore, answer d is incorrect.

## Question 57

The correct answer is *instance*.

# Part II

## Exam 310-012

# 13

# The Solaris Network Environment

## Terms you'll need to understand:

- ✓ OSI network model
- ✓ TCP/IP network model
- ✓ Ethernet address
- ✓ Network class
- ✓ TCP/IP configuration files
- ✓ Server and client
- ✓ Standalone workstation
- ✓ File server
- ✓ Diskless client
- ✓ AutoClient

## Techniques you'll need to master:

- ✓ Configuring TCP/IP on a Solaris 8 system
- ✓ Checking the status of a remote system
- ✓ Checking the status of the network interface
- ✓ Distinguishing between standalone, diskless, and AutoClient configurations

The first part of this chapter covers basic network concepts such as the OSI and TCP/IP network models along with details on the TCP/IP implementation. The *Solaris Network Environment* test objectives are covered by this part of the chapter.

The second part of this chapter covers the concepts and components of the different types of Solaris 8 configurations, including standalone systems, diskless clients, and AutoClients. This part of the chapter covers the *Client Server Relationship* test objectives.

# Networking Models

Although a variety of networking models have been developed over the years, most of the commercially available networks use one of the two following models:

- The Open System Interconnection (OSI) model
- The Transmission Control Protocol/Internet Protocol (TCP/IP) model

Of these two, the TCP/IP model predominates.

## The Open System Interconnection Model

The OSI network model developed by the International Standards Organization (ISO) consists of seven layers of services. Each layer is responsible for handling a different aspect of network communication.

When sending data, each layer performs its processing on the data and passes it to the next lower layer. When receiving data, each layer performs its processing on the data and passes it to the next higher layer.

This layered approach allows different types of processing (services) to be developed without having to develop all layers of the model. The new service is linked into the stack of layers or *protocol stack* at the appropriate layer.

The seven ISO/OSI layers (from lowest to the highest) are:

- *Physical*—The first layer is concerned with the physical interface between devices. It controls the transmission of a bit stream over the physical medium and has to deal with the mechanical and electrical characteristics of the physical medium.
- *Data Link*—The second layer provides error detection and control. It adds reliability to the Physical Layer by grouping bits into frames and providing synchronization, error control, and flow control over the frames. Basically, it controls the transfer of data across a network media.
- *Network*—The third layer is responsible for determining a path through the network between systems that wish to communicate. It understands the data communication and switching technologies used to interconnect systems.

- *Transport*—The fourth layer provides end-to-end error recovery and flow control. These services provide reliability to the layer and ensure that the data is delivered without errors and in sequence without duplication.
- *Session*—The fifth layer provides a control structure for communication between applications. It is responsible for establishing, maintaining, and terminating connections.
- *Presentation*—The sixth layer handles the differences in data representation or syntax. This layer maps data between formats so that the application can understand the data.
- *Application*—The seventh layer provides user utilities such as remote login, file transfers, and so on.

## The Transmission Control Protocol/Internet Protocol (TCP/IP) Model

Like the OSI network model, the TCP/IP network model consists of a stack of service layers. Unlike the OSI model, it provides the same functionality using five layers instead of seven. For the most part, the four lowest layers of the OSI and TCP/IP networks provide similar functionality; the top three OSI layers (Session, Presentation, and Application) are grouped into the TCP/IP Application Layer.

The five TCP/IP layers (from lowest to the highest) are:

- *Physical*—The first layer is concerned with the physical interface between devices. It controls the transmission of a bit stream over the physical medium and deals with the mechanical and electrical characteristics of the physical medium.
- *Data Link*—The second layer provides error detection and control. It adds reliability to the Physical Layer by grouping bits into *frames* and providing synchronization, error control, and flow control over the frames. This layer provides the deliver of data between system using a media or hardware address, such as the Ethernet or Media Access Control (MAC) address.
- *Network*—The third layer is responsible for determining a path across the Internet between systems that wish to communicate. It understands the data communication and switching technologies used to interconnect systems. This layer manages the network addressing and routing of data, locates the remote host based on its assigned Internet Protocol (IP) address, and determines the path through the network (the route) used to deliver data. Data at this layer typically is referred to as *datagrams*.
- *Transport*—The fourth layer provides end-to-end error recovery and flow control. These services provide reliability to the layer and ensure that the data

is delivered without errors and in sequence without duplication. This layer controls the exchange and flow of data. Data at this layer typically is referred to as *packets.*

- *Application*—The fifth layer provides user utilities such as remote login, file transfers, and so on. Data at this layer typically is referred to as *messages* or *streams.*

Figure 13.1 provides a side-by-side comparison the OSI and TCP/IP networking models.

# TCP/IP Networking

The Solaris operating system supports the TCP/IP networking model. Although Solaris can use several types of networking hardware architectures such as Ethernet, Token Ring, and Fiber Distributed Data Interface (FDDI) to communicate with other systems, Ethernet is the de facto networking architecture.

## Features and Functions of Ethernet

The Data Link Layer of the TCP/IP model controls the transfer of data across a network media. In an Ethernet Local Area Network (LAN), the Ethernet frame is used at the Data Link Layer to package and transmit the data.

The hosts on an Ethernet LAN are assigned unique addresses that are associated with the Data Link Layer. These addresses are referred to as *Ethernet* addresses, *hardware* addresses, *physical* addresses, or *MAC* addresses.

Typically, the corporation that manufactures the Network Interface Card (NIC) assigns these addresses, and a unique address is associate with each NIC. Thus

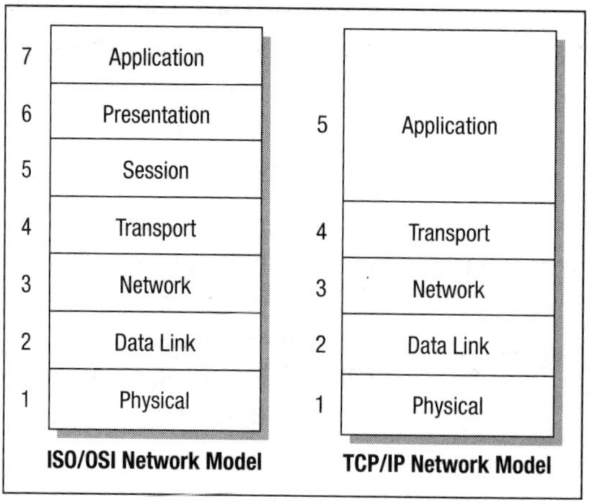


**Figure 13.1** OSI and TCP/IP network models.

the Ethernet address is associated with the NIC, not with a system. A system with two NICs (such as a router attached to two networks) will have two Ethernet addresses.

The Ethernet address consists of 48 bits (6 bytes of data). Typically, an Ethernet address is shown as six two-digit hexadecimal numbers separated by colons. For example, **00:40:05:37:9d:db** is the Ethernet address for the system used to generate most of the listings in this book.

The Ethernet frame transmitted on the LAN contains the Ethernet address of the NIC that should receive and respond to the frame. All hosts on a LAN receive all transmitted Ethernet frames. Any received frames with an Ethernet address that matches the Ethernet address of the NIC are read and processed.

The Ethernet addresses are used only on the LAN and do not pass through routers. Thus, any Ethernet frame sent to a host that is not on the current LAN will use the Ethernet address of the router as its destination. Likewise, an Ethernet frame sent from a router to a host will have the Ethernet address of the router as its source.

However, most TCP/IP applications address hosts using IP addresses. Typically, the IP address needs to be converted to an Ethernet address. Because each host has a unique IP address and a unique Ethernet address, a process is needed to map between these two addresses.

### The Address Resolution Protocol and the Reverse ARP

This process to map between Ethernet and IP addresses is referred to as *address resolution*. The protocol used to map from an IP address to an Ethernet address is referred to as the Address Resolution Protocol (ARP). The details of this process are specified in Request for Comment (RFC) 826, "An Ethernet Address Resolution Protocol."

In some cases, an Ethernet address is known, but the IP address needs to be determined. This process is known as the Reverse Address Resolution Protocol (RARP). The details of this process are specified in RFC 903, "A Reverse Address Resolution Protocol."

A host that needs to resolve an Ethernet address broadcasts an ARP request that contains the IP address as data. The message basically asks, *What is the Ethernet address of the host with this IP address?* Note that the ARP request is an Ethernet broadcast. That is, the destination Ethernet address of the Ethernet frame is all ones (FF:FF:FF:FF:FF:FF). The host that matches the specified IP address responds with an ARP reply that contains its Ethernet address. This address is part of the Data of the Ethernet frame.

The same process is used to resolve an IP address when the Ethernet address is known. An RARP request is broadcast (destination Ethernet address of

FF:FF:FF:FF:FF:FF) that contains an Ethernet address in the Data. The appropriate host responds with a RARP reply that contains the requested IP address.

Sometimes it may be necessary for a system to respond to an ARP or RARP request on behalf of another system. This process is referred to as *proxy ARP*; some protocol stacks (typically routers) are designed with this capability.

## Classes of IP Networks

In the TCP/IP network model, the IP at the Transport Layer is used to segregate networks into classes. The three most commonly used IP network classes are A, B, and C. Table 13.1 provides a summary of the characteristics of these different IP network classes.

Addresses with a first octet of 127 are not considered as part of either Class A or Class B. It is dedicated for a special use referred to as "loopback." The subnet mask is used to separate the network portion of an IP address from the host portion.

## TCP/IP Configuration Files

Solaris 8 uses several files to configure the TCP/IP environment. These files are used to identify both the hostname and the IP address of the system. The following three files are used to configure TCP/IP:

- /etc/inet/hosts
- /etc/nodename
- /etc/hostname.*interface*

The next few sections look at these files in depth.

### The /etc/inet/hosts File

The /etc/hosts file (which is a symbolic link to /etc/inet/hosts) contains a listing of hostnames and their associated IP addresses. This file is used to convert hostnames to IP addresses. Table 13.2 summarizes the format of the /etc/inet/hosts file.

**Table 13.1 IP address classes.**

| Class | First Octet | Default Subnet Mask | Maximum Theoretical Hosts |
|---|---|---|---|
| A | 1 through 126 | 255.0.0.0 | 16,777,216 |
| B | 128 through 191 | 255.255.0.0 | 65,536 |
| C | 192 through 223 | 255.255.255.0 | 256 |

| Table 13.2 /etc/inet/hosts file format. | |
|---|---|
| **Column** | **Description** |
| IP Address | IP address in dotted decimal notation |
| Host Name | Hostname or node name of the system |
| Alias | Alternate hostname(s) for the system |

The columns are separated by one or more tab or space characters. If more than one alias is defined, you should separate them using either spaces or tabs.

At a minimum, the /etc/inet/hosts file should contain an entry for the localhost (IP address 127.0.0.1) and an entry for each network interface installed on the system.

Additional entries can be added to the /etc/inet/hosts file for other systems. If a name service is not being used, doing so allows access to the remote systems using hostnames instead of IP addresses.

## The /etc/nodename File

The /etc/nodename file contains only one entry: the default hostname of the local system. You should assign the hostname or node name in accordance with RFC 952, "DOD Internet Host Table Specification."

## The /etc/hostname.*interface* File

One /etc/hostname.*interface* file exists for each network interface installed on the system. The *interface* portion of the file name reflects the manufacturer and type of network interface. For example, if an Intel x86–based system has a single 3COM Etherlink III network interface card installed, the file name is /etc/hostname.lex0. For a SPARC 5 platform with two network interfaces, the file names are /etc/hostname.le0 and /etc/hostname.le1.

The /etc/hostname.*interface* file(s) should contain only one entry: either the hostname or the IP address assigned to that interface.

If a hostname is used, that hostname must also be listed in the /etc/inet/hosts file. Also note that if more than one network interface is installed on the system, the /etc/hostname.*interface* files will contain different hostnames. Only the hostname (or IP address) that matches the hostname defined in the /etc/nodename file is considered the default hostname for the system.

## Checking Network Connectivity

Solaris 8 provides two commands for checking network connectivity between systems and the proper operation of the network interfaces on both systems: the **ping**(1M) command and the **spray**(1M) command.

### The ping Command

The **/usr/sbin/ping** command uses the Internet Control Message Protocol (ICMP) to send ECHO_REQUEST datagrams to another host. When a host receives an ECHO_REQUEST datagram, it responds with an ECHO_REPLY datagram. This basic echo mechanism is used to verify both the connectivity between two hosts and the proper operation of the network interfaces and protocol stacks (of both hosts) up to the Internet layer where the IP resides. The following listing sends one ICMP ECHO_REQUEST datagram using the **ping** command:

```
$ /usr/sbin/ping solaris8
solaris8 is alive
$
```

Table 13.3 lists some of the more frequently used command-line arguments supported by the **ping** command. See the **ping**(1M) manual page for more details.

At a minimum, a hostname or IP address must be specified. All these command-line arguments are specified before the hostname or IP address.

When you use the **ping** command without any command-line arguments (specifying only a hostname), you can specify a time-out after the host name. The default time-out is 20 seconds.

**Table 13.3 The ping command-line arguments.**

| Argument | Description |
|---|---|
| -i *interface* | Uses the specified interface address |
| -I *interval* | Specifies an interval between transmissions (default of 1 second) |
| -n | Displays addresses instead of hostnames |
| -r | Bypasses the routing tables (remote host is on the local network) |
| -R | Records the route in the IP header |
| -s | Sends ICMP packets until interrupted |
| -t *time* | Specifies a time to live (in seconds) for IP packets |
| -v | Displays detailed information (verbose mode) |

When you use **ping** with the **-s** command-line argument, you can specify a packet size and a count after the hostname. The following listing uses the **ping** command to send five packets (each with 60 bytes of data) to the sparc20 host:

```
$ /usr/sbin/ping -s sparc20 60 5
PING sparc20: 60 data bytes
68 bytes from sparc20 (192.168.99.208): icmp_seq=0. time=1. ms
68 bytes from sparc20 (192.168.99.208): icmp_seq=1. time=0. ms
68 bytes from sparc20 (192.168.99.208): icmp_seq=2. time=0. ms
68 bytes from sparc20 (192.168.99.208): icmp_seq=3. time=0. ms
68 bytes from sparc20 (192.168.99.208): icmp_seq=4. time=0. ms

---sparc20 PING Statistics---
5 packets transmitted, 5 packets received, 0% packet loss
round-trip (ms)  min/avg/max = 0/0/1
$
```

## The spray Command

The **/usr/sbin/spray** command sends a stream of User Datagram Protocol (UDP) packets to a host using the Remote Procedure Call (RPC) mechanism. On the remote end, the spray daemon, **sprayd**(1M), accepts these packets and acknowledges receiving them. The **spray** command, along with the **sprayd** program, is used to verify both the connectivity between two hosts and the proper operation of the network interfaces and protocol stacks (of both hosts) up to the Application Layer.

The following listing uses the **spray** command to test network connectivity:

```
$ /usr/sbin/spray sparc20
sending 1162 packets of length 86 to sparc20 ...
        706 packets (60.757%) dropped by sparc20
        1801 packets/sec, 154924 bytes/sec
$
```

Table 13.4 lists the command-line arguments supported by the **spray** command. See the **spray**(1M) manual page for more details.

At a minimum, you must specify a hostname or IP address. All these command-line arguments are specified before the hostname or IP address.

*Note: The **sprayd** program must be running on the remote system in order for the **spray** command to work properly.*

**Table 13.4 The spray command-line arguments.**

| Argument | Description |
|---|---|
| **-c *count*** | The number of packets to send (default is the number of packets required to send a total of 100KB) |
| **-d *delay*** | The number of microseconds to pause between packets (default is 0) |
| **-l *length*** | The length of the Ethernet packet (default is 86) |
| **-t *type*** | The class of transport (default is UDP) |

## Viewing the Network Interface Configuration and Statistics

Two commands are available to view the configuration of the network interfaces and network statistics. These are:

- **ifconfig**(1M)—Configures network interfaces
- **netstat**(1M)—Displays network statistics

The **ifconfig**(1M) command is used to configure parameters for the network interfaces. Although configuring network interfaces is beyond the scope of the exam, you can use the **ifconfig** command to view the configuration of the network interfaces. You do so either by specifying the **-a** command-line argument to list information about all network interfaces or by specifying the name of a particular interface as a command-line argument. The following listing uses these two command-line arguments:

```
# ifconfig -a
lo0: flags=1000849<UP,LOOPBACK,RUNNING,MULTICAST,IPv4> mtu 8232
     inet 127.0.0.1 netmask ff000000
elx0: flags=1000843<UP,BROADCAST,RUNNING,MULTICAST,IPv4> mtu 1500
     inet 192.168.99.8 netmask ffffff00 broadcast 192.168.99.255
     ether 0:a0:24:c:32:97
lo0: flags=2000849<UP,LOOPBACK,RUNNING,MULTICAST,IPv6> mtu 8252
     inet6 ::1/128
elx0: flags=2000841<UP,RUNNING,MULTICAST,IPv6> mtu 1500
     ether 0:a0:24:c:32:97
     inet6 fe80::2a0:24ff:fe0c:3297/10

# ifconfig elx0
elx0: flags=1000843<UP,BROADCAST,RUNNING,MULTICAST,IPv4> mtu 1500
     inet 192.168.99.8 netmask ffffff00 broadcast 192.168.99.255
     ether 0:a0:24:c:32:97
#
```

The **netstat**(1M) command is used to display network statistics and configuration information. Table 13.5 lists the command-line arguments supported by the **netstat** command.

ALERT: Note that you can use either the **ifconfig** or **netstat -p** command to display the Ethernet address associated with a network interface.

## Open Network Computing (ONC) and the Remote Procedure Call Mechanism

Sun Microsystems has developed an environment for supporting distributed services. This environment is referred to as Sun's Open Network Computing Plus (ONC+) Technologies. ONC+ Technologies is a family of technologies, services, and tools. The main components are:

- *Applications*—Network File System (NFS) and Network Information Service Plus (NIS+) services. They use RPCs to accomplish the client-server interaction.

**Table 13.5 The netstat command-line arguments.**

| Argument | Description |
|---|---|
| **-a** | Lists the status of all sockets, routing table entries, and network interfaces. |
| **-D** | Lists the status of DHCP-configured network interfaces. |
| **-f *family*** | Lists information only for the specified protocol family. Possible values are **inet** (IP version 4), **inet6** (IP version 6), or **unix** (Unix). |
| **-g** | Lists the multicast membership of each interface. |
| **-i** | Lists statistics for all network interfaces. |
| **-I *interface*** | Lists statistics only for the specified network interface. |
| **-m** | Lists STREAMS statistics. |
| **-M** | Displays the multicast routing table. |
| **-n** | Displays network addresses instead of network names. |
| **-p** | Displays hardware (Ethernet) addresses for each interface. |
| **-P *protocol*** | Lists statistics only for the specified protocol. |
| **-r** | Displays the dynamic routing table. |
| **-s** | Lists per-protocol statistics. |
| **-v** | Lists additional socket and routing table information. |

- *Remote Procedure Call (RPC)*—A mechanism that allows a client to request a remote server to execute a procedure or process.
- *External Data Representation (XDR)*—A machine-independent data representation. Both clients and servers translate data into and out of the XDR format. This mechanism provides a standardized format for all data to overcome differences in data byte ordering, data type size, and byte alignment between different hardware architectures.
- *Transport Layer Interface (TLI)*—An interface to TCP/IP that allows the RPC mechanism to be protocol independent. You can select either a connection-oriented protocol (such as TCP) or a connectionless protocol (such as UDP) without making changes to the client or server code.
- *Sockets*—Another mechanism that can be used to interface to TCP/IP that supports protocol-independent client and servers programming.

In the TCP/IP model, all the ONC+ components reside in the Application Layer. In terms of the OSI model, these components are distributed among the Session Layer (RPC), Presentation Layer (XDR), and Application Layer (NFS and NIS+). Note that the applications call XDR routines to translate the data. Once translated, the data is either processed locally or passed to RPC routines to send the data to a remote system.

## Registering RPC Services

In order for systems to use distributed services built on RPC, the programs that provide services must be identified (registered). The **rpcbind**(1M) daemon manages RPC services on a system. Each RPC program is assigned a unique number. When a RPC program starts, it contacts the local **rpcbind** daemon and provides its RPC program number, version, and so on. When a remote client attempts to use a local RPC service, it contacts the local **rpcbind** daemon to obtain information (based on RPC program number) about the service and to request a connection to the service. Thus the **rpcbind** daemon provides a method for local services to register their availability and remote clients to identify the services and establish a connection to the services.

You can use the **rpcinfo**(1) command to contact the local or a remote **rpcbind** daemon and request it to list the currently registered RPC services. The following listing uses the **rpcinfo** command to list local services and, because the name of a remote host is specified as a command-line argument, to list services on a remote system:

```
# rpcinfo
program version netid     address          service    owner
100000    4     ticots    solaris8.rpc     rpcbind    superuser
```

```
100000   3   ticots    solaris8.rpc    rpcbind   superuser
100000   4   ticotsord solaris8.rpc    rpcbind   superuser
100000   3   ticotsord solaris8.rpc    rpcbind   superuser
100000   4   ticlts    solaris8.rpc    rpcbind   superuser
100000   3   ticlts    solaris8.rpc    rpcbind   superuser
100000   4   tcp       0.0.0.0.0.111   rpcbind   superuser
100000   3   tcp       0.0.0.0.0.111   rpcbind   superuser
100000   2   tcp       0.0.0.0.0.111   rpcbind   superuser
100000   4   udp       0.0.0.0.0.111   rpcbind   superuser
.
.
.
# rpcinfo sparc20
program version netid  address         service   owner
100000   4   ticots    sparc8.rpc      rpcbind   superuser
100000   3   ticots    sparc8.rpc      rpcbind   superuser
100000   4   ticotsord sparc8.rpc      rpcbind   superuser
100000   3   ticotsord sparc8.rpc      rpcbind   superuser
100000   4   ticlts    sparc8.rpc      rpcbind   superuser
100000   3   ticlts    sparc8.rpc      rpcbind   superuser
100000   4   tcp       0.0.0.0.0.111   rpcbind   superuser
100000   3   tcp       0.0.0.0.0.111   rpcbind   superuser
100000   2   tcp       0.0.0.0.0.111   rpcbind   superuser
100000   4   udp       0.0.0.0.0.111   rpcbind   superuser
.
.
.
```

RPC services are typically listed in the /etc/rpc file. This file lists the common RPC service name, its RPC program number, and any aliases. See the **rpc**(4) manual page for more information.

## Controlling Network Services

Most of the Internet and RPC services are managed automatically by the **inetd**(1M) Internet Services daemon. These services are specified as entries in the /etc/inet/inetd.conf file (or /etc/inetd.conf, which is symbolically linked to /etc/inet/inetd.conf).

All Internet and RPC services controlled by the **inetd** daemon are started automatically at system boot, or you can start them all manually by executing the **/etc/init.d/inetd start** command. Likewise, all Internet and RPC services controlled by the **inetd** daemon are stopped automatically when the system is shut down, or you can stop them manually by executing the **/etc/init.d/inetd stop** command.

You can stop individual Internet and RPC services by using the **kill** command to send a signal to the process that provides the service. However, the **inetd** daemon should be reconfigured so that it will not retry to restart the service.

To reconfigure the **inetd** daemon, edit the /etc/inet/inetd.conf file and delete the entry for the service. Then, use the **kill** command to send the Hang Up signal (SIGHUP) to the **inetd** daemon. This signal will cause the **inetd** daemon to reread the /etc/inet/inetd.conf file. You can also use the /etc/init.d/inetd script (as previously described) to stop and restart the **inetd** daemon, or you can reboot the system.

# The Solaris Network Environment

The Solaris 8 network environment supports several different types of system configurations, including standalone, diskless, and AutoClient. These configurations provide different capabilities and impact deployment and support costs.

## Standalone Configuration

A *standalone* system has local disk space that is used to store all operating system files, applications, and user data. This data includes the root (/), /usr, /export/home, and /var file systems. Likewise, it provides local swap space for the system's virtual memory. A standalone system can function autonomously and can be either networked or non-networked. You can use a networked standalone system as a server, such as a file server, to provide remote access to shared or common data.

### File Server Concepts

A *file server* is a standalone system that functions as a server and allows clients to access files via the network. There are several kinds of file servers.

One important type of file server in the Solaris environment is the *operating system (OS) server*. The OS server provides access to client systems that do not have all or some of the operating system files available through local file systems on local hard disks.

An OS server can support more than one version of an operating system at a time. This support includes not only different releases of an operating system, such as Solaris 8, Solaris 7, and SunOS 2.5, but also different hardware platforms, such as SPARC and Intel x86 compatibles.

## Diskless Configuration

A *diskless client*, as the name implies, does not have a hard disk on which to store the operating system or applications locally. Storage is provided by a *diskless client server* that is accessible via the network. For a diskless client to boot and operate, it must remotely mount its root (/) and /usr file systems from an OS server.

In addition to providing a common set of operating system files for all the diskless clients (of the same version) through the network, the OS server provides hard disk space assigned for use by each client. This disk space is used for swap space for the diskless client's virtual memory system, and for the /home file system for user accounts that are unique to each diskless client.

Compared to the standalone configuration, the diskless configuration is cheaper and easier to maintain, because only a very small number of systems (the OS servers) require hard disks. Only one copy of common files is required, and this copy is shared among many clients. In addition, all data unique to each client is stored on an OS server, simplifying backup and restore procedures. Because no data is stored on the clients, the client hardware can be easily replaced or upgraded.

The main disadvantages of the diskless configuration are its dependence on the network and the load that it places on the network. If a diskless client cannot access the OS server via the network, it cannot operate at all. In addition, because all data (including that in swap space) is accessed remotely, the network is extremely loaded even under normal operating conditions.

## AutoClient Configuration

An *AutoClient* is similar to a diskless client, except that it has a limited amount of local storage space (minimum of 100MB) that is used for a specific purpose. Like the diskless client, the AutoClient must remotely access its root (/) and /usr file systems from an OS server configured as an AutoClient server. Unlike the diskless client, the AutoClient uses local disk space to store or cache the root (/) and /usr file systems.

In addition, the local hard disk is used for swap space. Like the diskless configuration, the OS server provides hard disk space for the /home and /var file systems that are unique to each diskless client.

Compared to the diskless configuration, the AutoClient configuration is somewhat more expensive, because its client requires a hard disk; but, the hard disk is small. Like the diskless configuration, only one copy of common files is required, and this copy is shared among the clients. In addition, all data unique to each client is stored on an OS server, simplifying backup and restore procedures. Thus, in terms of client hardware, AutoClients, like diskless clients, can be replaced or upgraded easily.

The disadvantages of the diskless configuration are reduced or, in some cases, eliminated by the AutoClient configuration. After the AutoClient has cached the operating system, it no longer requires access to the OS server for those files. In addition, the local swap space eliminates a significant portion of the network load.

## Comparison of Configurations

Table 13.6 provides a comparison of the significant differences among the various system configurations supported in the Solaris 8 network environment.

Standalone systems that function as servers typically provide file systems—such as /export/root, /export/home, and /export/swap—that store files remotely accessed by diskless clients and AutoClients. In addition, servers and standalone systems provide the /opt file system for storing application software.

**Table 13.6 A comparison of system configurations.**

| System Type | Local Swap | Local File Systems | Remote File Systems |
|---|---|---|---|
| Standalone | Yes | root, /usr, /var, /export/home | None |
| Diskless client | No | None | root, /usr, /var, /home |
| AutoClient | Yes | root, /usr | /var, /home |

# Practice Questions

## Question 1

Which of the following can be used as a file server?

- ❍ a. AutoClient
- ❍ b. Diskless client
- ❍ c. Non-networked standalone system
- ❍ d. Networked standalone system

Answer d is correct. A networked standalone system meets both of the basic requirements of a file server: It is networked, and it has storage space. An AutoClient has only a minimum amount of local storage space. Therefore, answer a is incorrect. A diskless client does not have any local storage space. Therefore, answer b is incorrect. A non-networked standalone system is not networked and cannot make its storage space available to other systems. Therefore, answer c is incorrect.

## Question 2

How many layers are in the TCP/IP network model?

- ❍ a. 4
- ❍ b. 5
- ❍ c. 6
- ❍ d. 7

Answer b is correct. The TCP/IP network model has five layers. The layers (bottom to top) are Physical, Data Link, Network, Transport, and Application. The OSI network model has seven layers.

## Question 3

Enter the name of the command used to display network statistics.

______________________________

The correct answer is **netstat**.

## Question 4

Which of the following have local swap space? [Select all that apply]

- ❑ a. Non-networked standalone system
- ❑ b. AutoClient
- ❑ c. OS server
- ❑ d. Diskless client
- ❑ e. Networked standalone system

Answers a, b, c, and e are correct. A non-networked standalone system, AutoClient, OS server, and networked standalone system all have a local hard disk that is used for swap space. Only a diskless client does not have a local disk and thus cannot have local swap space. Therefore, answer d is incorrect.

## Question 5

Which of the following commands can be used to determine the Ethernet address of a network interface? [Select all that apply]

- ❑ a. **ifconfig -a**
- ❑ b. **netstat -a**
- ❑ c. **netstat -p**
- ❑ d. **netstat -r**
- ❑ e. **netstat -e**

Answers a and c are correct. The **ifconfig -a** and **netstat -p** commands can be used to determine the Ethernet address of a network interface. **netstat -a** displays information about sockets and connections. Therefore, answer b is incorrect. **netstat -r** displays the routing table. Therefore, answer d is incorrect. **netstat -e** does not exist. Therefore, answer e is incorrect.

## Question 6

Which of the following layers are located between the Transport and Application Layers of the OSI network model? [Select all that apply]

- ❑ a. Session
- ❑ b. Data Link
- ❑ c. Presentation
- ❑ d. Network

Answers a and c are correct. Session provides connection management, and Presentation provides data format mapping. The Data Link and Network Layers are located below the Transport Layer. Therefore, answers b and d are incorrect.

## Question 7

Which of the following statements best describes RARP?

- ❍ a. The IP address is used to determine the Ethernet address.
- ❍ b. The Ethernet address is used to determine the IP address.
- ❍ c. The IP address is used to determine the network mask.
- ❍ d. The IP address is used to determine the hardware address.
- ❍ e. The Ethernet address is used to determine the network mask.

Answer b is correct. RARP uses the Ethernet address to determine the IP address. ARP uses IP address to determine the Ethernet address or hardware address. Therefore, answers a and d are incorrect. Neither is used to determine the network mask. Therefore, answers c and e are incorrect.

## Question 8

Enter the name of the file that is symbolically linked to the /etc/hosts file.

______________________________

The correct answer is /etc/inet/hosts.

# Need to Know More?

Finlayson, Mann, Mogul, and Thelmer, Request For Comment 903: "A Reverse Address Resolution Protocol" (June 1984). Available at **www.nic.mil/ftp/rfc/rfc903.txt**.

Plummer, David, Request For Comment 826, "An Ethernet Address Resolution Protocol" (November 1982). Available at **www.nic.mil/ftp/rfc/rfc826.txt**.

Sun Microsystems, *System Administration Guide, Volume 2*. Available in printed form (part number 805-7229-10), on the Web at **docs.sun.com**, and from the online documentation, AnswerBook2, provided with the Solaris 8 operating system.

Sun Microsystems, *System Administration Guide, Volume 3*. Available in printed form (part number 806-0916-10), on the Web at **docs.sun.com**, and from the online documentation, AnswerBook2, provided with the Solaris 8 operating system.

Sun Microsystems, *System Reference Manual, Section 1 - User Commands*. Available in printed form (part number 806-0624-10), on the Web at **docs.sun.com**, and from the online documentation, AnswerBook2, provided with the Solaris 8 operating system.

Sun Microsystems, *System Reference Manual, Section 1M - Administration Commands*. Available in printed form (part number 806-0625-10), on the Web at **docs.sun.com**, and from the online documentation, AnswerBook2, provided with the Solaris 8 operating system.

14

# Syslog and Auditing Utilities

**Terms you'll need to understand:**

- ✓ The syslog facility
- ✓ The syslog source facilities
- ✓ The syslog severity levels
- ✓ **m4** macros
- ✓ The **logger** command
- ✓ The **who**, **whodo** and **lastlogins** commands

**Techniques you'll need to master:**

- ✓ Configuring the syslog facility
- ✓ Enabling syslog messages to track use of the root login account
- ✓ Using the **who**, **whodo**, and **last** commands to audit login account usage

The first part of this chapter covers the Solaris 8 syslog facility. This mechanism provides the ability to log user and system messages in one or more files on either the local or a remote system. This chapter covers the *Solaris Syslog* test objectives.

The second part of this chapter describes three commands (**who**, **whodo**, and **last**) that are used to audit the usage of the login accounts.

# The syslog Facility

The **syslogd**(1M) command accepts messages sent to it from system (kernel and device driver) and user programs and handles them based on the entries in the /etc/syslog.conf file. These messages can be reporting anything from emergency situations to debugging details. Common uses include monitoring logins and recording hacking attempts. Typically, the **syslogd** command writes these messages to the specified log file, but other processing options are supported. A syslog message is categorized by its source, a *source facility*, and a priority, or *severity level*.

## Source Facilities

To provide better control over the handling of log messages, the facilities generating the messages can be used to determine where the messages are sent or stored. Thus you can maintain separate log files for different types of messages based on the source. Table 14.1 lists the keywords used in the /etc/syslog.conf file to identify the source of messages and control handling.

**Table 14.1 The syslog source facilities.**

| Keyword | Description |
|---|---|
| **auth** | Login authentication |
| **cron** | The **at**(1) and **cron**(1M) commands |
| **daemon** | System daemons |
| **kern** | The kernel |
| **lpr** | The line printer spooling system |
| **local0** through **local7** | As defined locally |
| **mail** | System mail |
| **mark** | Timestamp produced by **syslogd**(1M) |
| **news** | The USENET network news system |
| **user** | User programs |
| **uucp** | The UUCP system |
| * | All facilities except **mark** |

The **user** facility is the default and is used if the source does not specify a facility keyword in the syslog message.

## Priority (Severity) Levels

Along with the source facility, a syslog message can be identified by priority or severity. This identification provides a second mechanism (with finer granularity) for handling messages based on importance. Table 14.2 lists the keywords used in the /etc/syslog.conf file to identify the severity of messages and control handling. These keywords are ordered on the basis of severity (from most severe to least severe).

## Customizing System Message Handling

To control the handling of syslog messages, you add entries to the /etc/syslog.conf file. These entries take the form of one or more facility/severity keyword combinations followed by a tab character and an action. The facility and severity identify a particular source facility and message severity, whereas the action determines how the messages are handled. Facility/keywords and/or actions can be optionally defined using an **m4**(1) macro that can be used to determine if the current system is configured as a syslog host.

### Facility/Severity Keywords Combinations

The facility and severity keywords are separated by a period (.) and identify a particular source facility and severity of messages. For example, **kern.emerg** identifies emergency error messages from the kernel.

**Table 14.2 The syslog severity levels.**

| Keyword | Description |
|---|---|
| **emerg** | Panic conditions |
| **alert** | Conditions that need immediate attention |
| **crit** | Critical conditions |
| **err** | Other errors |
| **warning** | Warning messages |
| **notice** | Conditions that might require special handling |
| **info** | Nonurgent information |
| **debug** | Typically generated by debug messages in programs |
| **none** | Special keyword used to prevent logging of messages generated by specified sources |

Three special cases exist:

- A facility keyword is specified without being followed by a period and a severity keyword. This keyword is used to identify all levels of severity. For example, if the facility keyword **mail** is specified by itself, all severity levels of mail messages are processed.
- A facility keyword is followed by a period and the **none** severity keyword. This combination specifies that no messages from the specified facility should be processed. For example, **mail.none** indicates that no mail messages should be processed.
- The asterisk (*) facility is used. This facility specifies that all source facilities (except the **mark** facility) should be processed. For example, ***.notice** indicates that all messages of the **notice** level sent to syslog (from all sources except **mark**) should be processed.

You can specify more than one facility/severity combination in an /etc/syslog.conf entry by separating them with the semicolon (;) character.

## Actions

Each entry has an action associated with it. Table 14.3 lists the four forms of actions.

## Optional Entries Controlled by m4 Macros

You can define optional entries in the /etc/syslog.conf file using the **m4** macro

```
ifdef(condition, define_if_true, define_if_false)
```

specified in either the facility/keyword column or the action column.

**Table 14.3 The syslog actions.**

| Action | Description |
|---|---|
| ***/filename*** | The identified syslog messages are appended to the specified file (must begin with a slash (/) character). |
| ***@host*** | The identified syslog messages are forwarded to the **syslogd** daemon on the specified remote host (must begin with the at (@) character). |
| ***login account*** | The identified syslog messages are written to the standard out (typically the monitor) associated with the specified login account if the account is currently logged on to the system. Multiple login accounts can be specified (separated by commas). |
| * | The identified syslog messages are written to the standard out of all login accounts currently logged on to the system. |

The **ifdef()** macro provides a conditional control statement. If ***condition*** is true, then the ***define_if_true*** expression is in effect. If not, then the ***define_if_false*** expression is in effect.

The only relevant ***condition*** for the /etc/syslog.conf file is the *'LOGHOST'* keyword. This keyword is used to determine whether the local system has an alias of **loghost** in the /etc/hosts file. This alias indicates that the associated host is configured to store local syslog messages and possibly syslog message from remote hosts. The following /etc/hosts entry shows the solaris8 system as being identified as **loghost**:

```
192.168.99.8     solaris8     loghost
```

The following line shows a typical example of using an **m4 ifdef** macro in the action column of the /etc/syslog.conf file:

```
auth.notice   ifdef('LOGHOST', /var/log/authlog, @loghost)
```

This entry specifies that for an **auth.notice** message, if the local system is identified in the /etc/hosts file as **loghost**, the message should be added to the /var/log/authlog file. Or, if the local system is not identified as the **loghost**, the message should be forwarded to the system identified as the **loghost**.

The following listing shows using an **m4 ifdef** macro to optionally define entire /etc/syslog.conf file entries based on the local system *not* being the **loghost**:

```
ifdef('LOGHOST', ,
user.err        /dev/sysmsg
user.err        /var/adm/messages
user.alert      'root, operator'
user.emerg       *
)
```

This macro specifies that if the local system is defined as **loghost**, then nothing should be done (that is, the ***define_if_true*** expression is blank). If the local system is not **loghost**, then **user.err**, **user.alert**, and **user.emerg** messages should be processed locally.

## The /etc/syslog.conf File

Entries in the /etc/syslog.conf file determine the handling of syslog messages. The **syslogd** daemon reads the /etc/syslog.conf file whenever it is started, or when it is sent the **SIGHUP**(1) signal. Table 14.4 summarizes the default syslog message handling (/etc/syslog.conf contents) for systems that log messages locally. The previously described **m4** macro for **user** messages is also included.

**Table 14.4 The default /etc/syslog.conf file.**

| Facility/Severity | Action | Description |
|---|---|---|
| ***.err;kern.notice; auth.notice** | /dev/sysmsg | All **error**, **kernel.notice**, and **auth.notice** messages are written to the /dev/sysmsg file. |
| ***.err;kern.debug; daemon.notice; mail.crit** | /var/adm/messages | All **error**, **kern.debug**, **daemon.notice**, and **mail.crit** messages are written to the /var/adm/messages file. |
| ***.alert;kern.err; daemon.err** | operator | All **alert**, **kern.err**, and **daemon.err** messages are written to the operator login account (if currently logged in). |
| ***.alert** | root | All **alert** messages are written to the root account (if currently logged in). |
| ***.emerg** | * | All **emerg** messages are written to all login accounts currently logged in. |

Unless an entry exists for a particular facility/severity combination, messages generated using that particular combination are discarded. Be careful not to delete any of the existing entries unless those messages are being handled by a new entry. The most commonly used default log file is /var/adm/messages.

## Messages Generated by the **logger** Command

The **logger**(1) command can be used by users, shell scripts, or programs to generate syslog messages. Table 14.5 lists the command-line arguments for the **logger** command.

**Table 14.5 Command-line arguments for the logger command.**

| Argument | Description |
|---|---|
| ***message*** | Specifies the text of the message. |
| **-f *file*** | Uses the contents of ***file*** as the message. |
| **-i** | Includes the process ID (PID) of the **logger** command on each message. |
| **-p *priority*** | Specifies the priority of the message, which is specified as ***facility.level*** or a number. The default is **user.notice**. |
| **-t *tag*** | Includes ***tag*** on each message. |

The following example uses the **logger** command to log a message with a **user.err** priority:

```
$ logger -p user.err "This is a user error"

$ tail /var/adm/messages

Mar 31 20:09:38 solaris8 su: [ID 810491 auth.crit]
     'su root' failed for dla on /dev/pts/5
Mar 31 20:20:31 solaris8 su: [ID 810491 auth.crit]
     'su root' failed for dla on /dev/pts/5
Mar 31 20:38:12 solaris8 su: [ID 810491 auth.crit]
     'su dla' failed for dla on /dev/pts/7
Apr 19 00:41:02 solaris8 dla: [ID 702911 user.error]
     This is a user error

#
```

### Messages Generated by the login Command

The **login**(1) command, used to log on to the system, can be configured to generate **auth.notice** syslog messages when the root account logs on to the system. In addition, multiple failed attempts to log in as root are logged as **auth.crit** syslog messages. These messages are generated by the **login** command if the /etc/default/login file contains the following entry:

```
SYSLOG=YES
```

### Messages Generated by Internet Services

The Internet services daemon, **inetd**(1M), which is used to start the standard Internet services, can be configured to trace incoming TCP connections by logging the client IP address, TCP port number, and name of the service as a **daemon.notice** syslog message. To enable this logging, add the **-t** command-line argument to the **inetd** command at the end of the /etc/init.d/inetsvc file.

## Auditing Login Accounts and Processes

Several commands are available to monitor the use of system and user login accounts. In addition, you can use several commands to identify the processes currently running on the system and the associated login accounts.

### The who Command

You can use the **who**(1) command to determine which system and user accounts are currently logged in to the local system. Without arguments, the **who** command lists the login account name, terminal device, login date/time, and an indication of X window or origination:

```
$ who
root        console     Apr  4 18:57    (:0)
root        pts/5       Apr  8 22:13    (:0.0)
dla         pts/6       Apr 11 21:06    (winnt40)
$
```

When the **-q** command-line argument is specified, only the login account names and number of users currently logged on are displayed, as shown in the following listing:

```
$ who -q
root      root      dla
# users=3
$
```

## The whodo Command

The **whodo**(1M) command determines the processes that each login account is executing. The following listing shows (among other things) that the user dla is using the **vi**(1) command:

```
# whodo
Thu Apr 19 02:22:25 EDT 2001
solaris8

  console         root     16:16
      ?            423     0:00 Xsession
    pts/2          467     0:00 sdt_shell
    pts/2          483     0:00 ttsession
    pts/2          484     0:01 dtsession
      ?           1091     0:00 dtscreen
      ?            491     0:04 dtwm
      ?            507     0:00 dtaction
      ?            492     0:01 sdtperfmeter
    pts/2          470     0:00 sh
      ?            433     0:00 fbconsole
      ?            468     0:00 dsdm

    pts/3         root     16:17
    pts/3          515     0:00 sh

    pts/4          dla     11:02
    pts/4         1051     0:00 sh
    pts/4         1097     0:00 vi
```

When the -l command-line argument is specified, additional details are displayed, as shown in the following listing:

```
# whodo -l
2:23am  up 14 day(s), 7 hr(s), 27 min(s)  3 user(s)
User  tty        login@    idle     JCPU  PCPU what
root  console    4Apr01    4days          /usr/dt/bin/sdt_shell -c
root  pts/5      8Apr01    2days    1     -sh
dla   pts/6      11Apr01            8     whodo -l
#
```

In addition, if you specify the name of a login account after the -l command-line argument, only information on that login account is displayed.

The **w**(1) command (which is not listed as a test objective) can be used to list the users currently logged in to the system. Its output is similar to that of the **whodo** command.

## The last Command

The **last**(1) command displays login and logout information. You can use this command both to determine which accounts are logged in to the system and to display the last time accounts were used (starting with most recent). The following listing shows a partial output from the **last** command:

```
# last
dla       ftp          winnt40 Fri Apr  6 02:10 - 02:33 (5+00:22)
root      console      :0      Wed Apr  4 18:57   still logged in
reboot    system boot          Wed Apr  4 18:56
root      console      :0      Wed Apr  4 18:52 - 18:53  (00:01)
reboot    system boot          Wed Apr  4 18:51
root      console      :0      Tue Apr  3 21:46 - 18:49  (21:02)
```

As shown in the listing, the dla account logged in to the system from the "winnt40" system at 2:10 on April 6 and logged out at 2:33 the same day. The listing also shows the root account as still being logged on to the system from the console. To list information for only a particular login account, specify the account name as a command-line argument, as shown in the following listing:

```
# last dla
dla       ftp          winnt40 Fri Apr  6 02:10 - 02:33 (5+00:22)
#
```

# Practice Questions

## Question 1

Which of the following commands is used to determine when a particular login account was last used?

❍ a. **logins**

❍ b. **last**

❍ c. **whodo**

❍ d. **ps**

Answer b is correct. The **logins** command displays attributes about login accounts, not the usage of the login accounts. Therefore, answer a is incorrect. The **whodo** and **ps** commands list information regarding processes. Therefore, answers c and d are incorrect.

## Question 2

The /etc/syslog.conf file was modified to capture messages from a particular user application, but the log file still does not contain any of those messages. Which of the following reasons could explain this situation? [Select all that apply]

❑ a. A typographical error exists in the /etc/syslog.conf entry that was added.

❑ b. The **syslogd** program was not restarted.

❑ c. The user application does not generate the expected facility and/or severity of messages.

❑ d. The **syslogd** program is not running.

❑ e. The wrong log is being examined.

Answers a, b, c, d, and e are correct. All of these are reasons the syslog facility would not work as expected. Entries with typographical errors are either ignored or cause other entries to be misinterpreted. The **syslogd** command reads the /etc/syslog.conf file only when it is started or when it receives the SIGHUP signal. The /etc/syslog.conf entry must match the expected facility/severity being used by the user application to submit the messages. If the **syslogd** command is not running, it cannot receive and handle messages. Be certain that the messages are being sent to the intended log file.

## Question 3

Identify the name of the command that combines the **who** command with the **ps** command.

_______________________

The correct answer is **whodo**.

## Question 4

Which of the following are source facilities for syslog messages? [Select all that apply]

- ❑ a. **login**
- ❑ b. **news**
- ❑ c. **local8**
- ❑ d. **kern**

Answers b and d are correct. **news** and **kern** are source facilities for syslog messages. **auth** (not **login**) is the source facility associated with logging onto the system. Therefore, answer a is incorrect. The eight locally defined source facilities are **local0** through **local7**. Therefore, answer c is incorrect.

## Question 5

Which of the following are valid command-line arguments for the **logger** command? [Select all that apply]

- ❑ a. **-p** (Specifies a priority)
- ❑ b. **-l** (Sends the message to the **loghost** system instead)
- ❑ c. **-t** (Specifies a tag that is included with the message)
- ❑ d. **-L** (Specifies the log file that should be used)

Answers a and c are correct. The **-p** and **-t** command-line arguments are valid for the **logger** command. The **-l** and **-L** command-line arguments do not exist. Therefore, answers b and d are incorrect. Processing messages locally or sending them to **loghost** and log files are specified by the entries in the /etc/syslog.conf file.

## Question 6

Which of the following are valid uses for the asterisk (*) within the /etc/syslog.conf file? [Select all that apply]

- ❑ a. Represents all source facilities
- ❑ b. Represents all severity levels
- ❑ c. Represents all messages
- ❑ d. Writes message to all logged-on users

Answer d is correct. You can use an asterisk to write messages to all logged-in users. An asterisk can be used to represent all source facilities except **mark**. Therefore, answer a is incorrect. No symbol or keyword is available to represent all severity levels or all messages. Therefore, answers b and c are incorrect.

## Question 7

Identify the command used to list the login accounts currently logged in to the system.

_______________________________

The correct answer is either the **last** command or the **who** command.

## Question 8

Which of the following are severity levels? [Select all that apply]

- ❑ a. **alert**
- ❑ b. **notice**
- ❑ c. **none**
- ❑ d. **mail**

Answers a, b, and c are correct. **alert, notice,** and **none** are severity levels. **mail** is a source facility, not a severity level. Therefore, answer d is incorrect.

## Question 9

Enter the name of the default log file used for most of the syslog messages.

________________________________

The correct answer is /var/adm/messages.

## Question 10

Which of the following /etc/syslog.conf entries will cause user alert messages to be sent to the **loghost**?

- ❍ a. user.alert ifdef('LOGHOST',/var/adm/alerts,@loghost)
- ❍ b. usr.alert ifdef('LOGHOST',/var/adm/alerts,@loghost)
- ❍ c. usr.alert ifdef('LOGHOST',@loghost,/var/adm/alerts)
- ❍ d. user.alrt ifdef(@loghost,/var/adm/alerts.LOGHOST)

Answer a is correct. The /etc/syslog.conf entry

```
user.alert ifdef('LOGHOST',/var/adm/alerts,@loghost)
```

will cause user alert messages to be sent to the **loghost**. The other answers have an invalid facility (**usr**), severity level (**alrt**), or **m4** macro definition. Therefore, answers b, c, and d are incorrect.

# Need to Know More?

Sun Microsystems, *System Administration Guide, Volume 2*. Available in printed form (part number 805-7229-10), on the Web at **docs.sun.com**, and from the online documentation, AnswerBook2, provided with the Solaris 8 operating system.

Sun Microsystems, *System Reference Manual, Section 1 - User Commands*. Available in printed form (part number 806-0624-10), on the Web at **docs.sun.com**, and from the online documentation, AnswerBook2, provided with the Solaris 8 operating system.

Sun Microsystems, *System Reference Manual, Section 1M - Administration Commands*. Available in printed form (part number 806-0625-10), on the Web at **docs.sun.com**, and from the online documentation, AnswerBook2, provided with the Solaris 8 operating system.

15

# Advanced Disk Management

## Terms you'll need to understand:

- ✓ Virtual file systems
- ✓ Concatenation and Striping
- ✓ Mirroring
- ✓ Redundant Array of Inexpensive Disks (RAID)
- ✓ DiskSuite virtual disk manager
- ✓ Sun StorEdge Volume Manager

## Techniques you'll need to master:

- ✓ Identifying RAID levels
- ✓ Identifying virtual file system pathnames
- ✓ Distinguishing between DiskSuite and Volume Manager

This chapter covers the *Disk Management* test objectives. The first section of this chapter reviews basic disk management commands. The next section introduces and describes features of virtual file systems and defines some of the basic terminology.

The last two sections briefly describe the features and capabilities of two disk management software products that are available for the Solaris 8 operating system: Solstice DiskSuite and Sun StorEdge Volume Manager.

# Basic Disk Management

This section provides a brief review of the basic disk management commands provided with the Solaris 8 operating system. These commands are covered in more detail in Chapter 9.

*Note: Reviewing Chapter 9 should be considered part of your preparation for the Part II exam.*

Before you create a file system on a disk, the disk must be formatted using the **format** command. Next, you must define the volume table of contents (VTOC) using either the **fmthard** or **format** command. The VTOC includes the partition table that determines the number and size of partitions or disk slices. The **prtvtoc** command can be used to display the VTOC. For x86 platforms, the **fdisk** command is used to create or modify the partition table.

You can use the **mkfs** or **newfs** command to create a Unix File System (UFS) on the partition. The file system must fit within a partition, and only one file system can reside within a partition.

The **fsck** command checks and repairs file systems. Typically, a file system should be checked before it is made available for use.

You can use the **mount** or **mountall** command to mount the file system and make it available for use.

# Virtual File Systems

Virtual disk management systems let you use physical disks in different ways that are not supported by the standard Solaris file systems. This section summarizes these advantages and describes several techniques to provide virtual file systems.

## Advantages of Virtual Disk Management Systems

A virtual disk management system can overcome disk capacity and architecture limitations and improve performance and reliability. In addition, manageability is enhanced by the use of a graphical management tool.

### Overcoming Disk Limitations

Virtual disk management systems allow partitions on multiple disks to be combined and treated as a single partition. Not only can file systems be larger than the largest available physical disks, the entire storage area available on a physical disk can be used.

### Improved Performance

Typically, using multiple disks in place of a single disk increases performance by spreading the load across several physical disks.

### Improved Reliabilty

Virtual disk management systems typically support data-redundancy or high-availability features, such as mirroring and Redundant Array of Inexpensive Disks (RAID) configurations. In addition, features such as hot sparing and file system logging reduce recovery time.

### Enhanced Manageability

Virtual disk management systems typically provide a simple graphical user interface for disk management and administration. This interface allows simple, almost error-free administration of complex disk configurations and file systems.

The graphical interface usually includes a visual representation of the physical disks and virtual disk file systems. In addition, it typically supports drag-and-drop capabilities that allow quick configuration changes.

## Concatented Virtual Devices

Unlike the standard Solaris file system, which consists of a single partition (slice), a concatenated virtual file system consists of two or more slices. The slices can be on the same physical disk or on several physical disks. The slices also can be of different sizes.

Concatenation implies that the slices are addressed in a sequential manner. That is, as space is needed, it is allocated from the first slice in the concatenation. Once this space is completely used, space is allocated from the second slice, and so on.

The main advantage of a concatenated virtual device is that it provides a means for using slices that might otherwise be too small for use. In addition, concatenation using more than one physical disk provides some load balancing between the disks and can result in head-movement optimization.

However, using multiple disks increases the chance that a failure of any one disk will result in the failure of the virtual device.

## Striped Virtual Devices

A striped virtual device, like a concatenated virtual device, can consist of two or more slices. The slices can be on the same physical disk or on several physical disks. The slices can also be of different sizes.

Unlike a concatenated device, the slices are addressed in an interleaved manner. That is, as space is needed, it is allocated as a block from the first slice, then a block from the second slice, and so on.

The main advantage of a striped device is that when the slices are on several physical disks, it provides an increase in performance because it allows multiple simultaneous reads and writes. This concurrent activity is possible because each physical disk in the striped virtual device can be accessed at the same time. In addition, like concatenated virtual devices, a striped device provides a means for using slices that might otherwise be too small for use.

As with concatenated virtual devices, multiple disks increase the chance that a failure of any one disk will result in the failure of the virtual device.

*Note: A concatenated striped virtual device is a striped virtual device that has been expanded by concatenating additional slices to the end of the device.*

## Mirroring and Duplexing

*Mirroring* is the technique of copying data being written to an online device to another, offline device. This technique provides a realtime backup of data that can be brought online to replace the original device in the event the original device fails. Typically, the two disks share the same controller. However, if the controller fails, then neither disk can be accessed.

*Duplexing* is similar to mirroring, except that each disk has its own controller. This approach provides a little more redundancy and allows data to be accessed if either a single disk or a single controller fails.

## RAID Configurations

One approach to improving data availability is to arrange disks in various configurations known as Redundant Arrays of Inexpensive Disks. Table 15.1 lists the levels of RAID.

Virtual disk management systems implement one or more of these RAID levels but typically not all of them. The commonly supported RAID levels are 0, 1, and 5.

## UFS File System Logging

With UFS file system logging, updates to a UFS file system are recorded in a log before they are applied. In the case of system failure, the system can be

**Table 15.1 RAID levels.**

| Level | Description |
|---|---|
| 0 | Striping or concatenation |
| 1 | Mirroring and duplexing |
| 2 | Hamming Error Code Correction (ECC), used to detect and correct errors |
| 3 | Bit-interleaved striping with parity information (separate disk for parity) |
| 4 | Block-interleaved striping with parity information (separate disk for parity) |
| 5 | Block-interleaved striping with distributed parity information |
| 6 | Block-interleaved striping with two independent distributed parity schemes |
| 7 | Block-interleaved striping with asynchronous I/O transfers and distributed parity information |
| 10 | Mirrored striping or striped mirroring (combination of RAID 0 and RAID 1) |
| 53 | Similar to RAID 5, except data is taken from RAID 3 disks (the data on a set of RAID 3 disks is copied to another set of disks using the RAID 5 methodology) |

restarted, and the consistency of UFS file systems quickly restored using the log instead of the **fsck** command.

The **fsck** command is a time-consuming and not always 100-percent accurate method of recovering a file system. It reads and verifies the information that defines the file system. If the system crashed during an update, the update might have been only partially completed. The **fsck** command must correct the information by removing these partial updates.

With UFS file system logging, only logged updates are applied to the file system. If the system crashes, the log has a record of what should be complete; this log can be used to quickly make the file system consistent.

# Solstice DiskSuite

Solstice DiskSuite is a software product that can be used to increase storage capacity and data availability and, in some cases, to increase performance.

DiskSuite uses virtual disks, called *metadevices*, to manage the physical disks. A metadevice is a collection of one or more physical disk slices or partitions. You can use the basic disk-management commands, except the **format** command, with metadevices. In general, metadevices can be thought of as slices or partitions.

> **EXAM ALERT**
> Like the standard Solaris file systems that are accessible using raw (/dev/rdsk) and block (/dev/dsk) logical device names, virtual file systems under DiskSuite are accessed using either the raw or block device name under /dev/md/rdsk or /dev/md/dsk. The metadevices (that is, partition names) begin with the letter *d* followed by a number. For example, /dev/md/dsk/d0 is block metadevice *d0*.

Because you can build a metadevice that includes slices from more than one physical disk, it can be used to create a file system that is larger than the largest available physical disk. For SPARC platforms, metadevices can include IPI, SCSI, and SPARCStorage Array drives. For x86 platforms, metadevices can include SCSI and IDE devices. In addition, slices that are too small to be of any use can be combined to create usable storage.

DiskSuite supports four types of metadevices. They are listed in Table 15.2.

DiskSuite let's you expand metadevices dynamically by adding more slices. Then, a UFS file system on that metadevice can be expanded.

### Hot Spare Pools

A *hot spare pool* is a collection of slices that are substituted automatically for slices that fail. When a disk error occurs, DiskSuite locates a hot spare (slice) in the hot spare pool that is at least the size of the failing slice and allocates the hot spare as a replacement for the failing slice. Assuming a mirrored or RAID level 5 configuration, the data from the failed slice is copied to its replacement from the mirrored data or rebuilt using parity information.

## Administration

Two methods are available to manage the DiskSuite objects. The first is the DiskSuite Tool, which provides a graphical user interface. The second is a set of commands referred to collectively as the DiskSuite command-line interface.

**Table 15.2 Types of DiskSuite metadevices.**

| Metadevice | Description |
|---|---|
| Simple | Used directly or as a building block for mirror and trans metadevices (the three types of simple metadevices are stripes, concatenations, and concatenated stripes) |
| Mirror | Used to replicate data between simple metadevices to provide redundancy |
| RAID 5 | Used to replicate data with parity, allowing regeneration of data |
| Trans | Used for UFS file system logging |

### DiskSuite Tool

The DiskSuite Tool, also known as the **metatool** command, is used to set up and administer a DiskSuite configuration. It provides a graphical view of both the DiskSuite objects and the underlying physical disks. You can modify the DiskSuite configuration quickly by using drag-and-drop manipulation. However, the DiskSuite Tool does not support all DiskSuite operations. These operations must be performed using the command-line interface.

### DiskSuite Command-Line Interface

The command-line interface provides a set of commands to create and manage DiskSuite objects. Most of these commands start with the prefix *meta*, such as the **metainit** command used to initialize a metadevice. See the DiskSuite manuals for more information.

## Sun StorEdge Volume Manager

Sun StorEdge Volume Manager is a software product that, like DiskSuite, can be used to increase storage capacity and data availability. Unlike DiskSuite, Volume Manager includes performance analysis tools and dynamic online tuning to provide optimal use of storage.

*Note: Sun StorEdge Volume Manager is also known as the Solaris Enterprise Volume Manager and the Veritas Volume Manager. Sun Microsystems has been reselling the Veritas product under its own brand name since 1997. The Volume Manager supports the virtual file system referred to as the Veritas File System (vxfs).*

EXAM ALERT: Like the standard Solaris file systems that are accessible using raw (/dev/rdsk) and block (/dev/dsk) logical device names, virtual file systems under the Volume Manager are accessed using the either the raw or block device name under /dev/vx/rdsk or /dev/vx/dsk. Typically, disk groups and volumes are specified under these paths, such as /dev/vx/dsk/salesdg/salesvol for the storage space used by a sales organization. Names such as c0t0d0s3 and disk01 are also used to identify devices under the /dev/vx directory structure.

StorEdge Volume Manager uses a *VM disk* to manage storage. A VM disk is a physical disk partition that has been assigned to the Volume Manager. Each VM disk consists of a public region from which storage is allocated and a private region that stores configuration information. A *disk group* is a collection of VM disks that share a common configuration. Initially, a default disk group is used; however, additional groups can be defined to provide better management.

The public region of a VM disk is subdivided into *subdisks*; the subdisk is the basic unit used by the Volume Manager to allocate storage. A *plex* collection of subdisks can be organized to support the following approaches to data availability:

- Concatenated virtual device
- RAID level 0 (striping)
- RAID level 1 (mirroring)
- RAID level 5 (block-interleaved striping with distributed parity information)
- RAID 10 (RAID 1 + RAID 0)

A *volume* is a virtual disk device composed of up to 32 plexes. The volume is the virtual object that the operating system and applications view and manipulate.

### Hot Relocation

When a subdisk fails, Volume Manager automatically reacts by reconstructing the failed Volume Manager objects on a spare disk or free space within a disk group and then substituting the rebuilt subdisk for the failed subdisk.

## Administration

Volume Manager provides three methods to manage disk groups: a graphical user interface (Visual Administrator), a set of command-line utilities, and the **vxdiskadm** menu-oriented interface.

### Visual Administrator

Visual Administrator, also known as the **vxva** command, is used to set up and administer a Volume Manager configuration. It provides a graphical view of both the Visual Manager objects and the underlying physical disks. You can modify the Volume Manager configuration quickly by using drag-and-drop manipulation.

Visual Administrator lets you display statistics about the performance and activity levels of Volume Manager objects either graphically with colored icons or numerically with pop-up forms. Statistics that can be monitored include reads and writes, block reads and writes, total I/O, and average read and write times.

### Command-Line Utilities

The command-line utilities provide a set of commands to create and manage Volume Manager objects. Most of these commands start with the prefix *vx*, such as the **vxdiskadd** command used to add a physical disk to the Volume Manager configuration. See the Volume Manager manuals for more information.

### The vxdiskadm Menu Interface

The **vxdiskadm** command provides a menu-driven interface to the command-line utilities. It eliminates the need to be familiar with the **vx** commands and their command-line arguments.

# Practice Questions

## Question 1

Which of the following virtual devices or RAID levels does Volume Manager support? [Select all that apply]

- ❑ a. Concatenated virtual device
- ❑ b. RAID level 0
- ❑ c. RAID level 1
- ❑ d. RAID level 5
- ❑ e. RAID 10

Answers a, b, c, d, and e are correct. Volume Manager supports concatenated virtual devices as well as RAID levels 0, 1, 5, and 10.

## Question 2

Which of the following are types of virtual file system? [Select all that apply]

- ❑ a. Concatenated
- ❑ b. Aggregated
- ❑ c. Sliced
- ❑ d. Monolithic
- ❑ e. Striped

Answers a and e are correct. Concatenated and striped are two types of virtual file system. Aggregated, sliced, and monolithic do not relate to virtual file systems; they are simply appropriate sounding words. Therefore, answers b, c, and d are incorrect.

## Question 3

Identify the prefix used with most of the commands associated with the DiskSuite command-line interface.

____________________________

The correct answer is “meta”.

## Question 4

Which of the following are features of a virtual disk management system? [Select all that apply]

- ❑ a. Graphical administration tool
- ❑ b. Improved reliability
- ❑ c. Improved performance
- ❑ d. Ability to overcome physical disk limitations

Answers a, b, c, and d are correct. Virtual disk management systems provide all these features.

## Question 5

Enter the abbreviation for a multilevel system storage configuration that is used to improve data reliability.

____________________________

The correct answer is RAID.

## Question 6

Which of the following is a name for a virtual file system that is composed of several partitions and in which the partitions are allocated and used one at a time?

- ❍ a. RAID 5
- ❍ b. Striped
- ❍ c. Concatenated
- ❍ d. Hot spare

Answer c is correct. A concatenated virtual file system is composed of several partitions, and the partitions are allocated and used one at a time. RAID 5 is a configuration that uses a striped file system. Therefore, answer a is incorrect. A striped virtual file system uses all the slices in an interleaved fashion. Therefore, answer b is incorrect. A hot spare is not a type of file system. Therefore, answer d is incorrect.

## Question 7

Enter the word used to describe the technique of writing data to both an online disk and an offline disk to provide a realtime replacement disk if needed.

______________________________

The correct answer is mirroring.

## Question 8

Identify the pathname for virtual file systems associated with the DiskSuite disk manager.

- ❍ a. /dev/dsk/c0d0s0
- ❍ b. /dev/vx/dsk/mktdg/mktvol
- ❍ c. /dev/md/dsk/d0
- ❍ d. /dev/ds/dsk/d3

Answer c is correct. The pathname for virtual file systems associated with the DiskSuite disk manager is /dev/md/dsk/d0. The /dev/dsk/c0d0s0 pathname is associated with standard file systems. Therefore, answer a is incorrect. /dev/vx/dsk/mktdg/mktvol is associated with Volume Manager virtual file systems. Therefore, answer b is incorrect. /dev/ds/dsk/d3 does not exist. Therefore, answer d is incorrect.

## Question 9

Which of the following is the first command used to prepare a new disk for use?

❍ a. **mount**

❍ b. **newfs**

❍ c. **fsck**

❍ d. **format**

Answer d is correct. The **format** command is used first to prepare a new disk for use. The **mount** command is used to mount the file system. Therefore, answer a is incorrect. The **newfs** command is used to create a file system after the disk has been formatted. Therefore, answer b is incorrect. The **fsck** command is used to check the file system. Therefore, answer c is incorrect.

## Question 10

Which of the following administration methods can be used with Volume Manager? [Select all that apply]

❑ a. Graphical administration tool

❑ b. Command-line utilities

❑ c. Menu-driven command interface

❑ d. Client/server remote utility

Answers a, b, and c are correct. You can use the graphical administration tool, command-line utilities, and a menu-driven command interface with Volume Manager. The client-server remote utility does not exist. Therefore, answer d is incorrect.

# Need to Know More?

Sun Microsystems, *Solstice DiskSuite 4.2.1 Reference Guide.* Available in printed form (part number 806-3204-10) and on the Web at **docs.sun.com**.

Sun Microsystems, *Solstice DiskSuite 4.2.1 User's Guide.* Available in printed form (part number 806-3205-10) and on the Web at **docs.sun.com**.

Sun Microsystems, *Sun StorEdge Volume Manager 2.6 Administrator's Guide.* Available in printed form (part number 805-5706-10) and on the Web at **docs.sun.com**.

Sun Microsystems, *Sun StorEdge Volume Manager 2.6 User's Guide.* Available in printed form (part number 805-5705-10) and on the Web at **docs.sun.com**.

Sun Microsystems, *Sun StorEdge Volume Manager Storage Administrator 1.0 User's Guide.* Available in printed form (part number 805-5709-10), on the Web at **docs.sun.com**, and from the online documentation, AnswerBook2, provided with the Solaris 8 operating system.

16

# Pseudo File Systems and Swap Space

**Terms you'll need to understand:**

- ✓ Pseudo file systems
- ✓ proc tools
- ✓ Swap space

**Techniques you'll need to master:**

- ✓ Identifying pseudo file systems
- ✓ Using the proc tools to monitor process status
- ✓ Creating, adding, and deleting swap space

This chapter covers the *Solaris Pseudo File Systems and Swap Space* test objectives. The first section describes the Solaris pseudo file systems and provides information on the more important pseudo file systems. The second section covers managing swap space.

# Solaris Pseudo File Systems

Solaris supports several types of memory-based file systems. These are referred to as *pseudo file systems*. Because they are memory based, these file systems provide faster access to data stored in them. However, they are not permanent. In addition, any directories or files in pseudo file systems are lost when the file system is unmounted or the system is rebooted/shut down. Table 16.1 describes the pseudo file systems supported by Solaris 8.

Of these nine pseudo file systems, the following five file systems do not require any administration: FDFS, FIFOFS, NAMEFS, SPECFS, and SWAPFS. The other four pseudo file systems—CacheFS, LOFS, PROCFS, and TMPFS—are described in the following sections or in Chapter 17.

*Note: In some Solaris documentation, pseudo or memory-based file systems are referred to as "virtual file systems." However, this term is also used for file systems created and managed by virtual disk management systems (covered in Chapter 15). To avoid confusion, we refer to memory-based file systems only as pseudo file systems.*

**Table 16.1 Solaris 8 pseudo file systems.**

| Name | Abbreviation | Use |
|---|---|---|
| Cache File System | CacheFS | Local caching for remote file systems |
| File Descriptors File System | FDFS | Opening file using file descriptors with explicit names |
| First-In First-Out File System | FIFOFS | Accessing data (named pipes) |
| Loopback File System | LOFS | Providing alternate paths to existing data |
| Name File System | NAMEFS | Dynamic mounting of file descriptors by STREAMS modules |
| Process File System | PROCFS | Accessing process status and information |
| Special Device File System | SPECFS | Accessing special character or block devices |
| Swap File System | SWAPFS | Accessing system swap space |
| Temporary File System | TMPFS | Providing fast access to temporary files |

# Process File System (PROCFS)

The Process File System is a memory-based file system used to provide process status and information. One instance of PROCFS exists on a system by default; it is accessible as the /proc directory. This directory contains one directory for each active process on the system. The directory name is the process ID (PID) of the process. Files under each PID directory provide various status and other information about the process. The /proc directory is owned by the root account and has an access mode of 555 (read/execute for owner/group/other), because no user account (not even root) should attempt to modify the files. These files are managed directly by the kernel.

## The proc tools

You extract process status and other information from the /proc PROCFS instance using the proc tools, which are a collection of command-line utilities. These tools also provide stop/start capability.

The PID of the process to be examined is specified as a command-line argument. If more than one process is to be examined, the PIDs should be separated by spaces. Table 16.2 provides a list of the proc tools.

EXAM ALERT: Be familiar with the names and purposes of the proc tools. Memorizing Table 16.2 should be sufficient.

**Table 16.2 The proc tools.**

| Command | Purpose |
|---|---|
| **pcred** | Lists process credentials (effective and real UID and GID) |
| **pflags** | Displays tracing flags and pending and held signals, along with other information |
| **pfiles** | Lists information on all open files |
| **pldd** | Lists dynamic link libraries used |
| **pmap** | Displays the memory address space map |
| **prun** | Restarts the process |
| **psig** | Lists signal actions |
| **pstack** | Displays a stack trace |
| **pstop** | Stops the process |
| **ptime** | Displays the time of process execution |
| **ptree** | Displays the process tree (process and any child processes) |
| **pwait** | Waits for the process to terminate |
| **pwdx** | Displays the current working directory |

The following listing shows sample usage of some of the proc tools. They are used to examine the process (PID = 763) created by the **vi /etc/passwd** command executed by the dla user account (UID = 1001 and GID = 10). The system was accessed remotely from the "wint40" system using an X window terminal. The user is currently located under the dla home directory (/export/home/dla):

```
$ pflags 763
763:     vi /etc/passwd
         data model = _ILP32  flags = PR_ORPHAN
  /1:    flags = PR_PCINVAL|PR_ASLEEP [ read(0x0,0x8045d47,0x1) ]

$ pcred 763
763:     e/r/suid=1001  e/r/sgid=10

$ pfiles 763
763:     vi /etc/passwd
  Current rlimit: 256 file descriptors
   0: S_IFCHR mode:0620 dev:102,0 ino:429381 uid:1001 gid:7
      O_RDWR
   1: S_IFCHR mode:0620 dev:102,0 ino:429381 uid:1001 gid:7
      O_RDWR
   2: S_IFCHR mode:0620 dev:102,0 ino:429381 uid:1001 gid:7
      O_RDWR
   3: S_IFCHR mode:0666 dev:102,0 ino:429338 uid:0 gid:3
      O_RDWR
   4: S_IFREG mode:0600 dev:102,0 ino:880803 uid:1001 gid:10
      O_RDWR
   6: S_IFCHR mode:0620 dev:102,0 ino:429381 uid:1001 gid:7
      O_RDWR

$ ptree 763
759   /usr/openwin/bin/xterm -display winnt40:0
  760   sh
    763   vi /etc/passwd
$

$ pwdx 763
763:     /export/home/dla
$
```

## Temporary File System (TMPFS)

The Temporary File System is a memory-based file system used to improve the performance of file system reads and writes (because memory input/output is much faster than disk-based UFS input/output). Files in a TMPFS instance are not permanent and are lost when the file system is unmounted or the system is rebooted. Typically, TMPFS is used for temporary files (such as intermediate files created when a program is compiled). It can significantly speed up activities that require creating, reading, writing, and deleting temporary files.

The Solaris 8 operating system provides two TMPFS instances. The first is /tmp, which can be used by any user account or process that needs to use temporary files. The /tmp directory is owned by the root account and has an access mode of 1777 (read/write/execute for owner/group/other with the sticky bit set; see Chapter 5). The other TMPFS instance is the /var/run directory, which is used for temporary system files that are not needed across system reboots. This directory is owned by the root account and has an access mode of 755 (read/write/execute for owner and read/execute for group/other).

EXAM ALERT: Be sure you understand TMPFS and its use. Also be familiar with the two instances automatically provided by the Solaris 8 operating system.

## Loopback File System (LOFS)

The Loopback File System is a memory-based file system used to provide alternate path names to existing data. That is, the same copy of the data can be accessed using two different path names. Any file systems subsequently mounted in the original file system also appear in the LOFS. However, any subsequent file systems mounted in the LOFS do not appear in the original file system.

## Cache File System (CacheFS)

The Cache File System is a memory-based file system used to improve the performance of remote file systems and slow devices such as CD-ROM drives. It stores data previously read from the remote file system or slow device in the CacheFS on the local system. When that data is read again, the copy in the local CacheFS is used instead of the data on the remote file system or slow device.

The CacheFS is frequently used with the Network File System (NFS). It is described in more detail in Chapter 17.

# Swap Space

Solaris 8 supports the concept of virtual memory by using space on a hard disk to temporarily store the contents of memory that is currently not being used. When the contents are needed, the system swaps out some other area of memory to the swap file, and then swaps in the requested contents

As long as sufficient memory is available, swap space is not used. When the load on the system increases and resources (mainly memory) are in high demand, swapping may begin to occur.

Keep in mind that pseudo file systems (such as the /tmp TMPFS instance) use memory. As more /tmp space is used, the system will be forced to make more use of the swap space. Heavy use of the /tmp TMPFS instance may cause the system to run of swap space.

## Default Swap Space

When Solaris 8 is initially installed, a partition on a hard disk is defined as the default swap space. Its size is based on the amount of physical memory. Table 16.3 lists the recommended swap space sizes. The Solaris installation programs use these recommendations to determine the default size of the swap space.

If a system needs more swap space because additional memory is added or the system is heavily loaded, the size of the swap space partition cannot be increased without reinstalling Solaris 8 and resizing the swap space partition. However you can use available space from other file system partitions to add swap space.

## Adding More Swap Space

The **mkfile**(1M) command can configure additional swap space using available space from mounted partitions. This command creates a file of a specified size that internally has the appropriate layout. You can then use the **swap**(1M) command to add the file to the system swap space.

The **mkfile** command expects at least two command-line arguments. This first is a number that specifies the size of the file. The size should be followed by **k** or **K** for kilobyte, **b** or **B** for blocks, or **m** or **M** for megabyte, to identify the appropriate scale for the size. Be sure you do *not* place a space between the size and the scale. If a scale is not specified, then the size is assumed to be in bytes. The second command-line argument is the name of the file. You can create more than one file of the specified size by listing multiple file names as command-line arguments, separated by spaces. Two other command-line arguments are supported: **-n**, which indicates that the disk space should be allocated as needed up to the specified size (instead of all being allocated when the file is created), and **-v**, which specifies verbose reporting mode (file names and sizes are listed).

**Table 16.3 Recommended swap space sizes.**

| Equipped Memory | Recommended Swap Space Size |
|---|---|
| Less than 64MB | 32MB |
| 64 to 127MB | 64MB |
| 128 to 511MB | 128MB |
| 512MB or greater | 256MB |

A swap space file (or swap file) can be added to the system swap space using the **swap -a** command. At a minimum, the name of the file must be specified as a command-line argument. Be sure to use the full (absolute) path name for the file. To activate swap space files when the system is rebooted, list them in the /etc/vfstab file. The /etc/vfstab entry should contain the full path name to the swap file and be identified as a swap file system. The /sbin/swapadd script is executed for each swap file system listed in the /etc/vfstab file during system reboot.

> Understand the procedure and commands used to add, delete, and list swap space.

## Administering Swap Space

In addition to being used to add swap space, the **swap** command also supports command-line arguments to list swap space (**-l**), list swap space statistics (**-s**), and delete swap files (**-d**).

The following listing creates a 32MB swap file, adds to the system swap space, and uses the **swap** command to administer the swap space:

```
# swap -l
swapfile             dev  swaplo blocks   free
/dev/dsk/c0d0s1     102,1      8 1049320 1049320

# pwd
/

# mkfile 32m swapfile

# swap -a /swapfile

# swap -l
swapfile             dev  swaplo blocks   free
/dev/dsk/c0d0s1     102,1      8 1049320 1049320
/swapfile             -        8 65528    65528

# swap -s
total: 50732k bytes allocated + 12040k reserved = 62772k used,
585196k available

# swap -d /swapfile

# swap -l
swapfile             dev  swaplo blocks   free
/dev/dsk/c0d0s1     102,1      8 1049320 1049320
#
```

# Practice Questions

## Question 1

Match each pseudo file system with its use.

| | |
|---|---|
| a. CacheFS | 1. Temporary files |
| b. PROCFS | 2. Alternate path names |
| c. TMPFS | 3. Process information |
| d. LOFS | 4. Local caching of data |

Answers a-4, b-3, c-1, and d-2 are correct. CacheFS is used for local caching of data from remote file systems. PROCFS provides status and other information for active processes. TMPFS provides a storage area for fast access to temporary files. LOFS provides access to existing data using alternate path names.

## Question 2

Which **swap** command-line argument will add a swap file to the system swap space?

❍ a. **-a**

❍ b. **-d**

❍ c. **-l**

❍ d. **-s**

Answer a is correct. The **swap** command's **-a** command-line argument adds a swap file to the system swap space. **-d** deletes a swap file from the system swap space. Therefore, answer b is incorrect. **-l** lists the swap space partition and any swap files. Therefore, answer c is incorrect. **-s** lists statistics about swap space use. Therefore, answer d is incorrect.

## Question 3

The /tmp directory is one of two TMPFS instances typically found on a Solaris 8 system. Which of the following is the other?

- ❍ a. /etc/run
- ❍ b. /var/run
- ❍ c. /etc
- ❍ d. /var/tmp
- ❍ e. / (root)

Answer b is correct. /var/run is the other TMPFS instance typically found on a Solaris 8 system. /etc/run and /var/tmp do not exist. Therefore, answers a and d are incorrect. /etc and / (root) cannot be correct, because files stored in a TMPFS instance would be lost when the system was rebooted. If /etc or root was a TMPFS instance, the system could not boot after being shut down.

## Question 4

Which of the following commands are proc tools? [Select all that apply]

- ❑ a. **pstop**
- ❑ b. **pfiles**
- ❑ c. **pstart**
- ❑ d. **pwdx**
- ❑ e. **psig**
- ❑ f. **pmem**

Answers a, b, d, and e are correct. The **pstop** command stops the specified process(es). The **pfiles** command lists the file(s) opened by the specified process(es). The **pwdx** command displays the current working directory of the specified process(es). The **psig** command lists pending signals associated with the specified process(es). The **prun** command, not the **pstart** command, restarts the specified process(es). Therefore, answer c is incorrect. The **pmap** command, not the **pmem** command, displays memory usage of the specified process(es). Therefore, answer f is incorrect.

## Question 5

Which of the following is the correct syntax for the **mkfile** command?

- ❍ a. **mkfile -s 32m /swapfile**
- ❍ b. **mkfile 32 M swapfile**
- ❍ c. **mkfile 32m /swapfile**
- ❍ d. **mkfile 32m -f /swapfile**

Answer c is correct. The correct syntax for the **mkfile** command is **mkfile 32m /swapfile**. The **mkfile** command does not use command-line arguments such as -s or -f. Therefore, answers a and d are incorrect. The size scale (**m** or **M**) should not be separated from the size. Therefore, answer b is incorrect.

## Question 6

Which of the following conditions might require additional swap space? [Select all that apply]

- ❑ a. Physical memory is added.
- ❑ b. The /tmp file system is being heavily used.
- ❑ c. The load on the system increases.
- ❑ d. Several memory-intensive applications are added to the system.

Answers a, b, c, and d are correct. All these conditions may require additional swap space.

## Question 7

Which of the following pseudo file systems are used to provide fast local access to files and directories? [Select all that apply]

- ❑ a. TMPFS
- ❑ b. LOFS
- ❑ c. SWAPFS
- ❑ d. PROCFS
- ❑ e. CacheFS

Answers a and e are correct. TMPFS and CacheFS provide a local cache for data. A TMPFS instance is used for temporary data that is lost when the system is shut down or rebooted, and a CacheFS instance is used for data from remote file systems or slow devices. The LOFS provides alternate path names. Therefore, answer b is incorrect. The SWAPFS provides system swap space that is used to store memory contents. Therefore, answer c is incorrect. The PROCFS provides information about active processes. Therefore, answer d is incorrect.

# Need to Know More?

Mulligan, John P., *Solaris 8 Essential Reference* (New Riders, Indianapolis, IN, 2001), ISBN 0-7357-1007-4.

Sorbell, Mark G., *A Practical Guide to Solaris* (Addison-Wesley, Reading, MA, 1999), ISBN 0-201-89548-X.

Sun Microsystems, *System Administration Guide, Volume 1*. Available in printed form (part number 805-7228-10), on the Web at **docs.sun.com**, and from the online documentation, AnswerBook2, provided with the Solaris 8 operating system.

Sun Microsystems, *System Reference Manual, Section 1 - User Commands*. Available in printed form (part number 806-0624-10), on the Web at **docs.sun.com**, and from the online documentation, AnswerBook2, provided with the Solaris 8 operating system.

Sun Microsystems, *System Reference Manual, Section 1M - System Administration Commands*. Available in printed form (part number 806-0625-10), on the Web at **docs.sun.com**, and from the online documentation, AnswerBook2, provided with the Solaris 8 operating system.

17

# Role-Based Access Control (RBAC)

### Terms you'll need to understand:

- ✓ Roles
- ✓ Profiles
- ✓ Authorizations
- ✓ Privileged operations

### Techniques you'll need to master:

- ✓ Creating and assigning roles
- ✓ Displaying RBAC assignments

This chapter covers the *Role-Based Access Control* test objectives. The first section describes the purpose of role-based access. The second section provides details on the configuration files used to implement role-based access control. The last section summarizes the commands that you can use to manage the RBAC.

# Purpose of Role-Based Access Control

In the past, Solaris system administration has been performed using the root superuser account or a user account granted superuser privileges. Even if a user account needed to access only a few privileged operations or commands to perform a task, the account was granted complete control over the system. This all-or-nothing approach to system administration has always been a security issue. A new feature in Solaris 8, Role-Based Access Control (RBAC), addresses this issue.

The RBAC subsystem supports the concept of a special type of user account called a *role*. Roles are granted a set of superuser privileges to perform selected administrative tasks, such as printer management. Even though roles are a type of user account, they can only be accessed using the **su**(1) command. That is, a role cannot be used as a regular user account accessed directly with a normal login procedure such as **login**(1) or **telnet**(1). You grant superuser privileges to roles (and regular user accounts) by assigning them profiles and/or authorizations.

*Profiles* are sets of authorizations and privileged operations. You can think of a profile as a grouping mechanism used to simplify assigning sets of related superuser privileges. For example, the Device Management profile includes all the necessary authorizations to manage system devices.

*Authorizations* are rights to perform restricted functions, such as shutting down the system. An authorization may not correspond to a single Solaris command. For example, several commands can be used to shut down the system. If a user account has been assigned the authorization solaris.system.shutdown, then the user account can use any of the appropriate commands to perform the shutdown. The set of authorizations associated with the Solaris system have been defined by Sun Microsystems and cannot be modified.

On the other hand, *privileged operations* are Solaris commands that are executed with the UID and/or GID set to the appropriate value(s) to allow proper operation.

In summary, authorizations and privileged operations can be assigned to regular user accounts and roles to allow controlled delegation of superuser privileges. Profiles can be used to assign sets of authorizations and privileged operations.

# The RBAC Database

The RBAC database consists of four attribute databases or files. Collectively, these files define the attributes of the RBAC (roles, profiles, authorizations, and privileged operations). The RBAC database also provides a mechanism to associate profiles, authorizations, and privileged operations to regular user accounts and roles.

The four RBAC database files are:

- *User Attributes Database (user_attr)*—Defines roles and assigns authorizations and profiles to roles and regular user accounts. Also referred to as the Extended User Attributes Database.
- *Profile Attributes Database (prof_attr)*—Defines profiles.
- *Authorization Attributes Database (auth_attr)*—Defines the authorizations.
- *Execution Attributes Database (exec_attr)*—Defines privileged operations. Also referred to as the Profile Execution Attributes Database.

EXAM ALERT

The User Attributes Database (user_attr) is located under the /etc directory. The other three databases are under the /etc/security directory.

Figure 17.1 shows the relationships among the four database files. The User Attributes Database assigns profiles to user accounts and roles by referencing entries in the Profile Attributes Database. Likewise, the User Attributes Database assigns authorizations to user accounts and roles by referencing entries in the Authorization Attributes Database.

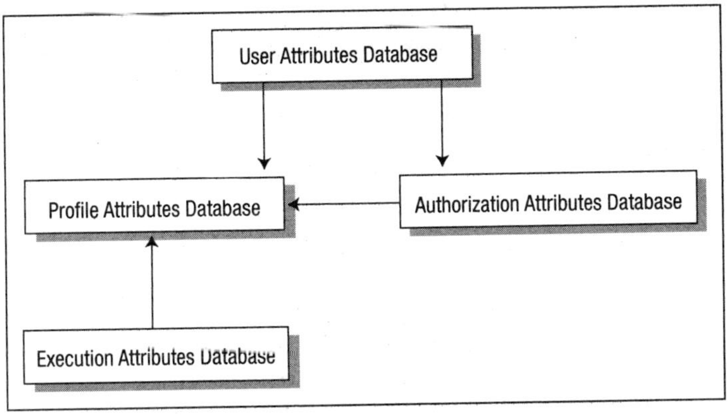


**Figure 17.1** Relationships among the RBAC database files.

The Profile Attributes Database assigns authorizations to profiles by referencing entries in the Authorization Attributes Database. The privileged operations defined in the Execution Attributes Database are associated with a profile by including the name of the profile in the Execution Attributes Database.

## The User Attributes Database (user_attr)

The /etc/user_attr file is the key database of the RBAC. It assigns profiles and/or authorizations to user accounts. It also defines roles (as one or more authorizations and/or profiles). Table 17.1 lists the colon-delimited fields of the user_attr file.

The following listing shows several sample entries from the /etc/user_attr file (wrapped lines are indented to improve readability):

```
prt_adm::::type=role;profiles=Printer Management;
           auths=solaris.system.date
prof_adm::::type=role;auths=solaris.profmgr.*
role_adm::::type=role;auths=solaris.role.*
amber::::type=normal;roles=prt_adm
morgan::::type=normal;roles=prof_adm,role_adm
dana::::type=normal;auths=solaris.jobs.*;
       profiles=Printer Management;roles= prof_adm,role_adm
```

The first entry defines the prt_adm role that is assigned the Printer Management profile. In addition, this role is assigned the authorization solaris.system.date, which allows the role to set the system date.

The second entry defines the prof_adm role, which is assigned all the authorizations relating to RBAC profile administration. Note that the asterisk (*) metacharacter can be used to denote *any* (like the shell metacharacter).

**Table 17.1 Fields of the User Attributes Database.**

| Field | Use |
|---|---|
| **Name** | Name of a user account (defined in the /etc/passwd file) or a role. |
| **Qualifier** | Reserved for future use (empty field). |
| **Res1** | Reserved for future use (empty field). |
| **Res2** | Reserved for future use (empty field). |
| **Attributes** | List of *key=value* pairs separated by semicolons that determines the attributes assigned to the user account or role. Valid keys are **auths** (one or more authorization names, separated by commas), **profiles** (one or more profile names, separated by commas), **roles** (one or more roles, separated by commas), and **type** (set to **normal** if the **name** field is a regular user account or **role** if **name** is a role). |

The third entry defines the role_adm role, which is assigned all the authorizations relating to RBAC role administration.

The fourth entry assigns the prt_adm role to the normal user account *amber*. Once logged in, *amber* can use the **su**(1) command to become the prt_adm and perform any tasks assigned to that role.

The fifth entry assigns the prof_adm and role_adm roles to the normal user account *morgan*. Once logged in, *morgan* can use the **su**(1) command to become the prof_adm and role_adm, and then perform any tasks assigned to those roles.

The sixth entry assigns a considerable amount of access control to the normal user account *dana*. This control includes all authorizations associated with solaris.jobs (**cron** and **at** job management), the Printer Management profile, the prof_adm role, and the role_adm role.

The following listing shows the only default entry in the user_attr file. This entry is for the root superuser account. Basically, it assigns all authorizations and profiles:

```
root::::type=normal;auths=solaris.*,solaris.grant;profiles=All
```

## The Execution Profile Attributes Database (prof_attr)

The /etc/security/prof_attr file is used to assign authorizations from the Authorization Attributes Database (auth_attr) and privileged operations from the Execution Attribute Database (exec_attr) to a single named entity referred to as an "execution profile" or just a "profile". You can then reference these profiles in the user_attr file to assign them to roles or directly to user accounts. Table 17.2 lists the colon-delimited fields of the prof_attr file.

The following listing shows two entries from the /etc/security/prof_attr file. The lines are broken and wrapped to improve readability.

**Table 17.2 Fields of the Profile Attributes Database.**

| Field | Use |
|---|---|
| **Name** | Profile name (case-sensitive). |
| **Res1** | Reserved for future use (empty field). |
| **Res2** | Reserved for future use (empty field). |
| **Description** | Description of profile. |
| **Attributes** | List of key=value pairs (separated by semicolons) that determines the authorizations and operations included in the profile. Valid keys are **auth** and **help**. |

```
Audit Review:::View the audit trail:auths=solaris.audit.read;
       help=AuditReview.html
Printer Management:::Control Access to Printer:
       help=PrinterMgmt.html
```

The first entry defines the Audit Review profile. The phrase "View the audit trail" is a somewhat terse but accurate description. The **Attributes** field references the solaris.audit.read authorization and identifies the help file (located under /usr/lib/help/profiles/locale/C directory). Any privileged operations identified by entries in the exec_attr file as being associated with the Audit Review profile also are allowed.

The second entry defines the Printer Management profile. Only the help file is identified in the **Attributes** field. However, any operations associated with Printer Management in the exec_attr field are allowed in this profile. Table 17.3 lists the default profiles defined by the prof_attr file. Note that the Device Management profile attributes uses the phrase solaris.device.*; this metacharacter expression implies that all solaris.device authorizations are included.

## The Authorization Attributes Database (auth_attr)

The /etc/security/auth_attr file is used to define authorizations (rights to use restricted functions) that can be granted on an individual user-account basis. You can then reference these authorizations in the user_attr file to assign them to roles or directly to user accounts. Table 17.4 lists the colon-delimited fields of the auth_attr file.

The following listing shows three entries from the /etc/security/auth_attr file:

```
solaris.grant:::Grant All Rights::help=PriAdmin.html
solaris.audit.:::Audit Management::help=AuditHeader.html
solaris.audit.config:::Configure Auditing::help=AuditConfig.html
```

**Table 17.3 Default RBAC profiles.**

| Name | Description | auths | help |
|---|---|---|---|
| All | Standard Solaris | N/A | All.html |
| Audit Control | Administers the audit subsystem | solaris.audit.config, solaris.jobs.admin | AuditControl.html |
| Audit Review | Views the audit trail | solaris.audit.read | AuditReview.html |
| Device Management | Controls access to removable media | solaris.device.* | DevMgmt.html |
| Printer Management | Controls access to printers | N/A | PrinterMgmt.html |

**Table 17.4 Fields of the Authorization Attributes Database.**

| Field | Use |
|---|---|
| **Name** | Name of the authorization, consisting of one or more keywords separated by periods (.) that identify a system, subsystem, and function. If the name ends with a period, then this entry is only a title that describes a group of related authorizations. |
| **Res1** | Reserved for future use (empty field). |
| **Res2** | Reserved for future use (empty field). |
| **Short Description** | A short description of the authorization. |
| **Long Description** | A long description of the authorization. |
| **Attributes** | List of zero or more *key=value* pairs (separated by semicolons) that describes the authorization. Currently, the only valid key is **help**; it defines the help file associated with the authorization. |

The first entry defines the solaris.grant authorization. The **Short Title** field identifies this authorization as Grant All Rights. The **Attributes** field identifies the help file (located under the /usr/lib/help/auths/locale/C directory).

The second entry defines the **Short Title** field for the audit management set of authorizations (note the period at the end of the **Name** field.) The third entry defines the solaris.audit.config authorization, which allows the system auditing to be configured (the help file is defined as AuditConfig.html).

Table 17.5 lists the default authorizations defined by the auth_attr file.

**Table 17.5 Default RBAC authorizations.**

| Name | Description | help |
|---|---|---|
| All | Standard Solaris | All.html |
| solaris.* | Primary administrator | PriAdmin.html |
| solaris.grant | Grants all rights | PriAdmin.html |
| solaris.audit.config | Configures auditing | AuditConfig.html |
| solaris.audit.read | Reads the audit trail | AuditRead.html |
| solaris.device.allocate | Allocates a device | DevAllocate.html |
| solaris.device.config | Configures device attributes | DevConfig.html |
| solaris.device.grant | Delegates device administration | DevGrant.html |
| solaris.device.revoke | Revokes or reclaims a device | DevRevoke.html |
| solaris.jobs.admin | **cron** and **at** administration | JobsAdmin.html |

*(continued)*

**Table 17.5 Default RBAC authorizations *(continued)*.**

| Name | Description | help |
|---|---|---|
| solaris.jobs.grant | Delegates **cron** and **at** administration | JobsGrant.html |
| solaris.jobs.user | Creates **cron** or **at** jobs | JobsUser.html |
| solaris.login.enable | Enables logins | LoginEnable.html |
| solaris.login.remote | Remote login | LoginRemote.html |
| solaris.profmgr.assign | Assigns profiles to users or roles | ProfmgrAssign.html |
| solaris.profmgr.write | Creates, modifies, and deletes profiles | ProfmgrWrite.html |
| solaris.role.assign | Assigns roles to users | RoleAssign.html |
| solaris.role.write | Adds, modifies, and deletes roles | RoleWrite.html |
| solaris.system | Machine administration | SysHeader.html |
| solaris.system.date | Sets the date and time | SysDate.html |
| solaris.system.shutdown | Shuts down the system | SysShutdown.html |

Note that all these authorizations are for the Solaris system (developed by Sun Microsystems). If new authorizations are added by other organizations, they should be identified using the reverse order Internet domain name of the organization that creates the authorization. For example, an authorization created by the unixcert.net organization would start with the *net.unixcert* prefix.

## The Execution Attributes Database (exec_attr)

The /etc/security/exec_attr file is used to associate privileged operations (commands executed with a specified UID and/or GID) with profiles. You can then assign these profiles to user accounts or roles. Table 17.6 lists the colon-delimited fields of the exec_attr file.

**Table 17.6 Fields of the Execution Attributes Database.**

| Field | Use |
|---|---|
| **Name** | Name of the associated profile (must match the profile name in the prof_attr file entry exactly). |
| **Policy** | Security policy. Currently, the superuser policy **suser** is the only valid entry. |
| **Type** | Type of entity. Currently, the command type **cmd** is the only valid entry. |
| **Res1** | Reserved for future use (empty field). |

*(continued)*

| Table 17.6 Fields of the Execution Attributes Database *(continued)*. | |
|---|---|
| **Field** | **Use** |
| **Res2** | Reserved for future use (empty field). |
| **ID** | Command to be executed (specified using a full path name or partial path with metacharacters). |
| **Attributes** | List of *key=value* pairs (separated by semicolons) that determines the attributes to apply to the command during execution. Valid keys are **euid** (set effective UID), **uid** (set real UID), **egid** (set effective GID), and **gid** (set real GID). Valid values are UIDs, user account names, GIDs, and group account names. |

The following listing shows two entries from the /etc/security/exec_attr file associated with the Printer Management profile.

```
Printer Management:suser:cmd:::/usr/bin/enable:euid=lp
Printer Management:suser:cmd:::/usr/bin/disable:euid=lp
```

The first entry defines execution of the **enable**(1) command as a privileged operation. It will be executed with an effective UID of lp. The second entry defines execution of the **disable**(1) command as a privileged operation. It also will be executed with an effective UID of lp.

Table 17.7 lists the default privileged operations defined by the exec_attr file. All have the **Policy** field set to **suser** and the **Type** field set to **cmd**.

| Table 17.7 Default RBAC execution attributes. | | |
|---|---|---|
| **Profile Name** | **Command** | **Attributes** |
| All | * | |
| Audit Control | /etc/init.d/audit | euid=0;egid=3 |
| Audit Control | /etc/security/bsmconv | uid=0 |
| Audit Control | /etc/security/bsmunconv | uid=0 |
| Audit Control | /usr/sbin/audit | euid=0 |
| Audit Control | /usr/sbin/auditconfig | euid=0 |
| Audit Control | /usr/sbin/auditd | uid=0 |
| Audit Review | /usr/sbin/auditreduce | euid=0 |
| Audit Review | /usr/sbin/praudit | euid=0 |
| Audit Review | /usr/sbin/auditstat | euid=0 |
| Printer Management | /etc/init.d/lp | euid=0 |
| Printer Management | /usr/bin/cancel | euid=0 |

*(continued)*

| Table 17.7 Default RBAC execution attributes *(continued)*. | | |
|---|---|---|
| **Profile Name** | **Command** | **Attributes** |
| Printer Management | /usr/bin/lpset | egid=14 |
| Printer Management | /usr/bin/enable | euid=lp |
| Printer Management | /usr/bin/disable | euid=lp |
| Printer Management | /usr/sbin/accept | euid=lp |
| Printer Management | /usr/sbin/reject | euid=lp |
| Printer Management | /usr/sbin/lpadmin | egid=14 |
| Printer Management | /usr/sbin/lpfilter | euid=lp |
| Printer Management | /usr/sbin/lpforms | euid=lp |
| Printer Management | /usr/sbin/lpmove | euid=lp |
| Printer Management | /usr/sbin/lpshut | euid=lp |
| Printer Management | /usr/sbin/lpusers | euid=lp |

Be familiar with the formats of all four RBAC database files and the purpose of each of the fields.

# Managing the RBAC

You can use the following commands to manage the RBAC:

- **auths**(1)—Displays authorizations assigned to a user account
- **profiles**(1)—Displays profiles assigned to a user account
- **roles**(1)—Displays roles assigned to a user account
- **roleadd**(1M)—Adds a role definition
- **roledel**(1M)—Deletes a role definition
- **rolemod**(1M)—Modifies a role definition

## Displaying RBAC Assignments

If you use the **auths, profiles,** and **roles** commands without a command-line argument, the authorizations, profiles, and roles assigned to the current user account are listed. To list the authorizations, profiles, and roles assigned to another user account, specify the user account as a command-line argument. For example:

```
$ auths root
solaris.*,solaris.grant
```

```
$ profiles root
All

$ roles root
roles: root : No roles
$
```

## Role Management

The **roleadd**, **rolemod**, and **roledel** commands are used to manage the RBAC roles.

### Creating a Role Using the roleadd Command

The **roleadd**(1M) command provides a quick method to add a new role. At a minimum, the name of the role must be specified as a command-line argument. Table 17.8 lists the command-line arguments supported by the **roleadd** command.

EXAM ALERT

The **roleadd** command supports command-line arguments that are identical to those of the **useradd** command, except **roleadd** does not support the **-R** command-line argument because a role cannot contain other roles.

**Table 17.8 Command-line arguments for the roleadd command.**

| Argument | Description |
|---|---|
| ***role*** | Specifies the name of the new role (required). |
| **-A *authorizations*** | Specifies one or more authorizations (separated by commas). |
| **-b *base*** | Defines a base directory. If a home directory (**-d**) is not specified, the role name is added to ***base*** and used as the home directory. |
| **-c *comment*** | Specifies a comment that is placed in the comment (**gcos**) field of the /etc/passwd file. |
| **-d *directory*** | Defines the home directory of the role. |
| **-e *date*** | Specifies an expiration date for the role. After the specified date, the role is disabled. |
| **-f *days*** | Specifies the maximum number of days the role can be inactive before it is disabled. |
| **-g *group*** | Defines the GID or name of an existing group that will be the primary group for the role. |
| **-G *group*** | Defines the GID or name of an existing group that will be a secondary group for the role |
| **-k *template_dir*** | Specifies the directory that contains a template (default) .profile used for the user profile. |

*(continued)*

**Table 17.8 Command-line arguments for the roleadd command *(continued).***

| Argument | Description |
|---|---|
| **-m** | Creates the home directory if it doesn't exist. The home directory is defined by **-b** and the role name or **-d**. |
| **-o** | Allows an existing UID to be specified. That is, allows a role to be created with a duplicate UID (see **-u**). |
| **-p *profiles*** | Specifies one or more execution profiles (separated by commas). |
| **-s *shell*** | Specifies the login shell; the default is the Bourne Shell (/bin/sh). |
| **-u *uid*** | Specifies the UID of the role. It must be a decimal integer. If not specified, the next highest available UID is assigned. |

The following example creates a role using the **roleadd** command:

```
# roleadd -A solaris.system.date -P "Printer Management" prt_adm
#
```

This command creates the prt_adm role. It assigns the solaris.system.date authorization and the Printer Management profile to the role.

To make life a little easier, the **roleadd** command also supports the **-D** command-line argument, which allows default values to be assigned to authorizations (**-A**), base directory (**-b**), group (**-g**), expiration date (**-e**), maximum inactivity (**-f**), and execution profile (**-P**). Subsequent uses of the **roleadd** command will use these default values if they are not specified.

EXAM ALERT

Roles created with the **roleadd** command do not have a password. These roles are locked and cannot be used until a password is defined for the role using the **passwd**(1) command.

## Modifying a Role Using the rolemod Command

The **rolemod**(1M) command modifies an existing role. The command-line arguments are identical to those of the **roleadd** command, with the following exceptions:

- The base directory (**-b**) is not available. Use **-d** to specify a new directory. Don't forget to include **-m** if the home directory doesn't exist.
- Set defaults (**-D**) is not available.
- The template directory (**-k**) is not available.
- A new role name is specified using **-l** ***role*** if the role name is being modified.

Keep in mind that if the role is changed, the name of the home directory does not change unless the **-d** and **-m** command-line arguments are used.

### Deleting a Role Using the roledel Command

The **roledel**(1M) command deletes a role. Not only is the role definition deleted from the user_attr file, all role assignments in other user_attr entries are modified. The role is specified as a command-line argument. Only one other command-line argument is supported: **-r** removes the home directory associated with the role.

# Practice Questions

## Question 1

Which of the following RBAC data files is not under /etc/security?

❍ a. auth_attr

❍ b. exec_attr

❍ c. prof_attr

❍ d. user_attr

Answer d is correct. The user_attr file is under the /etc directory. All the other files are under the /etc/security directory. Therefore, answers a, b, and c are incorrect.

## Question 2

Which of the following cannot be assigned to a role?

❍ a. A profile

❍ b. An authorization

❍ c. Another role

❍ d. More than one profile

Answer c is correct. A role cannot be assigned to another role. One or more authorizations and/or one or more profiles can be assigned to roles. Therefore, answers a, b, and d are incorrect.

## Question 3

The Execution Attributes Database file is associated with what other RBAC attributes database file?

❍ a. Authorization Attributes Database file

❍ b. Profile Attributes Database file

❍ c. User Attributes Database file

Answer b correct. Privileged operations listed in the Execution Attributes Database file are associated with profiles listed in the Profile Attributes Database file.

The Authorization Attributes Database defines privileged operations associated with a profile and does not relate directly to command execution. Therefore answer a is incorrect. The User Attributes Database associates users and roles with authorizations and profiles. These also do not directly relate to command execution. Therefore answer c id incorrect.

## Question 4

Which of the following keys are allowed in the **attribute** field of the User Attributes Database file? [Select all that apply]

- ❑ a. auths
- ❑ b. help
- ❑ c. profile
- ❑ d. roles
- ❑ e. type

Answers a, c, d, and e are correct. The **attribute** field of the User Attributes Database file can be used to assign authorizations, profiles, and roles. The **type** key identifies entries as being either normal user accounts or roles. The **help** key is supported only in the Authorization and Profile Attributes Database files. Therefore, answer b is incorrect.

## Question 5

Which of the following is the definition of a role?

- ❍ a. A special user account to which authorizations and profiles are assigned.
- ❍ b. A right used to grant access to a restriction function.
- ❍ c. A mechanism used to group authorizations and profile assignments.
- ❍ d. A user account that does not require a password.
- ❍ e. A user account that can be accessed via the login command.

Answer a is correct. *A right used to grant access to a restriction function* is the definition of an authorization. Therefore, answer b is incorrect. *A mechanism used to group authorizations and profile assignments* is the definition of a profile. Therefore, answer c is incorrect. Roles, like other user accounts, require a password and can only be accessed using the **su**(1) command. Therefore, answers d and e are incorrect.

## Question 6

Which of the following keys can be used in the **attribute** field of the RBAC Execution Attributes Database file? [Select all that apply]

- ❑ a. auths
- ❑ b. gid
- ❑ c. help
- ❑ d. profiles
- ❑ e. uid

Answers b and e are correct. The only valid keys for the **attribute** field of the Execution Attributes Database file are **egid**, **gid**, **euid**, and **uid**. The **auths** key can only be specified in the User and Profile Attributes Database files. Therefore, answer a incorrect. The **help** key is only supported in the Authorization and Profile Attributes Database files. Therefore, answer c incorrect. The **profiles** key can only be specified in the User Attributes Database file. Therefore, answer d incorrect.

## Question 7

Which of the following describes the format of the RBAC User Attributes Database file?

- ❍ a. name:qualifier:res1:res2:attributes
- ❍ b. name:res1:res2:description:attributes
- ❍ c. name:res1:res2:short description:long description:attributes
- ❍ d. name:policy:type:res1:res2:ID:attributes

Answer a is correct. The RBAC User Attributes Database file uses the format name:qualifier:res1:res2:attributes. name:res1:res2:description:attributes is the format of the Profile Attributes Database file. Therefore, answer b is incorrect. name:res1:res2:short description:long description:attributes is the format of the Authorization Attributes Database file. Therefore, answer c is incorrect. name:policy:type:res1:res2:ID:attributes is the format of the Execution Attributes Database file. Therefore, answer d is incorrect.

# Need to Know More?

Mulligan, John P., *Solaris 8 Essential Reference* (New Riders, Indianapolis, IN, 2001), ISBN 0-7357-1007-4.

Sun Microsystems, *System Administration Guide, Volume 2*. Available in printed form (part number 805-7229-10), on the Web at **docs.sun.com**, and from the online documentation, AnswerBook2, provided with the Solaris 8 operating system.

Sun Microsystems, *System Reference Manual, Section 1 - User Commands*. Available in printed form (part number 806-0624-10), on the Web at **docs.sun.com**, and from the online documentation, AnswerBook2, provided with the Solaris 8 operating system.

Sun Microsystems, *System Reference Manual, Section 1M - System Administration Commands*. Available in printed form (part number 806-0625-10), on the Web at **docs.sun.com**, and from the online documentation, AnswerBook2, provided with the Solaris 8 operating system.

18

# Network File System

### Terms you'll need to understand:

- ✓ Network File System (NFS)
- ✓ Resource sharing and mounting
- ✓ WebNFS
- ✓ Auto File System (AutoFS) service
- ✓ Cache File System (CacheFS) service

### Techniques you'll need to master:

- ✓ Sharing and unsharing NFS resources
- ✓ Mounting and unmounting NFS resources
- ✓ Determining NFS resources, shared or mounted
- ✓ Configuring AutoFS maps
- ✓ Managing a CacheFS cache

This chapter covers some final topics relating to file systems. The first part covers the Network File System (NFS) and the commands used to administer NFS. The next part describes the AutoFS and CacheFS services that support NFS. This chapter covers the *NFS*, *AutoFS*, and *CacheFS* test objectives.

# The NFS Environment

The NFS service uses the server/client model to allow systems to remotely access the storage of other systems. The NFS protocol is defined by Request For Comment (RFC) 1813, "NFS Version 3 Protocol Specification."

An NFS server allows computers of different architectures running different operating systems to access its storage space across a network. The NFS service also allows multiple systems to access the same information, thereby eliminating redundancy, improving consistency, and reducing administration.

An NFS client accesses this information in a somewhat transparent mode. That is, the remote resource appears and can be treated as local storage space for most operations and applications.

# NFS Administration

Before file systems or directories can be accessed (that is, *mounted*) by a client through NFS, they must be *shared* or, in older terminology, *advertised*. Once the resources are shared, authorized NFS clients can mount them.

> Another term used for sharing NFS resources is *exporting*. This term appears occasionally in Solaris documentation, but is most often seen as a directory name for NFS resources such as /export/home or /export/swap.

## Sharing NFS Resources

NFS resources can be shared using the **share**(1M) command and unshared using the **unshare**(1M) command. In addition, any resources identified in the /etc/dfs/dfstab file are automatically shared at system boot or when the **shareall**(1M) command is used. Shared resources are automatically recorded in the /etc/dfs/sharetab file. When the **unshareall**(1M) command is used, all resources listed in the /etc /dfs/sharetab file are automatically unshared.

> Actually, the NFS server is started and the identified resources are shared when the system enters system run level 3 as a result of system boot or administrator actions. The resources are unshared and the NFS server is stopped when the system run level changes to any level other than 3. Remember the NFS client is started at run level 2.

## The **share** Command

The **share** command shares NFS resources so that NFS clients can mount and access them. At a minimum, you must specify the full pathname of the directory (or mount point of the file system) to be shared as a command-line argument.

In addition, three other command-line arguments are supported. The **-d** command-line argument is followed by a description of the data being shared. The **-F nfs** command-line argument is used to specify the type of file system. If not specified, the default file system type listed in the /etc/dfs/fstypes file (NFS) is assumed. The **-o** command-line argument is followed by one or more NFS-specific options (separated by commas). The **share** command options for NFS are listed in Table 18.1. For details on the settings associated with these options, consult the **share**(1M) description in the *System Reference Manual.*

The following listing uses the **share** command to allow NFS clients to mount the /export/home file system, including WebNFS clients. All clients will have read-only access:

```
# share -F nfs -o public,ro /export/home
#
```

If you use the **share** command without any command-line arguments, the currently shared resources will be listed.

**Table 18.1 The share command's NFS-specific options.**

| Option | Description |
|---|---|
| **aclok** | Allows access control for NFS Version 2 clients |
| **anon=*uid*** | Assigns anonymous users the specified uid |
| **index=*file*** | Displays the contents of ***file*** instead of listing the directory for WebNFS clients |
| **nosub** | Prevents clients from mounting subdirectories of shared resources |
| **nosuid** | Prevents clients from setting setuid or setgid access modes on files |
| **public** | Specifies a public file handle |
| **ro** | Allows read-only access |
| **ro=*list*** | Allows read-only access to those clients specified by ***list*** |
| **root=*list*** | Allows root access to root users on clients specified by ***list*** |
| **rw** | Allows read/write access |
| **rw=*list*** | Allows only read/write access to those clients specified by ***list*** |
| **sec=*mode*** | Uses one or more of the security modes specified by ***mode*** to authenticate clients |
| **window=*value*** | Sets the maximum lifetime for a client's credentials to ***value*** seconds |

## The **unshare** Command

The **unshare** command stops the sharing of NFS resources so that NFS clients can no longer mount and access them. At a minimum, you must specify the full pathname of a directory (or mount point of the file system) that is currently shared as a command-line argument.

Only one other command-line argument is supported: **-F nfs**, which is used to specify the type of file system. If not specified, the default file system type listed in the /etc/dfs/fstypes file (NFS) is assumed.

The following listing uses the **unshare** command to stop the sharing of the /export/home file system:

```
# unshare -F nfs /export/home
#
```

## The /etc/dfs/dfstab File

The /etc/dfs/dfstab file specifies resources that should be shared automatically when the system is changed to run level 3 or when the **shareall** command is used.

This file can be modified using any text editor. To automatically share a resource, add a line to the /etc/dfs/dfstab file that contains the **share** command with the desired command-line arguments and options that would have been entered manually. To remove automatic sharing of a resource, delete the appropriate **share** command from /etc/dfs/dfstab. See the previously described **share** commands for examples.

*Note: You might wonder why some of the directories, files, and even commands associated with NFS use the phrase dfs or df. This usage comes from the System V (5) version of the Unix operating system. Originally, Distributed File Systems (DFS) had two variations: NFS and the Remote File System (RFS). Directories, files, and commands that contained the dfs phrase were used to manage and configure both types of file systems. Since then, RFS has disappeared, leaving behind the DFS legacy.*

## The **shareall** and **unshareall** Commands

The **shareall** command shares one or more resources. If the **-F nfs** command-line argument is not specified, the default file system type (NFS) is assumed. If the name of a file (that contains one or more **share** commands) is not specified as a command-line argument, the /etc/dfs/dfstab file is used by default.

The **unshareall** command unshares all currently shared resources. If the **-F nfs** command-line argument is not specified, the default file system type (NFS) is assumed.

### The **dfshares** Command

The **dfshares**(1M) command lists shared resources on either the local or a remote system. If the hostname (or IP address) of a remote system is specified as a command-line argument, the resources shared on that system are listed.

In addition, two other command-line arguments are supported. The **-F nfs** command-line argument is used to specify the type of file system. If not specified, the default file system type listed in the /etc/dfs/fstypes file (NFS) is assumed. If the **-h** command-line argument is specified, the header describing the columns of the resource listing is not displayed.

In addition, you can obtain information on locally shared resources from the /etc/dfs/sharetab file. This file is updated by the **share**, **shareall**, **unshare**, and **unshareall** commands to reflect the currently shared resources.

## Mounting NFS Resources

NFS resources that have been shared by an NFS server can be mounted by an NFS client using the **mount**(1M) command and unmounted using the **umount**(1M) command. In addition, any NFS resources identified in the /etc/vfstab file are automatically mounted at system boot or when the **mountall**(1M) command is used. Likewise, the NFS resources listed in the /etc/mnttab file are unmounted by using the **umountall**(1M) command.

### The **mount** Command

The **mount** command is used to mount NFS resources like any other standard Solaris file system so that NFS clients can mount and access them. For NFS, you specify the hostname (or Internet Protocol [IP] address) and pathname of the currently shared directory as a command-line argument followed by a mount point. The hostnames and pathnames are separated by a colon (:).

The generic **mount** command-line arguments are listed in Table 18.2. A few of the more significant NFS-specific options used with the **-o** command-line argument are listed in Table 18.3 (multiple NFS-specific options are separated by commas.) For additional information, see the **mount_nfs**(1M) page in the *System Reference Manual.*

**Table 18.2 The mount command-line arguments.**

| Argument | Description |
|---|---|
| -F *fstype* | Specifies the file system type |
| -m | Mounts the file system without creating an /etc/mnttab entry |
| -o | Specifies NFS-specific options (see Table 18.3) |
| -O | Overlays an existing mount point |
| -r | Mounts the file system read-only |

**Table 18.3 The mount command's NFS-specific options.**

| Option | Description |
|---|---|
| **hard** | If the server does not respond, continues to try to mount the resource |
| **intr** | Allows keyboard interrupts to kill the process while waiting on a **hard** mount |
| **nointr** | Does not allow keyboard interrupts to kill the process while waiting on a **hard** mount |
| **public** | Specifies a public file handle |
| **retrans=*n*** | Retransmits NFS requests ***n*** times |
| **retry=*n*** | Retries the mount operation ***n*** times |
| **ro** | Mounts resource read-only |
| **rw** | Mounts resource read/write |
| **soft** | If the server does not respond, returns an error and exits |
| **timeo=*n*** | Sets the NFS time-out to ***n*** tenths of a second |

The following listing uses the **mount** command to mount the /export/home file from the sun system on the /sun_home mount point. The resource is soft mounted (1,000 attempts) with read-only access:

```
# mount -F nfs -o soft,retry=1000,ro sun:/export/home /sun_home
#
```

If you use the **mount** command without any command-line arguments, all currently mounted file systems (standard Solaris file systems and NFS resources) are displayed.

## The umount Command

The **umount** command is used to unmount local file systems and remote NFS resources so that local users can no longer access them. For NFS, you specify one or more *system:pathname* pairs (or file system mount points) that are currently mounted as command-line arguments.

Two other command-line arguments are supported. The first is **-V**, which displays instead of executes the command line used to perform the unmount (used to verify the command line). The second is the **-a**, which performs parallel unmount operations if possible.

The following listing uses the **umount** command to unmount the /export/home file system being shared from the **solaris** host:

```
# umount solaris:/export/home
#
```

## The /etc/vfstab File

The /etc/vfstab file, referred to as the *file system table*, specifies resources that should be automatically mounted when the system is booted or when the **mountall** command is used.

You can modify this file using any text editor. To automatically mount an NFS resource, add a line to the /etc/vfstab file that contains the appropriate options that would have been entered manually with a **mount -F nfs** command. To remove automatic mounting of an NFS resource, delete the appropriate line from the /etc/vfstab file.

Table 18.4 lists the (tab-separated) fields and the appropriate values of an entry in the /etc/vfstab file as they pertain to mounting an NFS resource. A hyphen (-) indicates no entry in a field.

NFS supports *client-side failover*. That is, if an NFS resource becomes unavailable, the client can switch to another NFS server that provides a "replicated" copy of the resource. You enable this failover capability by adding an entry in the /etc/vfstab file for the resource. In the **Device To Mount** field, list the systems that provide the replicated resource, separated by commas. You should also specify the read-only option (**-o ro**) in the **Mount Options** field. For example, to provide client-side failover for the /export/local resource that is available from either the **alpha** or the **beta** NFS server and mounted at /usr/local, add the following entry to the /etc/vfstab file:

```
alpha,beta:/export/local - /usr/local nfs - no -o ro
```

**Table 18.4 Fields of an NFS resource /etc/vfstab entry.**

| Field | Description |
|---|---|
| **Device To Mount** | Uses the *system:resource* format, where *system* is a hostname or IP address and *resource* is the full path name of the shared NFS resource |
| **Device To fsck** | Uses a hyphen (-) to indicate no entry, because NFS clients should not check remote NFS resources with the **fsck** command |
| **Mount Point** | Specifies the subdirectory where the NFS resource should be mounted |
| **FS Type** | Uses **nfs** to indicate an NFS resource |
| **fsck Pass** | Uses a hyphen (-) to indicate no entry |
| **Mount At Boot** | Uses **yes** to indicate that the resource should be mounted at boot or when the **mountall** command is executed; otherwise, **no** |
| **Mount Options** | Specifies any desired NFS mount options; see Table 18.3 or the manual page for the **mount** command |

The read-only resources (**-o ro** mount option) should be configured for client-side failover. Also be certain that the system hostnames or IP addresses are valid and separated by commas.

## The **mountall** and **umountall** Commands

The **mountall** command is used to mount one or more local file systems and/or remote (NFS) shared file systems or directories. If the name of a file (containing information on one or more resources) is not specified as a command-line argument, the /etc/vfstab is used by default. The **mountall** command will mount only the resources in the file system table (or specified file) that have the **Mount At Boot** column set to **yes**.

If a file system type is specified using the **-F** command-line option, only file systems of that type are mounted. If the **-l** command-line argument is specified, only local file systems or directories are mounted. If the **-r** command-line argument is specified, only remote shared file systems or directories are mounted.

The **umountall** command is used to unmount all currently mounted resources. It also supports the **-F**, **-l**, and **-r** command-line arguments supported by the **mountall** command. In addition, it supports the **-h** ***host*** command-line argument to specify that only the resources mounted from that host should be unmounted. The **-k** command-line argument can be used to kill processes using the **fuser**(1M) command to allow unmounting. Also the **-s** command-line argument, which prevents unmount operations from being performed in parallel. Currently mounted file resources are typically listed in the /etc/mnttab file.

## The **dfmounts** Command

The **dfmounts**(1M) command lists currently mounted resources on either the local or a remote system (and its clients). If you specify the hostname (or IP address) of a remote system as a command-line argument, the resources mounted on that system (and its clients) are listed.

In addition, two other command-line arguments are supported. The **-F nfs** command-line argument is used to specify the type of file system. If not specified, the default file system type listed in the /etc/dfs/fstypes file (NFS) is assumed. If the **-h** command-line argument is specified, the header describing the columns of the listing is not displayed. The following listing uses the **dfmounts** command to list the NFS resources on the local system named **solaris**:

```
# dfmounts
RESOURCE   SERVER PATHNAME           CLIENTS
   -       solaris /export/home   uxsys2.ambro.org
```

## WebNFS

WebNFS extends the NFS protocol to allow Web browsers or Java applets to access NFS shared resources. It allows client systems to access NFS resources without requiring them to be NFS clients. Browsers can access NFS resources by using an NFS Uniform Resource Locator (URL) that takes the form **nfs://*server*/*path***. The WebNFS server and client specifications are defined by RFCs 2054 and 2055.

The **share** command supports two NFS-specific options that pertain to WebNFS access. The first is the **public** option. Each server has one public file handle that is associated with the root file system of the server. NFS URLs are relative to the public file handle. For example, accessing the target directory under the /usr/data shared resource on the host server requires using the **nfs://server/usr/data/target** NFS URL. However, if the **public** option is specified when the /usr/data directory is shared, the public file handle is associated with the /usr/data directory; this association allows using the **nfs://server/target** NFS URL to access the same data.

The second option is **index**, which is used to specify a file that contains information that should be displayed instead of a listing of the directory. The following listing uses the **share** command to enable read/write NFS and WebNFS access relative to the /export/home directory:

```
# share -F nfs -o rw,public,index=index.html /export/home
#
```

# The Auto File System Service

The Auto File System (AutoFS) service is a client-side service that is used to automatically mount and unmount NFS resources on demand. This service simplifies keeping track of resources manually and can reduce network traffic. In addition, AutoFS eliminates the need to add NFS mounts in the /etc–/vfstab file. It allows faster booting and shutdown, and users need not know the root password to mount/unmount NFS resources.

The **automount**(1M) command runs when the system is booted (system run level 2) and initializes the AutoFS service. In addition, the **automountd**(1M) command is started at this time. The **automountd** command is a daemon process that runs continuously and provides the automatic mounting and unmounting.

By default, a resource is unmounted if it is not accessed for 10 minutes. You can modify this default time by using the **automount** command and including the **-t** command-line argument followed by a number representing a time (in seconds).

The configuration of the AutoFS service is controlled by *AutoFS maps* that define local mount points and associate remote NFS resources with the mount points. These maps are read by the **automount** command during initialization.

## AutoFS Maps

The three types of AutoFS (or automount) maps are auto_master, direct, and indirect. All these maps are under the /etc directory.

### The /etc/auto_master File

The auto_master file associates directories with indirect maps. In addition, the auto_master file references one or more direct maps.

Entries in the auto_master file consist of three fields:

- *Mount point*—The initial portion of a full pathname to a local directory where an NFS resource should be mounted.
- *Map name*—The file name of a map (direct or indirect) or a special built-in map. You can identify a built-in map by the first character in its name, which is a hyphen (-).
- *Mount options*—Zero or more (comma-separated) NFS-specific mount options, as described earlier in Table 18.3.

A special mount point that uses the notation /- indicates that the map listed in the map name field is a direct map that actually contains the mount points. In addition, a special entry that consists of only the keyword **+auto_master** is used to include AutoFS maps that are part of Network Information Service (NIS) or NIS+.

The following listing shows the contents of the /etc/auto_master file:

```
# Master map for automounter
#
+auto_master
/net            -hosts          -nosuid,nobrowse
/home           auto_home       -nobrowse
/xfn            -xfn
/-              auto_direct
```

As previously described, the **/net** and **/xfn** entries reference built-in maps. The **/home** entry references the indirect map /etc/auto_home, and the / entry references the direct map /etc/auto_direct.

The **-hosts** built-in map uses the hosts database. The **-xfn** built-in map uses resources shared thorough the Federated Naming Service (FNS).

### Direct Maps

A direct map provides both mount point and NFS resources. Entries in a direct map consist of three fields:

- *Key*—Typically a full pathname that is to be used as a mount point.
- *Mount options*—Zero or more (comma-separated) NFS-specific mount options, as described earlier in Table 18.3.
- *NFS resource*—Files that take the form *server:file system*, which identifies a file system shared by the system server. Because more than one NFS server might be providing the same resource, multiple resources can be specified (separated by spaces). The first available resource is used.

The following listing shows the contents of the /etc/auto_direct file that is referenced in the /etc/auto_master file:

```
/usr/local/bin                        nfsserver:/usr/local/bin
/usr/games          -ro               nfsserver:/usr/games
```

In this example, the /usr/local/bin and /usr/games directories shared by the host named **nfsserver** are mounted on the local system under mount points using the same names.

EXAM ALERT

The default name for the initial direct map is *auto_direct*.

## Indirect Maps

An indirect map provides the remainder of the /etc/auto_master mount point and identifies the NFS resource that should be mounted on the client. Entries in an indirect map consist of three fields:

- *Key*—Typically a directory that provides the remainder of the mount point.
- *Mount options*—Zero or more (comma-separated) NFS-specific mount options, as described earlier in Table 18.3.
- *NFS resource*—Files that take the form *server:file system*, which identifies a file system shared by the system server.

The following listing shows the contents of the /etc/auto_home file:

```
dla                                  solaris:/export/home/dla
guest       -rw,nosuid               nfsserver:/export/home/guest
```

In this example, the indirect map is referenced by the **/home** entry in the auto_master file. It contains two entries. The first entry identifies the /home/dla mount point, which is used to mount the /export/home/dla directory from the host named **solaris**. The second entry identifies the /home/guest mount point, which is used to mount the /export/home/guest directory from the host named **nfsserver**.

The default name for the initial direct map is auto_home.

### Running the **automount** Command

When changes are made to the AutoFS maps, you may need to execute the **automount** command manually. Any changes to the /etc/auto_master file require that the **automount** command be executed to put the changes into effect. The command also must be executed when an addition or a deletion is made to a direct map.

## The Cache File System Service

The Cache File System (CacheFS) is a client-side service that provides the ability to cache a remotely accessed NFS resource locally on the NFS client. Doing so not only speeds up client access to the data but also decreases network traffic and load on the NFS server.

After you create a cache, a remote NFS resource can be mounted "in" the cache. The first time the NFS resource is accessed, data is copied from the remote NFS server into the local cache. Subsequent accesses are from the local cache instead of the remote NFS server. Like other types of file systems, the remote NFS resource can be mounted manually using the **mount** command, at system boot, by adding it to the /etc/vfstab file, or as needed using the AutoFS mechanism (described in the previous section).

*Note: The root (/) and /usr file systems cannot be cached using the CacheFS mechanism. However, these two file systems can be cached using the AutoClient configuration, which is briefly described in Chapter 13.*

### Configuring a Cache

The **cfsadmin**(1M) command is used to create, check, tune, and delete caches.. The **cachefsstat**(1M) command can also be used to display cache statistics.

You specify the **-c** command-line argument to create a cache, followed by the full pathname of a directory to be used for the cache. In addition, multiple options (separated by commas) can be specified using the **-o** command-line argument.

The following listing uses the **cfsadmin** command to create a cache under the /cache directory. The size of the largest file that can be cached is set to 10MB:

```
# cfsadmin -c -o maxfilesize=10 /cache
#
```

To list the file systems mounted in the cache and the cache status, use the **-l** command-line argument. Additional command-line arguments include **-s** to perform a consistency check, **-u** to update cache parameters, and **-d** to delete a cache. All of these command-line arguments should be followed by the full pathname of the cache directory.

Mounting a remote NFS resource in the cache using the **mount** command requires specifying the remote file system, the local cache, and a local mount point.

The **-F** command-line argument should be used to identify the file system type as CacheFS. In addition, at least two cache-specific mount options need to be specified using the **-o** command-line argument: **backfstype**, which is used to identify the type of file system being mounted (typically NFS); and **cachedir**, which is used to identify the cache directory. The following listing uses the **mount** command to mount the /export/home file system from the host **sparc20** on the /home mount point (referred to as the *front file system*) using /cache as the cache directory. The line is wrapped to improve readability:

```
# mount -F cachefs -o backfstype=nfs,cachedir=/cache
  sparc20:/export/home /home
#
```

### Checking the Status of a Cache

To display the status of a cached file system, use the **cfsadmin** command and specify the **-l** command-line argument followed by the name of the cache.

The following information about the cache is displayed:

- **maxblocks**—The maximum amount of storage space the cache can use (expressed as a percentage of blocks in the front file system).
- **minblocks**—The minimum amount of storage space the cache can use (expressed as a percentage of blocks in the front file system).
- **threshblocks**—The threshold at which additional resources cannot be claimed after **minblocks** is reached (expressed as a percentage of blocks in the front file system).
- **maxfiles**—The maximum number of files the cache can use (expressed as a percentage of blocks in the front file system).

- **minfiles**—The minimum number of files the cache can use (expressed as a percentage of blocks in the front file system).
- **threshfiles**—The threshold at which additional inodes cannot be claimed after **minfiles** is reached (expressed as a percentage of inodes in the front file system).
- **maxfilesize**—Size of the largest file allowed in the cache.
- **mount info**—The resource being mounted and its local mount point. The slash (/) characters are displayed as underscore (_) characters.

The maximum, minimum, and threshold parameters can be modified using the **cfsadmin** -*u* command. The following listing uses the **cfsadmin -l** command to display the cache status:

```
# cfsadmin -l /cache
cfsadmin: list cache FS information
   maxblocks     90%
   minblocks      0%
   threshblocks  85%
   maxfiles      90%
   minfiles       0%
   threshfiles   85%
   maxfilesize    3MB
  sparc20:_export_home:_home
#
```

## Displaying Cache Statistics

To display statistical information about the performance of the cached file system, use the **cachefsstat**(1M) command and specify the mount point of the cached file system.

The following statistics about the cached file are displayed:

- **cache hit rate**—Percentage of attempts to locate files or directories in the cached file system that were successful, followed by a count of the actual hits and misses
- **consistency checks**—Number of consistency checks performed, followed by the count of passed and failed checks
- **modifies**—Number of modify operations
- **garbage collection**—Number of attempts to reclaim resources that are no longer used

The following listing uses the **cachefsstat** command to display the cached file system statistics:

```
# cachefsstat /home

    /home
                  cache hit rate:    57% (8 hits, 6 misses)
              consistency checks:     14 (14 pass, 0 fail)
                        modifies:      0
              garbage collection:      0
#
```

Note that the **cfsadmin -l** command reports on the configuration status (tunable parameters) of the cache, whereas the **cachefsstat** reports on the contents of the cache (cached file system statistics).

## Checking the Consistency of a Cache

To be certain that the information in a cache is up to date, periodic consistency checks are performed automatically. These checks may create a large amount of network activity. To reduce the amount of network traffic, you can disable the automatic consistency checking and check the consistency manually (on demand).

To disable automatic consistency checking (that is, to request on-demand consistency checking), specify the **demandconst** option when the file system is mounted. The line is wrapped to improve readability:

```
# mount -F cachefs -o backfstype=nfs,cachedir=/cache,demandconst
sparc20:/export/home /home
#
```

To perform a consistency check on demand, use **cfsadmin -s** followed by a mount point of the cached files system as a command-line argument:

```
# cfsadmin -s /home
#
```

## Managing a Cache Log

The **cachefslog**(1M) command is used to set up, verify, and halt CacheFS logging. The **cachefswssize**(1M) command is used to analyze the log to determine a recommended working set size for the cache. A cache that's too small will cause access delays and higher network traffic (a low cache hit rate). A cache that's too large will waste file system space.

To set up a CacheFS log, use the **cachefslog** command with the **-f** command-line argument followed by the file name to be used for the log and the name of directory where the cached file system is mounted (not the name of the cache itself).

For example, to setup a log named /var/tmp/home_log on a cached file system mounted at /home, use the following **cachefslog** command:

```
# cachefslog -f /var/tmp/home_log /home
/var/tmp/home_log: /home
#
```

To verify cache logging, use the **cachefslog** command and specify only the mount point of the cached file system as a command-line argument:

```
# cachefslog /home
/var/tmp/home_log: /home
#
```

To halt logging, use the **cachefslog** command with the **-h** command-line argument followed by the mount point of the cached file system:

```
# cachefslog -h /home
not logged: /home
#
```

To determine the appropriate size for the cache, set up CacheFS logging and allow it to run for an appropriate time period (such as a day or week) to provide a snapshot of the representative work load. Then, stop logging and use the **cachefswssize** with the file name of the log as a command-line argument:

```
# cachefswssize /var/tmp/home_log

    /home
                end size:             72k
         high water size:             72k

    total for cache
            initial size:          53888k
                end size:             72k
         high water size:             72k
#
```

The **end size** (cache working set size when logging was halted) and **high water size** (largest cache working set size) are displayed for each file system mounted in the cache. In this example, only one file system (/home) is mounted.

The **total for cache** summary includes the **initial size** of the cache. If the **high water size** is the same as the **initial size**, then the cache is probably too small. If the **high water size** is much smaller than the **initial size**, then the cache is probably too large.

# Practice Questions

## Question 1

Which of the following commands can be used to mount the /export/home file system from the solaris system (IP address of 192.168.39.7) on the /mnt mount point?

❍ a. **mount -F nfs -h solaris /export/home /mnt**

❍ b. **mount -F nfs 192.168.39.7:/export/home /mnt**

❍ c. **mount -F nfs /mnt solaris:/export/home**

❍ d. **mount -F nfs /export/home@solaris /mnt**

Answer b is correct. The first argument following the -F file system type should be the hostname or IP address of the system sharing the resource. None of the other answers uses the appropriate syntax or command-line arguments. Therefore, answers a, c, and d are incorrect.

## Question 2

Enter the name of the file system type used to temporarily store a remote NFS resource on a local disk.

____________________________

The correct answer is CacheFS.

## Question 3

Which of the following are types of AutoFS maps? [Select all that apply]

❑ a. direct

❑ b. indirect

❑ c. linked

❑ d. auto_master

❑ e. auto_home

Answers a, b, and d are correct. Direct, indirect, and auto_master are types of AutoFS maps. The name *linked* is not associated with the AutoFS capability. Therefore, answer c is incorrect. Auto_home is a commonly used name for an indirect map. Therefore, answer e is incorrect.

## Question 4

Which of the following situations requires that the automount command be manually executed? [Select all that apply]

- ❑ a. Addition to auto_master
- ❑ b. Addition to a direct map
- ❑ c. Addition to an indirect map
- ❑ d. Deletion from auto_master
- ❑ e. Deletion from a direct map
- ❑ f. Deletion from an indirect map

Answers a, b, d, and e are correct. You must manually execute **automount** after additions to or deletions from auto_master or a direct map. Changes to indirect maps do not require running the **automount** command. Therefore, answers c and f are incorrect.

## Question 5

Which of the following commands is used to create a CacheFS configuration?

- ❍ a. **cfsadm**
- ❍ b. **cachefsinit**
- ❍ c. **cfsadmin**
- ❍ d. **newcache**
- ❍ e. **cfscreate**

Answer c is correct. The **cfsadmin** command creates a CacheFS configuration. None of the other commands exists. Therefore, answers a, b, d, and e are incorrect.

## Question 6

Identify the command used to make an NFS resource available for mounting or to list those resources already available.

______________________________

The correct answer is **share**.

## Question 7

Match each command with its operation:

| | |
|---|---|
| a. **cachefswssize** | 1. Displays cache file system statistics |
| b. **cachefslog -h** | 2. Displays the cache status |
| c. **cachefslog -f** | 3. Displays the cache working set size |
| d. **cachefsstat** | 4. Starts cache logging |
| e. **cfsadmin -l** | 5. Stops cache logging |

Answers a-3, b-5, c-4, d-1, and e-2 are correct. The **cachefswssize** command displays the size of the cache working set. For the **cachefslog** command, **-h** stops logging and **-f** starts logging. The **cachefsstat** command displays statistics relating to the cache contents, and **cfsadmin -l** displays the status of the cache itself.

## Question 8

Which of the following commands can be used to determine any mounted NFS resources? [Select all that apply]

- ❑ a. **share**
- ❑ b. **dfmounts**
- ❑ c. **nfsmounts**
- ❑ d. **mountall**
- ❑ e. **mount**

Answers b and e are correct. You can use the **dfmounts** and **mount** commands to determine any mounted NFS resources. **share** is used to share NFS resources. Therefore, answer a is incorrect. **nfsmounts** does not exist. Therefore, answer c is incorrect. **mountall** is used to mount resources, not to list NFS resources. Therefore, answer d is incorrect.

## Question 9

When using NFS, which of the following results are true? [Select all that apply]

- ❑ a. Introduces redundancy
- ❑ b. Improves consistency
- ❑ c. Reduces administration
- ❑ d. Reduces network traffic

Answers b and c are correct. Using NFS improves consistency and reduces administration. NFS eliminates redundancy by making a single copy of data available to multiple clients. Therefore, answer a is incorrect. NFS is a network application, and using it will increase network traffic. Therefore, answer d is incorrect.

## Question 10

Identify the NFS-specific option used with the **-o** command-line argument of the share command to change the public file handle.

______________________________

The correct answer is **public**.

## Question 11

Which file contains one or more share commands used with the **shareall** command?

- ❍ a. /etc/nfs/nfstab
- ❍ b. /etc/nfs/shares
- ❍ c. /etc/dfs/dfstab
- ❍ d. /etc/dfs/sharetab

Answer c is correct. The /etc/dfs/dfstab file contains one or more **share** commands used with the **shareall** command. The /etc/nfs/nfstab and /etc/nfs/shares files do not exist. Therefore, answers a and b are incorrect. /etc/dfs/sharetab is the file that contains information on shared resources. Therefore, answer d is incorrect.

## Question 12

The command **cfsadmin** -s xyz fails. Which of the following is probably the reason?

- ❍ a. xyz is a mount point. It should be the name of a cache.
- ❍ b. The **demandconst** option was not specified when mounting xyz.
- ❍ c. Cache logging has not been started.
- ❍ d. The size of the cache is too small.

Answer b is correct. The **cfsadmin -s xyz** command probably failed because the **demandconst** option was not specified when mounting xyz. xyz must be a point mount, not a cache name. Therefore, answer a is incorrect. The -s command-line argument performs a consistency check; it does not have anything to do with logging or cache size. Therefore answers c and d are incorrect.

# Need to Know More?

Stern, Hal, *Managing NFS and NIS* (O'Reilly & Associates, Sebastopol, CA, 1991), ISBN 0-937175-75-7.

Sun Microsystems, *System Administration Guide, Volume 1*. Available in printed form (part number 805-7228-10), on the Web at **docs.sun.com**, and from the online documentation, AnswerBook2, provided with the Solaris 8 operating system.

Sun Microsystems, *System Administration Guide, Volume 3*. Available in printed form (part number 806-0916-10), on the Web at **docs.sun.com**, and from the online documentation, AnswerBook2, provided with the Solaris 8 operating system.

Sun Microsystems, *System Reference Manual, Section 1M - Administration Commands*. Available in printed form (part number 806-06253-10), on the Web at **docs.sun.com**, and from the online documentation, AnswerBook2, provided with the Solaris 8 operating system.

Sun Microsystems, *System Reference Manual, Section 4 - File Formats*. Available in printed form (part number 806-0633-10), on the Web at **docs.sun.com**, and from the online documentation, AnswerBook2, provided with the Solaris 8 operating system.

Callaghan, B. J., Request For Comments 2054, "WebNFS Client Specification" (October 1996). Available at **www.nic.mil/ftp/rfc/rfc2054.txt**.

Callaghan, B. J., Request For Comments 2055, "WebNFS Server Specification" (October 1996). Available at **www.nic.mil/ftp/rfc/rfc2055.txt**.

Callaghan, B. J., "WebNFS" (April 1997). Available at **www.sun.com/webnfs**.

Callaghan, B. J., B. Pawlowski, and P. Staubach, Request For Comments 1813, "NFS Version 3 Protocol Specification" (June 1995). Available at **www.nic.mil/ftp/rfc/rfc1813.txt**.

19

# Name Services

## Terms you'll need to understand:

- ✓ Name services
- ✓ The /etc files configuration
- ✓ Domain Name System (DNS)
- ✓ Network Information Service (NIS)
- ✓ Network Information Service Plus (NIS+)
- ✓ Lightweight Directory Access Protocol (LDAP)
- ✓ Authentication and authorization
- ✓ The name service switch

## Techniques you'll need to master:

- ✓ Configuring the name service switch
- ✓ Configuring NIS master and slave servers
- ✓ Configuring NIS clients
- ✓ Updating and adding NIS maps

This chapter describes the name services supported by the Solaris 8 operating system. The first part provides an overview. The second part covers the Network Information Service (NIS) in more detail. The third part summarizes the Network Information Service Plus (NIS+). This chapter covers the *Naming Services* and *NIS* test objectives.

# Solaris Name Services

A *name service* or *naming service* provides a centralized location for information used by users and systems to communicate with each other across the network. The name service not only stores the information but also provides mechanisms to manage and access that information.

The information is referred to as a *namespace* and typically includes the following:

- Hostnames and their IP addresses
- User accounts and their passwords
- Access permissions

Without a centralized name service, each system would have to maintain its own copy of the information. For example, by default the Solaris 8 system uses the /etc/hosts file to resolve hostnames to IP addresses. This approach is fine for a small number of systems, but for a large number of systems it becomes a maintenance nightmare. A centralized name service eliminates redundancy, improves consistency, and reduces administration.

## Supported Naming Services

The Solaris 8 operating system supports five naming services:

- The original Unix name configuration, referred to as the */etc files*
- The Domain Name Service (DNS)
- The Network Information Service (NIS)
- The Network Information Service Plus (NIS+)
- The Federated Naming Service (FNS), which conforms to the X/Open Federated Naming Specification (XFN)

The /etc/files, NIS, and NIS+ are considered enterprise-level naming services. That is, they work adequately within an intranet environment, but are not scalable to the global level (Internet environment). To address this scaling issue, FNS can be used to *federate* or link NIS or NIS+ with a global-level naming service such as X.500 via the Lightweight Directory Access Protocol (LDAP) or DNS.

By linking these naming services, the information managed by the enterprise-level name service is accessible globally.

Currently, Sun Microsystems does not fully embrace X.500/LDAP as a naming service or provide an LDAP server as part of the Solaris 8 distribution. However, it does provide an LDAP client and an LDAP data caching mechanism.

> **EXAM ALERT** Of these naming services, NIS and NIS+ are covered in the most detail on the exam. The /etc files and DNS are covered briefly. FNS will probably not be mentioned. But, be sure to understand the significance of enterprise-level (NIS and NIS+) versus global-level (DNS and LDAP) naming services.

## Domain Name System (DNS)

DNS is part of the TCP/IP protocol suite and is the name service used by the Internet. It provides hostname-to-IP-address resolution as well as IP-address-to-hostname resolution. The DNS namespace is divided into domains that in turn are divided into subdomains (or zones). One or more DNS servers can be responsible (authoritative) for a zone. All the DNS servers work together to provide name resolution services across the entire namespace.

The DNS server provided with Solaris 8 is version 8.1.2 of the Berkeley Internet Name Domain (BIND) program that is referred to as the *Internet name daemon* (in.named).

Information on the namespace is stored in text files using a predefined syntax known as *records*. The in.named program uses the following data files:

- */etc/named.conf*—The BIND configuration file that identifies zones over which the DNS server is authoritative and the associated data files
- */etc/resolv.conf*—When configured as a DNS client, a file that identifies the DNS server that should be used for name resolution
- *named.ca*—The names and IP addresses of the Internet root DNS servers
- *hosts*—The DNS address (A type) records used for resolving hostnames to IP addresses (not to be confused with the /etc/hosts file)
- *hosts.rev*—The DNS pointer (PTR type) records used for resolving IP addresses to hostnames
- *named.local*—The DNS records for the localhost or the loopback interface

The named.ca, hosts, hosts.rev, and named.local files are typically located under the /var/named directory but can be in any directory specified by the /etc/named.conf file.

## Network Information Service (NIS)

NIS is a distributed name service. It is a mechanism for identifying and locating network objects and resources. It provides a uniform storage and retrieval method for networkwide information in a platform-independent manner. The data files (called *maps*) can be distributed among NIS servers to improve availability but can still be managed and updated from a central location. The second part of this chapter provides additional details regarding NIS.

## Network Information Service Plus (NIS+)

NIS+ is very similar to NIS but includes many more features. Unlike NIS, the NIS+ namespace is dynamic because updates can take effect at any time by any authorized user.

The NIS+ namespace is hierarchical and is similar to a Unix file system. This structure allows the namespace to conform to the hierarchy of an organization and can be divided into multiple domains that can be administrated separately.

Whereas NIS has weak security, NIS+ includes a security system that uses both authentication and authorization to maintain the integrity of its namespace. *Authentication* is a method to restrict access to specific users when accessing a remote system. Authentication can be set up at both the system level and the network level. Credentials are used to verify the identity of a user. For NIS+, every request for access is authenticated by checking the credentials of the user. *Authorization* is a method to restrict the operations that a user can perform on the remote system once the user has gained access (been authenticated). For NIS+, every component in the namespace specifies the type of operations that it will accept from each user.

## The Name Service Switch

Because Solaris 8 supports five different naming services, we need a method to select which name services should be used and in which order. This capability is provided by the *name service switch*, which consists of the /etc/nsswitch.conf file and five templates that can be used to simplify the setup of the nsswitch.conf file.

Applications use standardized routines to obtain name resolution and other system and network information. These routines consult the /etc/nsswitch.conf file to determine which name service(s) should be queried.

The /etc/nsswitch.conf file contains entries for each type of data supported by the name services. An entry consists of a keyword that identifies the type of information, followed by one or more information sources. The source keywords are separated from the information keyword and other source keywords by one or more space characters. Table 19.1 lists the 17 types of information keywords. In addition to the five name services supported by Solaris, three additional name

| Table 19.1 The /etc/nsswitch.conf information keywords. | |
|---|---|
| **Information Keyword** | **Description** |
| **aliases** | Mail aliases |
| **automount** | Information on the Auto File System (AutoFS) configuration |
| **bootparams** | Location of root, swap, and dump partitions for diskless workstations |
| **ethers** | Ethernet addresses of systems |
| **group** | Group name and member information |
| **hosts** | Hostnames and network (IP version 4) addresses |
| **ipnodes** | Hostnames and network (IP version 6) addresses |
| **netgroup** | Network groups and members defined in the domain |
| **netmasks** | Netmasks associated with known networks |
| **networks** | Networks and their associated names |
| **passwd** | Password information for user accounts |
| **printers** | Printer alias database |
| **protocols** | IP protocols used within the domain |
| **publickey** | Public keys used for authentication |
| **rpc** | Remote Procedure Call (RPC) program numbers for RPC services used within the domain |
| **sendmailvars** | Variables used by the **sendmail**(1M) program |
| **services** | Names of IP services and their port numbers |

resolution methods are supported via the information source field of name service switch. These are *compat,* which is used for passwords and group information; *ldap* for using an external LDAP service; and *users,* which is used for printers. Table 19.2 lists the 8 information source keywords.

| Table 19.2 The /etc/nsswitch.conf source keywords. | |
|---|---|
| **Source Keyword** | **Description** |
| **compat** | Uses old-style syntax for password and group information |
| **dns** | Uses DNS to resolve queries |
| **files** | Uses /etc/ files to resolve queries |
| **ldap** | Uses LDAP to resolve queries |
| **nis** | Uses NIS to resolve queries |
| **nisplus** | Uses NIS+ to resolve queries |
| **users** | Valid only for printers |
| **xfn** | Valid only for printers |

When these name services (DNS, /etc files, LDAP, and NIS or NIS+) are queried or searched, they will return one of four search status messages:

- *SUCCESS*—The requested information was located.
- *UNAVAIL*—The service is not responding.
- *NOTFOUND*—The requested data does not exist.
- *TRYAGAIN*—The service is busy; try again later.

For each of these four search status messages, an action can be associated with each source. The action is either *return* (stop looking) or *continue* (try the next source). For example, the following listing shows a hosts entry in the /etc/nsswitch.conf file:

```
hosts:    nisplus dns files
```

The default action for a SUCCESS status message is to return the information. The default action for the other status messages (NOTFOUND, TRYAGAIN, and UNAVAIL) is to continue to the next source if one exists or to return if one does not exist.

When an application attempts to resolve a hostname to an IP address, first NIS+ is searched. If the information is found, it is returned to the application. If it is not found, DNS is searched. If the information is found, it is returned to the application. If it is not found, the /etc files configuration (/etc/hosts file) is searched. If the information is found, it is returned to the application; otherwise, an error is returned.

**EXAM ALERT** Note that the name service search order proceeds from left to right. That is, the search will start with the leftmost service and, if necessary, continue until the rightmost service is queried.

Five templates are included with the Solaris 8 distribution to simplify setting up the /etc/nsswitch.conf file. These templates provide a standardized setup for the most commonly used name services in the Solaris 8 environment. They are:

- DNS (/etc/nsswitch.dns)
- LDAP (/etc/nsswitch.ldap)
- NIS (/etc/nsswitch.nis)
- NIS+ (/etc/nsswitch.nisplus)
- Original Unix /etc files configuration (/etc/nsswitch.files)

During system installation, the contents of one of these files is copied to the /etc/nsswitch.conf file based on the name service selected (if any). Listing 19.1 shows the default contents of the /etc/nsswitch.nisplus file. To use this configuration, copy this file to the /etc/nsswitch.conf file. Comments are preceded by the pound (#) character. An action can be defined for a status message by using a *message=action* statement within square brackets ([]) after the source keyword.

**Listing 19.1 The contents of the /etc/nsswitch.nisplus file.**

```
#
# /etc/nsswitch.nisplus:
#
# An example file that could be copied over to /etc/nsswitch.conf;
# it
# uses NIS+ (NIS Version 3) in conjunction with files.
#
# "hosts:" and "services:" in this file are used only if the
# /etc/netconfig file has a "-" for nametoaddr_libs of "inet"
# transports.

# the following two lines obviate the "+" entry in /etc/passwd
# and /etc/group.
passwd:     files nisplus
group:      files nisplus

# consult /etc "files" only if nisplus is down.
hosts:      nisplus [NOTFOUND=return] files
ipnodes:    files
# Uncomment the following line and comment out the above to
# resolve
# both IPv4 and IPv6 addresses from the ipnodes databases. Note
# that
# IPv4 addresses are searched in all of the ipnodes databases
# before
# searching the hosts databases. Before turning this option on,
# consult
# the Network Administration Guide for more details on using IPv6.
#ipnodes:    nisplus [NOTFOUND=return] files

#Uncomment the following line, and comment out the above, to use
# both DNS
#and NIS+.  You must also set up the /etc/resolv.conf file for DNS
# name
#server lookup.  See resolv.conf(4).
#hosts:      nisplus dns [NOTFOUND=return] files
```

```
services:    nisplus [NOTFOUND=return] files
networks:    nisplus [NOTFOUND=return] files
protocols:   nisplus [NOTFOUND=return] files
rpc:         nisplus [NOTFOUND=return] files
ethers:      nisplus [NOTFOUND=return] files
netmasks:    nisplus [NOTFOUND=return] files
bootparams: nisplus [NOTFOUND=return] files

publickey:  nisplus

netgroup:   nisplus

automount:  files nisplus
aliases:    files nisplus
sendmailvars:   files nisplus

printers:       user nisplus files xfn

auth_attr:  files nisplus
prof_attr:  files nisplus
project:    files
```

# Network Information Service (NIS)

NIS, like other network applications, follows the client/server architecture model. This section of the chapter describes the components of NIS, how to configure these components, and how to add and update NIS maps.

## NIS Components

NIS consists of a master server, possibly slave servers, and one or more clients. The servers store NIS maps and make the information contained in the maps available to clients on request.

### NIS Maps

NIS stores information in a set of files called *maps*, which are two-column tables. The first column is used as a key, and the second column is the information associated with that key. Because the maps are organized by key, the same information might appear in more than one map. For example, host and associated IP addresses appear in two maps: hosts.byname (where the hostname is the key and the IP address is the information) and hosts.byaddr (where the IP address is the key and the hostname is the information). Table 19.3 lists the NIS maps. These maps are physically located under the /var/yp directory along with several other NIS files.

**Table 19.3 The NIS maps.**

| Keyword | Maps | Description |
|---|---|---|
| **aliases** | mail.aliases, mail.byaddr | Mail addresses and aliases |
| **bootparams** | bootparams | Location of root, swap, and dump partitions for diskless workstations |
| **ethers** | ethers.byaddr, ethers.byname | Ethernet addresses of systems |
| **group** | group.bygid, group.byname | Group name, group ID (GID), and member information |
| **hosts** | hosts.byaddr, hosts.byname | Hostnames and network (IPv4) addresses |
| **ipnodes** | ipnodes.byaddr, ipnodes.byname | Hostnames and network (IPv6) addresses |
| **netgroup** | netgroup, netgroup.byhost, netgroup.byuser | Network groups and members defined in the domain |
| **netmasks** | netmasks.byaddr | Netmasks associated with known networks |
| **networks** | networks.byaddr, networks.byname | Networks and their associated names |
| **passwd** | netid.byname, passwd.adjunct.byname, passwd.byname, passwd.byuid | Password information for user accounts |
| **protocols** | protocols.byname, protocols.bynumber | IP protocols used within the domain |
| **rpc** | rpc.bynumber | RPC program numbers for RPC services used within the domain |
| **services** | services.byname, services.byservice | IP services and their port numbers |

EXAM ALERT

NIS was previously known as Yellow Pages. For this reason, many of the NIS files and commands contain the *yp* prefix.

## NIS Master and Slave Servers

Each NIS environment, or domain, must have only one NIS master server. The NIS maps reside on the master server. To provide load distribution and redundancy, one or more slave servers can be configured. Whenever the NIS maps are updated on the master server, they are propagated to the slave servers.

### NIS Clients

NIS clients request information contained in the maps from NIS servers. The clients do not make any distinction between the master server and slave servers.

> **EXAM ALERT** NIS servers can also be NIS clients, depending on the configuration of the /etc/nsswitch.conf file. Keep in mind that NIS servers also need to resolve host names, network addresses, and so on for their own use.

## Configuring NIS Servers and Clients

The procedures used to configure an NIS master server, slave server, and client are somewhat similar. The steps to do each are given in this section.

Each system should be identified as a member of the domain. You do so by using the **domainname**(1M) command and specifying the domain name as an argument. For example, if a system will be part of the sun.com domain, you use the following command to set the domain:

```
# domainname sun.com
#
```

### NIS Master Server

Before you can configure an NIS master server, you must prepare the data used to build the maps. By default, the maps will be built from the /etc files. However, it is recommended that you copy the /etc files to another directory so that you can make any necessary changes to these source files without affecting the local system. Use the following procedure to prepare the data:

1. Verify that the /etc files are up to date. These files are auto_home, auto_master, bootparams, ethers, group, hosts, netgroup, netmasks, networks, passwd, protocols, rpc, service, and shadow.

2. Select a directory to be used to build most of the maps (the DIR directory) and another directory for building the passwd map (the PWDIR directory).

3. Copy all the files (except /etc/passwd) to the DIR directory and copy the /etc/passwd file to the PWDIR directory.

4. Verify that the /etc/mail/aliases file is up to date, but do not copy it to the DIR directory.

5. Remove comments and other unnecessary information from the copied source files. Verify that the file formats are correct.

6. Modify the /var/yp/Makefile to identify the selected DIR and PWDIR directories.

Use the following procedure to configure an NIS master server. As part of the procedure, the maps will be built automatically:

1. To be sure that the system is using the /etc files configuration for the name service switch, copy the /etc/nsswitch.files file to the /etc/nsswitch.conf file.

2. Add entries to /etc/hosts for each NIS slave server.

3. If necessary, use the **domainname**(1M) command to set the domain name.

4. Run the **ypinit**(1M) command to initialize the NIS master server and build the maps, as shown here:

   ```
   ypinit -m
   ```

5. Provide the information in response to the prompts from the **ypinit** command. This information includes a list of NIS slave servers, and whether the **ypinit** command should exit if an error is encountered.

6. Enable NIS by copying the /etc/nsswitch.nis file to the /etc/nsswitch.conf file.

To start the NIS master server, either reboot the system or run the **ypstart**(1M) command as shown here:

```
/usr/lib/netsvc/yp/ypstart
```

### NIS Slave Server

You can configure a system as an NIS slave server using the following procedure:

1. Configure the system as an NIS client. If necessary, use the **domainname** command to set the domain name.

2. Update the /etc/nsswitch.conf file to use NIS either by copying the /etc/nsswitch.nis template file to it or by manually editing the appropriate configuration.

3. Log in to the system as the root account and run the **ypinit** command as shown here:

   ```
   ypinit -c
   ```

4. The **ypinit** command will prompt for one or more NIS servers. Enter the hostnames of the closest NIS servers. This step completes the client setup.

5. Add an entry for the NIS master server to the /etc/hosts file.

6. If the **ypbind**(1M) command is running, stop it by using the following command:

```
/usr/lib/netsvc/yp/ypstop
```

7. Restart the **ypbind** command using the following command:

```
/usr/lib/netsvc/yp/ypstart
```

8. Run the **ypinit** command from the /var/yp directory, as shown here (where *master* is the hostname of the NIS master server):

```
# cd /var/yp
# ypinit -s master
```

To start the NIS slave server, either reboot the system or repeat Steps 6 and 7.

Only the maps generated on the master server are copied to the slave server. The original files used to generate the maps reside only on the master server.

### NIS Client

You can configure a system as an NIS client using the following procedure:

1. If necessary, use the **domainname** command to set the domain name.
2. Update the /etc/nsswitch.conf file to use NIS either by copying the /etc/nsswitch.nis template file to it or by manually editing the appropriate configuration.
3. Log in to the system as the root account and run the **ypinit** command as shown here:

```
ypinit -c
```

4. The **ypinit** command will prompt for one or more NIS servers. Enter the hostnames of the closest NIS servers.

## Updating and Adding NIS Maps

Updating one of the default maps (one automatically generated when the master server is configured) is fairly straightforward. Edit the appropriate source file, and then execute the **make**(1) command from the /var/yp directory. The name of the map being updated must be specified as a command-line argument to the **make** command. The **make** command updates the map and automatically propagates the updated map to any slave servers. The following listing shows the commands used to update the hosts map and propagate it to slave servers:

```
# cd /var/yp
# make hosts
```

To add a new map (referred to as a *nondefault map*), create a text file in the /var/yp directory on the master server with the appropriate information. Then, run the **makedbm**(1M) command to add the map. The **makedbm** command expects two command-line arguments: the name of the source file and the name of the map that should be created. The **ypxfr**(1M) command is used to distribute a new map that does not currently exist on the slave servers. The name of the new map is specified as a command-line argument. The following lines create the new map, apps, from the apps.txt source file:

```
# cd /var/yp
# makedbm apps.txt apps
# /usr/lib/netsvc/yp/ypxfr apps
```

To update and propagate a nondefault map, edit the source file, and then run the **makedbm** command to rebuild the map. To propagate the updated map, use the **yppush**(1M) command and specify the map name as a command-line argument. The following lines rebuild the apps map from the apps.txt source file and propagate it to the slave servers:

```
# cd /var/yp
# makedbm apps.txt apps
# /usr/lib/netsvc/yp/yppush apps
```

### Verifying the NIS Configuration

Several commands provide access to NIS configuration information. You can use these commands to verify a client configuration and check the contents of the maps. Consult the *System Reference Manual* for additional details:

- **ypcat**(1)—Lists the contents of the specified map.
- **ypmatch**(1)—Returns data that matches the specified key from the specified map.
- **ypwhich**(1)—Returns the name of the NIS server or map master. When used with the **-m** command-line argument, the **ypwhich** command returns a list of all available maps.

## Network Information Service Plus (NIS+)

NIS+ is similar to NIS but provides additional features. In addition to providing centralized administration and access to domain data, it also supports a hierarchical domain that can be configured to reflect the structure of an organization. NIS provides only a flat domain. Whereas NIS provides no authentication, NIS+

provides Data Encryption Standard (DES) authentication. In addition, whereas NIS propagates updated information in a batch mode, NIS+ propagates incremental updates immediately. Like NIS, NIS + supports the optional use of redundant servers (referred to as *replicas*). These replicas provide load balancing and alternate servers in case the master NIS+ server fails.

Whereas NIS stores its data in files referred to as *maps*, NIS+ stores its data in files referred to as *tables*. NIS+ provides tables for all the data stored in NIS maps, plus some additional tables for credential, time zone, and automount information. Table 19.4 lists the NIS+ tables.

The tables are stored under a directory by the name of the domain. This directory contains three other directories: ctx_dir.*domain*, which is used for xfn (FNS) data; org_dir.*domain*, which is used to store the tables; and groups_dir.*domain*, which is used for group information.

**Table 19.4 NIS+ tables.**

| Table | Description |
|---|---|
| auto_home | Location of users' home directories |
| auto_master | AutoFS map information |
| bootparams | Location of root, swap, and dump partitions for diskless workstations |
| cred | Credentials for NIS+ principals |
| ethers | Ethernet addresses of systems |
| group | Group name, GID, and member information |
| hosts | Hostnames and network (IP) addresses |
| mail_aliases | Mail addresses and aliases |
| netgroup | Network groups and members defined in the domain |
| netmasks | Netmasks associated with known networks |
| networks | Networks and their associated names |
| passwd | Password information for user accounts |
| protocols | IP protocols used within the domain |
| rpc | RPC program numbers for RPC services used within the domain |
| services | IP services and their port numbers |
| timezone | Time zone of workstations in the domain |

# Practice Questions

## Question 1

Which of the following naming services requires the data to be configured manually on every system on which it is used?

❍ a. NIS

❍ b. NIS+

❍ c. DNS

❍ d. /etc files

Answer d is correct. NIS requires the data to be configured manually on every system on which it is used. All the other naming services provide a means to update one master database and propagate changes to every system that needs them. Therefore, answers a, b, and c are incorrect. Although using /etc files is simple and quick for a small number of systems, using NIS, NIS+, or DNS for a large number of systems reduces maintenance.

## Question 2

Enter the name of a method to restrict access to NIS+ resources based on the credentials of the user.

______________________________

The correct answer is authentication.

## Question 3

Which of the following are features provided by NIS+? [Select all that apply]

❑ a. Authentication

❑ b. Time zone support

❑ c. Batch propagation of updates

❑ d. Hierarchical domain architecture

❑ e. Flat domain architecture

Answers a, b, and d are correct. NIS+ provides authentication, time zone support, and a hierarchical domain architecture. Batch propagation of updates and flat domain architecture are characteristics of NIS. Therefore, answers c and e are incorrect.

## Question 4

Which of the following name services are supported by the Solaris 8 operating system? [Select all that apply]

- ❑ a. NIS
- ❑ b. NIS+
- ❑ c. FNS
- ❑ d. DNS
- ❑ e. /etc files configuration

Answers a, b, c, d, and e are correct. The Solaris 8 operating system supports NIS, NIS+, FNS, DNS, and /etc files configuration.

## Question 5

Which of the following commands is used to configure an NIS client?

- ❍ a. **ypinit -m**
- ❍ b. **ypinit -c**
- ❍ c. **ypinit -s**
- ❍ d. **nisclient**
- ❍ e. **nisinit -c**

Answer b is correct. The **ypinit -c** command is used to configure an NIS client. **ypinit -m** is used to configure a master server. Therefore, answer a is incorrect. **ypinit** -s is used to configure a slave server. Therefore, answer c is incorrect. The commands in answers d and e do not exist.

## Question 6

Which of the following is *not* a valid type of search status message?

❍ a. SUCCESS

❍ b. NOTFOUND

❍ c. TRYLATER

❍ d. UNAVAIL

Answer c is correct. TRYLATER does not exist; the correct keyword is TRYAGAIN. SUCCESS, NOTFOUND, and UNAVAIL are valid search status messages. Therefore, answers a, b, and d are incorrect.

## Question 7

Identify the name of the BIND program used to provide DNS services.

________________________

The correct answer is the in.named program.

## Question 8

Which of the following are information-type keywords that can be used in the /etc/nsswitch.conf file? [Select all that apply]

❑ a. hosts

❑ b. ipaddr

❑ c. protocols

❑ d. services

Answers a, c, and d are correct. The hosts, protocols, and services keywords can be used in the /etc/nsswitch.conf file. ipaddr is not a valid keyword. IP addresses are a portion of the hosts information. Therefore, answer b is incorrect.

## Question 9

The files NIS uses to store the information that NIS clients request are collectively referred to as what?

______________________________

The correct answer is maps.

## Question 10

Which of the following commands is used to propagate a new NIS map to NIS slave servers?

❍ a. **yppush**

❍ b. **ypupdate**

❍ c. **yppropagate**

❍ d. **ypxfr**

❍ e. **ypmaps**

Answer d is correct. The **ypxfr** command is used to propagate a new NIS map to NIS slave servers. **yppush** is used to propagate an existing map that has been updated. Therefore, answer a is incorrect. The commands in answers b, c, and e do not exist.

## Question 11

Which of the following naming services can operate in the Internet environment and are considered global naming services? [Select all that apply]

❑ a. NIS+

❑ b. DNS

❑ c. NIS

❑ d. X.500/LDAP

Answers b and d are correct. DNS and X.500/LDAP are considered global naming services. NIS and NIS+ are enterprise-level naming services and do not scale globally. Therefore, answers a and c are incorrect.

# Need to Know More?

Albtiz, Paul and Cricket Liu, *DNS and BIND* (O'Reilly & Associates, Sebastopol, CA, 1998), ISBN 1565925122.

Stern, Hal, *Managing NFS and NIS* (O'Reilly & Associates, Sebastopol, CA, 1991), ISBN 0-937175-75-7.

Sun Microsystems, *Solaris Naming Administration Guide*. Available in printed form (part number 806-1387-10), on the Web at **docs.sun.com**, and from the online documentation, AnswerBook2, provided with the Solaris 8 operating system.

Sun Microsystems, *Solaris Naming Setup and Configuration Guide*. Available in printed form (part number 806-1386-10), on the Web at **docs.sun.com**, and from the online documentation, AnswerBook2, provided with the Solaris 8 operating system.

Howard, L., Request For Comment 2307, "An Approach for Using LDAP as a Network Information Service" (March 1998). Available at **ftp.isi.edu/in-notes/rfc2307.txt**.

Wahl, M. et al., Request For Comment 2251, "Lightweight Directory Protocol (v3)" (December 1997). Available at **ftp.isi.edu/in-notes/rfc2251.txt**.

# 20

# Solaris Management Console and Solstice AdminSuite

**Terms you'll need to understand:**

- ✓ Solaris Management Console
- ✓ Solstice AdminSuite
- ✓ Host Manager
- ✓ Storage Manager
- ✓ Database Manager
- ✓ Serial Port Manager
- ✓ User Manager
- ✓ Group Manager
- ✓ Printer Manager

**Techniques you'll need to master:**

- ✓ Identifying the functionality and features of the Management Console
- ✓ Identifying the functionality and capabilities of AdminSuite
- ✓ Identifying the types of systems supported by the Host Manager
- ✓ Identifying the functionality of two tools of the Storage Manager
- ✓ Identifying the data managed by the Database Manager

This chapter covers the *Solaris Management Console* and the *Solstice AdminSuite* test objectives by briefly describing the functionality and features of these tools.

# Solaris Management Console

The Solaris Management Console is an administrative tool used to remotely manage multiple domains consisting of Solaris systems. A set of graphical user interface (GUI) administrative tools is integrated into a single interface framework. The Solaris systems registered with the Management Console are viewed as a tree of icons representing hosts and services. These tools include:

- *User Manager*—User account administration
- *Process Manager*—Active process management
- *Log Viewer*—View content Console log
- *Job Scheduler*—View and manage scheduling of tasks
- *Mounts and Shares Manager*—View and modify Network File Systems (NFS) mounts and shares
- *Disk/Partition Manager*—View and modify disk and partition configurations
- *Serial Port Manager*—View and modify serial port configuration

## Other Features

The Management Console provides a *single login* capability. By logging in to the Management Console, you can access all hosts and services managed by the Console. This single login eliminates the need to log in to each host separately.

The new Role-Based Access Control (RBAC) feature can be managed using the Management Console, allowing you to delegate specific rights to multiple administrators while maintaining centralized control.

The Management Console enables applications to be executed on remote hosts and monitored using local GUIs. It eliminates the need to install the applications on the local system.

# The Solstice AdminSuite

The graphical management tool AdminSuite is a collection of the following tools:

- *Host Manager*—Manages AutoClient servers, standalone servers, and diskless clients
- *Storage Manager*—Manages partitions and file systems
- *Database Manager*—Manages network-related data

- *Serial Port Manager*—Manages the configuration of serial ports
- *User Manager*—Manages user accounts
- *Group Manager*—Manages group accounts
- *Printer Manager*—Manages printers and print servers

Many of the functions performed by AdminSuite can also be performed by the **admintool** command. These include serial port management, user and group account management, and printer management. For these cases, the AdminSuite GUIs (windows) look very similar to the windows provided by the **admintool** command.

EXAM ALERT: The Solstice AdminSuite is not covered in detail on Part II of the exam. However, you should be familiar with the capabilities of the seven AdminSuite manager tools and the two tools that compose the Storage Manager.

## Host Manager

The Host Manager provides the ability to add and maintain server and client support. You can use it to perform tasks including the following:

- Adding and modifying system support for all types of system configurations (AutoClients, diskless clients, operating system [OS] servers, and standalone systems), including converting system types
- Setting root passwords for AutoClients or diskless clients

System support includes providing software services such as boot and install services for installation and OS services for systems with limited disk space. The Host Manager provides the ability to convert a standalone system to an OS server, an AutoClient to a standalone system, and so on. In addition, you can use the Host Manager to add OS services to an OS server (for example, to add support for another type of operating system) or to remove OS services that are no longer needed. Another function of the Host Manager is to set up install, boot, and profile servers that are used to perform over-the-network installation.

AdminSuite provides command-line equivalents for the following operations of the Host Manager:

- **admhostadd**—Adds support for a new system or OS server
- **admhostdel**—Deletes support for an existing system or OS server
- **admhostmod**—Modifies an existing system
- **admhostls**—Lists existing hosts

## Storage Manager

The Storage Manager consists of two tools: the Disk Manager and the File System Manager. The Disk Manager allows viewing and editing of partition-related information. You can use it for the following:

- Viewing and modifying x86 and SPARC slice parameters (that is, changing the starting and ending addresses of the slices)
- Specifying a disk label
- Viewing and modifying x86 fdisk partitions
- Copying the characteristics of a disk to one or more similar disks

The File System Manager supports creating and modifying file systems. You can use it for the following:

- Creating file systems
- Creating mount points
- Mounting and unmounting file systems
- Sharing and unsharing Network File System (NFS) resources
- Modifying the /etc/vfstab file on one or more systems
- Adding entries to existing Auto File System (AutoFS) maps

The File Manager also provides the ability to select mount and share options, such as the NFS-specific mount options.

AdminSuite does not provide any command-line equivalents for the Storage Manager, because you can use standard Solaris commands to perform disk and file system tasks.

## Database Manager

The Database Manager is used to view and modify network-related system information. This information can be stored on a selected host (in /etc files), in Network Information Service (NIS), or in Network Information Service Plus (NIS+). You can use the Database Manager to view and modify the files, maps, or tables (depending on name service) that contain the following types of information:

- System aliases
- AutoFS map contents
- Boot parameters
- Ethernet addresses

- Groups
- Host names and IP addresses
- Locale information
- Network groups
- Network masks
- Network names
- User account information
- Network protocols
- RPC configuration
- Network services
- Timezone information

AdminSuite does not provide any command-line equivalents for the Database Manager. For the /etc files name service, you can use any text editor to modify the information. For NIS and NIS+, use the appropriate procedures to modify the maps and tables as necessary.

## Serial Port Manager

The Serial Port Manager provides AdminSuite with a graphical interface to view and modify the settings of serial ports on the selected host. Using the Serial Port Manager, you can perform the following operations:

- View serial port settings
- Add a terminal
- Add a modem
- Disable a port service
- Delete a port service

AdminSuite provides command-line equivalents for the following operations of the Serial Port Manager:

- **admserialdel**—Deletes a port service
- **admserialls**—Lists a port service
- **admserialmod**—Modifies a port service

## User Manager

The User Manager is used to view and modify user account information. This information can be stored on the selected host (in /etc files), in NIS, or in NIS+. You can use the User Manager to view and modify the files, maps, or tables (depending on name service) that contain the following types of information:

- System aliases
- AutoFS map contents for home directories
- User credential information
- Group account information
- User account information
- Password information

AdminSuite provides the following command-line equivalents for the User Manager:

- **admuseradd**—Adds a user account
- **admuserdel**—Deletes a user account
- **admuserls**—Lists user accounts
- **admusermod**—Modifies a user account

## Group Manager

The Group Manager is used to view and modify group account information. This information is stored on a selected host (in the /etc/group file), a NIS map, or a NIS+ table. AdminSuite provides the following command-line equivalents for the Group Manager:

- **admgroupadd**—Adds a group account
- **admgroupdel**—Deletes a group account
- **admgroupls**—Lists group accounts
- **admgroupmod**—Modifies a group account

## Printer Manager

The Printer Manager provides AdminSuite with a graphical interface to perform the following operations:

- Install a printer on a print server
- Install a network printer

- Give print clients access to a printer
- Modify existing information for a printer
- Delete access to a printer
- Delete a printer from a print server

AdminSuite does not provide any command-line equivalents for the Printer Manager. You can manage printers using the Solaris LP Service commands on the appropriate system.

# Practice Questions

## Question 1

Enter the name of one of the two tools included in the Storage Manager.

______________________________

The correct answer is either Disk Manager or File System Manager.

## Question 2

AdminSuite consists of seven tools. Six of these are the Printer Manager, Host Manager, User Manager, Database Manager, Storage Manager, and Serial Port Manager. Name the seventh tool.

______________________________

The correct answer is Group Manager.

## Question 3

Which of the following AdminSuite managers is used to mount a file system?

- ❍ a. Volume Manager
- ❍ b. Disk Manager
- ❍ c. File System Manager
- ❍ d. Mount Manager
- ❍ e. Partition Manager

Answer c is correct. The File System Manager is used to mount a file system. The Disk Manager is used to manage disk partitions. Therefore, answer b is incorrect. The managers in answers a, d, and e do not exist.

## Question 4

Which of the following are Management Console tools? [Select all that apply]

- ❑ a. User Manager
- ❑ b. Mounts and Shares Manager
- ❑ c. USB Port Manager
- ❑ d. Job Scheduler
- ❑ e. Serial Port Manager

Answers a, b, d, and e are correct. The User Manager, Mounts and Shares Manager, Job Scheduler, and Serial Port Manager are Management Console tools. The Management Console does not provide the ability to manage USB ports. Therefore, answer c is incorrect.

## Question 5

Identify the name of the AdminSuite manager that can be used to modify the /etc/protocols file.

______________________________

The correct answer is the Database Manager.

## Question 6

Which of the following is not a tool provided with AdminSuite?

- ❍ a. Database Manager
- ❍ b. Storage Manager
- ❍ c. Parallel Port Manager
- ❍ d. Printer Manager

Answer c is correct. AdminSuite includes a Serial Port Manager, not a Parallel Port Manager. The Database Manager, Storage Manager, and Printer Manager all are included in AdminSuite. Therefore, answers a, b, and d are incorrect.

## Question 7

Which of the following tasks can be performed with the Host Manager? [Select all that apply]

- ❑ a. Add OS services
- ❑ b. Remove OS services
- ❑ c. Convert an AutoClient to a standalone system
- ❑ d. Set up a boot server
- ❑ e. Set the root password of an AutoClient system

Answers a, b, c, d, and e are correct. You can perform all these tasks with the Host Manager.

## Question 8

Identify the name of the Management Console capability that eliminates the need to log in to every host managed by the Console.

_______________________________

The correct answer is the single login.

## Question 9

Which of the following commands is provided with AdminSuite?

- ❍ a. **admsliceadd**
- ❍ b. **admfilesysdel**
- ❍ c. **admdbls**
- ❍ d. **admserialmod**
- ❍ e. **admprinteradd**

Answer d is correct. AdminSuite includes the **admserialmod** command. The commands listed in answers a, b, c, and e don't exist.

# Need to Know More?

Sun Microsystems, *Solstice AdminSuite 2.3 Administration Guide*. Available in printed form (part number 802-7048) and on the Web at **docs.sun.com**.

Sun Microsystems, *Solstice AdminSuite 2.3 Installation and Release Notes*. Available in printed form (part number 805-3027) and on the Web at **docs.sun.com**.

# 21

# Over-the-Network Installation and JumpStart

**Terms you'll need to understand:**

- ✓ Installation phase
- ✓ Installation method
- ✓ Software packages, clusters, and groups
- ✓ Over-the-network installation
- ✓ Install server
- ✓ Boot server
- ✓ Custom JumpStart
- ✓ JumpStart rules file and profile files

**Techniques you'll need to master:**

- ✓ Installing systems
- ✓ Preconfiguring system installation information
- ✓ Setting up and using over-the-network installation
- ✓ Setting up a JumpStart configuration directory

The first part of this chapter covers concepts and terms related to system installation, specifically over-the-network installation. Some of this information was covered in Chapter 3 as it pertained to the exam objectives for the Part I exam. Some of the information in Chapter 3 is repeated here with a slightly different emphasis.

The second part of this chapter covers automating over the network installation using the JumpStart feature. The *JumpStart - Automatic Installation* test objectives are covered by this chapter.

# Server Installation

This section includes the phases of an installation, the software configurations that can be installed on a system, and over-the-network installation.

## Installation Phases

Installation consists of three phases: The *system configuration* phase identifies the necessary system information, the *system installation* phase copies the software onto the system, and the *post-installation* phase updates system software as required.

### System Configuration Phase

During the system configuration phase, basic information about the system, such as hostname and domain, is identified. Optionally, this information can be set up ahead of time, or *preconfigured*. You can use two methods to preconfigure system information. The first uses the sysidcfg file, and the second uses a name service.

If a system is not preconfigured, the **sysidtool**(1M) is executed during installation to prompt for the information. The **sysidtool** command consists of five programs: **sysidnet**, **sysidnis**, **sysidsys**, **sysidroot**, and **sysidpm**.

### System Installation Phase

During the system installation phase, the selected Solaris 8 software group (covered later in this chapter) is installed using one of the four installation methods:

- SunInstall (standard interactive installation)
- Web Start
- JumpStart
- Custom JumpStart

The two interactive installation methods (SunInstall and Web Start) are Part I exam objectives and were discussed in Chapter 3. The two automatic installation methods (JumpStart and custom JumpStart) are Part II exam objectives and are described later in this chapter.

> All four of these installation methods can use over-the-network installation as described later in this chapter. However, exam 310-012 only addresses over-the-network installation in terms of its use with JumpStart.

### Post-Installation Phase

During the post-installation phase, any appropriate patches are installed, along with any separately purchased applications. In addition, any custom configurations, such as user accounts and environments, are applied to the system. Typically, system security hardening is also performed during the post-installation phase.

## Preconfiguring System Information

As previously described, during the system configuration phase, basic information about the system (such as hostname and domain) is identified. This information can be defined in the sysidcfg file, in the name service being used (NIS or NIS+), or manually during an interactive dialog.

### Using the sysidcfg File

To use the sysidcfg file method, you create a file for each system containing a set of lines in the form ***keyword=value***, such as **timezone=US/CENTRAL**. The file can be available either over the network (via Network File System [NFS]) or on diskette mounted in the local diskette drive.

The following information can be defined in the sysidcfg file:

- Name service (NIS, NIS+, DNS, or none), along with the hostname and Internet Protocol (IP) address of the server
- Domain name
- Network interface (enable use of DHCP or specify IP address and netmask; enable IPv6)
- Root password
- System locale
- Terminal (keyboard, mouse, monitor, and graphics card type)
- Timezone (timezone and timeserver)

### Using NIS

For the name service method, entries for each system are added to the Network Information Service (NIS) or Network Information Service Plus (NIS+) database. Name services are described in Chapter 19.

The following system definition information can be defined using NIS/NIS+:

- Name service (implied)
- Hostname and IP address
- System locale
- Timezone (timezone and timeserver)

A lot of information can be defined in the sysidcfg file that cannot be defined in a name service, including the domain name, most of the network interface parameters (netmask, DCHP usage, and IPv6 usage), the root password, and terminal information (monitor, keyboard, mouse, and so on).

The system locale (specific language and region) is stored in the /etc/locale file and can be specified for either the system name or the domain name. For NIS, you can build a locale.byname map by modifying and executing the NIS makefile. The /etc/locale file is used as a source of information for the local.byname map. For NIS+, you use the **nistbladm**(1M) command to build the locale table and add entries.

## Software Configurations

The Solaris 8 system software is distributed in several different configurations, as described in the following sections.

### Software Packages

Solaris 8 system and application software are delivered as collections of files and directories, referred to as *software packages*. These packages can be copied onto the system from CD-ROM or magnetic tape as a single compressed file and then uncompressed for installation.

Included with the package is information regarding the package, such as title, storage requirements, and version. Also included are any custom scripts needed to properly install the software.

## Software Clusters

Sometimes, system software is distributed in more than one package, but the packages need to be distributed and installed as a unit. A collection of two or more related packages is referred to as a *software cluster*. A software cluster is a logical grouping of packages.

## Software Groups

*Software groups* (also referred to as *software configuration clusters*) are collections of software clusters. Depending on the intended use of the system, the most appropriate software group should be selected for installing an operating system. Table 21.1 describes the five software groups.

**Table 21.1 Solaris 8 software groups.**

| Software Group | Contents |
|---|---|
| Core | Minimum files required for the operating system. |
| End User Support System | Typical configuration for a system that supports general users. Consists of the Core software group plus:<br>Windowing software: Common Desktop Environment (CDE) and Open Windows<br>Basic networking and printer support<br>Standard Unix and patch utilities<br>Java Virtual Machine |
| Developer System Support | Intended as a software development environment. Consists of the End User Support System software group plus:<br>Programming tools and libraries<br>Extended terminal, X, and kernel probing support<br>CDE/Motif developer software and runtimes<br>Online manual pages |
| Entire Distribution | All files included with the Solaris 8 distribution. Consists of the Developer System Support software group plus:<br>AnswerBook2 (online Web-based documentation)<br>Enhanced security features, including disk quotas and system accounting<br>Enhanced network support, including Unix-to-Unix Copy Protocol (UUCP), Dynamic Host Configuration Protocol (DHCP) server, Point-to-Point Protocol (PPP), and the Network Information Service (NIS) |
| Entire Distribution Plus OEM System Support | Includes modules and drivers for optional hardware components. Consists of the Entire Distribution software group plus:<br>PCI drivers<br>SunFastEthernet and FastWide SCSI adapter drivers |

# Over-the-Network Installation

Typically, Solaris is installed directly from the Solaris distribution CD. Doing so requires that each system be equipped with a CD-ROM drive. However, another approach is available: Solaris can be installed over the network using a remote server that has either the Solaris distribution CD in its CD-ROM drive or a copy of the files from the Solaris distribution CD on its hard disk.

The over-the-network installation can be used with the two interactive installation methods (Solaris interactive installation or Web Start, covered in Chapter 3) or the two automatic installation methods (JumpStart and custom JumpStart).

To perform over-the-network installation, you must set up one or more network servers, consisting of an install server and possibly a boot server. In addition, you must add information about the install clients in the local NIS or NIS+ name service or in the /etc files of the appropriate install servers.

## Install Server

An *install server* is a system that provides the distribution files necessary for the installation of the Solaris operating system on an install client during an over-the-network installation. The files can be provided directly from the Solaris distribution CD mounted in a local CD-ROM drive or from a local hard disk.

If you copy the distribution files to a local hard disk, a single install server can be used to provide the files for multiple releases (Solaris 8, Solaris 7, Solaris 2.6, and so on) and/or for multiple platforms (SPARC and Intel x86). In addition, a local hard disk typically provides faster access to the distribution files than a local CD-ROM drive.

To set up a system as an install server, mount the Solaris 8 Software (1 of 2) distribution CD in the local CD-ROM drive. Then use the **setup_install_server** command, under the Solaris_8/Tools directory on the Solaris distribution CD, to copy the distribution files to the local hard disk of the install server. One command-line argument is required: the full pathname to a target directory to which the distribution files will be copied. Although you can use any directory, by convention the directory is named /export/install. The following line executes the **setup_install_server** command from the Solaris_8/Tools directory of the distribution CD to set up an install server:

```
# ./setup_install_server /export/install
```

The **setup_install_server** command copies the CD image of the software to the specified directory. Both the Product and Tools directories are copied. In addition, a **netmask**(4) file that contains the network subnet mask for the server is created in the Tools directory.

Once an install server is set up, you can add products from the other Solaris distribution CDs, such as Solaris 8 Software (2 of 2) or Solaris 8 Languages, to the install server. The directory used for the files associated with the install server must be specified as a command-line argument. To add to the install server, insert the supplemental CD into the local CD-ROM drive and execute the **add_to_install_server**(1M) command on the CD. The following line executes the **add_to_install_server** command from the Solaris_8/Tools directory of the distribution CD to add to the install server:

```
# ./add_to_install_server /export/install
```

The **add_to_install_server** command supports two additional command-line arguments. The first is **-s**, which allows selection of the products to install. By default, all products are installed. The second is **-p** ***product_path***, where *product_path* is an alternate directory for products to be installed into.

By default, the install server supports the SunInstall installation program (see Chapter 3). However, the install server can be modified to use the Solaris Web Start program instead. The **modify_install_server**(1M) command (located on the Solaris 8 Installation CD) can be used to copy the Web Start–enabled miniroot from the CD to the install server configuration.

To modify the install server, insert the Solaris 8 Installation CD into the local CD-ROM drive and execute the **modify_install_server** command on the CD. The following line executes the **modify_install_server** command from the mount point of the distribution CD to modify the install server:

```
# ./modify_install_server /export/install
```

The **modify_install_server** command supports the **-p** command-line argument, which preserves the existing miniroot by copying it to the /Solaris_8/Tools/Boot.orig location under the install server configuration before the CD miniroot is installed.

## Boot Server

A *boot server* is a system that contains the files necessary to boot a SPARC install client over the network during an over-the-network installation. After an install client has booted, the boot server has completed its function. The remainder of the installation is supported by an install server. Because Intel-compatible install clients boot from local diskette or local CD-ROM, they do not use a boot server for installation.

Typically, an install server and a boot server reside on the same system. In fact, when a system is set up as an install server, it is also set up as a boot server.

However, if install clients are on a different subnet than an install server, a boot server must be set up on the same subnet as the install clients.

A boot server is required to be on the same subnet as SPARC install clients because the clients obtain booting information from the boot server using the Boot Protocol (BOOTP). Typically, this protocol is not passed by routers (which interconnect subnets).

To set up a system only as a boot server, the system must have access to the Solaris software distribution CD through a local CD-ROM drive or a remotely shared CD-ROM drive.

The **setup_install_server** command, under the Solaris_8/Tools directory on the Solaris software distribution CD, copies the boot software to the boot server. Two command-line arguments are required: **-b**, which specifies that a boot server is being set up; and the full pathname to an empty directory to which the boot files will be copied. Although any directory can be used, by convention the directory is named boot and is located under the /export/install directory. The following line executes the **setup_install_server** command from the Solaris_8/Tools directory of the distribution CD to set up a boot server:

```
# ./setup_install_server -b /export/install/boot
```

## Adding Install Clients

When a system or install client is installed over the network, basic information about the install clients needs to be available through a name service (NIS/NIS+) or in the files under the /etc directory on the install server or boot server.

You can use the Solstice Host Manager program to add this information or, if Host Manager is not available, the **add_install_client** command.

The **add_install_client** command can only be used to update the /etc files on an install server or boot server. Use the appropriate NIS or NIS+ procedures to add client information to these name services. At minimum, you must add the hostname, IP address, and Ethernet address of the client.

Depending on the environment, you can modify the following /etc files to support over the network installation:

- /etc/**bootparams**(4)—An entry for each client, to define various pathnames and parameters required to boot the client
- /etc/dfs/**dfstab**(4)—Entries for any NFS resources that should be shared
- /etc/**ethers**(4)—An entry mapping the Ethernet address to the system hostname

- **/etc/exports**(4)—Entries for any NFS resources that should be shared
- **/etc/hosts**(4)—An entry mapping the hostname to an IP address
- **/etc/inetd.conf**(4)—An entry to enable the Trivial File Transfer Protocol (FTP) daemon

The following line uses the **add_install_client** command to set up a system for over-the-network installation. This command is executed from the Solaris_8/Tools directory of the Solaris 8 Software (2 of 2) distribution CD or from the mount point of the Solaris 8 Installation CD. The name of the system to be installed is identified by the **host** command-line argument followed by the platform group of the system.

In this example, the command-line argument **sun4m** is used to identify the system to be installed as a SPARC5 platform:

```
# add_install_client host sun4m
```

Table 21.2 lists the command-line arguments supported by the **add_install_client** command.

## Install/Boot Server Daemons

Several network daemons are used by the install and boot servers to support over-the-network installation:

- **in.rarpd**(1M)—The Reverse Address Resolution Protocol (RARP) daemon provides Ethernet-address-to-IP-address resolution. Clients use this service to determine their IP address based on their assigned Ethernet address.

**Table 21.2 Command-line arguments for the add_install_client command.**

| Argument | Description |
|---|---|
| -c ***server:path*** | Specifies the profile ***server*** and ***path*** of the JumpStart directory. |
| -d | Defines the client as a DHCP client. |
| -e ***address*** | Specifies an Ethernet address. |
| -i ***address*** | Specifies an IP address. |
| -n ***server:service netmask*** | Specifies the name ***service*** and the name service ***server***. The ***netmask*** also can be defined. |
| -p ***server:path*** | Specifies the ***server*** on which the sysidcfg file is located and the absolute ***path*** to the sysidcfg file. |
| -s ***server:path*** | Specifies the install ***server*** and ***path*** to the CD image (needed only when you're adding a client to the boot server). |

- **in.tftpd**(1M)—The Trivial File Transfer Protocol (TFTP) daemon provides a method for SPARC install clients to obtain bootable images from a server without logging in to the server.
- **nsfd**(1M)—The NFS daemon provides clients remote access to file systems over the network.
- **rpc.bootparamd**(1M)—The Boot Protocol (BOOTP) daemon provides clients with boot information from the /etc/bootparams file.

## The RARP Daemon (in.rarpd)

The /etc/sbin/in.rarpd daemon provides Ethernet-address-to-IP-address resolution. When a RARP request is received, the **in.rarpd** program attempts to determine the IP address assigned to the specified Ethernet address. The look-up procedure consists of first looking up the Ethernet address to obtain the hostname of the system, and then looking up the hostname to determine its IP address.

The procedure used to look up the hostname (based on the Ethernet address) is determined by the configuration of the *ethers* keyword in the name service switch (/etc/nsswitch.conf) file. It may be obtained from NIS (ethers.byaddr map), NIS+ (ethers table), or the /etc/ethers file. See **ethers**(4) for the format of the /etc/ethers file.

The procedure used to look up the IP address (based on the obtained host name) is determined by the configuration of the *hosts* keyword in the name service switch (/etc/nsswitch.conf) file. It may be obtained from DNS, NIS (hosts.byname map), NIS+ (hosts table), or the /etc/hosts file. See **hosts**(4) for the format of the /etc/hosts file.

## The TFTP Daemon (in.tftpd)

The /usr/sbin/in.tftpd daemon provides a simple method for SPARC install clients to obtain the boot image from the install/boot server using the Trivial File Transfer Protocol (TFTP). Unlike the standard File Transfer Protocol (FTP), TFTP does not require user authentication (account name and password) to access files. The boot images are typically stored under the/tftpboot directory.

## The NFS Server Daemon (nsfd)

The /usr/lib/nfs/nfsd daemon provides network access to the Solaris 8 distribution files via NFS. These files are identified by the boot parameters provided by the **rpc.bootparamd** daemon.

## The Boot Parameter Server Daemon (rpc.bootparamd)

The /user/sbin/rpc.bootparamd daemon provides NFS share names and other information necessary to boot install clients. The source of the information is determined by the configuration of the *bootparams* keyword in the name service switch (/etc/nsswitch.conf) file. It may be obtained from NIS (bootparams map), NIS+ (bootparams table), or the /etc/bootparams file. See **bootparams**(4) for the format of the /etc/bootparams file.

EXAM ALERT: Because these four daemons are required to support over-the-network installation (with or without JumpStart), the **add_install_client** command will configure and start them (on the install/boot server) if required when a network install client is configured.

# Automating Installation with JumpStart

The JumpStart feature provides a mechanism to automatically install the Solaris operating system. The two JumpStart methods are JumpStart and custom JumpStart.

EXAM ALERT: Not only does JumpStart automate installation, it can be used to automate the installation of large numbers of systems that are identically configured. If you need to install 100 servers using the same configuration, JumpStart provides a way to simplify this task.

JumpStart lets you automatically install the Solaris operating system on new SPARC platforms by inserting the Solaris distribution CD into the local CD-ROM drive and powering on the system or booting via the network. The software that is installed is determined by a default profile. The default profile is selected based on the hardware model and the size of the hard disks. The software installed cannot be manually selected.

All new SPARC platforms have a preinstalled JumpStart boot image. This boot image can be copied to an existing SPARC platform by using the **re-preinstall**(1M) command.

Custom JumpStart lets you automatically install the Solaris operating system on new SPARC or Intel x86 platforms by inserting the Solaris distribution CD into the local CD-ROM drive and powering on the system or booting via the network. The software that is installed is determined by a custom profile. Using this method, you can automatically install groups of systems in an identical manner. The custom profile, along with other JumpStart configuration files, is located in the JumpStart configuration directory.

## JumpStart Configuration Directory

The JumpStart configuration directory contains the files used to customize a JumpStart installation. It provides a means to automate the system configuration phase of an installation for groups of similar systems. This directory can reside either on a floppy diskette, referred to as a *profile diskette*, or on a network server, referred to as a *profile server*. The profile server provides access to the custom JumpStart configuration files over the network and eliminates the need to create and distribute multiple profile diskettes during installation of a large number of systems. The two basic types of files in the JumpStart directory are a rules file and one or more profile files.

> The Part II Exam (310-012) continues to refer to the *profile file* as the *class file*, even though it was renamed way back in the Solaris 2.6 system documentation. Keep this in mind when you see JumpStart questions that refer to the class file.

## The Rules File

The rules file is a text file that contains an entry or *rule* for each system or group of systems that are to be automatically installed. Each rule identifies the system (or group of systems) based on one or more attributes and identifies a unique profile file that provides the configuration details for that system or group of systems.

Each rule consists of one or more keywords and values followed by the name of a begin script, the profile file, and then the finish script (all separated by tabs or spaces). Keywords (and associated values) include the following:

- **any**
- **arch** (followed by a processor-type value)
- **disksize** (followed by a disk name value)
- **hostaddress** (followed by an IP address value)
- **hostname** (followed by a hostname value)
- **memsize** (followed by a physical memory value)
- **model** (followed by a platform name value)

One or more of these keywords and associated values are specified per rule to uniquely identify a system or group of systems.

Following the keywords and values is the name of a begin script. This is a Bourne shell script that executes before installation begins. If a begin script is not required, a hyphen (-) should be specified instead. Following the begin script is the name of a profile file in the JumpStart configuration directory that provides the configuration details for that system or group of systems. Following the profile file is the name of the finish script. The finish script is a Bourne shell script that is executed after installation is complete. If a finish script is not required, a hyphen (-) should be specified instead.

The following listing is an example of several entries from a rules file:

```
hostname sample_host    -           host_class    set_root_pw
network 924.222.43.0 && \
        karch sun4c     -           net924_sun4c  -
arch i386               x86-begin   x86-class     -
any -                   -           any_machine   -
```

The first entry lists the JumpStart installation for the host named sample_host. No begin script is specified, the host_class file is used as the profile or class file, and the finish script set_root_pw is called after installation to set the password of the root account.

The second entry is actually listed on two lines. The backslash (\) character at the end of the first line continues the entry to the next line. For systems located on network 924.222.43.0 and are SPARC sun4c platforms, the net924_sun4c profile or class file is used. No begin or finish script is specified.

The third entry is for all i386 or Intel-compatible platforms. The x86-begin script is executed first, and then the x86-class profile or class file is used to direct the installation. No finish script is specified.

The fourth entry provides a default. Any systems not covered by the other rules are installed using the any_machine profile file. No begin or finish script is specified.

## The Profile Files

A profile (or class) file is a text file that defines how to install the Solaris 8 software on a system. Like the rules file, a profile file contains keywords and associated values that guide the installation. Keywords and associated values include the following:

- **boot_device** (followed by the partition to use as a boot device)
- **cluster** (followed by the name of the software group to install, add, or delete)
- **filesys** (followed by pathname and mount point of a remote file system to mount)
- **install_type** (followed by the type of install: initial_install or upgrade)
- **package** (followed by the name of a software package to add or delete)
- **partitioning** (followed by the type of disk partitioning: default, existing, or explicit)
- **root_device** (followed by the partition to use as the root device)
- **system_type** (followed by the system type: standalone or server)

The following lists the contents of the any_machine profile provided as a JumpStart sample on the Solaris 8 distribution CD:

```
install_type    initial_install
system_type     standalone
partitioning    default
cluster         SUNWCuser
cluster         SUNWCxgl delete
package         SUNWaudmo add
filesys         any 40 swap
filesys         any 50 /opt
```

The **install_type** entry must be specified as the first entry in a profile. This example identifies the installation as an initial instead of an upgrade. The system type is standalone with default disk partitioning. The End User Support software group or cluster will be installed, but the xgl cluster will be deleted and the audmo package will be added. For the file system layout, any partition will be used for swap (40MB in size), and any partition will be used for the /opt file system (50MB in size).

## Validation

Before you can use the rules file and profile files, you must validate them by using the **check**(1M) command (located on the Solaris 8 distribution CD under the Tools directory). If the rules file and all the profile files are set up correctly, a rules.ok file is created in the JumpStart configuration directory.

## Booting the JumpStart Client

When booted, the JumpStart client attempts to locate the rules and profile files associated with the system. If a diskette is mounted in the diskette drive that contains the JumpStart configuration directory, the client will use it.

Otherwise, the client will contact the in.rarpd daemon running on an install/boot server using a RARP broadcast and obtain its client name or IP address based on its Ethernet address. Then the client will contact the in.bootparamd daemon running on an install/boot server using BOOTP. The request includes the name of the client or IP address. Based on this information, the in.bootparamd daemon provides the boot parameters from /etc/bootparam, NIS, or NIS+. One of these parameters is install_config, which defines the profile server and path to the JumpStart configuration directory. Other parameters including the name of the TFTP server that will provide the boot image (SPARC only) and NFS server that will provide the distribution of the Solaris 8 software over the network are also obtained using this same procedure. Once the JumpStart Directory is located, the rules file determines the appropriate profile or class file to use. The details in the profile file are used to direct the installation.

The install files will be obtained from the distribution CD mounted in a local CD-ROM drive or from an install server and path identified by the install boot parameter.

# Practice Questions

## Question 1

Which of the following commands is used to set up an install server?

- ❍ a. **setup_install_server**
- ❍ b. **setup_install_server -b**
- ❍ c. **install_server_setup**
- ❍ d. **server_setup -i**

Answer a is correct. The **setup_install_server** command is used to set up an install server. The **-b** command-line argument is used to install a boot server. Therefore, answer b is incorrect. The commands in answers c and d do not exist.

## Question 2

Which of the following is a reason to set up a boot server on a separate system than an install server?

- ❍ a. A boot server cannot reside on an install server.
- ❍ b. One or more install clients are not on the same subnet as the install server.
- ❍ c. All install clients are not on the same subnet.
- ❍ d. NIS or NIS+ cannot locate a boot server that resides on an install server.

Answer b is correct. If one or more install clients are not on the same subnet as the install server, you should set up a boot server on a separate system than the install server. A boot server can reside on an install server. Therefore, answer a is incorrect. The location of clients in relation to other clients does not determine the need for boot servers; the location of the clients in relation to the install server determines the need for a separate boot server. Therefore, answer c is incorrect. NIS and NIS+ do not locate things but serve only as databases of information. Therefore, answer d is incorrect.

## Question 3

Enter the name of the command (without command-line arguments) used to add install client information to an install or a boot server.

______________________________

The correct answer is **add_install_client**.

## Question 4

Which of the following install methods can use over-the-network installation resources? [Select all that apply]

- ❑ a. Custom JumpStart
- ❑ b. Web Start
- ❑ c. JumpStart
- ❑ d. Interactive installation

Answers a, b, c, and d are correct. All four installation methods can use over-the-network installation resources.

## Question 5

Which of the following are automatic installation methods? [Select all that apply]

- ❑ a. SunInstall
- ❑ b. Custom JumpStart
- ❑ c. Web Start
- ❑ d. JumpStart

Answers b and d are correct. Custom JumpStart and JumpStart are automatic installation methods. SunInstall and Web Start are interactive installation methods. Therefore, answers a and c are incorrect.

## Question 6

Enter the name of the command used to add the contents of the Solaris 8 Software (2 of 2) CD or the Solaris 8 Languages distribution CD to an install server.

____________________

The correct answer is **add_to_install**.

## Question 7

Which of the following files should be in a JumpStart configuration directory? [Select all that apply]

- ❑ a. One or more JumpStart profile files
- ❑ b. **check**
- ❑ c. rules file
- ❑ d. rules.ok file

Answers a, c, and d are correct. The profile files and the rules file are the two types of file that must be created in the JumpStart configuration directory. If they are set up correctly, the rules.ok file is created in the JumpStart configuration directory. The **check** command, which is located on the Solaris 8 distribution CD, must be executed to validate the rules and profile files. Therefore, answer b is incorrect.

## Question 8

Match each **add_install_client** command-line argument with its purpose.

| | |
|---|---|
| a. **-c** | 1. Specifies the install server and path |
| b. **-d** | 2. Specifies the profile server and JumpStart configuration directory path |
| c. **-p** | 3. Specifies client is a DHCP client |
| d. **-s** | 4. Specifies the server and path for the sysidcfg file |

Answers a-2, b-3, c-4, and d-1 are correct. The **-c** ***server:path*** command-line argument specifies the profile server and JumpStart configuration directory where the rules and profile (class) files reside. The **-d** command-line argument specifies that the client will use DHCP to determine the IP address, netmask, and so on. The **-p** *server:path* command-line argument specifies a server and the full path name to the sysidcfg file. The **-s** *server:path* command-line argument specifies the install server and path to the install images.

## Question 9

Enter the file used by a custom JumpStart installation to define how a system is installed.

________________________________

The correct answer is profile.

## Question 10

Which of the following are Solaris 8 software groups? [Select all that apply]

- ❑ a. Entire Distribution
- ❑ b. Basic
- ❑ c. End User Support
- ❑ d. Java Development Environment

Answers a and c are correct. Entire Distribution and End User Support are Solaris 8 software groups. The groups in answers b and d do not exist.

## Question 11

Enter the name of the file that contains boot parameters and is updated by the **add_install_client** command.

________________________________

The correct answer is /etc/bootparams.

# Need to Know More?

Becker, George, Mary E. S. Morris, and Kathy Slattery, *Solaris Implementation* (SunSoft Press, 1995), ISBN 0-13-353350-6.

Sun Microsystems, *Solaris Advanced Installation Guide.* Available in printed form (part number 806-0957-10), on the Web at **docs.sun.com**, and from the online documentation, AnswerBook2, provided with the Solaris 8 operating system.

Sun Microsystems, *System Reference Manual, Section 1 - User Commands.* Available in printed form (part number 806-0624-10), on the Web at **docs.sun.com**, and from the online documentation, AnswerBook2, provided with the Solaris 8 operating system.

Sun Microsystems, *System Reference Manual, Section 1M - Administration Commands.* Available in printed form (part number 806-0625-10), on the Web at **docs.sun.com**, and from the online documentation, AnswerBook2, provided with the Solaris 8 operating system.

Sun Microsystems, *System Reference Manual, Section 4 - File Formats.* Available in printed form (part number 806-0633-10), on the Web at **docs.sun.com**, and from the online documentation, AnswerBook2, provided with the Solaris 8 operating system.

22

# Sample Test II

This chapter provides 61 questions on the topics that pertain to Exam 310-012, "Certified Solaris Administrator Examination for the Solaris 8 Operating Environment." This exam must be completed in 90 minutes.

Keep in mind that to become certified, you must pass both the 310-011 exam and this one. The sample test for the other exam is in Chapter 11. See that chapter for test-taking tips, as well.

# Sample Test

## Question 1

Enter the name of the command used to add the contents of the Solaris 8 Software (2 of 2) distribution CD to an install server.

______________________________

## Question 2

Which of the following virtual devices or RAID levels does the DiskSuite support? [Select all that apply]

- ❑ a. Concatenated virtual device
- ❑ b. RAID level 0
- ❑ c. RAID level 1
- ❑ d. RAID level 5
- ❑ e. RAID level 10

## Question 3

Which of the following commands is used to set up a system to be installed over the network?

- ❍ a. **setup_network_client**
- ❍ b. **network_install**
- ❍ c. **add_install_client**
- ❍ d. **install_network_client**

## Question 4

Which of the following /etc/nsswitch.conf file entries would cause DNS, then NIS+, followed by the /etc files, to be searched when trying to resolve a hostname?

❍ a. hosts: dns nisplus files

❍ b. hosts: files nisplus dns

❍ c. ipaddress: file nisplus dns

❍ d. ipaddress: dns nisplus files

## Question 5

Which of the following commands can be used to mount the /export/home file system from the solaris system (IP address 192.168.39.7) on the /mnt mount point? [Select all that apply]

❑ a. **mount solaris:/export/home /mnt**

❑ b. **mount 192.168.39.7:/export/home /mnt**

❑ c. **mount -F nfs solaris:/export/home /mnt**

❑ d. **mount -F nfs -o soft,retry=1000,ro 192.168.39.7:/export /home /mnt**

## Question 6

Which of the following is a reason to set up a boot server on a separate system from an install server?

❍ a. A boot server cannot reside on an install server.

❍ b. One or more install clients are not on the same subnet as the install server.

❍ c. All install clients are not on the same subnet.

❍ d. NIS or NIS+ cannot locate a boot server that resides on an install server.

## Question 7

Which of the following are proc tools? [Select all that apply]

- ❑ a. **ptree**
- ❑ b. **pwd**
- ❑ c. **ptime**
- ❑ d. **psignal**

## Question 8

Which of the following commands is used to propagate an updated NIS map to NIS slave servers?

- ❍ a. **yppush**
- ❍ b. **ypupdate**
- ❍ c. **yppropagate**
- ❍ d. **ypxfr**
- ❍ e. **ypmaps**

## Question 9

Where is CacheFS used—on the NFS server or on the NFS client?

______________________________

## Question 10

Arrange the seven layers of the OSI Network Model in order from highest to lowest.

| | |
|---|---|
| a. | 1. Network |
| b. | 2. Session |
| c. | 3. Physical |
| d. | 4. Presentation |
| e. | 5. Transport |
| f. | 6. Data Link |
| g. | 7. Application |

## Question 11

Which of the following steps are *not* used to add a new NIS map? [Select all that apply]

- ❑ a. Create a text file with the appropriate information
- ❑ b. Use the **make** command
- ❑ c. Use the **makedbm** command
- ❑ d. Use the **yppush** command

## Question 12

Which of the following are valid entries for an AutoFS direct map? [Select all that apply]

- ❑ a. /usr/local/bin nfsserver:/usr/local/bin
- ❑ b. /usr/games -ro nfsserver:/usr/games
- ❑ c. /usr/bin nfsserver1:/usr/bin nfsserver2:/usr/bin
- ❑ d. /- nfsserver:/usr/data
- ❑ e. /usr/data nfsserver:/usr/data -ro

## Question 13

Which of the following are features of a virtual disk management system? [Select all that apply]

- ❑ a. Graphical administration tool
- ❑ b. Improved reliability
- ❑ c. Improved performance
- ❑ d. Overcomes physical disk limitations

## Question 14

Which of the following are fields in a custom JumpStart rules file? [Select all that apply]

- ❑ a. Rule keyword
- ❑ b. Rule value
- ❑ c. Begin script
- ❑ d. Profile script
- ❑ e. End script

## Question 15

Which of the following functions can be performed using the AdminSuite Host Manager?

- ❍ a. Mounting a local hard disk
- ❍ b. Editing any NIS+ table
- ❍ c. Adding support for a network client
- ❍ d. Booting a network client

## Question 16

Which of the following situations do not require the **automount** command to be executed manually? [Select all that apply]

- ❑ a. Addition to the auto_master
- ❑ b. Addition to a direct map
- ❑ c. Addition to an indirect map
- ❑ d. Deletion from the auto_master
- ❑ e. Deletion from a direct map
- ❑ f. Deletion from an indirect map

## Question 17

Which of the following client information must be added to NIS/NIS+ to support JumpStart installation? [Select all that apply]

- ❑ a. Host name
- ❑ b. IP address
- ❑ c. System locale
- ❑ d. Ethernet address
- ❑ e. Name service

## Question 18

Which of the following commands is used to start the **ypbind** program?

- ❍ a. **ypinit**
- ❍ b. **ypstop**
- ❍ c. **ypstart**
- ❍ d. **ypcrank**
- ❍ e. **ypwhich**

## Question 19

Which of the following is the default source facility for syslog messages if a source is not specified?

- ❍ a. mail
- ❍ b. auth
- ❍ c. user
- ❍ d. kern

## Question 20

What is the collective name for the files NIS+ uses to store the information that NIS+ clients request?

______________________________

## Question 21

Which of the following **cfsadmin** command-line arguments are required to create a CacheFS configuration? [Select all that apply]

❑ a. NFS server name and resource

❑ b. **-c**

❑ c. **-o**

❑ d. Full pathname of the cache directory

❑ e. Name of the local host

## Question 22

Which of the following statements is true about an Ethernet address associated with a network interface?

❍ a. It is displayed in the **xx:xx:xx:xx:xx** format (five 8-bit bytes) using the **ifconfig** command.

❍ b. It is displayed in the **xx:xx:xx:xx:xx:xx** format (six 8-bit bytes) using the **ping** command.

❍ c. It is displayed in the **xx:xx:xx:xx:xx** format (five 8-bit bytes) using the **ping** command.

❍ d. It is displayed in the **xx:xx:xx:xx:xx:xx** format (six 8-bit bytes) using the **ifconfig** command.

## Question 23

Which of the following are interactive installation methods? [Select all that apply]

❑ a. SunInstall

❑ b. Custom JumpStart

❑ c. Web Start

❑ d. JumpStart

## Question 24

Which of the following are valid command-line arguments for the **cfsadmin** command? [Select all that apply]

❑ a. **-c** (create a cache)

❑ b. **-C** (perform a consistency check on a cache)

❑ c. **-d** (delete a cache)

❑ d. **-o** (set cache options)

## Question 25

Which of the following name services uses ASCII text files, supports hostname-to-IP-address resolution and IP-address-to-hostname resolution, and is used on the Internet?

❍ a. NIS

❍ b. NIS+

❍ c. DNS

❍ d. /etc files

## Question 26

Which of the following is a name for a virtual file system that is composed of several partitions that are allocated and used in an interleaved fashion?

❍ a. RAID 1

❍ b. Striped

❍ c. Concatenated

❍ d. Hot spare

## Question 27

Which of the following are valid actions that can be specified in the /etc/syslog.conf file? [Select all that apply]

❑ a. The name of a file

❑ b. An exclamation mark (!)

❑ c. The name of a host

❑ d. The name of a user account

## Question 28

Which of the following commands can be used to determine shared NFS resources? [Select all that apply]

- ❑ a. **share**
- ❑ b. **dfmounts**
- ❑ c. **dfshares**
- ❑ d. **mountall**
- ❑ e. **mount**

## Question 29

Which of the following is the best procedure for generating the data files used to create NIS maps?

- ❍ a. Edit the /etc files to remove any information not needed by NIS.
- ❍ b. Copy the /etc files to a directory and clean up the copy for use in building NIS maps.
- ❍ c. Create a new set of data files by using the **makenisdata** command.
- ❍ d. Run the **buildmap** command for each map and enter the appropriate data when prompted.

## Question 30

Identify the file used by Custom JumpStart installation to define which profile a system or group of systems should use for installation.

______________________________

## Question 31

Enter the word used to describe the technique of writing data across multiple disks to improve performance and to overcome disk limitations.

______________________________

## Question 32

Identify the command used to create a CacheFS log.

______________________________

## Question 33

Identify the command used to make an NFS resource unavailable for mounting.

______________________________

## Question 34

Enter the name of the command used to add a role to the RBAC database.

______________________________

## Question 35

The Solaris 8 operating system supports five types of name services. Four of these are /etc files, DNS, NIS, and NIS+. Enter the name of the fifth name service.

______________________________

## Question 36

Which of the following is the most severe level of syslog message?

❍ a. alert

❍ b. notice

❍ c. emerg

❍ d. crit

## Question 37

Which of the following commands is used to configure an NIS master?

- ❍ a. **ypinit -m**
- ❍ b. **ypinit -c**
- ❍ c. **ypinit -s**
- ❍ d. **nisclient**
- ❍ e. **nisinit -c**

## Question 38

Which file is used to automatically mount NFS resources during system boot or when the **mountall** command is used?

- ❍ a. /etc/dfs/dfstab
- ❍ b. /etc/vfstab
- ❍ c. /etc/mnttab
- ❍ d. /etc/dfs/sharetab

## Question 39

Which of the following pathnames is associated with the Volume Manager?

- ❍ a. /dev/dsk
- ❍ b. /dev/vx/dsk
- ❍ c. /dev/md/dsk
- ❍ d. /dev/ds/dsk

## Question 40

Identify the name of the NIS+ table that contains the Ethernet addresses of systems in the domain.

____________________________

## Question 41

Name the command used to add a new NIS map.

__________________________________

## Question 42

You use the **domainname** command to set the domain name for a system using /etc files, but after the system is rebooted, the domain name is lost. Why?

- ❍ a. The domain name must be re-entered after every reboot.
- ❍ b. You didn't use the **-p** command-line argument to make the domain name permanent.
- ❍ c. You forgot to edit the /etc/defaultdomain file and enter the domain.

## Question 43

Which /etc file contains a list of the servers (and paths) that provide boot, root, and swap areas for network/install clients?

- ❍ a. bootparams
- ❍ b. ethers
- ❍ c. timezone
- ❍ d. hosts
- ❍ e. vfstab

## Question 44

Identify the NFS-related protocol that can be used to access NFS resources using a Web browser.

__________________________________

## Question 45

Which of the following commands is used to check and repair a file system?

❍ a. **mount**

❍ b. **newfs**

❍ c. **fsck**

❍ d. **format**

## Question 46

From which of the following system run levels will the NFS server program be started? [Select all that apply]

❑ a. 0

❑ b. s

❑ c. 2

❑ d. 3

❑ e. 6

## Question 47

Which of the following are Solaris 8 software groups? [Select all that apply]

❑ a. Entire Distribution

❑ b. Entire Distribution Plus OEM System Support

❑ c. End User Support

❑ d. Developer System Support

## Question 48

Name the graphical management tool that supports single sign-on.

______________________________

## Question 49

Which of the following is included with Volume Manager but not DiskSuite? [Select all that apply]

- ❑ a. Graphical administration tool
- ❑ b. Command-line utilities
- ❑ c. Performance analysis tools
- ❑ d. Dynamic online tuning

## Question 50

Enter the command-line argument used with the **setup_install_server** command to set up a boot server.

_______________________________

## Question 51

Enter the name of the file used to configure the syslog facility.

_______________________________

## Question 52

Which of the following is not a tool provided with AdminSuite?

- ❍ a. Database Manager
- ❍ b. Storage Manager
- ❍ c. Network Client Manager
- ❍ d. Serial Port Manager

## Question 53

Which file should always contain the currently shared NFS resources?

❍ a. /etc/nfs/nfstab

❍ b. /etc/nfs/shares

❍ c. /etc/dfs/dfstab

❍ d. /etc/dfs/sharetab

## Question 54

Which of the following pathnames is associated with standard Solaris file systems?

❍ a. /dev/dsk

❍ b. /dev/vx/dsk

❍ c. /dev/md/dsk

❍ d. /dev/ds/dsk

## Question 55

Identify the facility used to capture and log messages from system components and user programs.

______________________________

## Question 56

Which of the following are keywords that can be defined in a profile or class file? [Select all that apply]

❑ a. **install_type**

❑ b. **cluster**

❑ c. **package**

❑ d. **system_type**

## Question 57

Which of the following install clients use Trivial FTP to obtain a bootable image over the network? [Select all that apply]

- ❑ a. Intel clients only
- ❑ b. SPARC clients only
- ❑ c. Both Intel and SPARC clients
- ❑ d. Any client on a subnet different than the install server

## Question 58

Arrange the five layers of the TCP/IP Network Model in order from highest to lowest.

a. 1. Network

b. 2. Data Link

c. 3. Physical

d. 4. Application

e. 5. Transport

## Question 59

Which of the following NFS mount options should be specified in the /etc/vfstab file to support failover? [Select all that apply]

- ❑ a. Read-only (ro)
- ❑ b. Read-write (rw)
- ❑ c. No interrupts allowed (nointr)
- ❑ d. Advertise as public (public)

## Question 60

Identify the **share** command-line argument used to allow remote root access to a NFS share.

______________________________

## Question 61

Which of the following swap-related operations can be performed by the **swap** command? [Select all that apply]

- ❑ a. Create swap space
- ❑ b. Add swap space
- ❑ c. List swap space
- ❑ d. Delete swap space

23

# Answer Key II

1. **add_to_install_server**
2. a, b, c, d
3. c
4. a
5. a, b, c, d
6. b
7. a, c
8. a
9. NFS client
10. a-7, b-4, c-2, d-5, e-1, f-6, g-3
11. b, d
12. a, b, c
13. a, b, c, d
14. a, b, c, d, e
15. c
16. c, f
17. a, b, d
18. c
19. c
20. tables
21. b, d
22. d
23. a, c
24. a, c, d
25. c
26. b
27. a, c, d
28. a, c
29. b
30. rules
31. striping
32. **cachefslog**
33. **unshare**
34. **roleadd**
35. FNS
36. c
37. a
38. b
39. b
40. ethers
41. **makedbm**
42. c
43. a
44. WebNFS
45. c
46. d
47. a, b, c, d
48. Solaris Management Console
49. c, d
50. -b
51. /etc/syslog.conf
52. c
53. d
54. a
55. syslog or syslogd
56. a, b, c, d
57. b
58. a-4, b-5, c-1, d-2, e-3
59. a
60. **root**
61. b, c, d

## Question 1

The correct answer is **add_to_install_server**.

## Question 2

Answers a, b, c, and d are correct. The DiskSuite supports concatenated virtual devices and RAID levels 0, 1, and 5. DiskSuite does not support RAID level 10. Therefore, answer e is incorrect.

## Question 3

Answer c is correct. The **add_install_client** command is used to set up a system to be installed over the network. The commands in the other answers do not exist.

## Question 4

Answer a is correct. The hosts: *dns nisplus files* entry will cause DNS, then NIS+, and then /etc files to be searched when trying to resolve a hostname. The *hosts files nisplus dns* has all the name services, but in the incorrect order; the search order is from left to right. Therefore, answer b is incorrect. Answers c and d use an invalid keyword (ipaddress) and therefore are incorrect.

## Question 5

Answers a, b, c, and d are correct. The system sharing an NFS resource can be identified by either hostname or IP address. If the file system type is not specified using the -F command-line argument, NFS is assumed. NFS-specific options can be specified using the **-o** command-line argument.

## Question 6

Answer b is correct. A boot server can reside on an install server. Therefore, answer a is incorrect. The location of clients in relation to other clients does not determine the need for boot servers. It is the location of the clients in relation to the install server that determines the need for a separate boot server. Therefore, answer c is incorrect. NIS and NIS+ do not locate things, but serve only as a database of information. Therefore, answer d is incorrect.

## Question 7

Answers a and c are correct. **ptree** and **ptime** are proc tools. **pwd** is used to display the current working directory. The proc tool equivalent is the **pwdx** command. Therefore, answer b is incorrect. The proc tool command to list signal actions is **psig**, not **psignal.** Therefore, answer d is incorrect.

## Question 8

Answer a is correct. **yppush** is used to propagate an updated NIS map to NIS slave servers. **ypxfr** is used to propagate a new map. Therefore, answer d is incorrect. The commands in answers b, c, and e do not exist.

## Question 9

The correct answer is the NFS client.

## Question 10

Answers a-7, b-4, c-2, d-5, e-1, f-6, and g-3 are correct. The layers of the OSI Network Model from highest to lowest are: Application, Presentation, Session, Transport, Network, Data Link, and Physical.

## Question 11

Answers b and d are correct. The **make** command is used when updating a default map. The **yppush** command is used for propagating an updated nondefault map. The text file is used to add a new map. Therefore, answer a is incorrect. Likewise, the **makedbm** command is used for new maps. Therefore, answer c is incorrect.

## Question 12

Answers a, b, and c are correct. If more than one NFS server provides the same resource, as in answer c, multiple servers can be listed (separated by spaces). The first available resource is used. /- nfsserver:/usr/data does not provide a valid mount point. Therefore, answer d is incorrect. The format for a direct map entry is mount point, options, and then resource. The format of answer e is mount point, resource, and then options. Therefore, answer e is incorrect.

## Question 13

Answers a, b, c, and d are correct. Virtual disk management systems provide all these features.

## Question 14

Answers a, b, c, d, and e are correct. A rules entry consists of one or more rule keywords and rule values followed by the name of a begin script and then a profile script and an end script. The begin and end scripts are optional. If either is not specified, a hyphen (-) is used in place of the script name.

## Question 15

Answer c is correct. The AdminSuite Host Manager can add support for a network client. The Host Manager cannot be used to mount a disk. Therefore, answer a is incorrect. It also cannot edit any NIS+ table or boot a network client. Therefore, answers b and d are incorrect.

## Question 16

Answers c and f are correct. Changes to indirect maps do not require running the **automount** command. Changes to the auto_master and direct maps require that the **automount** command be executed manually. Therefore, answers a, b, d, and e are incorrect.

## Question 17

Answers a, b, and d are correct. The host name, IP address, and Ethernet address of the client need to be added to NIS/NIS+ to support JumpStart installation. The system locale is not required to install a client. Therefore, answer c is incorrect. Because the client information is added to the appropriate name service, you don't need to identify the name service. Therefore, answer e is incorrect.

## Question 18

Answer c is correct. The **ypstart** command is used to start the **ypbind** program. **ypinit** is used to initialize NIS servers and clients. Therefore, answer a is incorrect. **ypstop** is used to stop the **ypbind** program. Therefore, answer b is incorrect. **ypcrank** does not exist. Therefore, answer d is incorrect. **ypwhich** is used to identify the NIS server. Therefore, answer e is incorrect.

## Question 19

Answer c is correct. The user source facility is used for messages from user programs. If a source is not specified, user is assumed. The mail source is used for messages related to mail. Therefore, answer a is incorrect. The auth source is used for messages related to login authentication. Therefore, answer b is incorrect. The kern source is used for messages related to the kernel. Therefore, answer d is incorrect.

## Question 20

The correct answer is tables.

## Question 21

Answers b and d are correct. The **-c** command-line argument and the full pathname of the cache directory are required to create a CacheFS configuration. The NFS server name and resource, along with the name of the local host, cannot be specified using command-line arguments. Therefore, answers a and e are incorrect. The **-o** command-line argument can be used to specify options but is not required. Therefore, answer c is incorrect.

## Question 22

Answer d is correct. The Ethernet address is six 8-bit bytes or 48 bits long. It can be displayed using the **ifconfig** command. The Ethernet address is six, not five 8-bit bytes long, and the **ping** command cannot be used to display the Ethernet address of a network interface. Therefore, answers a, b, and c are incorrect.

## Question 23

Answers a and c are correct. SunInstall and Web Start are interactive installation methods. Custom JumpStart and JumpStart are automatic installation methods. Therefore, answers b and d are incorrect.

## Question 24

Answers a, c, and d are correct. **-c**, **-d**, and **-o** are valid command-line arguments for **cfsadmin**. The **-s** command-line argument is used to perform a consistency check, not **-C**. Therefore answer b is incorrect.

## Question 25

Answer c is correct. Although some of the name services use ASCII files and/or provide both hostname and IP address resolution, DNS is the only one used on the Internet. Therefore, answers a, b, and d are incorrect.

## Question 26

Answer b is correct. A striped virtual file system is composed of several partitions that are allocated and used in an interleaved fashion. RAID 1 is a configuration that uses mirroring in an identical (not interleaved) fashion. Therefore, answer a is incorrect. A concatenated virtual file system uses one partition at a time. Therefore, answer c is incorrect. Hot spare is not a type of virtual file system. Therefore, answer d is incorrect.

## Question 27

Answers a, c, and d are correct. If a file name is specified, the message is appended to the file. If a hostname is specified, the message is sent to the host. If a user account name is specified, the message is displayed on the standard output of the logged-in user. The only other valid action is an asterisk (*), which causes the message to be displayed on the standard output device of all logged-in user accounts. Therefore, answer b is incorrect.

## Question 28

Answers a and c are correct. The **share** command, used without arguments, lists all locally shared NFS resources. The **dfshares** command can be used to list locally or remotely shared resources. The **dfmounts** command is used to list locally or remotely mounted resources. Therefore, answer b is incorrect. The **mountall** command is used to mount local file systems. Therefore, answer d is incorrect. The **mount** command is used to mount or list currently mounted local file systems and NFS resources. Therefore, answer e is incorrect.

## Question 29

Answer b is correct. To generate the data files used to create NIS maps, you should copy the /etc files to a directory and clean up the copy. The /etc files can be modified, but the editing may adversely affect the system and is not the best approach. Therefore, answer a is incorrect. The **makenisdata** and **buildmap** commands do not exist. Therefore, answers c and d are incorrect.

## Question 30

The correct answer is rules.

## Question 31

The correct answer is striping.

## Question 32

The correct answer is **cachefslog**.

## Question 33

The correct answer is **unshare**.

## Question 34

The correct answer is **roleadd**.

## Question 35

The correct answer is FNS.

## Question 36

Answer c is correct. The rank order of severity levels is emerg, alert, crit, err, warning, notice, info, debug, and none.

## Question 37

Answer a is correct. The **ypinit -m** command is used to configure an NIS master. **ypinit -c** is used to configure a NIS client, and **ypinit -s** is used to configure a NIS slave server. Therefore, answers b and c are incorrect. The commands in answers d and e do not exist.

## Question 38

Answer b is correct. The /etc/vfstab file is used to automatically mount NFS resources during system boot or when the **mountall** command is used. The /etc/dfs/dfstab file is used to automatically share NFS resources. Therefore, answer a is incorrect. The /etc/mnttab file lists the currently mounted file systems and NFS resources. Therefore, answer c is incorrect. The /etc/dfs/sharetab file lists the NFS resources currently shared. Therefore, answer d is incorrect.

## Question 39

Answer b is correct. The /dev/vx/dsk pathname is associated with the Volume Manager. /dev/dsk is associated with the standard file systems. Therefore, answer a is incorrect. /dev/md/dsk is associated with DiskSuite virtual file systems. Therefore, answer c is incorrect. The pathname in answer d does not exist.

## Question 40

The correct answer is ethers.

## Question 41

The correct answer is **makedbm**.

## Question 42

Answer c is correct. The /etc/defaultdomain file is used to store the default system domain. If this file is used, then the domain name does not have to be defined after every reboot. Therefore, answer a is incorrect. The **domainname** command does not support a **-p** command-line argument. Therefore, answer b is incorrect.

## Question 43

Answer a is correct. The bootparams file contains a list of the servers (and paths) that provide boot, root, and swap areas for network/install clients. Either contains network client Ethernet addresses and associated hostnames. Therefore, answer b is incorrect. timezone contains network client time zone information. Therefore, answer c is incorrect. hosts contains system hostnames and IP addresses. Therefore, answer d is incorrect. vfstab contains a list of file systems to be mounted automatically. Therefore, answer e is incorrect.

## Question 44

The correct answer is WebNFS.

## Question 45

Answer c is correct. The **fsck** command is used to check and repair a file system. The **mount** command is used to mount the file system. Therefore, answer a is incorrect. The **newfs** command is used to create a file system after the disk has been formatted. Therefore, answer b is incorrect. The **format** command is used to format a file system. Therefore, answer d is incorrect.

## Question 46

Answer d is correct. The NFS server program is started at run level 3. Run level 0 is the power down state; services are being shut down in this state. Therefore, answer a is incorrect. Run level s is used for administration, and users are not allowed to access the system. Therefore, answer b is incorrect. All network services except the NFS server are started at run level 2. Therefore, answer c is incorrect. Run level 6 is the reboot state, and the system is being restarted. Therefore, answer e is incorrect.

## Question 47

Answers a, b, c, and d are correct. From smallest to largest, the software groups are End User Support, Developer System Support, Entire Distribution, and Entire Distribution Plus OEM System Support.

## Question 48

The correct answer is Solaris Management Console.

## Question 49

Answers c and d are correct. Volume Manager includes performance analysis tools and dynamic online tuning, but DiskSuite does not. Both Volume Manager and DiskSuite provide a graphical administration tool and command-line utilities. Therefore, answers a and b are incorrect.

## Question 50

The correct answer is **-b**.

## Question 51

The correct answer is /etc/syslog.conf.

## Question 52

Answer c is correct. AdminSuite includes a Host Manager that is used to manage network clients, not a Network Client Manager. Database Manager, Storage Manager, and Serial Port Manager all are included in AdminSuite. Therefore, answers a, b, and d are incorrect.

## Question 53

Answer d is correct. The /etc/dfs/sharetab file should always contain the currently shared NFS resources. The files in answers a and b do not exist. The /etc/dfs/dfstab file contains resources that should be shared automatically during system boot or when the **shareall** command is used. Therefore, answer c is incorrect.

## Question 54

Answer a is correct. The pathname /dev/dsk is associated with standard Solaris file systems. /dev/vx/dsk is associated with the Volume Manager virtual file systems. Therefore, answer b is incorrect. /dev/md/dsk is associated with DiskSuite virtual file systems. Therefore, answer c is incorrect. The pathname in answer d does not exist.

## Question 55

The correct answer is syslog or syslogd.

## Question 56

Answers a, b, c, and d are correct. All of these keywords can be defined in a profile file. The **install_type** keyword must be defined and must be the first entry in the profile file.

## Question 57

Answer b is correct. Intel clients typically obtain a bootable image from a local diskette or local CD-ROM. Only SPARC clients use TFTP to obtain a bootable image. Therefore, answers a and c are incorrect. Intel clients can be configured to use the Remote Program Load (RPL). The subnet has no impact on the use of TFTP. Therefore, answer d is incorrect.

## Question 58

Answers a-4, b-5, c-1, d-2, and e-3 are correct. The layers of the TCP/IP Network Model from highest to lowest are: Application, Transport, Network, Data Link, and Physical.

## Question 59

Answer a is correct. Only the read-only (ro) NFS mount option should be specified to set up failover. Therefore, answers b, c, and d are incorrect.

## Question 60

The correct answer is **root**. The **root=***list* command-line argument is used to specify a list of clients that have root access.

## Question 61

Answers b, c, and d are correct. The **swap** command is used to add, list, and delete swap space. The **mkfile** command is used to create swap space. Therefore, answer a is incorrect.

# Glossary

### Access Control List (ACL)

Solaris 8 extends the standard Unix file permissions by adding an Access Control List capability. ACLs provide the ability to add permissions for specific users and groups along with a default permission (mask). In addition to supporting the standard read/write/execute permission for owner, group, and other, ACLs can be used to set read/write/execute permissions for additional user accounts and group accounts and to define a mask capability that controls the maximum allowed permissions given to user and group accounts. The ACL for a directory includes default entries that determine the permissions assigned to files and subdirectories created under the directory. The **setfacl**(1M) command is used to set ACLs, and the **getfacl**(1M) command is used to display ACLs.

### Address Resolution Protocol (ARP)

A protocol used to map from an IP address to an Ethernet address.

### architecture

The variation of the platform. For SPARC platforms, types of architecture include sun4c and sun4m.

### authorization (for role-based access control)

The right to perform restricted administrative functions such as shutting down the system.

### AutoClient

A type of network client that uses a small local disk for swap space and a cached copy of the root and user file systems.

### AutoFS

A network service and type of file system. AutoFS resources are mounted automatically when an attempt is made to access them and are then unmounted automatically after a period of being idle.

### AutoFS map

A file used to configure the AutoFS service. The three types of AutoFS maps are the /etc/auto_master file that identifies other maps, direct maps that identify full pathnames to mount points and associated NFS resources, and indirect maps that identify partial pathnames to mount points and associated NFS resources.

**boot server**
A network server that provides the files necessary to boot an install client over the network during an over-the-network installation. After an install client has booted, the boot server has completed its function. The remainder of the installation is supported by an install server. Typically, an install server and a boot server reside on the same system. However, if install clients are on a different subnet than an install server, a boot server must be set up on the same subnet as the install clients.

**Bourne shell**
A version of the Unix shell developed by Steven Bourne from AT&T Bell Labs. It is referred to as *sh*. The Bourne shell is the default shell for the Solaris operating system.

**C shell**
A version of the Unix shell developed at the University of California at Berkeley. It is referred to as *csh*.

**CacheFS**
A storage service and a type of file system. CacheFS is used to store a copy of a remote NFS resource locally. Doing so allows faster access and less network traffic.

**client**
A networked computer system that uses services provided by a server.

**client/server**
An operation model used by computer systems in which services are centralized on a server and accessed by one or more clients via a network.

**client-side failover**
Automatic switch to another NFS server that provides a "replicated" copy of a resource when the original NFS server becomes unavailable.

**Common Desktop Environment (CDE)**
A graphical user interface.

**concatenated striped virtual device**
A striped virtual device that has been expanded by concatenating additional slices to the end of the device.

**concatenated virtual device**
A device consisting of two or more slices. The slices can be on the same physical disk or on several physical disks. The slices also can be of different sizes. The slices are addressed in a sequential manner; that is, as space is needed, it is allocated from the first slice in the concatenation. Once this space is used completely, space is allocated from the second slice, and so on.

**csh**
See **C shell**.

**Custom JumpStart**
An automated installation method that uses a predefined rules file and one or more profile files to determine the system configuration to install, depending on architecture, equipped hardware, or other defined characteristics. These files are located in the JumpStart Configuration directory.

**daemon**
A task or process that appears to be executing all the time (and typically provides a service on demand).

**dataless client**
A type of network client that uses a small local disk for swap space and a root file system. Other file systems are accessed remotely.

**device aliases**
An OpenBoot feature that lets you assign a short, easy-to-use name to a full physical device pathname.

**device driver**
Software modules that interface with physical resources and understand how to communicate with hardware devices and control their operation. Typically, each device has a unique driver that is provided with the hardware and identified by hardware manufacturer, model, and sometimes hardware version.

**direct map**
A type of AutoFS configuration file that identifies the full path to mount points and associated NFS resources.

**directory**
A folder used to organize files.

**disk group**
A collection of Volume Manager (VM) disks that share a common configuration.

**disk label**
See **volume table of contents**.

**diskless client**
A type of network client that does not have any local storage. All file systems along with swap space are accessed remotely.

**domain**
A group of systems managed as a single entity using a name service such as NIS or NIS+.

**Domain Name System (DNS)**
The name service used on the Internet to resolve hostnames to IP addresses and IP addresses to hostnames.

**duplexing**
The technique of copying data being written to one online device to another, offline device. Duplexing provides a realtime backup of data that can be brought online to replace the original device in the event that it fails. Each disk has its own controller.

**Dynamic Host Configuration Protocol (DHCP)**
A protocol used by DHCP clients to request host configuration information from a DHCP server. The requested information includes IP address, subnet mask, default router(s), and so on.

**dynamic reconfiguration**
A system capability that supports hot plugging by allowing the system to recognize the new hardware (or even software) configuration without rebooting the system.

**Enterprise Volume Manager**
A virtual disk management system. In addition to supporting disk mirroring and several RAID configurations, it provides statistics and dynamic tuning capability.

### /etc files

The original name service provided with the Unix operating system. Information about other systems is stored in files located under the /etc directory.

### Ethernet address

A unique 48-bit Data Link Layer address of a network interface. Also referred to as a hardware address, physical address, or Media Access Control (MAC) address.

### Federated Naming Service (FNS)

A name service that conforms to the X/Open Federated Naming Specification (XFN).

### file

A group of bytes treated as a unit for storage, retrieval, and manipulation.

### file server

A networked standalone system used to provide remote access to shared or common data.

### file system

A logical collection of files and directories contained in a partition. The file system can be treated as a single entity when making it available for use (mounting), checking, and repairing.

### group account

A unique name and associated group ID used to manage a collection of user accounts.

### group ID (GID)

A unique numeric ID assigned to a group account used for group ownership and permissions.

### host

A computer system that provides resources to locally and/or remotely logged-on users.

### hot plugging

A hardware capability that allows system components to be changed without shutting down the system.

### hot relocation

The process the Volume Manager uses to reconstruct a failed subdisk on a spare disk or free space within a disk group and then substitute the rebuilt subdisk for the failed subdisk.

### hot spare

A disk slice that DiskSuite automatically substitutes for a slice that has failed.

### hot spare pool

A collection of hot spares managed by DiskSuite.

### indirect map

A type of AutoFS configuration file that identifies partial pathnames to mount points and associated NFS resources. The partial pathnames are relative to the directory identified in the /etc/auto-master file.

### initialization file templates

Login and shell startup initialization files for each user account are copied from templates under the /etc/skel directory when the home directory for the user account is created.

### initialization files

Several initialization files are associated with each user account home directory. These files are used to specify commands to be executed when the associated event occurs.

Depending on the login shell being used, there might be a login initialization file, a shell startup file, or a logout file. Commands in the login initialization file are executed when the user logs in. All three common shells provide a login initialization file. Commands in the shell startup file are executed whenever the logged-in user starts a shell. Both csh and ksh provide this capability. The **ENV** parameter is used to define the ksh shell startup initialization file. Only csh provides a file for automatic execution of commands when a user logs out.

### install client

A system that will be installed over the network. Basic information about the install clients needs to be available through a name service (NIS/NIS+) or in the files under the /etc directory on the install server or boot server.

### install server

A network server that provides the distribution files necessary for the installation of the Solaris operating system on an install client during an over-the-network installation. The files can be provided directly from the Solaris distribution CD mounted in a local CD-ROM drive or from the local hard disk.

### installation

The four installation methods are SunInstall, WebStart, JumpStart, and Custom JumpStart. All four methods can use either a local CD-ROM or over-the-network installation resources to obtain the distribution files. The installation process is divided into three phases: system configuration, system installation, and postinstallation.

### JumpStart

An automated installation process that uses standardized configurations based on system architecture and hardware to determine the system configuration to install.

### JumpStart configuration directory

A directory that contains the files used to customize a JumpStart installation. It provides a means to automate the system configuration phase of an installation for groups of similar systems. This directory can reside either on a floppy diskette, referred to as a *profile diskette*, or on a network server, referred to as a *profile server*. The two basic types of files in the JumpStart directory are a rules file and one or more profile files.

### kernel

A collection of software that manages the physical and logical resources of a computer. These management services include controlling the allocation of memory and other storage devices, controlling access to peripheral devices (input/output), and controlling the scheduling and execution of processes or tasks. The kernel is one of the three parts of an operating system (the other parts are the shell and the file system).

### kernel modules

Kernel software divided into groups of related functions. Some modules are part of a small, common core of the operating system, some modules provide platform-specific operations, and other modules are device drivers. This architecture allows portions of the kernel to be included or excluded on the basis of the desired functionality or allows portions of the kernel to be updated without replacing the entire kernel. The device drivers are loaded when the device is accessed.

**Korn shell**
A version of the Unix shell developed by David Korn from AT&T Bell Labs and referred to as *ksh*. It combines the best features of the Bourne shell and the C shell.

**Lightweight Directory Access Protocol (LDAP)**
A common protocol used by many vendors to provide access to directory services.

**localhost**
The loopback IP address for the local system; typically 127.0.0.1, but can be any address starting with 127.

**logical device name**
A naming convention used to identify disk, tape, and CD-ROM devices and provide either raw access (one character at a time) or block access (via a buffer for accessing large blocks of data). All logical device names reside under the /dev directory, and the /dev/dsk subdirectory identifies the device as a block disk device (the /dev/rdsk subdirectory indicates a raw disk).

**m4 macro**
An interpreted command syntax used to control the execution of conditional statements.

**man page**
A page from the Solaris 8 System Reference Manual that describes a command, system call, library routine, file format, and so on.

**mandatory locking**
A special file permission that prevents a program from reading or writing a file while another program has the file open.

**memory management**
A means of keeping track of available memory, allocating it to processes as needed, and reclaiming it as processes release it or terminate.

**metadevice**
The basic virtual disk used by DiskSuite to manage physical disks.

**mirroring**
The technique of copying data being written to one online device to another, offline device. Mirroring provides a realtime backup of data that can be brought online to replace the original device in the event that the original device fails. Typically, the two disks share the same controller.

**mount point**
A directory in a mounted file system that serves as an access point for another file system.

**mounting**
The process of associating a file system or NFS resource with a directory (mount point) so that it can be accessed by users and programs.

**multitasking**
The ability to execute more than one process or task at a time.

**multiuser**
The ability of a system to support multiple simultaneous users.

**name service**
A network service that provides a centralized location for information used by users and systems to communicate with each other across the network. The name service not only stores the information but also provides mechanisms to manage and access that information.

**name service switch**
A configuration file that is used to select which name services to use and in what order.

**namespace**
A collection of information regarding systems within the domain of a name service.

**network client**
A system that contains little to no local storage space. Some or all of the necessary files for booting and operation are accessed remotely via the network.

**Network File System (NFS)**
A network service and type of file system. This service allows local storage, such as file systems, to be accessible by other systems via the network. The version 3 of the NFS protocol is defined by RFC 1813.

**Network Information Service (NIS)**
A name service that stores information in maps and makes it available to NIS clients that request it.

**Network Information Service Plus (NIS+)**
An enhanced version of NIS that stores information in tables. Security is provided using authentication and authorization.

**nonvolatile random access remory (NVRAM)**
An area of memory used to store OpenBoot parameters that is not affected by powering down or rebooting the system.

**Open System Interconnection (OSI) network model**
The network model developed by the International Standards Organization (ISO), consisting of seven layers of services. Each layer is responsible for handling a different aspect of network communication.

**Open Windows**
A graphical user interface.

**OpenBoot**
The standard firmware for Sun Systems. OpenBoot is used to boot the operating system, run diagnostics, and modify boot-related parameters stored in nonvolatile RAM (NVRAM), and it provides a Forth interpreter. OpenBoot firmware pertains only to SPARC platforms, but some limited functionality is available on Intel x86 platforms.

**operating system release**
The version of an operating system, such as 7 or 8 for Solaris.

**operating system (OS) server**
A network server that provides network clients with access to operating system files as required.

### operating system (OS) service

A set of files needed to support a particular network client. An OS service is identified and configured for a combination of platform, system architecture, and OS release.

### over-the-network installation

Solaris can be installed over the network using an install server that has either the Solaris distribution CD in its CD-ROM drive or a copy of the files from the Solaris distribution CD on its hard disk. A boot server may also be required.

### partition

A contiguous collection of disk sectors as defined by the partition table. Once a partition is defined in the partition table, a file system can be created within the partition.

### partition table

A table in the VTOC that contains an entry for each partition on the disk.

### password aging

The parameters of the /etc/shadow file determine the password aging policy. These parameters enforce a policy for protecting the integrity of passwords.

### Peripheral Component Interconnect (PCI)

A slot- and card-based bus mechanism used to connect video adapters, network cards, sound cards, and so on to a computer system.

### platform

The particular type of hardware—either SPARC or Intel x86 compatible.

### plex

A collection of Volume Manager subdisks organized to support various levels of RAID.

### postinstallation phase

The installation phase during which any appropriate patches and applications are installed and custom configurations such as user accounts and environments are set up.

### preconfigured system information

Two methods are available for preconfiguring system information: using the sysidcfg file and using a name service.

### privileged operation

A Solaris command that is executed with the UID and/or GID set to the appropriate value to allow proper operation.

### process

A task or program currently being executed by the computer system.

### profile (role-based access control)

A mechanism used to assign authorizations and/or privileged operations to roles.

### profile diskette

A diskette that contains the JumpStart configuration directory; that is, a rules file and one or more profile files.

### profile file

A text file that defines how to install the Solaris 8 software on a system. Like the rules file, a profile file contains keywords and associated values that guide the installation.

### profile server
A server that provides access to a custom JumpStart configuration directory over the network and eliminates the need to create and distribute multiple profile diskettes during installation of large numbers of systems.

### pseudo file system
A memory-based file system.

### RAID
Redundant Array of Inexpensive Disks.

### remote authentication database
Used to determine which remote hosts and users are considered to be trusted. The **rlogin**, **rsh**, and **rcp** commands use the remote authentication database. This database consists of two types of files: the /etc/host.equiv file, which applies to the entire system, and the .rhosts files, which apply to individual user accounts and are located in the home directories of user accounts.

### Remote Procedure Call (RPC)
A mechanism that allows a client to request a remote server to execute a procedure or process.

### Request For Comment (RFC)
A document used to publish networking-related policies and protocols so that interested parties can submit comments and recommend changes. After a period of time, the RFC may be adopted as a standard by the U.S. government and industry. Protocols such as TCP/IP and NFS have been defined by RFCs.

### Reverse Address Resolution Protocol (RARP)
A protocol used to map from an Ethernet address to an IP address.

### role
A special type of user account provided by the Role-Based Access Control mechanism to grant a set of superuser privileges to perform some administrative tasks.

### Role-Based Access Control (RBAC)
A mechanism used to grant access to privileged operations or commands to accounts as needed to perform a task.

### rules file
A text file that contains an entry or rule for each system or group of systems that is to be automatically installed. Each rule identifies the system (or group of systems) based on one or more attributes and identifies a unique profile file that provides the configuration details for that system or group of systems. Each rule consists of one or more keywords and values followed by the name of the profile file.

### run control (rc) script
A shell script (typically Bourne) written to start and stop various processes and services. An rc script is usually written in two portions: a start portion and a stop portion. The appropriate portion is executed when the system is booted or shut down.

### server
A computer system that provides resources to remote clients.

**setgid**
A special file access mode that sets the effective GID of the user account executing a program to the GID of the program group owner. The setgid permission has an absolute mode of 2000 and a symbolic mode of **s**.

**setuid**
A special file access mode that sets the effective UID of the user account executing a program to the UID of the program owner. The setuid permission has an absolute mode of 4000 and a symbolic mode of **s**.

**SGML**
The Standard Generalized Markup Language used to provide a generic method of encoding the contents of a document without associating it with a particular format. See **Bourne shell**.

**share**
The process of making an NFS resource available for mounting by remote NFS clients.

**shell**
A software module that provides the interface between users and the kernel. One of the three parts of an operating system (the other parts are the kernel and the file system).

**signal**
A notification sent to a process to indicate an event or an action that should be performed. Signals can be used to terminate processes.

**slice**
See **partition**.

**small computer system interface (SCSI)**
A bus-based peripheral device connection mechanism typically used for disk drives and tape drives.

**software cluster**
A logical grouping of software packages. Clusters are necessary because some software is distributed in more than one package, but all the packages need to be distributed and installed as a unit.

**software configuration cluster**
See **software group**.

**software group**
A collection of software clusters. Depending on the intended use of the system, the most appropriate software group should be selected for installing an operating system.

**software package**
An easily installable collection of Solaris 8 system and application software. These packages consist of files and directories that can be copied onto the system from CD-ROM or magnetic tape as a single compressed file and then uncompressed for installation. Included with the package is information regarding the package, such as its title, storage requirements, and version. Also included are any custom scripts needed to properly install the software.

**software patch**
An easily installable collection of file and directories intended to update or fix a problem with an installed software package.

### SPARC
A computer architecture developed by Sun Microsystems. It uses a reduced instruction set processor, which provides superior performance over processors that operate using a standard instruction set.

### standalone system
A system that uses local disk space to store all operating system files, applications, and user data, including the root (/), /usr, /export/home, and /var file systems. Likewise, a standalone system provides local swap for the system's virtual memory. A standalone system can function autonomously and can be either networked or non-networked.

### sticky bit
A special file permission that, when set on a directory that allows write permission for everyone, allows only the user account that created the files and subdirectories under that directory to remove those files and subdirectories. A sticky bit is especially useful for the /tmp directory, which is available from any user account. The sticky bit permission has an absolute mode of 1000 and a symbolic mode of **t**.

### striped virtual device
A device consisting of two or more slices. The slices can be on the same physical disk or on several physical disks. The slices also can be of different sizes. They are addressed in an interleaved manner. That is, as space is needed, it is allocated as a block from the first slice, then a block from the second slice, and so on.

### subdisk
The basic unit used by the Volume Manager to allocate storage. A subdisk is a portion of the public region of a VM disk.

### SunInstall
An interactive Open Windows installation program that can be used to install the Solaris 8 software but does not support installation of co-packaged software.

### superuser
A special administrative account that provides the ultimate in terms of access to data and services, because it can override any file permissions on the system.

### swap space
Disk space used as virtual memory. Swap space can be on a local disk or on a remote disk that is accessed via the network.

### syslog
A facility used to collect messages from system programs and applications. These messages are identified by a source facility and priority level. The /etc/syslog.conf file assigns an action to each combination of source and priority level.

### syslog actions
The action that should be performed when a syslog message of the identified *source.priority* is received by the **syslogd** daemon.

### syslog priority levels
A syslog message can be identified by priority level or severity. This identification provides a second mechanism

(with finer granularity) for handling messages on the basis of importance.

**syslog source facilities**
The facilities generating syslog messages can be used to determine where the messages are sent or stored. Doing so allows separate log files for different types of messages based on source.

**system configuration phase**
The installation phase during which basic information about the system, such as hostname and domain, is identified. This information can optionally be set up ahead of time, or preconfigured.

**system installation phase**
The installation phase during which the system software is installed. The system software is one of the Solaris 8 software groups.

**system profile**
For user accounts that use sh (Bourne shell) or ksh (Korn shell) as a login shell, commands in the system profile (/etc/profile) are executed before the user's login initialization file.

**system run levels**
Eight defined levels, each associated with specific functions used to shut down or reboot the system and control system services and resources.

**Transmission Control Protocol/Internet Protocol (TCP/IP) network model**
A network model consisting of five layers of services. Each layer is responsible for handling a different aspect of network communication.

**UFS file system logging**
Updates to a UFS file system are recorded in a log before they are applied. In the case of system failure, the system can be restarted, and the UFS file system can quickly use the log instead of having to use the **fsck** command.

**user account**
A unique name and user ID that control an individual's access to a computer and its resources.

**user ID (UID)**
A unique numeric ID assigned to a user account that is used for file and process ownership and access permissions.

**Veritas File System (vxfs)**
The type of virtual file system supported by the Enterprise Volume Manager.

**virtual disk management system**
A software package that allows the use of physical disks in different ways that are not supported by the standard Solaris file systems. It can overcome disk capacity and architecture limitations and improve performance and reliability. In addition, manageability is enhanced by the use of a graphical management tool.

**virtual file system**
An enhanced file system that provides improved performance and data reliability.

**volume**
An Enterprise Volume Manager virtual disk device composed of up to 32 plexes. The volume is the virtual object that the operating system and applications view and manipulate.

### Volume Manager (VM) disk
A physical disk partition or slice that has been assigned to the Enterprise Volume Manager.

### volume table of contents (VTOC)
Contains the partition table and various geometry data about the disk, such as sectors per track, tracks per cylinder, available cylinders, and so on.

### WebNFS
A protocol that allows Web browsers to access NFS resources. This protocol is defined by RFCs 2054 and 2055.

### Web Start
An interactive installation method that uses a Web browser interface.

### x86 Intel compatible
A computer architecture based on a microprocessor originally designed by the Intel Corporation, which used the 286, 386, 486 series of numbers to denote versions.

### X/Open Federated Naming Specification (XFN)
The specification for the Federated Naming Service (FNS) as defined by the X/Open Consortium.

### zone
A portion of a domain delegated to a DNS server.

# Index

**Bold page numbers indicate sample exam questions.**

## A



## B

## E



## F

## G



## H



## I



## J



## K



## L

## T



## U

## V



## W



## Z